International and Development Education

The *International and Development Education Series* focuses on the complementary areas of comparative, international, and development education. Books emphasize a number of topics ranging from key international education issues, trends, and reforms to examinations of national education systems, social theories, and development education initiatives. Local, national, regional, and global volumes (single authored and edited collections) constitute the breadth of the series and offer potential contributors a great deal of latitude based on interests and cutting edge research. The series is supported by a strong network of international scholars and development professionals who serve on the International and Development Education Advisory Board and participate in the selection and review process for manuscript development.

SERIES EDITORS
John N. Hawkins
Professor Emeritus, University of California, Los Angeles
Co-Director, Asian Pacific Higher Education Research Partnership (APHERP), East West Center

W. James Jacob
Associate Professor, University of Pittsburgh
Director, Institute for International Studies in Education

PRODUCTION EDITOR
Weiyan Xiong
Program Coordinator, Institute for International Studies in Education

INTERNATIONAL EDITORIAL ADVISORY BOARD
Clementina Acedo, *Webster University, Switzerland*
Philip G. Altbach, *Boston University, USA*
Carlos E. Blanco, *Universidad Central de Venezuela*
Oswell C. Chakulimba, *University of Zambia*
Sheng Yao Cheng, *National Chung Cheng University, Taiwan*
Ruth Hayhoe, *University of Toronto, Canada*
Wanhua Ma, *Peking University, China*
Ka Ho Mok, *Hong Kong Institute of Education, China*
Christine Musselin, *Sciences Po, France*
Yusuf K. Nsubuga, *Ministry of Education and Sports, Uganda*
Namgi Park, *Gwangju National University of Education, Republic of Korea*
Val D. Rust, *University of California, Los Angeles, USA*
Suparno, *State University of Malang, Indonesia*
John C. Weidman, *University of Pittsburgh, USA*
Husam Zaman, *Taibah University, Saudi Arabia*
Yuto Kitamura, *Tokyo University, Japan*

Institute for International Studies in Education
School of Education, University of Pittsburgh
5714 Wesley W. Posvar Hall, Pittsburgh, PA 15260 USA

Center for International and Development Education
Graduate School of Education & Information Studies, University of California, Los Angeles
Box 951521, Moore Hall, Los Angeles, CA 90095 USA

Titles:

Higher Education in Asia/Pacific: Quality and the Public Good
Edited by Terance W. Bigalke and Deane E. Neubauer

Affirmative Action in China and the U.S.: A Dialogue on Inequality and Minority Education
Edited by Minglang Zhou and Ann Maxwell Hill

Critical Approaches to Comparative Education: Vertical Case Studies from Africa, Europe, the Middle East, and the Americas
Edited by Frances Vavrus and Lesley Bartlett

Curriculum Studies in South Africa: Intellectual Histories & Present Circumstances
Edited by William F. Pinar

Higher Education, Policy, and the Global Competition Phenomenon
Edited by Laura M. Portnoi, Val D. Rust, and Sylvia S. Bagley

The Search for New Governance of Higher Education in Asia
Edited by Ka-Ho Mok

International Students and Global Mobility in Higher Education: National Trends and New Directions
Edited by Rajika Bhandari and Peggy Blumenthal

Curriculum Studies in Brazil: Intellectual Histories, Present Circumstances
Edited by William F. Pinar

Access, Equity, and Capacity in Asia Pacific Higher Education
Edited by Deane Neubauer and Yoshiro Tanaka

Policy Debates in Comparative, International, and Development Education
Edited by John N. Hawkins and W. James Jacob

Curriculum Studies in Mexico: Intellectual Histories, Present Circumstances
Edited by William F. Pinar

Increasing Effectiveness of the Community College Financial Model: A Global Perspective for the Global Economy
Edited by Stewart E. Sutin, Daniel Derrico, Rosalind Latiner Raby, and Edward J. Valeau

The Internationalization of East Asian Higher Education: Globalizations Impact
Edited by John D. Palmer, Amy Roberts, Young Ha Cho, and Gregory Ching

University Governance and Reform: Policy, Fads, and Experience in International Perspective
Edited by Hans G. Schuetze, William Bruneau, and Garnet Grosjean

Mobility and Migration in Asian Pacific Higher Education
Edited by Deane E. Neubauer and Kazuo Kuroda

Taiwan Education at the Crossroad: When Globalization Meets Localization
Edited by Chuing Prudence Chou and Gregory Ching

Higher Education Regionalization in Asia Pacific: Implications for Governance, Citizenship and University Transformation
Edited by John N. Hawkins, Ka Ho Mok, and Deane E. Neubauer

Post-Secondary Education and Technology: A Global Perspective on Opportunities and Obstacles to Development
Edited by Rebecca Clothey, Stacy Austin-Li, and John C. Weidman

Education and Global Cultural Dialogue: A Tribute to Ruth Hayhoe
Edited by Karen Mundy and Qiang Zha

The Quest for Entrepreneurial Universities in East Asia
By Ka Ho Mok

The Dynamics of Higher Education Development in East Asia: Asian Cultural Heritage, Western Dominance, Economic Development, and Globalization
Edited by Deane Neubauer, Jung Cheol Shin, and John N. Hawkins

Leadership for Social Justice in Higher Education: The Legacy of the Ford Foundation International Fellowships Program
Edited by Terance W. Bigalke and Mary S. Zurbuchen

Curriculum Studies in China: Intellectual Histories, Present Circumstances
Edited by William F. Pinar

The Transnationally Partnered University: Insights from Research and Sustainable Development Collaborations in Africa
By Peter H. Koehn and Milton Odhiambo Obamba

Curriculum Studies in India: Intellectual Histories, Present Circumstances
Edited By William F. Pinar

Private Universities in Latin America: Research and Innovation in the Knowledge Economy
Edited by Gustavo Gregorutti and Jorge Enrique Delgado

Private Universities in Latin America

Research and Innovation in the Knowledge Economy

Edited by
Gustavo Gregorutti and
Jorge Enrique Delgado

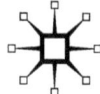

PRIVATE UNIVERSITIES IN LATIN AMERICA
Copyright © Gustavo Gregorutti and Jorge Enrique Delgado, 2015.

All rights reserved.

First published in 2015 by
PALGRAVE MACMILLAN®
in the United States—a division of St. Martin's Press LLC,
175 Fifth Avenue, New York, NY 10010.

Where this book is distributed in the UK, Europe and the rest of the world, this is by Palgrave Macmillan, a division of Macmillan Publishers Limited, registered in England, company number 785998, of Houndmills, Basingstoke, Hampshire RG21 6XS.

Palgrave Macmillan is the global academic imprint of the above companies and has companies and representatives throughout the world.

Palgrave® and Macmillan® are registered trademarks in the United States, the United Kingdom, Europe and other countries.

ISBN: 978–1–137–47937–2

Library of Congress Cataloging-in-Publication Data

    Private universities in Latin America : research and Innovation in the knowledge economy / edited by Gustavo Gregorutti, Jorge Enrique Delgado.
        pages cm.—(International and development education)
        Summary: "Using policy analysis and case study approaches, Private Universities in Latin America examines the significant amounts of research and innovation being made available from private universities in Latin America"—Provided by publisher.
    Includes bibliographical references and index.
    ISBN 978–1–137–47937–2 (hardback)
    1. Private universities and colleges—Latin America. 2. Education, Higher—Research—Latin America. I. Gregorutti, Gustavo.
II. Delgado, Jorge Enrique.

LB2328.52.L29I58 2015
378'.04098—dc23
                                                     2014044276

A catalogue record of the book is available from the British Library.

Design by Newgen Knowledge Works (P) Ltd., Chennai, India.

First edition: May 2015

10 9 8 7 6 5 4 3 2 1

Contents

List of Figures	ix
List of Tables	xi
Series Editors' Preface	xiii
List of Abbreviations and Acronyms	xv

1 Introduction   1
   Jorge Enrique Delgado and Gustavo Gregorutti

Part I Regulatory Environment Impacting Research Productivity in Latin America

2 Research as a New Challenge for the Latin American Private University   9
   Claudio Rama and Gustavo Gregorutti

3 Latin American Private Universities in the Context of Competition and Research Productivity   27
   Jorge Enrique Delgado

4 Quality Assurance and Public Policy Research Funding: Their Impact on Private Universities in Argentina   51
   Ana García de Fanelli and Ángela Corengia

5 Institutional Frameworks and Scientific Productivity in Chile and Colombia, 1950–2012   79
   Pedro Pineda

Part II Successful Cases of Research Productivity at Private Universities

6 A Research and Innovation Ecosystem Model for Private Universities: The Monterrey Institute of Technology Experience 109
Francisco J. Cantú-Ortiz

7 The Emergence of the Puebla State Popular Autonomous University as a Successful Mexican Research University 131
Stephen P. Wanger and Édgar Apanecatl-Ibarra

8 Central American Outliers: Leveraging International Cooperation for Research Productivity 157
Nanette Svenson

9 Research and Knowledge Production in the Private Sector: The Brazilian Experience 185
Elizabeth Balbachevsky and Antonio José Botelho

10 Contributions from a Private University in Peru: The Case of the Cayetano Heredia Peruvian University 205
José Anicama and José Livia

11 Research and Incentives: The Case of Two Private Universities in Argentina 225
Marcelo Rabossi

12 Private University Strategies to Promote Knowledge Production: Development of a Graduate Program in Biotechnology in Uruguay 251
Enrique Martínez Larrechea and Adriana Chiancone

13 Conclusion 273
Gustavo Gregorutti and Jorge Enrique Delgado

Appendix 279

List of Contributors 281

Index 287

Figures

4.1	Trends in the Argentinian expenditure on R&D by sector (in constant pesos of 1999)	60
6.1	Components of a research and innovation ecosystem for private universities	118
13.1	Promoting research among private universities in Latin America	276

Tables

4.1	Characteristics of the two universities selected	56
4.2	Number of CONICET researchers and doctoral fellows at Argentinian private universities, 2004 and 2012	61
5.1	Knowledge production of private universities in Chile and Colombia	86
6.1	ITESM publications and citations in Scopus since 2002	122
7.1	Key performance indicators	139
8.1	Central American public and private universities by country, 2012	160
8.2	Central America: select development statistics, 2012	161
9.1	Highest teaching level and degree of commitment with the research by subsector	191
10.1	Academics by faculty with PhD, master's, and professional degrees	211
11.1	BU: faculty body satisfaction with research activities according to type of contract in percentage of responses	238
11.2	GU: satisfaction with research activities to the faculty body according to type of contract in percentage of responses	238
11.3	BU: recognition of faculty body research activities according to type of contract in percentage of responses	240
11.4	GU: recognition of faculty body research activities according to type of contract in percentage of responses	240
12.1	Academic production of ORT by category (select years)	261

Series Editors' Preface

We are pleased to introduce another volume in the Palgrave Macmillan International and Development Education book series. In conceptualizing this series we took into account the extraordinary increase in the scope and depth of research on education in a global and international context. The range of topics and issues being addressed by scholars worldwide is enormous and clearly reflects the growing expansion and quality of research being conducted on comparative, international, and development education (CIDE) topics. Our goal is to cast a wide net for the most innovative and novel manuscripts, both single-authored and edited volumes, without constraints as to the level of education, geographical region, or methodology (whether disciplinary or interdisciplinary). In the process, we have also developed two subseries as part of the main series: one is cosponsored by the East West Center in Honolulu, Hawaii, drawing from their distinguished programs, the International Forum on Education 2020 (IFE 2020) and the Asian Pacific Higher Education Research Partnership (APHERP); and the other is a publication partnership with the Higher Education Special Interest Group of the Comparative and International Education Society that highlights trends and themes on international higher education.

The issues that will be highlighted in this series are those focused on capacity, access, and equity, three interrelated topics that are central to educational transformation as it appears today around the world. There are many paradoxes and asymmetries surrounding these issues, which include problems of both excess capacity and deficits, wide access to facilities as well as severe restrictions, and all the complexities that are included in the equity debate. Closely related to this critical triumvirate is the overarching concern with quality assurance, accountability, and assessment. As educational systems have expanded, so have the needs and demands for quality assessment, with implications for accreditation and accountability. Intergroup relations, multiculturalism, and gender issues comprise another cluster of concerns facing most educational systems in differential ways when one looks at the change in educational systems in an international context. Diversified notions of the structure of knowledge and curriculum development occupy another important niche in educational change at both the precollegiate and collegiate levels. Finally, how systems are managed and governed are key policy issues for educational policymakers worldwide. These and other key elements of the education and social change environment have guided this series and are reflected in the books that have already appeared and those that will appear in the future. We welcome proposals on these and other topics from as wide a range of scholars and practitioners as possible. We believe that the world of educational change is dynamic, and our goal is to reflect the very best work being done in these and other areas.

JOHN N. HAWKINS
University of California, Los Angeles

W. JAMES JACOB
University of Pittsburgh

Abbreviations and Acronyms

AI	Appreciative inquiry
ANII	National Research and Innovation Agency (Uruguay)
ANPCYT	National Agency for the Promotion of Science and Technology (Argentina)
ARWU	Shanghai Jiao Tong University Academic Ranking of World Universities
BCIE	Central American Bank for Economic Integration
BKCI	Book Citation Index
CAPES	Coordination for Improvement of Higher Education Personnel (Brazil)
CATIE	Center for Tropical Agricultural Research and Education (Costa Rica)
CIE	ORT University, Centre for Innovation and Entrepreneurism
CINDA	Inter-University Center for Andean Development (Chile)
CIP	Interdisciplinary Center of Graduate Programs (Mexico)
CLACDS	Latin American Center for Competitiveness and Sustainable Development
CLACSO	Latin American Council of Social Sciences
Colciencias	Department of Science, Technology, and Innovation (Colombia)
CONACYT	National Council for Science and Technology (Mexico)
CONCYTEC	National Council for Science and Technology (Peru)
CONEAU	National Commission for University Evaluation and Accreditation (Argentina)
CONI	National Council of Researchers (Peru)
CONICET	National Council of Scientific and Technological Research (Argentina)
CONICYT	National Commission for Scientific and Technological Research (Chile)

CONUP	National Peruvian University Council
CORFO	Corporation for Production Improvement
CRUCH	Council of Chilean University Presidents
DI	Pontifical Catholic University of Rio de Janeiro, Department of Computer Science (Brazil)
DSR	Cayetano Heredia Peruvian University, Department of Scientific Research
DUICT	Cayetano Heredia Peruvian University, University Research, Science, and Technology Office
EARTH	School of Tropical Agriculture (Costa Rica)
EPGE	Getulio Vargas Foundation, Graduate School of Economics (Brazil)
ETP	Pontifical Catholic University of Rio de Janeiro, Entrepreneur Training Program
FCIU	Fund for Construction and University Research
FGV	Getulio Vargas Foundation (Brazil)
FLACSO	Latin American School of Social Sciences
FONCYT	Fund for Scientific and Technological Research (Argentina)
FONDECYT	National Fund for Scientific and Technological Development (Chile)
FONTAR	Argentinian Technological Fund
GDP	Gross domestic product
HEI	Higher education institutions
HRC	United Nations Human Rights Centre
HTLV-1	*T-lymphotropic virus*
IADB	Inter-American Development Bank
IBRE	Law School of Rio de Janeiro, the Institute of Economics (Brazil)
ICTs	Information and communication technologies
IESALC	UNESCO International Institute for Higher Education in Latin America and the Caribbean
IGERO	Cayetano Heredia Peruvian University, Gerontology Institute
IICA	Inter-American Institute of Cooperation on Agriculture (Costa Rica)
IMT	Institute of Tropical Medicine Alexander Von Humboldt (Peru)
INCAE	Central-American Business School (Costa Rica)
INIA	National Research Institute of Farming (Uruguay)
ITAM	Technological Autonomous Institute of Mexico

ITESM	Monterrey Institute of Technology and Higher Education (Mexico)
ITS	Pontifical Catholic University of Rio de Janeiro, Institute of Software Technology
IVIC	Venezuelan Institute for Scientific Research
LES	Pontifical Catholic University of Rio de Janeiro, Laboratory of Software Engineering
MEC	Ministry of Education and Culture (Uruguay)
MEN	National Ministry of Education (Colombia)
MINCYT	Ministry of Science, Technology, and Productive Innovation (Argentina)
NGO	Non-governmental organization
NIE	New institutional economic theory
OAS	Organization of American States
OECD	Organisation for Economic Co-operation and Development
ORT	ORT University (Uruguay)
PEACE	University for Peace
PEDECIBA	ORT University, Basic Sciences Development Program
Petrobras	Brazilian Petroleum Corporation
PNPC	National Program of Quality Programs (Mexico)
PUCC	Pontifical Catholic University of Chile
PUCRJ	Pontifical Catholic University of Rio de Janeiro
PUCV	Pontifical Catholic University of Valparaiso (Chile)
PUJ	Pontifical Javeriana University
R&D	Research and development
REDES	Center for the Study of Science, Development, and Education (Argentina)
RICYT	Network for Science and Technology Indicators
RIE	Research and innovation ecosystem
SACS	Southern Association of Colleges and Schools
SCI	Science Citation Index
SECYT	Secretariat of Science and Technology (Argentina)
SIDISI	Cayetano Heredia Peruvian University, Decentralized Research Monitoring and Information System
SINEACE	National Evaluation, Accreditation, and Quality Assurance in Education System (Peru)
SIR	SCImago Institutions Rankings
SNI	National Researcher System (Mexico)
SNI-Uru	National System of Researchers (Uruguay)
SPU	Secretariat of University Policy (Argentina)

SSCI	Social Science Citation Index
STI	Science, technology, and innovation
TBC	Tuberculosis
TecGraf	Pontifical Catholic University of Rio de Janeiro, Laboratory of Graphic Computing
THE	Times Higher Education World University Ranking
UAustral	Austral University (Argentina)
UCA	Argentinean Pontifical Catholic University Santa Maria de Los Buenos Aires
UChi	University of Chile
UCUDAL	Catholic University of Uruguay "Dámaso Antonio Larrañaga"
UFRG	Federal University of Rio de Janeiro (Brazil)
UNAM	National Autonomous University of Mexico
UNDP	United Nations Development Programme
UNESCO	United Nations Educational, Scientific and Cultural Organization
Uniandes	University of the Andes (Colombia)
Unicamp	State University of Campinas (Brazil)
Uninorte	University of the North (Colombia)
UPAEP	Puebla State Popular Autonomous University (Mexico)
UPCH	Cayetano Heredia Peruvian University
UPEACE	University for Peace (Costa Rica)
UR	University of the Republic (Uruguay)
USAID	US Agency for International Development
USP	University of Sao Paulo (Brazil)
UTFS	Technical University Federico Santa Maria
UVG	University of the Valley of Guatemala
VRI	Cayetano Heredia Peruvian University, Vice-Chancellor for Research
WEF	World Economic Forum
WIPO	World Intellectual Property Organization
WoS	Web of Science

Chapter 1

Introduction

Jorge Enrique Delgado and Gustavo Gregorutti

The current scientific and technological paradigm gives knowledge an essential role for social and economic development. Hence, supporting research and innovation has become imperative. In this context, applied research has become more important than basic inquiry, and the whole scientific endeavor converges with the advancement of technology, so knowledge can be transferred to benefit societies and propel economies. Governments, non-for-profit organizations, and private businesses can use knowledge generation to become more competitive and to hold up in the national and international arenas. Under these circumstances, productivity is required to efficiently use resources in order to obtain the highest benefits.

Traditionally, Latin American participation in the global science, technology, and innovation (STI) has been modest. In the past two decades, however, its scientific outcomes have increased significantly because many governments have made important investments and implemented policies to promote research and development. In many cases, funding and other resources are mostly or exclusively available for public universities where most research in the region originates. Nevertheless, the private sector has been the major contributor to the expansion of higher education in the past four decades. Private institutions have focused more on teaching (preparing professionals) than on developing capabilities and generating new knowledge from research. There are exceptions though. As a response, some governments have started to create strategies to encourage private universities to develop their research. They include accreditation and quality assurance systems, access to some funding with public monies, fiscal incentives, support of professional organizations, and stimuli to develop government-university private-sector initiatives. Mechanisms vary from country to country.

Now, how can private universities adapt and generate research that leads to innovation and economic progress? This is a central question that guides *Private Universities in Latin America: Research and Innovation in the Knowledge Economy*. We start by recognizing that many private universities in Latin America have a longer tradition than their public counterparts. Several of those institutions are actors that make important contributions to STI at the national, regional, and even international levels. On the other side, there are other private institutions that emerged recently and can, in many cases, adapt more easily to changes and challenges than public universities. We provide several positive examples of private universities that are adapting to current demands and generating mechanisms to develop research focused on innovation and economic progress. Some institutions have had to overcome teaching-oriented cultures and limited public funding in order to open the door to research in their missions. Others already had a research tradition that is expanding. Those institutions have learned to look for opportunities for collaboration and projects beyond the institutional and national context.

This book analyzes, on the one side, the context of STI and higher education in Latin America (in the region and selected countries) and the role of private universities in generating research and innovation. On the other side, the book introduces cases of Latin American private institutions that are developing interesting research strategies and how they turn them into productive ventures. Accordingly, we have divided the book in two broad parts.

Part I is titled "Regulatory Environment Impacting Research Productivity in Latin America" and includes four chapters. In chapter 2, "Research as a New Challenge for the Latin American Private University," Claudio Rama and Gustavo Gregorutti discuss how Latin American private higher education has evolved over the past 30 years toward an increasing segmentation where some institutions prioritize research as a distinctive characteristic while others focus on absorbing higher education demand. Rama and Gregorutti also analyze what being a research university means and the requirements to become one. Jorge Enrique Delgado, in chapter 3, "Latin American Private Universities in the Context of Competition and Research Productivity," analyzes the development of STI policy in Latin America in the past 20 years and how it has moved from prioritizing building capacity and infrastructure to incentivizing productivity and evaluating performance. Delgado also reviews the main university rankings regarding competitiveness and productivity and identifies the best ranked private universities. As a conclusion, he analyzes characteristics of successful private universities in a context of productivity and competitiveness and the emphasis on innovation for the future of universities. Chapter 4, "Quality Assurance and Public Policy Research Funding: Their Impact on Private Universities in Argentina," authored by Ana García de Fanelli and Ángela Corengia, looks at answering the question: do quality assurance and research funding public policies promote research activity in the Argentine private university sector? Using Clark's internal approach and DiMaggio and Powell's new institutionalism as analytical perspectives, García de Fanelli and Corengia explain the impact of policies in relation to institutional characteristics. They conclude that the result of policy in Argentina is institutional and program isomorphism in terms of minimum quality standard (quality as a "floor," not as a "ceiling"), but it has not affected interorganizational diversity; the accreditation of undergraduate programs had a greater impact on change than the institutional assessment; and the research funding policies had a greater impact on those private universities and fields of knowledge whose missions give significant weight to research. In the last chapter under this section, "Institutional Frameworks and Scientific Productivity in Chile and Colombia, 1950–2012," Pedro Pineda compares the institutional frameworks of higher education and research performance in Chile and Colombia. Public funding seems to be a central feature that has also segmented universities in both countries. The author suggests policy options for advancing more research involvement in both countries.

Part II of the book titled "Successful Cases of Research Productivity at Private Universities" intends to give some practical examples of institutions that have made significant changes to strengthen research. The section starts with chapter 6, "A Research and Innovation Ecosystem Model for Private Universities: The Monterrey Institute of Technology Experience," in which Francisco J. Cantú-Ortiz maps the evolution of the Monterrey Institute of Technology and Higher Education (ITESM: *Instituto Tecnológico y de Estudios Superiores de Monterrey*) in Mexico from a mainly teaching-oriented institution to one that stimulates innovation through the creation of spin-offs and jobs. Cantú-Ortiz presents the "research and innovation ecosystem" approach that ITESM used in this transformation. He argues that this perspective could be helpful for those administrators who are looking for models to implement in institutional reforms oriented to develop research and innovation. In chapter 7, "The Emergence of the Puebla State Popular Autonomous University as a Successful Mexican Research University," Stephen P. Wanger and Édgar Apanecatl-Ibarra present the case of a Catholic private institution.

The Puebla State Popular Autonomous University (*Universidad Popular Autónoma del Estado de Puebla*) exemplifies how even religious universities can become research-intensive institutions if the right leadership and internal policies are strategically applied. Nanette Svenson, in chapter 8, "Central American Outliers: Leveraging International Cooperation for Research Productivity," explores how some Central American private institutions are using their international networks to advance regional innovation. She concludes that autonomous and nonpublic academic governance, along with limited development-oriented course offerings, resources from international organizations and universities, and localized knowledge and experience, can be strategically leveraged to produce sustainable, innovative, and knowledge-generating institutions.

Elizabeth Balbachevsky and Antonio José Botelho describe the Brazilian prominent private higher education system in chapter 9, "Research and Knowledge Production in the Private Sector: The Brazilian Experience." To do that, they explore two cases to show how different degrees of commitment to research and graduate education entail a differentiation inside the private sector that, in turn, advance more research. Professors José Anicama and José Livia in chapter 10, "Contributions from a Private University in Peru: The Case of the Cayetano Heredia Peruvian University," portray the historical development of Cayetano Heredia Peruvian University and the mechanisms this Peruvian institution has been using to increase faculty research outcomes. It is interesting how this institution since its founding has been establishing visionary strategies to produce important scientific contributions in a very unstable national political and economic context. This emphasis has brought prestige and international visibility to the institution. Marcelo Rabossi, in chapter 11, "Research and Incentives: The Case of Two Private Universities in Argentina," analyzes differing private universities in Argentina. One is a research-oriented and the other is a more teaching-oriented institution. Rabossi's study explores the mechanisms these institutions put into practice to select their best human resources and the type of promotion and salary strategies they follow to increase faculty research productivity. Part II closes with the case from Uruguay, a country with a small private higher education sector. In chapter 12, "Private University Strategies to Promote Knowledge Production: Development of a Graduate Program in Biotechnology in Uruguay," Enrique Martínez Larrechea and Adriana Chiancone present the case of biotechnology program at ORT University, one of the only four private universities in Uruguay. The ORT University has been a teaching-oriented institution in technology and job-oriented fields. Martínez Larrechea and Chiancone's study analyzes the strategic decisions this private university made to open the biotechnology program and the strategies implemented to develop human resources, promote applied and transferable knowledge, and contribute to the national economy.

Finally, as this book fills an important research gap for English-speaking readers, it also represents a comprehensive discussion of some of the trends regarding research development and knowledge generation among Latin American private universities. It provides both an overview and analysis of the main issues and a detailed discussion of regional and national case studies. With contributors from a wide range of backgrounds, this book includes several models used by institutions in the region to develop research and innovation capabilities and outcomes. We expect to contribute to the understanding of the conditions that can help private universities to be more proactive in supporting research and of the implications for institutional and national development.

This book may be of interest not only for university professors and students concerned about higher education, particularly from international and comparative perspectives, but also for practitioners, policy analysts, higher educational specialists, governmental officials, and senior managers in the higher education sector. We also hope this book encourages Latin American private universities to support STI because of the positive impact it can have on the economy and on the society.

Part I

Regulatory Environment Impacting Research Productivity in Latin America

Chapter 2

Research as a New Challenge for the Latin American Private University

Claudio Rama and Gustavo Gregorutti

Introduction

This chapter presents a global overview of how private higher education has expanded and evolved toward research productivity over the past 30 years in Latin America. Its exponential growth in the early stages can be understood through a multifactorial combination of variables such as the promotion of neoliberal policies, as a response to the increasing demand for access in a context of shrinking national budgets for education in the region (Gaffikin and Perry 2009; Rama 2012a,b). That expansion of private universities initially focused on the training of professionals in traditional disciplines, which did not require high investment but had high demand (Gascón and Cepeda 2007). However, as private universities multiplied and, more importantly, enlarged, they evolved by adding new functions. Over the years, and through the stages described in this chapter, it has been possible to see that new policies created by different actors have addressed quality as a dominant concern about higher education in Latin America. This can be observed in the interaction of government regulations and the increasing influence of international organizations that have promoted, in addition to training, the creation of new knowledge as a central function of higher education in the region. Knowledge generation became a new mission for many institutions that have been carrying on education with almost no research productivity (Gregorutti et al. 2014).

Notions of quality have been changing throughout the period of this study. At the beginning, the almost total absence of legislation to regulate private universities prompted a dominant concern over quality as an opposite paradigm to the growing commercialization of educational services in the region (Monckeberg 2012). As new issues and challenges emerged, quality was understood and enriched with new models that embraced more and more research as a defining feature for distinguished and qualified universities. This represented an important paradigm shift that has driven many reactions that ended up in substantial reforms of higher education in Latin American countries. Producing discoveries and transferring the resulting knowledge to generate jobs and economic growth has been increasingly assumed as a meaningful role universities must take upon for the current knowledge-driven society (Toakley 2004). Accrediting agencies and collegial bodies, along with all kinds of national and international organizations, mirrored these trends and tried different models of quality assessment that reconfigured the higher education landscape. Furthermore, many leading private universities have also taken research as a marketing tool to reposition themselves in the most prominent rankings (Burness 2008; Marginson and Van der Wende 2007; Rauhvargers 2011). Thus, rankings reinforced the idea that research is a stamp of quality and differentiation for institutions that look for visibility through innovation. These trends resulted in powerful forces that stratified universities allowing the top runners to become more and more entrepreneurial accessing increasing amounts of external funding to advance research. Several decades ago, Robert Merton (1968) observed similar trends in higher education and called this type of polarization the "Matthew effect" to describe how accumulated advantage helps productive institutions to receive more resources and recognition.

Another goal for the second part of this chapter is to describe basic elements of the emerging research university, as well as some of the challenges administrators may face to advance knowledge production. Toward the end, the discussion section includes some crucial issues leaders need to address to become a research university in a globalized world.

Private Higher Education in Latin America

The Expansion Phase (1975–1999)

Since mid-1970s and toward the end of the twentieth century, private universities have been steadily multiplying in number, allowing the sector a dynamic positioning in the region (Altbach 2002). This stage was characterized by a strong expansion and transformation centered around new institutions to supply the demand with more flexible access through less requirements, innovative programs (for instance, among others, business administration, informatics, tourism, and marketing), and a more differentiated administration that considered students as costumers as opposed to the public university under the free tuition education. In this new context, the emerging private university flourished enrolling the "left out" students providing alternative schooling systems during evenings, weekends, and online classes. In addition, many of these institutions built campuses closer to students, facilitating easier access to the working class and adults relatively excluded from traditional universities (Rama 2009a,b,c). According to Daniel Levy's (1995) taxonomy, this phase was related to the third wave in which private universities absorbed the nonelite demand and the students rejected from public universities (see also Silas 2005). This was a natural consequence of the policies that had increased quotas and screening entrance processes in state-funded universities (Brunner 1985; García Guadilla 1998; Krotch 2001; Rama 2006). The expansion of new private universities occurred in the context of disarticulated higher education systems with elite private initiatives that had created their own universities due to disenchantment with government-funded institutions and public universities running on their own track and structure with little questioning regarding the quality of education they provided (Holm-Nielsen et al. 2005). Even though this new wave was very much criticized, it helped to reduce the demand of students at public universities, facilitating an initial restoration of quality among them as well (Rodríguez 2005). Many of these public institutions refocused, with better budgets, on developing more research and catching up with international trends, as they had less students lining up for enrollment every year. In the context of financial constraints, and without the demand-absorbing private university, the free or almost free Latin American public university would have had much more difficulty to enhance its quality. This dynamic situation was more intensive in countries where higher education demand and expansion was more recent and rapid. In the case of older and more developed tertiary education systems (e.g., Argentina and Uruguay), and with lesser jumps in demand, the private sector was also less prominent (Barsky et al. 2004). On the contrary, when the exceeding demand was not covered by the private sector, quality was severed in countries such as Bolivia, Honduras, or Guatemala (UNESCO—International Institute for Higher Education in Latin America and the Caribbean—IESALC 2006).

The growth of new private tertiary education was also associated with the transformation of the labor market that increased the demand for qualified workers with higher salaries for university-trained employees. From a systemic point of view, this association of more formal education equals better income was seen as a second university reform (Rama 2006) that promoted in the region a growth of private universities as much as four times larger than public counterparts during the 1980s and 1990s. Toward the end of the twentieth century, the private sector had reached about 47 percent of the tertiary enrollment in Latin America (Rama 2012a; Silas 2013) and that in the midst of multiple economic crises. During those years, tertiary institutions doubled their quantity to reach almost 10,000 units in the region with a growth of about 1.3 institutions per day. Moreover, this remarkable expansion had a high impact in terms of investment, employment of new faculty members, more programs, modernization of facilities, and human resources available for more competitive markets (Inter-University Center for Andean Development—CINDA 2009). As already mentioned, this dynamic enlargement of private higher education reshaped the traditional landscape of public-elite private universities, allowing multiple models and systems of institutions to absorb the increasing demand of training from new comers.

However, it is important to remark that these changes did not take place without many challenges. One of the most noticeable was the lack of regulation that generated serious quality and institutional complications. In many countries, private universities were authorized without minimum quality controls creating problems for graduates and families that invested in dubious education. Many institutions operated as diploma mills without an educational project to ensure quality training (Espinoza and González 2013). This situation has been changing and new regulations are trying to correct and counterbalance past mistakes using accreditation and external assessments. Accrediting bodies are pressing institutions to add qualified professors, better facilities, and research productivity (Gregorutti 2010). Although research productivity was not a critical goal for these new private universities, it is becoming an important mission in many of them as internal and external factors combine to promote knowledge production.

A New Phase: More Regulations and Controls (2000–2010)

Throughout this decade many Latin American countries improved their economies, which resulted in a higher per capita income that helped families invest more in private education. In consequence, the sector continued to expand, even though it took place in a slower pace. At the same time, several governments opened new public universities increasing enrollments that jumped from 11.3 million students in 2000 to 21.5 million in 2010, with an annual growth rate of 7 percent for both sectors combined. That boost in regional enrollment that higher education coverage went from 23.5 percent in 2000 to 41 percent at the end of the decade (UNESCO IESALC 2006; Rama 2009a).

As it was mentioned earlier, toward the end of the twentieth century a wave of new regulations and increasing governmental controls took place in most Latin American countries. New policies intended to adjust growth by emphasizing a regulated expansion of the private sector. One of the reasons for the increasing supervision of private higher education was the need for professionals prepared with new skills for the fast-tracking globalized economy that was transforming the region (Rama 2012a). With the expansion of public universities, some policies only allowed teaching-oriented institutions, like in the case of Brazil where the for-profit sector and more requirements and controls on the opening of new private institutions led to a higher concentration and growth of several private universities. Concentration became a central characteristic of this decade (Rama 2012b). This situation facilitated an increment in research productivity especially among the elite and more traditional institutions. Additionally and as part of their market strengthening, several private universities developed internal incentives to free professors from teaching loads and give them more resources to get involved in research. Moreover, these trends were reinforced by new government policies and funding to support research projects conducted in nonpublic universities through competitive grants. Brazil and Chile are two remarkable cases. On the one hand, the Brazilian Petroleum Corporation—Petrobras[1] invests 1 percent of its revenue in STI in 29 universities, including some private ones. On the other side, the Chilean government subsidizes multimillion dollar grants for the advancement of research and it does to a vast majority of private universities, although most of them are elite type institutions (Ginsburg et al. 2005). These funding mechanisms with public monies to advance knowledge played a relevant role in the emerging research trends in private universities that otherwise would have had to constrain themselves within internal resources. This is especially true for tuition-driven institutions that do not have the extra funds to invest on expensive and complex projects. However, very few universities seemed to engage in applying and pursuing external funding (Gregorutti 2011a).

Little by little, throughout this decade, an emerging segmentation is taking place among private universities in Latin America. This means that some institutions reorganized their internal cultures and resources to advance STI, and others continued with a mainly teaching or training approach while trying to develop some research. The Argentinian case study that Marcelo Rabossi presents in this book is a good example of this polarization among private universities. In short, it is possible to see a growing distance between teaching-oriented institutions and universities that are strongly focusing on research. The latter type of private university tends to be well equipped and accredited, have more full-time faculty, offer several graduate programs, and be more in tune with global competition. These institutions are emerging as private research universities.

Actual Phase: Growing Segmentation

The surplus of new institutions at the beginning of the twenty-first century, combined with the consolidation of universities in expansion during recent years, seems to be pushing higher education toward more segmentation in Latin America. For instance, universities are compelled to demonstrate higher quality levels, through obtaining accreditation and numerous certifications that, at the same time, press them to look for an important position in a very stressful and competitive market (Silas 2013). Strategies that range from scholarships for best students to better facilities and growing interest in research as a distinguishing stamp are used to differentiate institutions (Silas 2009; Rama 2012b). Producing knowledge is a central variable for comparison in national and international rankings (Huang 2011). Universities are increasing their competitiveness by creating new journals (Delgado 2014; Delgado and Fischman 2014), boosting financial support for researchers, and even changing their academic structures to encourage productivity. More advanced institutions are expanding into new centers of research and incubators along with companies that finance their cutting-edge technology programs (Cantú et al. 2009). An outstanding example of this is the Monterrey Institute of Technology (ITESM: *Instituto Tecnológico de Monterrey*), in Mexico. Francisco Cantú-Ortiz's chapter 10 in this book explains how ITESM has evolved from a little research generating institution to a front-runner in the region, which differentiates it from other private institutions.

While a group of universities look for ways to be part of the mainstream, there is another group of higher education institutions absorbing demand. The latter are moving rapidly toward for-profit models and positioning themselves at the other extreme with less prestige. Although already existing in previous years, these national and, in some cases, transnational institutions are bringing in new types of training oriented to develop job skills and competencies for local and global markets (Rama 2009a; Salmi 2009). When big and international consortiums support for-profit institutions, they tend to promote higher levels of quality than local for-profit units. Examples of this can be found in Chile and Costa Rica where the purchase of local universities has brought higher standards of quality with accreditations and even research developments (Rama 2012b). Although some scholars have questioned their validity and quality (Monckeberg 2012; Espinoza 2005), these institutions follow and allow a rationale of more market and more State (Fukuyama 2004).

In this new context of polarization regarding institutional models and their products, different components of quality seem to be of concern among all universities. Although there have been significant quality improvements and a remarkable research development, knowledge production has leaned more toward publications and less to breakthrough innovation and patent registration. This is also a problem between public universities if they are compared with peers in more developed countries (Rama 2009c, 2014). In short, large private universities seem to look for ways to distance themselves from mass education to a better position in national and international rankings. This strategic direction has helped some of them to compete with public universities, a scenario unthinkable some years ago (Gregorutti 2011b; Rama 2009c). At the same time, smaller and less prestigious institutions continue to have their share in a segmented market.

Discussion

Even though for years some Latin American private universities have been reorienting their missions to knowledge production, newest institutions have not. As a result, the growing importance of STI in the globalized economy is evidenced in the implementation of international and national policies that use research achievement as a powerful marketing tool (Bok 2010). This is a new university paradigm that is reshaping the higher education landscape in the region and worldwide. Therefore, many private universities have undergone deep mission challenges that prompted shifts from their traditional teaching-oriented approach, which increases pressure on administrators. Throughout this book, there are several cases that illustrate how some institutions have been able to successfully stand out as productive examples amid the mounting challenges. This means that they are after becoming *research universities*, mirroring Anglo-Saxon models. According to Altbach (2009, p. 15), research universities are

> institutions committed to the creation and dissemination of knowledge in a range of disciplines and fields and featuring the appropriate laboratories,

libraries, and other infrastructures that permit teaching and research at the highest possible level. Research universities educate students, usually at all degree levels—an indication that the focus extends beyond research. Indeed, this synergy of research and teaching is a hallmark of these institutions, which employ mainly full-time academics who hold doctoral degrees.

These institutions are seeking to gain prominent positions in national and international rankings in order to enjoy prestige, which is a dominant factor for competition. Now, what characteristics should a university that wants to advance knowledge and become a research university have? Philip Altbach (2009) created a list of key challenges leaders may face to transform private institutions from teaching-oriented to emerging research universities. These basic points may be useful for Latin American private universities that are looking for ways to advance a global agenda in STI starting from institutional missions, namely:

1. *Funding.* As is well documented, this type of institution is highly expensive and requires substantial sources of income to maintain and develop the multiple dimensions of research. Universities with high levels of research attract more resources, such as investments for facilities, endowments, equipment for research, internal budgetary resources, grants, and scholarships for students (Lee and Rhoads 2004). However, and since most of the private institutions are tuition-driven, it is difficult to develop long-term research projects depending on students' fees. This is a challenging area for most private universities in the region (Gregorutti 2011b). Operational costs of any complex institution are high and even more for research that demands full-time professors and researchers who would teach a few classes. Some administrators may see research as a luxury, if no aggressive external funding is incorporated as a key budgetary strategy. Latin American governments provide several types of grants and support for researchers. However, going after grants and money from companies is not a simple task and requires the development of strategic decision-making to be effective.
2. *Research culture.* Faculty research productivity and innovation in advanced institutions is also a by-product of internal cultures that support these activities (Bleiklie 2005). It may be especially difficult to implement cultural changes in the context of institutions that are deeply rooted in teaching traditions. However, through policies that promote monetary and career incentives, departments can facilitate internal cultural changes. Hiring new faculty members with doctoral degrees will promote research. Since these new professors have

passed through intense socialization experiences in which they have assumed the role of researchers, administrators can involve them in advancing new projects and peer-reviewing publication with students (Austin 2002). In addition, by encouraging collegial discussions, professors develop research areas that have potential impact. Most of the Latin American countries have some possible strength in agriculture and alternative technologies for mineral and ocean resources. These areas, along with other regional needs, can become a nexus to companies that may want to use some of the services universities provide.

3. *Commercialism and the market.* As private universities explore relationships with companies and external sources of funding, they may risk academic autonomy. This is an international issue that impacts especially the development of patents with a high potential for financial return and that compete with similar inventions in a given market. Many universities may have to adjust to a different logic when it comes to publishing some of their researchers' findings (Slaughter et al. 2004). Here universities need to carefully assess through legal partners how to deal with these stressful situations to protect researchers, inventions, and relationships with external funders.

4. *Autonomy and accountability.* As an extension of the previous point, a truly research university looks into the potential impact its discoveries can have over a region or even globally. But it must always do it maintaining a strong academic autonomy. This is a problematic and complex task. As universities develop new ideas with economic implications, their discoveries and contributions are no longer an exclusive institutional asset. They actually belong to a community of researchers since in many cases projects are carried out through teams from several institutions, the funding party, and the broader society that will assimilate a specific knowledge or technology. The increasing interchange of scientific information that circulates through highly specialized networks of researchers may create some stress to private institutions. Current globalized scholarship is becoming more intertwined with a paradigm of internal and external networks. This requires an unfamiliar mindset for some private universities that makes scholarly work more intricate and socially constructed (Ylijoki 2003). Therefore, this attitude should be nurtured throughout all levels of university actors to have a successful and realistic contribution to the existing knowledge-based society.

5. *Meritocracy.* One of the central pillars for advancing scholarly work is to select and promote the best possible human resources available.

Some private Latin American universities suffer from corruption, cronyism, and nepotism. Universities may justify decisions based on political and ideological reasons. This is a challenging issue since it is impossible to have academic excellence if the best human resources are not recognized and promoted according to their outstanding performance. Selection and promotion mechanisms must favor the best. Transparent and fair academic structures are essential to recruit and retain the most prolific professors. Internal policies and practices should assure that meritocracy is a core value; otherwise, it will be difficult for a private university to really engage in serious research developments.

6. *Academic freedom.* This is another key value for an institution committed to advancing knowledge under the model of research university. It means that a professor has the freedom to carry out a research project and teach in a class or publish his or her findings to share ideas. In this way universities allow faculty members to freely distribute and exchange ideas regardless their content. This can be very controversial and challenging for some universities, especially confessional ones. Although there is no "neutral" model for scholarly work, every institution needs to ensure the maximum possible openness to develop research. If religious beliefs interfere with some aspects of this value, administrators must provide alternatives to avoid tensions.

7. *Academic profession.* This aspect is linked to a previous point that looks at providing the best possible conditions for outstanding faculty members with competitive salaries and advanced work settings. The tenure figure is also an essential component for stability and institutional commitment. Higher faculty research productivity has been shown to correlate with full-time professors (Baker and Wiseman 2008; Bunton and Mallon 2007; Johnsrud 2008; Schwartzman 2008). Professors need a collegial type of academic structure to freely discuss and develop their professional interests in association with inside and outside peers. Administrators should promote this to facilitate academic innovation and professional development (García de Blas and Mora Caballero 2014). A faculty member who produces research and collaborates within and between institutions can be a main source of research for a growing institution, bringing prestige to that professor's department and university (Moore et al. 2001).

8. *Students and graduate programs.* Students are a key component for advancing research that in turns may bring prestige and a broader recognition, making the university more attractive to good prospect

students. They can carry on many responsibilities to help professors in large research projects. Some private universities in Latin America, like ITESM in Mexico, have been adding new graduate programs to recruit also outstanding students who are actively involved in research with their professors (Cantú et al. 2009). Graduate programs facilitate research as they link professors, students, and academic degrees (Golde and Walker 2006).

The issues discussed here can be a starting point to shifting into serious research as a model for institutions that are really willing to make significant changes. As Schwartzman (2008) summarized, Latin American universities that want to produce knowledge must face central questions regarding: (a) sustained research funding; (b) the promotion of a clear development plan for professors to expand scholar activities; (c) avoiding tensions with copyright as new ideas and patents are produced. These three dimensions represent matters that leaders of private universities need to address as they unfold new research strategies (Powers 2004). However, a transformation that would take into considerations all these elements will require a deep reengineering of purposes and methods of management. Administrators will need multiple agreements with faculty, alumni, and board members that can be summarized in the following steps:

1. *Negotiate the model.* It seems an obvious step, but often a few top officers try to implement a model that the majority does not understand or like and they will naturally oppose. This is especially true when cultural changes imply revising traditions built for many years and that in some cases trace back to the foundation of the institution. Most universities can carry on some levels of research, but becoming a research university is not necessarily a good fit for all good intentioned institutions (Scott 2006). As it was discussed earlier, producing knowledge involves more than having good laboratories and hiring specialized scholars. This is a model of openness with a mindset that implies a radical metamorphosis for some universities that are accustomed to manage personnel and activities as high schools. Professors and general constituencies can see some of these changes as threatening and beyond bearable (Serow 2000). According to some case studies presented in this book, it is possible to conclude that a few universities have been repositioning as research oriented from their local or regional context with a global agenda in mind. All this requires maturity and collegial discussions to ponder options and possibilities. This is probably one of the most difficult decisions to become a research university in Latin America.

2. *Management and structure.* Even though the most advanced and consolidated institutions have more resources and strategies to reorganize research innovation, there is always room for other institutional peers to reposition. However, the task will not be simple as they confront organizational challenges. One of them has to do with their management structure, as it was already mentioned. Many have command chains that are top-down with several disconnections between academic decision-making and professors. Faculties/schools and their departments have little word in their economic and administrational involvement. Departments tend to have reduced spaces to restructure their needs, and sometimes they must implement academic plans without much discussion. In some cases, administrators who do not understand what is happening at the departmental level and their research development design top-down strategies (Gregorutti 2011b). Situations like these can be stressful and counterproductive to the promotion of the research model for a private university. More autonomy and trust needs to be given to lower levels of administration. That means more freedom and accountability for hiring new personnel, spending budgets, and strategies to increase faculty research productivity.
3. *Leadership.* Several chapters of this book describe real cases of top leaders that have set forward innovative and exciting plans to reinvent their universities after a research-intensive model of institution. However, these transformational changes were far from imposed. If policies are implemented without an overall understanding and agreement, it is possible to predict that results will not be positive. In addition, leaders have to develop strategies that include long-term plans to give a clear sense of direction throughout years. Any change will demand new thinking and revision of previous vision statements. Here the cohesive influence of solid leadership is a necessity.

In short, private universities that are interested in developing research should consider finding diverse sources of funding, developing a research culture, working with private companies and understanding the markets, balancing autonomy and accountability, creating product-based meritocratic systems, rethinking the academic profession, and developing graduate education. In addition, this requires renegotiating institutional models, transforming management and organizational structures, and promoting leadership. The next section includes some conclusions about the reflections presented in this chapter.

Final Thoughts

As we have described, Latin American private universities have gone through different stages and increasing challenges to achieve higher quality and research levels. This situation has generated institutional segmentation where traditional teaching-oriented and research-intensive universities coexist. This is the product of long-term policies that international and national organizations and agencies have been promoting (Gregorutti et al. 2014).

Whether institutions accept those policies or not, it is undeniable that issues around quality and research productivity have impacted Latin American private universities. These trends have also prompted an increasing segmentation not between public and private, but within the same private sector. Universities are adopting new forms of elitism through STI and positions in rankings. This isomorphism after the research university model represents and brings challenges and opportunities for Latin American private higher education. One of them is to produce a positive impact in the region as they engage in serious research projects (Bensimon et al. 2004). This suggests that private universities have the potential to make significant contributions to improve Latin American economies and societies. On the other side, demand-absorbing and less prestigious universities should consider the cost of producing highly competitive research, as they see this the research university as the "want-to-be" model. Reconverting a mainly teaching institution may not be the best fit even for the region. If training is done with minimum quality standards, less research-oriented universities can make contributions to this globalized and knowledge society. After all, deciding strategies to handle all these trends in a proactive way may be one of the most difficult tasks university leaders must face (Rama 2010).

Note

1. The largest government oil company that runs the extraction of petroleum in Brazil.

References

Altbach, Philip G. 2002. *Educación Superior Privada* (Private Higher Education). México City, Mexico: National Autonomous University of Mexico.

———. 2009. "Peripheries and Centers: Research Universities in Developing Countries." *Asia Pacific Education Review* 10 (1): 15–27.

Austin, Ann. 2002. "Preparing the Next Generation of Faculty: Graduate School as Socialization to the Academic Career." *The Journal of Higher Education* 73 (1): 94–122.

Baker, David, and Alexander W. Wiseman, editors. 2008. *The Worldwide Transformation of Higher Education*. Bingley, UK: Emerald.

Barsky, Osvaldo, Victor Sigal, and Mabel Davila. 2004. *Los Desafíos de la Universidad Argentina* (Challenges of Argentinean Universities). Buenos Aires, Argentina: Siglo XXI.

Bensimon, Estela, Donald Polkinghorne, Georgia Bauman, and Edlyn Vallejo. 2004. "Doing Research that Makes a Difference." *Journal of Higher Education* 75 (1): 104–126.

Bleiklie, Ivar. 2005. "Organizing Higher Education in a Knowledge Society." *Higher Education* 49 (1–2): 31–59.

Bok, Derek. 2010. *Universidades a la Venta* (Universities on Sale). Valencia, Spain: University of Valencia.

Brunner, José Joaquín. 1985. *Universidad y Sociedad en América Latina: Un Esquema de Interpretación* (University and Society in Latin America: A Model for Interpretation). Caracas, Venezuela: UNESCO Regional Center for Higher Education in Latin America.

Bunton, Sarah, and William Mallon. 2007. "The Impact of Centers and Institutes on Faculty Life: Findings from a Study of Life Sciences Faculty at Research-Intensive Universities' Medical Schools." *Innovative Higher Education* 32 (2): 93–103.

Burness, John. 2008. "The Rankings Game: Who's Playing Whom?" *The Chronicle of Higher Education* 55 (2): A80.

Cantú, Francisco, Alberto Bustani, Arturo Molina, and Héctor Moreira. 2009. "Knowledge-Based Development Model: The Research Chair Strategy." *Journal of Knowledge Management* 13 (1): 154–170.

Centro Interuniversitario de Desarrollo Andino (CINDA: Inter-University Center for Andean Development). 2009. *La Educación Superior en Ibero América. Informe 2007* (Higher Education in Iberic-America. 2007 Report). Santiago, Chile: CINDA.

Delgado, Jorge Enrique. 2014. "Scientific Journals of Universities of Chile, Colombia, and Venezuela: Actors and Roles." *Education Policy Analysis Archives* 22 (34, Special issue: The Future of Educational Research Journals). Available online at: http://dx.doi.org/10.14507/epaa.v22n34.2014, accessed on June 20, 2014.

Delgado-Troncoso, Jorge Enrique, and Gustavo Enrique Fischman. 2014. "The Future of Latin American Academic Journals." In *The Future of the Academic Journal* (2nd edition), edited by Bill Cope and Angus Phillips (pp. 379–400). Oxford: Chandos Elsevier.

Espinoza, Oscar. 2005. "Privatization and Commercialization of Chilean Higher Education: A Critical Perspective" ("Privatización y Comercialización de La Educación Superior en Chile: Una Visión Crítica"). *Revista de La Educación Superior* (Journal of Higher Education) XXXIV (135): 41–60.

Espinoza, Óscar, and Luis Eduardo González. 2013. "Accreditation in Higher Education in Chile: Results and Consequences." *Quality Assurance in Education* 21 (1): 20–38.

Fukuyama, Francis. 2004. *La Construcción del Estado. Hacia un Nuevo Orden Mundial en el Siglo XXI* (Construction of the State. Toward a New Order in the XXI Century). Madrid, Spain: Ediciones B.

Gaffikin, Frank, and David Perry. 2009. "Discourses and Strategic Visions: The US Research University as an Institutional Manifestation of Neoliberalism in a Global Era." *American Educational Research Journal* 46 (1): 115–144.

García de Blas, Elsa, and Antonio Jesús Mora Caballero. 2014. "La Endogamia Enferma el Campus" ("Endogamy Sickens the Campus"). *Diario El País*. Available online at: http://sociedad.elpais.com/sociedad/2014/03/23/actualidad/1395604536_271638.html, accessed on February 20, 2014.

García Guadilla, Carmen. 1998. *Situación y Principales Dinámicas de Transformación de la Educación Superior en América Latina* (Situation and Main Dynamics of Latin American Higher Education Transformation). Caracas, Venezuela: UNESCO Regional Center for Higher Education in Latin America.

Gascón Muro, Patricia, and José Cepeda Dovala. 2007. "El Comercio de Servicios Educativos y la Educación Superior" ("Commerce of Education Services and Higher Education"). *Reencuentro (Reunion)* 50 (December): 73–82.

Ginsburg, Mark, Oscar Espinoza, Simona Popa, and Mayumi Terano. 2005. "Globalization and Higher Education in Chile and Romania: The Roles of the International Monetary Fund, World Bank, and World Trade Organization." In *International Handbook on Globalization, Education, and Policy Research. Global Pedagogies and Policies*, edited by Joseph Zaida (pp. 221–234). New York: Springer.

Golde, Chris, and George Walker. 2006. *Envisioning the Future of Doctoral Education: Preparing Stewards of the Discipline*. San Francisco, CA: Jossey Bass.

Gregorutti, Gustavo. 2010. "La Acreditación de los Posgrados en Instituciones Privadas de Educación Superior Mexicanas" ("Accreditation of Graduate Programs in Mexican Private Higher Education Institutions"). *Reencuentro (Reunion)* 59 (December): 61–69.

———. 2011a. *Following the Path, from Teaching to Research University*. Newcastle, UK: Cambridge Scholars Publishing.

———. 2011b. "La Producción de Investigación en las Universidades Privadas: Estudio de un Caso" ("Research Production among Private Universities: Case Study"). *Enfoques XIII* (Approaches XIII) 2 (Spring): 5–20.

Gregorutti, Gustavo, Óscar Espinoza, Luis Eduardo González, and Javier Loyola. 2014. "What if Privatising Higher Education Becomes an Issue? The Case of Chile and Mexico." *Compare: A Journal of Comparative and International Education* 14: 1–23.

Holm-Nielsen, Lauritz B., Kristian Thorn, José Joaquín Brunner, and Jorge Balán. 2005. "Regional and International Challenges to Higher Education in Latin America." In *Higher Education in Latin America: The International Dimension*, edited by Hans de Wit, Isabel Christina Jaramillo, Jocelyne Gacel-Ávila, and Jane Knight. Washington, DC: The World Bank.

Huang, Mu-Hsuan. 2011. "A Comparison of Three Major Academic Rankings for World Universities: From a Research Evaluation Perspective." *Journal of Library and Information Studies* 9 (1): 1–25.

Johnsrud, Linda. 2008. "Faculty Work: Making Our Research Matter-More." *Review of Higher Education* 31 (4): 489–509.

Krotch, Pedro. 2001. *Educación Superior y Reformas Comparadas (Higher Education and Compared Reforms)*. Buenos Aires, Argentina: Quilmes National University Press.

Lee, Jenny, and Robert Rhoads. 2004. "Faculty Entrepreneurialism and the Challenge to Undergraduate Education at Research Universities." *Research in Higher Education* 45 (7): 739–760.

Levy, Daniel. 1995. *El Estado y la Educación Superior en América Latina: Desafíos Privados al Predominio Público* (The State and Higher Education in Latin America: Private Challenges to the Public Dominance). México City, Mexico: National Autonomous University of Mexico, Latin American School of Social Sciences, and Porrúa.

Marginson, Simon, and Marijk van der Wende. 2007. "Top Rank or to Be Ranked: The Impact of Global Rankings in Higher Education." *Journal of Studies in International Education* 11 (3/4): 306–329.

Merton, Robert. 1968. "The Matthew Effect in Science." *Science* 159 (3810): 56–63.

Monckeberg, Maria Olivi. 2012. *Con Fines de Lucro. La Escandalosa Historia de la Universidades Privadas de Chile* (For Profit. Scandalous History of Private Universities in Chile). Santiago, Chile: Editorial Debate.

Moore, William, Robert Newman, and Geoffrey Turnbull. 2001. "Reputational Capital and Academic Pay." *Economic Inquiry* 39 (4): 663–671.

Powers, Joshua. 2004. "R&D Funding Sources and University Technology Transfer: What Is Stimulating Universities to Be More Entrepreneurial?" *Research in Higher Education* 45 (1): 1–23.

Rama, Claudio. 2006. *La Tercera Reforma de la Educación Superior en América Latina* (Third Higher Education Reform in Latin America). Buenos Aires, Argentina: Fondo de Cultura Económica.

———. 2009a. "La Tendencia a la Masificación de la Cobertura de la Educación Superior en América Latina" ("Access Massification Trends of Latin American Higher Education"). *Revista Iberoamericana de Educación* (Iberic-American Journal of Education) (50): 173–195.

———. 2009b. *Paradigmas Emergentes, Competencias Profesionales y Nuevos Modelos Universitarios en América Latina* (Emerging Paradigms, Professional Competencies, and New University Models in Latin America). San Luis, Argentina: Nueva Editorial Universitaria.

———. 2009c. "La Tendencia a la Propietarización de la Investigación" ("Proprietarizing Trends of Research"). *Revista Sudamericana de Educación y Sociedad—RSEUS* (South American Journal of Education and Society) 1 (1): 54–72.

———. 2010. *La Universidad Latinoamericana en la Encrucijada de sus Tendencias* (Crossroads of Latin American University Trends) (3rd edition). México City, Mexico: Latin American Institute for Education Communication.

———. 2012a. *La Nueva Fase de la Universidad Privada en América Latina* (New Phase of Latin American Private University). Montevideo, Uruguay: Magro.

———. 2012b. "El Negocio Universitario 'For-Profit' en América Latina" ("Latin American for-Profit University Business"). *Revista de Educación Superior* (Journal of Higher Education) 41 (164): 59–95.

———. 2014. "El Cambio en las Lógicas del Conocimiento y la Transformación de las Revistas Académicas" ("Change in Knowledge Logics and Transformation of Academic Journals"). *Revista Cuaderno de Investigación en la Educación* (Notebook of Education Research Journal) 29 (Diciembre): 97–111.

Rauhvargers, Andrejs. 2011. *Global University Rankings and Their Impact*. Brussels, Belgium: European University Association.

Rodríguez, Francisco. 2005. *El Financiamiento de la Educación Superior en América Latina. Estudio Comparativo* (Financing Higher Education in Latin American. Comparative Study). Caracas, Venezuela: Instituto Internacional para la Educación Superior en América Latina y el Caribe de la UNESCO (IESALC: UNESCO International Institute for Higher Education in Latin America and the Caribbean).

Salmi, Jamil. 2009. *The Challenge of Establishing World-Class Universities*. Washington, DC: The World Bank.

Schwartzman, Simon. 2008. *Universidad y Desarrollo en Latinoamérica: Experiencias exitosas de Centros de Investigación* (University and Development in Latin America: Successful Experiences among Research Centers). Caracas, Venezuela: IESALC.

Scott, John. 2006. "The Mission of the University: Medieval to Postmodern Transformations." *Journal of Higher Education* 77 (1): 1–39.

Serow, Robert. 2000. "Research and Teaching at a Research University." *Higher Education* 40 (4): 449–463.

Silas, Juan Carlos. 2005. "Realidades y Tendencias en la Educación Superior Privada Mexicana" ("Realities and Trends in Mexican Private Higher Education"). *Perfiles Educativos* (Educational Profiles) 27 (109–110): 7–37.

———. 2009. "Context and Regulation Matter: Mexican Private Higher Education 1990-2007." Paper presented at 6th International Workshop on Higher Education Reforms. Mexico City, Mexico: Center for Research and Advanced Studies.

———, editor. 2013. *Estado de la Educación Superior en América Latina. El Balance Público-Privado* (Situation of Latin American Higher Education. Public-Private Balance). Mexico City, Mexico: Asociación Nacional de Universidades e Instituciones de Educación Superior (ANUIES: National Association of Universities and Higher Education Institutions), ITESO.

Slaughter, Sheila, Cynthia Archerd, and Teresa Campbell. 2004. "Boundaries and Quandaries: How Professors Negotiate Market Relations." *The Review of Higher Education* 28 (1): 129–165.

Toakley, Arthur. 2004. "Globalization, Sustainable Development and Universities." *Higher Education Policy* 17 (3): 311–324.
UNESCO IESALC. 2006. *La Metamorfosis de la Educación Superior. Informe de la Educación Superior 2000–2005* (Metamorphosis of Higher Education. Report on Higher Education 2000–2005). Caracas, Venezuela: IESALC.
Ylijoki, Oili-Helena. 2003. "Entangled in Academic Capitalism? A Case-Study on Changing Ideals and Practices of University Research." *Higher Education* 45 (3): 307–335.

Chapter 3

Latin American Private Universities in the Context of Competition and Research Productivity

Jorge Enrique Delgado

Introduction

For several decades, science and technology systems in Latin America prioritized infrastructure and capacity development. In the past 20 years, attention moved towards incentivizing research productivity and developing mechanisms to evaluate individual and institutional performance (Aupetit 2007; Delgado 2011a). Research in Latin America has been traditionally concentrated in major public universities, in particular, megauniversities (Didriksson et al. 2008). However, there are also successful private universities that have, in some cases, a longer tradition and often more flexibility than their public counterparts to respond to pressures from the knowledge-based economies. In addition, private higher education institutions (HEIs) have been one of the drivers of higher education expansion, when governments have been incapable of providing access to postsecondary education to the growing numbers of high school graduates (Rama 2006). The wide spectrum of private HEIs shows that these entities have evolved in different ways and their mission purposes do not always promote faculty and/or institutional research. However, some Latin American private universities are among the best placed in international rankings that incorporate analysis of indicators such as competitiveness and science, technology, and innovation (STI) productivity (Altbach and Balán 2007; Delgado and Weidman 2012; Salmi 2009).

Research on private universities in Latin America has not been abundant in terms of productivity and successful cases, even though some of them have reached world-class status. In 2004, Alma Maldonado-Maldonado and her colleagues published a book titled, *Private Higher Education: An International Bibliography*, where they compiled a list of titles of the most relevant publications published between 1967 and 2004 on the topic. The book includes 185 references (books, reports, conference papers, journal articles, and dissertations) on Latin American private higher education that cover themes such as religion-affiliated universities (Catholic—Jesuit and LaSallist—and other Christian institutions—Adventist and Lutheran); relations between government, public policy and the markets; comparisons between public and private higher education; trends on quality, evaluation, and accreditation; history, trends, and future; issues of expansion and coverage; and a few ones on think tanks and research centers. As issues of research, productivity, competitiveness, globalization, and rankings become more relevant, they appear more frequently in the education scholarship. However, those issues are not much studied in the context of Latin American higher education, particularly private universities. This could be observed, for instance, in the bibliography that the *Comparative Education Review* publishes every year (Comparative and International Education Society 2009, 2010, 2011, 2012, 2013). The few references on private university productivity primarily describe individual institutional cases.

Purpose and Structure of This Chapter

Despite their importance, private HEIs have not received enough attention from the international scholarship about their participation in the knowledge-based societies and economies. The purpose of this chapter is to describe the context of higher education and STI in which Latin American private universities are immersed. The framework is developed to show the environment and outcomes in terms of competitiveness and productivity. The first part of the chapter describes the situation of STI in Latin America. It includes current global trends and regional indicators. The second section analyzes the context of higher education in Latin America. It briefly depicts the history of higher education in the region and analyzes its role and insertion in the economic models and STI systems. The third part reviews some of the main university rankings that show the current emphasis and interest in competitiveness and productivity and identifies which private universities are among the best ranked. The conclusion looks at some characteristics that successful private universities could have in a context of STI productivity and competitiveness and reviews the growing emphasis on innovation for the future of universities.

Context of Science, Technology, and Innovation in Latin America

Globalization of the world economy is based on a market-oriented model that emphasizes competitiveness and where knowledge plays a key role (some consider that knowledge has become a commodity). The globalization of information, communication, and other technologies also boost knowledge generation and dissemination (Delgado 2010). In this context of knowledge-based societies and economies, the sectors of education (Rama 2006) and STI (Vessuri et al. 2008) acquire a new dimension, which have become essential for the competitiveness of nations. Thus, governments are responsible for creating public policy and the conditions necessary to articulate education and STI to other sectors of the economy. Education has the role of integrating different societal actors and developing national identity; it is one of the drivers of human capital development and compensation of social inequalities (Inter-American Development Bank—IADB 2010; Rama 2006; Task Force on Higher Education and Society 2000; World Bank 2002). Along with STI, education, particularly the graduate levels of higher education, supports the advancement of the productive sector and economic competitiveness through innovation. Academia is seen to work in alliance with the private sector and the government in a model that is called the triple helix of innovation (García Guadilla 2010; Marins et al. 2012; Rama 2006, 2009).

Globalization and competitiveness also imply internationalization. Globalization associated to internationalization of universities shows the following policy trends: (a) incentives through government funding; (b) normative for faculty promotion; and (c) competitive public funding for research groups and centers. In this context, the new scenario of knowledge includes: (a) normative changes: global competition of research; (b) copyright: knowledge property; and (c) research depending on funding and external alliances. Pressure for research also increases institutional differentiation and it is concentrated in world-class universities (Rama 2009).

Current Status of STI in the Region

Indicators Used to Evaluate STI

Actors, activities, and outcomes of the scientific enterprise are usually evaluated through indicators related to institutional capacity, research capacity, and productiveness and quality. Variables associated with the institution include faculty/student relation, library development, support for teaching, education level of professors, faculty salaries, full-/part-time student enrollment, and students' cultural capital (IADB 2010; Rama 2006; Task Force on Higher Education and Society 2000; World Bank 2002). In the context of productiveness, other variables have become more relevant. Some are indicators used to measure research capacity, such as expenditure on research and development (R&D), STI personnel, and number of researchers with higher degrees, mainly doctorates. However, publications (mainly articles published in indexed journals) and patents are the most used variables to "determine" not only productiveness but also the quality of the scientific/scholarly enterprise: the number of articles published in indexed journals and recognized scientific/scholarly journals for the former (Delgado 2011a, 2011b; Delgado and Weidman 2012; Santa and Herrero 2010) and the amount of requested and obtained patents for the latter (Aupetit 2007). Some indicators like innovation through technology transfer and contribution to sustainable or social development due to the growth of STI are more difficult to assess.

Scientific Research in Latin America

One of the main publications on the status of science in Latin America is the annual report published by the Center for the Study of Science, Development, and Education (REDES: *Centro de Estudios sobre Ciencia, Desarrollo y Educación*) that is located in Buenos Aires, Argentina. The main indicators related to productivity that REDES uses include (Albornoz et al. 2012): (a) context indicators like R&D investment in terms of purchasing power parity; (b) human resources with reference to full-time STI employees; and (c) productivity as measured by publications (data from the Science Citation Index—SCI and Pascal databases) and patents (data provided by the national industrial property agencies) (Aguirre-Bastos and Gupta 2009; Albornoz et al. 2012).

In 1999, José Joaquín Brunner synthesized scientific research in Latin America in eight points. Even though there has been some progress in the past decade, these points still seem to be relevant to understand the challenges that the Latin American scientific endeavor needs to overcome:

- Academic community in R&D is small, science grows slowly in the international arena, and it is concentrated in a few countries.
- Graduate education, a possible source for local researchers, grows slowly.
- There is a low investment in R&D as a percentage of the gross domestic product (GDP).
- There is almost an exclusive reliance on public funding for research that is starting to become competitive.
- There is a separation between the industries and higher education, which is evident with a low private investment in R&D.
- Mainstream scientific productivity from Latin America has a modest participation in the global context.
- There is disequilibrium between the imported technology and the one that is locally produced.

In short, STI in Latin America needs more support from the governments, increase the basis of highly trained researchers, diversify sources of funding, get the private sector more involved, emphasize products (e.g., publications and patents) with a global impact, and push for more balance in the transfer to society of foreign- and locally generated technology.

R&D Investment

With respect to resource allocation, several attempts to diversify funding for research have shown modest results with the exception of some experiences in Brazil, Colombia, and Uruguay (Aupetit 2007; IADB 2006). The countries with the highest investment in R&D in 2003 (IADB 2006) were Panama, Venezuela, and Chile, while the lowest ones were Honduras and Argentina (for different reasons, like the 2000–2003 financial crisis in Argentina).

The most recent report was published by REDES in 2012 and covers the period of 2001–2010. The report describes how Latin America showed steady economic growth between 2002 and 2007, which slowed down with the 2008 global crisis and started to recover in 2009 mainly influenced by the accelerated growth of Brazil and Mexico. In 2010, Latin America had a 3.1 percent share of government investment on R&D with a growth rate larger than any other region in the world. At the end of the 2001–2010 decade, R&D investment doubled. However, the distribution of R&D investment was not balanced among countries: Brazil represented

60 percent, Mexico 20 percent, and Argentina 9.7 percent of the total. The mean R&D investment in the region was 0.75 percent GDP with only Brazil showing R&D investment that surpasses the 1 percent threshold (1.16 percent) (Albornoz et al. 2012).

Human Resources

With respect to human resources, when compared with more developed countries, Latin America has traditionally performed modestly in indicators such as the proportion of researchers regarding economically active population (human resources with reference to full-time STI employees), the percentage of granted doctoral degrees compared to the total enrollment in higher education, and the concentration of STI activities in research universities that mostly depend on public funding. The amount of researchers and technicians in Latin America grew 80 percent between 2001 and 2010 to reach around 270,000, which represents 3.7 percent of the share of researchers worldwide. Analyzed by countries, Brazil has more than 50 percent of the researchers and technicians in the region. Argentina, Brazil, and Mexico together account for more than 90 percent.

One of the obstacles for the development of research in Latin American universities has been the low number of full-time faculty. Universities in the region have traditionally attracted part-time instructors who are active in the professions and the government. Recently, some indicators show how the percentage of full- and part-time professors has increased among public universities in Latin America, even though part-timers are still the majority (Bernasconi 2008).

The number of students completing undergraduate and higher levels of education is another indicator of the human resources category. In Latin America the number of alumni from undergraduate programs showed a larger growth in the social sciences, but it was steady in agricultural, natural, and basic sciences. At the master's level, there was also a larger growth of social sciences and humanities graduates, followed by engineering, technology-associated majors, and medical sciences; the number of graduates from master's programs tripled between 2001 and 2010. Most doctors graduated from programs in the natural and basic sciences, followed by social sciences, humanities, and medical sciences (Albornoz et al. 2012). At the doctoral level, 71 percent students are concentrated in Brazil (50 percent) and Mexico (21 percent) (García Guadilla 2010).

Publications and Patents

Productivity indicators showed different trends. The number of publications from Latin America doubled in SCI between 2001 and 2010. However, the publication-researcher ratio has remained constant during this period. Growth of publications was notable mostly in the databases: CAB Index (agriculture), SCI (interdisciplinary), Biosis (biology), Pascal (interdisciplinary), Medline (biomedical), Compendex (engineering), and Inspec (physics). It was lower in Chemical Abstracts (Albornoz et al. 2012; Aupetit 2007; Brunner and Ferrada 2011). A study on publications by country carried out by Jorge Enrique Delgado and John C. Weidman (2012) showed how Brazil, Mexico, Argentina, and Chile had the largest number of publications in SCI (year interval: 1990–2010) and the interdisciplinary database Scopus (year interval: 1996–2010), dominance that increased in that period. However, the dynamics of publications varied among countries; for instance, Colombia showed the largest growth of publications in both indexes (1,245 percent in SCI and 706 percent in Scopus), becoming the fifth country with most publications in Latin America. Publications are concentrated in public megauniversities (García Guadilla 2010).

On the other side, in the past two decades, patents grew 30 percent in Brazil and 7 percent in Mexico but decreased 20 percent in Argentina. Most patent requests came from nonresidents and foreign companies (Albornoz et al. 2012; Aupetit 2007).

As it has been described, research productivity assessments tend to emphasize publication of journal articles and patents. However, along with the interest and pressures to publish in journals that are included in the indexes with the best international reputation, such as SCI (and other indexes included in the Thomson Reuters Web of Science—WoS) and Scopus (by Elsevier), scientific and scholarly journals from Latin America show an important quantitative and qualitative growth in the past two decades. Prompted by the creation of regional and national repositories and indexes and the enactment of STI policy, journals in Latin America serve the purpose of providing scholars and researchers from the region with forums in their spoken languages (mainly Spanish and Portuguese) and areas of intellectual production. Most of these journals are published by academic units (schools or research centers) within universities.[1] With a few exceptions, the characteristics and dynamics of journal publication by Latin American universities, public and/or private, have not been studied (Alperin et al. 2008, 2011; Delgado 2010, 2011a, 2014; Delgado-Troncoso and Fischman 2014; Fischman et al. 2010).

Higher Education Systems, Private Universities, and Productivity

As explained earlier, even though there is recent evidence of some progress, STI outcomes from Latin America have been historically modest.

With a few exceptions, research in Latin America has been concentrated in a few universities, mostly public. This section briefly describes the context, history, and evolution of higher education in the region, its context and role within the STI systems, and the participation and characteristics of private universities.

Latin American Higher Education after Independence

Spanish America had 25 universities when declared independence from the crown, and there were no universities in Brazil. University systems suffered changes as the countries experienced several transformations and crises. The first public universities in the republican era were created in the 1840s in Chile and Uruguay (Balán 2013), where education in the professions (Napoleonic model) continued to be the main mission of the university even though there was some interest in turning them into centers of intellectual debate, places for research and scholarship, and forums to discuss national issues. Jorge Balán confirms the lack of emphasis on research among the initial universities in Latin America: "Applied research, technological innovation, and links with industrial and agricultural sectors were unusual, as they were perceived to be most properly the function of autonomous government institutes and laboratories outside of the university" (p. x). This was a defining characteristic that still has an impact in the region.

Economic Models, Higher Education, and Science Systems

Scientific development of a country can be understood through the economic model in place in a specific time frame. When analyzing the history of STI policy in Latin America since the twentieth century, Carlos Aguirre-Bastos and Mahabir P. Gupta (2009) explain how most policies have taken place within three economic models: import substitution, liberalization and privatization, and twenty-first-century socialism. After the period of the import substitution of the 1930s, there were numerous efforts to modernize and reform the national universities between 1950 and 1975 (Levy 2005). Often convinced of the role of research, industrialization, and economic development, universities sought to achieve transformations that would help them better serve national development. Reforms were promoted by international aid agencies following university models from English-speaking countries. They included the professionalization and full-time commitment of faculty to research, the formalization of graduate education, and the strengthening of discipline-based departments and the central administration (Balán 2013; Levy 2005). However, reform and expansion of higher education systems was difficult to carry out due to the great amount of resources required and a great deal of institutional reluctance to change. Therefore, universities tended to be underfunded and governments and administrators found it hard to make key decisions. Some of the options were to create new HEIs, strengthen agencies to fund and coordinate STI outside of the university sector (Balán 2013), and develop policy to allow the expansion of private subsector, which had an early development in Chile, Brazil, and Colombia (Balán 2013; Levy 1986).

Vertical differentiation of Latin American higher education has occurred through the growth of research funding and graduate education provided through the STI agencies that the most competitive universities take the most advantage of. This has been particularly important in Brazil and Chile, followed by in Mexico and Argentina, and less in the other countries. More recently, with the increased pressure to get the private sector involved in supporting applied research, technology development, and innovation via knowledge transfer, more collaboration between public and private HEIs, governments, and the productive sectors has been sought (triple helix model mentioned earlier) (Balán 2013).

As it was stated early in this chapter, pressures for competitiveness have grown in recent years, in part because of the visibility and interest that international and local league tables and rankings attract. In this context, knowledge has become a commodity, and it is concentrated in some dominant economies that also tend to absorb the most talented people from other regions. Knowledge is also concentrated in what are called world-class universities that occupy the top positions in international rankings. Leading English-speaking countries (United States, United Kingdom, Canada, Australia, and New Zealand) and Western Europe concentrate 65 percent of the world's publications, 76 percent of international students, and 93 percent of top 100 positions in rankings (García Guadilla 2010). In Latin America, leading universities "are known to do poorly in international rankings, given the weakness or low intensity of their research activities" (Balán 2013, p. xvii). Within the region, there is also concentration of scientific outputs and outcomes in Brazil, Mexico, and Argentina. The next sections explore the history, characteristics, and conditions of Latin American private universities for the development of STI.

Private Universities in Latin America

History of Private Universities in the Region

The University of Santo Domingo was the first institution founded in the New World (1538). In the eighteenth century there were six universities in Latin America: Santo Domingo, Quito, Bogotá, Lima, La Paz, and Mexico (Rama 2006). The first private universities of the republican era were founded in Chile and Brazil. They had functions similar to their public counterparts but enjoyed more "freedom in administration, governance, and finance, while only occasionally receiving a direct public subsidy" (Balán 2013, p. ix). The increasing demand for higher education during the twentieth century was the opportunity for Jesuits to return to Latin America.[2] In 2000, there were 280 religious universities (80 percent Catholic) enrolling 1.3 million students. Many of the best Latin American private universities, in terms of research productivity and development, are affiliated to the Catholic Church (Rama 2006).

Enrollment Trends and Institutions

One of the main obstacles to perform a comparative analysis of the current situation of higher education in Latin America is the lack of up-to-date indicators. One of the most recent compilations was carried out by Carmen García Guadilla (2010) from the UNESCO Institute for Higher Education in Latin America. In 2007, private universities and other HEIs accounted for 40 percent of student enrollment (17.43 million students) in Spanish- and Portuguese-speaking Latin America, even though there are substantial differences between countries. For example, in Brazil and Chile enrollment was more than 70 percent of students; institutions from Colombia, Costa Rica, El Salvador, Nicaragua, Paraguay, Peru, Dominican Republic, and Venezuela attracted between 43 and 66 percent of the students; and Argentina, Bolivia, Cuba, and Uruguay enrolled 25 percent or less of the students. The size of the higher education subsystems also varies from country to country. Brazil had nearly 5.27 million students; Argentina and Mexico more than 2.2 million; Colombia and Venezuela more than 1.3 million; Chile, Cuba, and Peru more than 753,000; Ecuador 443,509; Dominican Republic 286,134; and the rest of the countries less than 159,000 students.

Data about institutions are even more out of date. Between 2000 and 2002, there were 7,514 HEIs and 1,213 universities in Latin America of which 65.1 and 69.2 percent, respectively, were private. With the exception of Cuba, where there are not private universities, in all of the countries in the region private HEIs accounted for more than 50 percent. In the smaller systems (e.g., El Salvador, Guatemala, and Honduras), private universities were the great majority and the only type of HEIs. In more diversified systems (e.g., Brazil, Chile, Colombia, and Peru), private universities were majority but less dominant (García Guadilla 2010).

Conditions for the Development of STI in Private Universities

There are some private universities with research programs, but most institutions depend on external funding mainly because revenue comes from tuition. However, most countries have competitive funding to which universities can apply for (Rama 2006, 2009).

Regarding human capital, only 6 percent of faculty members of private universities hold doctoral degrees. The new economic paradigm links faculty salaries to their productivity and not only to the time in the faculty position as it used to be until recently (Delgado 2011a; Rama 2006). There are different models to determine who does research in Latin America. For instance, in Venezuela, the Organic Law of Science and Technology established that all university professors were considered researchers per se (Delgado 2011a). The model of professor-researcher is changing to one that values more specialized researchers, and this is an important trend that has been taking place in Venezuela at the Venezuelan Institute for Scientific Research (IVIC: *Instituto Venezolano de Investigación Científica*) (Delgado 2011a). However, most research is highly concentrated in public universities in Venezuela, and even the public system has been changing since 2009 (Delgado 2011a, 2014). Several countries like Mexico and Argentina have created researcher promotion and evaluation systems. Mexico has the National Researcher System (SNI: *Sistema Nacional de Investigadores*) and Argentina the Scientific Researcher Career Program at the National Council of Scientific and Technological Research (*Consejo Nacional de Investigaciones Científicas y Tecnológicas*). Affiliated researchers, most of them with doctoral degrees, receive compensations that complement their salaries and bring to institutions prestige and possibility to obtain external funding for research projects (Aupetit 2007). However, participation of researchers from private HEIs in research systems is low. For instance, in Mexico, in 2010, there were 12,674 researchers in the SNI of whom only 646 (5.6 percent) worked in private universities. They exclusively belong to 13 institutions out of more than 800 that exist in the country, namely: Monterrey Institute of Technology (ITESM: *Instituto Tecnológico de Estudios Superiores Monterrey*) (40.9 percent), Iberic-American University (*Universidad Iberoamericana*) (16.1 percent), Technological Autonomous Institute of Mexico (ITAM: *Instituto Tecnológico Autónomo de México*)

(10.7 percent), University of the Americas (*Universidad de Las Américas*) (8.2 percent), and Pan-American University (*Universidad Panamericana*) (7.6 percent) (de Garay 2012).

The following section looks at examples of successful private universities from Latin America. To do so, it utilizes university rankings as source of information, since these types of surveys use indicators to measure research productivity and competitiveness.

Private Universities and the Rankings

Universities compete for faculty, students, funding, and social recognition. With the growth of the higher education market internationally, particularly since the 1990s, ranking surveys have been increasingly used to determine organizational effectiveness and evaluate quality of higher education (Shin and Toutkoushian 2011). Rankings or league tables are usually critiqued because universities differ in mission, focus, size, academic programs, and available resources. In addition, higher education systems and history vary between regions and from one country to another. However, universities and governments often use rankings to reinforce the environment of competition and to make policy (Shin and Toutkoushian 2011).

University rankings are published mainly by commercial media and research institutions. Jung Cheol Shin and Robert K. Toutkoushian (2011) reported that in 2009 there were 33 league tables worldwide. The most well-known are the Times Higher Education World University Ranking (THE), the Shanghai Jiao Tong University Academic Ranking of World Universities (ARWU), the QS University Rankings, the Leiden University Ranking, and the Taiwan Higher Education and the Accreditation Council Ranking. This chapter reviews the first three and one of the most recently created, the SCImago Institutions Rankings (SIR) to identify some of the most prestigious private universities in Latin America and to attempt to determine patterns among those institutions. Even though the evaluation criteria and their weights vary between rankings, all of them include indicators of productivity. The following paragraphs identify the best positioned Latin American private universities in some of the most prestigious rankings worldwide.

THE World University Ranking

The THE World University Ranking evaluates 13 performance indicators that are grouped into five categories: teaching (learning environment), research (volume, income, and reputation), citations (research influence), international outlook (staff, students, and research), and industry income (innovation) (Times Higher Education 2012). The 2012–2013 THE Ranking includes four Latin American universities, three public megauniversities (University of Sao Paulo [USP: *Universidade de São Paulo*, #158] and the State University of Campinas [Unicamp: *Universidade Estadual de Campinas*, #251–275 group] from Brazil, and the National Autonomous University of Mexico [UNAM: *Universidad Nacional Autónoma de México*, #351–400 group]), and one private university (University of the Andes [Uniandes: *Universidad de los Andes*, #351–400 group] from Colombia).

University missions and strategic planning are useful to see how universities emphasize and develop their research. For instance, the Uniandes's 2011–2015 Plan for Integral Development prioritizes producing high quality research under the quality and differentiation strategic axes through increasing external funding, creating new partnerships with the productive sector, promoting collaborative projects with internationally recognized universities, strengthening artistic creation, and increasing quality of research products. In addition, the university has 18 doctoral programs with around 276 students (Uniandes 2011). It is interesting to notice that, even though they can be subject of several interpretations and controversy, Uniandes international outlook and citation indicators are higher than the three top public universities in this ranking.

Shanghai Jiao Tong University ARWU

The Shanghai Jiao Tong University publishes annually the ARWU. Even though they could be disputed, ARWU uses six indicators that include the number of alumni and staff winning Nobel Prizes and Fields Medals, number of highly cited researchers selected by Thomson Scientific, number of articles published in the journals *Nature* and *Science*, number of articles indexed in the SCI-Expanded and Social Sciences Citation Index, and per capita performance with respect to the size of an institution (Shanghai Jiao Tong University 2012a). In 2012, the ARWU included ten institutions from Latin America among the top 500: USP, Unicamp, the Federal University of Minas Gerais (*Universidade Federal de Minas Gerais*), the Federal University of Rio de Janeiro (UFRJ: *Universidade Federal do Rio de Janeiro*), the State University of Sao Paulo (*Universidade Estadual do São Paulo*), and the Federal University of Rio Grande do Sul (*Universidade Federal do Rio Grande do Sul*) from Brazil; UNAM from Mexico; the University of Buenos Aires (*Universidad de Buenos Aires*) from Argentina; the University of Chile (*Universidad de Chile*), and the Pontifical Catholic

University of Chile (PUCC: *Pontificia Universidad Católica de Chile*) (Shanghai Jiao Tong University 2012b).

The PUCC is the only private university in the ranking (Shanghai Jiao Tong University 2012b). When reviewing planning documents, in its 2010–2015 Development Plan the PUCC highlights its achievements at introducing innovative projects and promoting research through increasing funding, creating doctoral programs in many fields, and developing infrastructure. An important proportion of funding for PUCC research comes from the government, which generates around 1,000 articles published in journals included in indexes of the WoS and an average of 5.1 citations per year. The PUCC also has 800 students enrolled in its 30 doctoral programs (PUCC 2010).

The QS University Rankings

With more presence of universities from Latin America than the THE and the ARWU, the QS University Rankings developed by Quacquarelli Symonds (2012a) are established through six basic indicators that are assigned different weights: academic reputation (survey to academicians, 40 percent), employer reputation (survey to employers, 10 percent), citations per faculty member (exported from Scopus and combines research productivity and quality, 20 percent), faculty/student ratio (20 percent), international students (5 percent), and international faculty (5 percent). The 2012 version of the World University Ranking (2012c) shows the PUCC (rank #195) as the first private university and third top university from Latin America after USP (#139) and UNAM (#146). Placing sixth, seventh, eighth, and tenth among other Latin American universities in the World University Ranking there are four private universities, the Argentinean Pontifical Catholic University Santa Maria de Los Buenos Aires (UCA: *Pontificia Universidad Católica Argentina Santa María de Los Buenos Aires*, #305), the ITESM from Mexico (#306), the Austral University (UAustral: *Universidad Austral*, #327) of Argentina, and Uniandes (#335).

QS also develops rankings by region. The 2012 version of the Latin American University Ranking (Quacquarelli Symonds 2012b) includes 250 institutions. Among the top 50 universities of this ranking, there are 17 private institutions from six countries,

- Argentina: UCA (#20), UAustral (#27), and San Andrés University (*Universidad de San Andrés*, #49).
- Brazil: Pontifical Catholic University of Rio de Janeiro (PUCRJ: *Pontificia Universidade Católica de Rio de Janeiro*, #18), Pontifical

Catholic University of Sao Paulo (*Pontificia Universidade Católica de São Paulo*, #28), and Pontifical Catholic University of Rio Grande do Sul (*Pontifícia Universidade Católica do Rio Grande do Sul*, #40).
- Chile: PUCC (#2), *Pontificia Universidad Católica de Valparaíso* (PUCV, Pontifical Catholic University of Valparaiso, #34), and Technical University Federico Santa Maria (UTFS: *Universidad Técnica Federico Santa María*, #36).
- Colombia: Uniandes (#6), Pontifical Javeriana University (PUJ: *Pontificia Universidad Javeriana*, #23), and Rosary University (*Universidad del Rosario*, #47).
- Mexico: ITESM (#7), ITAM (#19), Iberic-American University (#30), and University of the Americas Puebla (#32).
- Peru: Pontifical Catholic University of Peru (*Pontificia Universidad Católica del Perú*, #31).

SCImago Institutional Rankings

The SIR includes the Iberic-American and the Global rankings that report indicators of scientific impact, thematic specialization, output size, and international collaboration networks of institutions. The rankings have been published since 2009 by the SCImago Research Group whose members include the Spanish Institute for Policy and Public Goods (*Instituto de Política y Bienes Públicos*), the Universities of Granada, Carlos III, Extremadura, and Alcalá de Henares from Spain, the University of Porto from Portugal, and the publisher Elsevier (SCImago Lab 2013a). The 2013 version of the Iberic-American SIR analyzes information from articles published in journals included in Scopus between 2007 and 2011. Among the top 150 universities, there are eight private institutions: PUCC (#32), UTFS (#118), and PUCV (#135) from Chile; PUCRJ (#79) and the Pontifical Catholic University of Parana (*Pontificia Universidade Católica do Paraná*, #128) from Brazil; Uniandes (#92) and PUJ (#137) from Colombia; and ITESM (#107) from Mexico (SCImago Lab 2013b).

As it can be appreciated, even though the presence of universities from Latin America in the global league tables is modest, public institutions dominate the terrain; however, there is a select group of private universities that frequently appears in the four university rankings analyzed in this chapter. Some of them are even ahead of their public counterparts. They are universities mostly from Brazil, Chile, Colombia, and Mexico, countries where private higher education has a larger share. It is interesting that Pontifical Catholic universities have an important participation, which confirms the influence this type of universities have historically had in Latin America.

Conclusion: Leading Universities and the Future

The last section in this chapter attempts to identify those features that could describe successful private universities. Several of these characteristics are associated with faculty qualifications and the way they are positioned at and supported by the institutions. Others are related to the characteristics of the institutions and their decisions and institutional arrangements to promote and develop research (Delgado 2011a, 2014). A final reflection looks at the role that innovation through university-private sector partnerships could play in propelling research in private universities in Latin America making them more productive and competitive.

Successful Universities

What characteristics should or do private universities from Latin America have in order to be competitive and successful in the national and international arenas? First, research productivity has been traditionally an activity that requires full- or, at least, half-time professors. However, private universities tend to emphasize teaching over research because it is less expensive and is mainly performed largely by adjunct or part-time instructors (Rama 2006). For instance, Colombian data show how adjuncts made up to 74 percent of faculty. In those institutions the relationship student/faculty was 66:1 in 2002, which is twice the proportion of their public counterparts (33:1) (Cárdenas and Gutiérrez 2005); this suggests that faculty probably did not have time or were not hired to work on research. This situation is similar in Mexico, Argentina, and other Latin American countries (de Garay 2012; Pérez Lindo 2005; Rama 2006). Second, research and scholarly work takes place primarily in larger research-intensive universities (Alperin et al. 2011) that offer programs in a wide range of disciplines and all levels of training (undergraduate degrees, specialties, master's, doctorates, and beyond). As it was mentioned earlier, Axel Didriksson and his colleagues (2008) call macrouniversities to those institutions that have big enrollments, are complex and heterogeneous, and often have multiple campuses. Even though these authors apply this category to public universities, it could be used to describe major successful private universities. Third, regarding the academic level, usually faculty members in HEIs hold the same program degrees they are teaching and it is expected that professors with doctorates are mainly affiliated with academic units that promote research activities (Mollis et al. 2010). Low percentages of professors with master's and doctorate degrees are found in universities of Argentina, Chile, Colombia, Cuba, Mexico, and El Salvador (Brunner and Ferrada 2011; Perez Lindo 2005). Fourth, private universities that also prioritize research are older or more traditional; however, more recently founded but progressive institutions could also be successful. Fifth, successful private institutions can also be flexible and work in strategic partnerships with the government and the private sector, which assures a variety of funding sources for the STI endeavors.

In short, productive and successful private universities from Latin America should result of a combination of factors that include high proportion of professors with doctoral degrees and full-time appointments who work at large traditional/progressive universities that offer programs in a variety of academic fields and through different levels of training. These institutions have also the capacity and vision to develop partnerships and attract funding from different sources.

What Is Next: Innovation and the Context of Competitiveness

Innovation is one of the forces that promote economic development. The STI policies in Latin America have taken place within three economic models: import substitution, liberalization and privatization, and twenty-first-century socialism. Regardless of the economic model, all countries in the region face similar challenges: conduct world-class scientific research and create innovative capacities (Aguirre-Bastos and Gupta 2009; Delgado and Weidman 2012). Innovation is defined as a new or improved product (good or service), process, method of commercialization, or organizational method, in the internal practices of a company, the organization in the workplace, or external relationship (Marins et al. 2012). Innovation is a key element to develop relationships between the private sector, the government, and the universities (triple helix model). This could be a fertile terrain for private universities to explore in terms of productivity because most of them rely on revenue from tuition and developing a productive environment for research and technology, and knowledge transfer would benefit improving university quality and reputation.

In recent decades universities have been under enormous pressure to increase research funding from industry. Several authors call it the third mission of the universities: knowledge transfer from university to industry.

For that reason, universities are seen as engines of economic growth through commercialization of intellectual property through technology transfer (Siegel et al. 2004; Viana Barceló et al. 2011). There are two channels in which technology transfer takes place: formal (patents and joint research and licensing agreements, more at the institutional level) and informal (consulting by faculty, contacts in conferences, and joint publications, more at the individual level). Evidence shows that institutions supporting university-industry technology transfer have created technological parks, enterprise incubators, technology transfer offices, and research centers for university-industry cooperation. This type of technology transfer is known as vertical as it takes place from basic to applied research, from research for development to research for production, and it takes place in both directions between levels of research and between universities and industries. Universities with higher royalties generate higher revenue from licensing; it suggests that private institutions could be more effective in terms of transfer with commercial purposes. There are some factors that create an environment for interactions university-industries: academic quality, high levels of patenting, and R&D investment from the industry and the university (Viana Barceló et al. 2011). This is an area that still needs to be studied with respect to higher education in Latin America and particularly among private universities.

Private universities have in innovation an interesting opportunity to improve their research productivity and competitiveness. Innovation through strengthened relations with the private sector is possible due to universities' flexibility and adaptability to changing economic environments. That could be a key for private universities to gain recognition as world-class institutions and to have a wider impact on societies.

Acknowledgments

The author expresses his gratitude to his colleagues Diane Hardy-Saran and Daniel Narey from the University of Pittsburgh, as well as Gustavo Gregorutti from Andrews University for reviewing and providing feedback during the writing of this chapter.

Notes

1. Worldwide, scientific/scholarly publication has been primarily developed by scientific societies, universities and research centers, and commercial publishers.

In Latin America, in general, associations have not been historically strong as drivers for the generation and dissemination of local knowledge. Therefore, most of the academic publications come from universities where an important portion of the knowledge taught has been imported (Delgado 2012).
2. Jesuits were expelled from the colonies in 1767.

References

Aguirre-Bastos, Carlos, and Mahabir P. Gupta. 2009. "Science, Technology and Innovation Policies in Latin America: Do They Work?" *Interciencia* (Interscience) 34 (12): 865–872.

Albornoz, Mario, Rodolfo Barrere, Agustina Roldán, Manuel Crespo, and María Laura Trama. 2012. *El Estado de la Ciencia. Principales Indicadores de Ciencia y Tecnología Iberoamericanos / Interamericanos 2012* (Status of Science. Main Iberic-American/Inter-American Science and Technology Indicators). Buenos Aires, Argentina: Centro de Estudios sobre Ciencia, Desarrollo y Educación Superior (REDES: Center for the Study of Science, Development, and Higher Education). Available online at: http://www.ricyt.org, accessed on February 20, 2014.

Alperin, Juan Pablo, Gustavo Fischman, and John Willinsky. 2008. "Open Access and Scholarly Publishing in Latin America: Ten Flavours and a Few Reflections." *Liinc em Revista* 4 (2): 172–185. Available online at: http://www.ibict.br/liinc, accessed on February 20, 2014.

———. 2011. "Scholarly Communication Strategies in Latin America's Research-Intensive Universities." *Educación Superior y Sociedad* (Higher Education and Society) 16 (2). Available online at: http://ess.iesalc.unesco.org.ve/index.php/ess /article/view/409/347, accessed on February 20, 2014.

Altbach, Philip G., and Jorge Balán, editors. 2007. *World Class Worldwide: Transforming Research Universities in Asia and Latin America*. Baltimore, MD: Johns Hopkins University Press.

Aupetit, Silvie Didou. 2007. "Evaluación de la Productividad Científica y Reestructuración de los Sistemas Universitarios de Investigación en América Latina" ("Evaluation of Scientific Productivity and Restructuring of University Research Systems in Latin America"). *Educación Superior y Sociedad* (Higher Education and Society) 12 (1): 1–18.

Balán, Jorge. 2013. "Latin American Higher Education Systems in a Historical and Comparative Perspective." In *Latin America's New Knowledge Economy. Higher Education, Government, and International Collaboration*, edited by Jorge Balán (pp. vii–xx). New York: Institute for International Education.

Bernasconi, Andrés. 2008. "Is There a Latin American Model of the University?" *Comparative Education Review* 52 (1): 27–52.

Brunner, José Joaquín. (1999). *Educación Superior en América Latina. Cambios y Desafíos* (Higher Education in Latin America. Changes and Challenges). Santiago, Chile: Fondo de Cultura Económica.

Brunner, José Joaquín, and Rocío Ferreda Hurtado. 2011. *Educación Superior en Iberoamérica. Informe 2011* (Higher Education in Iberic America. 2011 Report). Santiago, Chile: Centro Interuniversitario para el Desarrollo Andino (CINDA: Inter-University Center for Andean Development), Universia.

Cárdenas B., Jorge Hernán, and María Lorena Gutiérrez B. 2005. *La Educación Superior Privada en Colombia* (Private Higher Education in Colombia). Bogotá, Colombia: Instituto Internacional para la Educación en América Latina y el Caribe de la UNESCO (IESALC: UNESCO International Institute for Higher Education in Latin America and the Caribbean, Digital Observatory for Higher Education in Latin America and the Caribbean).

Comparative and International Education Society (CIES). 2009. "Comparative and International Education: A Bibliography (2008)." *Comparative Education Review* 53 (S1): S1–S125.

———. 2010. "Comparative and International Education: A Bibliography (2009)." *Comparative Education Review* 54 (S1): S1–S132.

———. 2011. "Comparative and International Education: A Bibliography (2010)." *Comparative Education Review* 55 (S3): S1–S140.

———. 2012. "Comparative and International Education: A Bibliography (2011)." *Comparative Education Review* 56 (S3): S1–S139.

———. 2013. "Comparative and International Education: A Bibliography (2012)." *Comparative Education Review* 57 (S2): S1–S162.

de Garay, Adrián. January 6, 2012. "La Participación de los Académicos de las Universidades Privadas en el Sistema Nacional de Investigadores del Conacyt" ("Participation of Academicians from Private Universities in the Conacyt's National System of Researchers"). *Avance y Perspectiva (Cinvestav)* (Advance and Perspective). Available online at: http://educacionadebate.org/30046/, accessed on February 20, 2014.

Delgado, Jorge Enrique. 2010. "Trends in the Publication of Refereed Journals in Spanish- and Portuguese-Speaking Latin America." *Comparative & International Higher Education* 2: 43–49.

———. 2011a. *Journal Publication in Chile, Colombia, and Venezuela: University Responses to Global, Regional, and National Pressures and Trends*. Doctoral dissertation. Pittsburgh, PA: University of Pittsburgh. Available online at: http://d-scholarship.pitt.edu/9049/, accessed on February 20, 2014.

———. 2011b. "Las Revistas Científicas en Colombia: Logros, Oportunidades y Riesgos" ("Scientific Journals in Colombia: Achievements, Opportunities, and Risks"). *Unilibros de Colombia* (18): 90–91.

———. 2012. "Academic Journals, Scientific Associations, and the Academia." *Universitas Odontologica* 31 (66): 15–17.

Delgado, Jorge Enrique. 2014. "Scientific Journals of Universities of Chile, Colombia, and Venezuela: Actors and Roles." *Education Policy Analysis Archives* 22 (34, Special issue: The Future of Educational Research Journals). Available online at: http://dx.doi.org/10.14507/epaa.v22n34.2014, accessed on February 20, 2014.

Delgado-Troncoso, Jorge Enrique, and Gustavo Enrique Fischman. 2014. "The Future of Latin American Academic Journals." In *The Future of the Academic*

Journal (2nd edition), edited by Bill Cope and Angus Phillips (pp. 379–400). Oxford, UK: Chandos Elsevier.

Delgado, Jorge Enrique, and John C. Weidman. 2012. "Latin American and Caribbean Countries in the Global Quest for World Class Academic Recognition: An Analysis of Publications in Scopus and the Science Citation Index between 1990 and 2010." *Excellence in Higher Education* 3 (2): 111–121.

Didriksson, Axel, Efraín Medina, Miguel Rojas Mix, Lincoln Bizzorezo, and Javier Pablo Hermo. 2008. "Global and Regional Contexts of Higher Education in Latin America and the Caribbean." In *Trends in Higher Education in Latin America and the Caribbean*, edited by Ana Lúcia Gazzola and Axel Didriksson (pp. 20–50). Caracas, Venezuela: IESALC.

Fischman, Gustavo E., Juan Pablo Alperin, and John Willinsky. 2010. "Visibility and Quality in Spanish-Language Latin American Scholarly Publishing." *Information Technologies & International Development* 6 (4): 1–21.

García Guadilla, Carmen. 2010. *Educación Superior Comparada: El Protagonismo de la Internacionalización* (Comparative Higher Education: Protagonism of Internationalization). Caracas, Venezuela: IESALC, Central University of Venezuela—Center for Development Studies.

Inter-American Development Bank (IADB). 2006. *Education, Science and Technology in Latin America and the Caribbean. A Statistical Compendium of Indicators*. Washington, DC: IADB.

———. 2010. *Science, Technology, and Innovation in Latin America and the Caribbean. A Statistical Compendium of Indicators*. Washington, DC: IADB.

Levy, Daniel C. 1986. *Higher Education and the State in Latin America: Private Challenges to Public Dominance*. Chicago, IL: University of Chicago Press.

———. 2005. *To Export Progress: The Golden Age of University Assistance in the Americas*. Bloomington, IN: Indiana University Press.

Maldonado-Maldonado, Alma, Yingxia Cao, Philip G. Altbach, Daniel C. Levy, and Hong Zhu. 2004. *Private Higher Education: An International Bibliography*. Chestnut Hill, MA: Boston College.

Marins, Luciana, Guillermo Anlló, and Martin Schaaper. 2012. "Estadísticas de Innovación: El Desafío de la Comparabilidad" ("Statistics of Innovation: The Challenge of Comparability"). In *El Estado de la Ciencia. Principales Indicadores de Ciencia y Tecnología Iberoamericanos/Interamericanos 2012* (Status of Science. Main Iberic-American/Inter-American Science and Technology Indicators), edited by Mario Albornoz, Rodolfo Barrere, Agustina Roldán, Manuel Crespo, and María Laura Trama (pp. 65–79). Buenos Aires, Argentina: REDES. Available online at: http://www.ricyt.org/files/2_2_Estadisticas_de_innovacion.pdf, accessed on February 20, 2014.

Mollis, Marcela, Jorge Núñez Jóver, and Carmen García Guadilla. 2010. *Políticas de Posgrado y Conocimiento Público en América Latina. Desafíos y Perspectivas* (Graduate Policies and Public Knowledge in Latin America. Challenges and Perspectives). Buenos Aires, Argentina: Consejo Lationamericano de Ciencias Sociales (CLACSO: Latin American Council of Social Sciences), Instituto de Investigación Gino Germani (Gino Germani Research Institute).

Pérez Lindo, Augusto. 2005. *Políticas de Investigación en las Universidades de Argentina* (Research Policies in Argentinean Universities). Buenos Aires: IESALC, Digital Observatory for Higher Education in Latin America and the Caribbean.

Pontificia Universidad Católica de Chile (PUCC). 2010. *2010–2015 Development Plan* (Plan de Desarrollo 2010–2015). Santiago, Chile: PUCC.

Quacquarelli Symonds. 2012a. *QS Intellingence Unit*. London: Quacquarelli Symonds. Available online at: http://www.qs.com, accessed on February 20, 2014.

———. 2012b. *QS Latin American University Rankings—2012*. London: Quacquarelli Symonds. Available online at: http://topuniversities.com, accessed on February 20, 2014.

———. 2012c. *QS World University Rankings—2012*. London: Quacquarelli Symonds. Available online at: http://topuniversities.com, accessed on February 20, 2014.

Rama, Claudio. 2006. *La Tercera Reforma de la Educación Superior en América Latina* (The Third Higher Education Reform in Latin America). Mexico City, Mexico: Fondo de Cultura Económica.

———. 2009. *Tendencias de la Educación Superior en América Latina y el Caribe en el siglo XXI. Desautonomización, Desgratuitarización, Desnacionalización, Despresencialización* (Higher Education Trends in Latin America and the Caribbean in the Twenty-First Century. De-autonomization, De-gratuitousness, De-nationalization, De-presentialization). Lima, Peru: Asamblea Nacional de Rectores (National Assembly of University Presidents).

Salmi, Jamil. 2009. *The Challenge of Establishing World-Class Universities*. Washington, DC: The World Bank. Available online at: http://documents.worldbank.org, accessed on February 20, 2014.

Santa, Salamy, and Víctor Herrero Solana. July–December 2010. "La Producción Científica de América Latina y el Caribe: una Aproximación a través de los Datos de Scopus (1996–2007)" ("Scientific Production of Latin America and the Caribbean: An Approach through Scopus Data [1996–2007]"). *Inter-American Journal of Library Science* (*Revista Interamericana de Bibliotecología*) 33 (2): 379–400.

———. 2013a. *SCImago Institutions Rankings*. Madrid, Spain: SCImago Group. Available online at: http://www.scimagoir.com/pdf/SCImago%20Institutions%20Rankings%20IBER%20en.pdf, accessed on February 20, 2014.

———. 2013b. *SIR Iber 2013. 2007–2011*. Madrid, Spain: SCImago Group. Available online at: http://www.scimagoir.com/pdf/SIR%20Iber%202013.pdf, accessed on February 20, 2014.

Shanghai Jiao Tong University, Center of World-Class Universities, and Institute of Higher Education. 2012a. *About ARWU*. Shanghai, China: Shanghai Jiao Tong University. Available online at: http://www.arwu.org, accessed on February 20, 2014.

———. 2012b. *Academic Ranking of World Universities*. Shanghai, China: Shanghai Jiao Tong University. Available online at: http://www.arwu.org, accessed on February 20, 2014.

Shin, Jung Cheol, and Robert K. Toutkoushian. 2011. "The Past, Present, and Future of University Rankings." In *University Rankings: Theoretical Basis, Methodology and Global Higher Education*, edited by Jung Cheol Shin, Robert K. Toutkoushian, and Ulrich Teichler (pp. 1–16). Dordrecht, Netherlands: Springer.

Siegel, Donald S., David A. Waldman, Leanne E. Atwater, and Albert N. Link. 2004. "Toward a Model of Effective Transfer of Scientific Knowledge from Academicians to Practitioners: Qualitative Evidence from the Commercialization of University Technologies." *Journal of Engineering and Technology Management* 21 (1–2): 115–142.

Task Force on Higher Education and Society. (2000). *Higher Education in Developing Countries. Peril and Promise*. Washington, DC: International Bank for Reconstruction and Development, The World Bank.

Times Higher Education. 2012. *World University Rankings*. London, UK: Thomson Reuters. Available online at: http://www.timeshighereducation.co.uk/world-university-rankings, accessed on February 20, 2014.

Universidad de los Andes (Uniandes) (University of the Andes). 2011. *Plan de Desarrollo Integral 2011–2015 (2011–2015 Plan for Integral Development)*. Bogotá, Colombia: Uniandes.

Vessuri, Hebe, José Miguel Cruces, Renato Janine Ribeiro, and José Luis Ramírez. 2008. "Overtaken by the Future: Foreseeable Changes in Science and Technology." In *Trends in Higher Education in Latin America and the Caribbean*, edited by Ana Lúcia Gazzola and Axel Didriksson (pp. 51–81). Caracas, Venezuela: IESALC.

Viana Barceló, Rafael Antonio, Claudia Patricia Cote Peña, Jorge Luis Navarro España, and Jairo Orlando Villabona Robayo. 2011. "Análisis de los Factores que influencian la Disponibilidad de los Investigadores Universitarios a participar en los Procesos de Transferencia de Tecnología Universidad-Industria" ("Analysis of Factors Influencing Availability of University Researchers to Participate in University-Industry Technology Transfer Processes"). In *Agenda 2011. Temas de Indicadores de Ciencia y Tecnología* (Agenda 2011. Topics of Science and Technology Indicators), edited by Mario Albornoz and Luis Plaza (pp. 353–369). Buenos Aires, Argentina: REDES. Available online at: http://www.ricyt.org/files/Capitulo%205.pdf, accessed on February 20, 2014.

The World Bank. 2002. *Constructing Knowledge Societies: New Challenges for Tertiary Education*. Washington, DC: The World Bank, International Bank for Reconstruction and Development.

Chapter 4

Quality Assurance and Public Policy Research Funding
Their Impact on Private Universities in Argentina

Ana García de Fanelli and
Ángela Corengia

Introduction

This chapter examines the institutional framework and the incentive structure that developed as a consequence of quality assurance and government research funding policies. It also analyzes the way these policies have influenced the current functioning and configuration of the private university sector in Argentina.

While the oldest antecedent of the Argentinian public university sector dates back to the *Universidad de Córdoba* (Cordoba University), established by the Company of Jesus in 1610, the first private universities were not authorized until 1958. Successive periods of rapid institutional growth followed although restrictions on the creation of private institutions were in effect between 1973 and 1989 (Del Bello et al. 2007; Rabossi 2011). A key moment in the private university sector was the sanction of the Higher Education Act in 1995, which gave rise to the creation of the first agency for quality assurance, the National Commission for University Evaluation and Accreditation (CONEAU: *Comisión Nacional de Evaluación y Acreditación Universitaria*). Among other responsibilities, the CONEAU passes judgment on new private institutions for their provisional authorization and for their final recognition six years after their creation.

In the mid-1990s, the central government established the National Agency for the Promotion of Science and Technology (ANPCYT: *Agencia Nacional de Promoción Científica y Tecnológica*), an organization designed to distribute public funds to advance research activities both in the public and private higher education sector. This agency, along with the growing number of doctoral research scholarships and more vacancies to join the National Scientific and Technical Research Council (CONICET: *Consejo Nacional de Investigaciones Científicas y Técnicas*) career, facilitated the advancement of research activity at a national level. From the point of view of private universities, accessing public funds has been always a key factor to develop research since these institutions have scarce resources to do so. This is due to factors such as fewer years in the higher education system, the underdevelopment of basic sciences, and the limited amount of researchers (Balán and García de Fanelli 1997; Del Bello et al. 2007).

This chapter studies whether the policies implemented to assure quality (CONEAU) and research funding (ANPCYT and CONICET) actually promoted the development of organizational strategies to strengthen the research function at private universities. We begin by characterizing the private university sector in Argentina and the theoretical approaches used in order to understand its change. We then present the methodology employed for collecting and analyzing the data. The last two sections focus on the main findings. First, we analyze the 1990s' and 2000s' regulatory framework (quality assurance) and the incentive structure (research funding policies), showing how they have impacted on private universities. Second, using a case study method, we examine how the institutional assessment (self-assessment and external review) policy, undergraduate program accreditation, and the ANPCYT funding policies have helped research activities at two private universities.

An Overview of the Private University Sector in Argentina

In 2010, the Argentinian higher education sector was composed of 55 public university institutions and 59 private ones with almost 1.7 million students. Although the private sector has more institutions, it represents only 20 percent of the total student body. However, enrollment at private institutions grew by 5.8 percent, faster than public universities that expanded at a 1.8 percent rate for the period of 2000–2010 (Ministry of Education 2012).

The 1995 Higher Education Act facilitated a common framework to formulate policies to coordinate private and public universities as one higher education system. However, the federal government has encountered some limitations to accomplish this task due to the autonomy universities enjoy. This is especially true for public institutions whose autonomy and autarchy are established in their individual charters or statutes. The Argentinian Constitution supports this. Moreover, the 1995 Higher Education Act also recognizes the autonomy not only of public universities but also of private ones from the moment they acquire final recognition, six years after their performance has been evaluated (García de Fanelli 2006).

Even though public and private universities are similar in terms of autonomy, they differ in the way they finance and govern themselves. The federal government is the principal and almost only source of funding for public universities. Instead, private universities are nonprofit organizations that depend almost entirely on student tuition, fees, and other private sources of income (Del Bello et al. 2007). Nonetheless, these institutions may receive federal funds to support research groups through competitive grants. In addition, their faculty can join the CONICET researcher career and their graduate students can obtain CONICET doctoral scholarships.

Collegial and executive bodies govern public universities and the assembly is the highest authority. The assembly, composed of all the executive and collegial bodies of each school or *facultad* (faculty), is in charge of the construction of, approval of, and amendments to the university statute, as well as the election of the president. Professors, students, and alumni elect members of the university councils of each school. Unlike public universities, private universities are more hierarchical in their organization and management. They are generally governed by a board of directors or trustees that appoints executive and collegial authorities. It also participates in decisions concerning the university's major goals. Faculty representation is very limited; university presidents appoint deans and other administrative staff (Del Bello et al. 2007).

Beyond these common funding and governance features, the private sector in Argentina is quite heterogeneous. In particular, as a result of increasing pressure to attract students, private universities differentiate student programs and other facilities. As a consequence of its resource dependence on student tuition and fees, we can distinguish different segments of the private university market that target diverse students. Institutions within these niches compete for students, faculty, and reputation. According to Levy's (1986) typology of Latin American private higher education, the traditional sector with its "confessional" character was joined by an elite sector that imitated the American research university, even though they lacked the proper resources for research and student financial aid. On the other hand, a demand-absorbing sector was consolidated, serving students who opted for an alternative to higher education with fewer bureaucratic obstacles, more personalized attention, better infrastructure, and, on occasion, fewer academic demands. In Argentina since the 1990s some of the confessional private universities have been competing with secular universities in the academic market niche of the demand-absorbing type, while others have been trying to improve the quality of the educational service to contend for a place in the elite niche.

Theoretical Approach

Bearing in mind the autonomy of Argentinian universities, since the mid-1990s the government has been trying to promote an improvement in the university sector and the institutional innovation using mechanisms that can indirectly steer it via financial or quality assessment measures (García de Fanelli 2005; Van Vught 1989). To understand the relationship between these government policies and the change in the Argentinian private university sector, we consider DiMaggio and Powell's (1983) "new institutionalism" approach and Clark's (1983, 2004) "internal" approach.

Both perspectives share the view that organizations, like universities, are open systems, strongly influenced by their environments (Scott 2003). But while the new institutionalism emphasizes that the institutional environments demanding conformity are dominant, the internal approach of Burton Clark (1983 p. 128) highlights that "changes are strongly guided by the underlying internal features and the beliefs of internal groups which help mold responses to external pressures." The result, in Clark's view, is adaptation to the environment and increasing institutional differentiation.

One of the central concepts of the new institutionalism is the process of "institutional isomorphism" in the organizational field.[1] According to this approach, organizational characteristics change in the direction of increasing compatibility with environmental features to acquire political power and institutional legitimacy. DiMaggio and Powell (1983) identify three mechanisms through which institutional isomorphic change takes place.[2] The first, coercive isomorphism, occurs when some organizations exert formal and informal pressures on others. These pressures can take the shape of a force, persuasion, or invitation to collude. In some circumstances, organizational change is the direct response to a government mandate. For example, for the CONEAU to accredit their undergraduate and graduate programs, the universities may have to reform the syllabus, change hiring practices, or create a research and development (R&D) office. But institutional isomorphism does not always stem from a coercive authority. Uncertainty is also a powerful influence that may trigger imitation. This second isomorphic mechanism is called mimetic isomorphism. When organizational technologies are not well understood, when goals are ambiguous, or when the environment creates symbolic uncertainty, organizations can function better following another institution's model. Universities, like companies, adopt these "innovations" to reinforce their legitimacy, to demonstrate that, at least, they are trying to improve. Then, in order to minimize the risk of uncertainty, these organizations tend to copy others in similar fields, which they deem more successful. Finally the normative isomorphism is a consequence of professionalization (Di Maggio and Powell 1983). For instance, in the accreditation of engineering and medical programs, professional boards participate in the definition of the accreditation standards. The result was an isomorphic production of professional programs. Briefly, universities and other organizations that must interact with professional boards and the State are more vulnerable to isomorphic pressures (Thornton 2011).

Though the new institutionalism is a useful theoretical framework to comprehend some transformations in the Argentinian private university sector, we consider, following Clark's (1983, 2004) approach, that the existence of external demands on universities does not imply that they are going to respond to them equally. Therefore, it is important to analyze the different responses to common policies that universities provided as autonomous institutions of learning. Clark highlighted that the restrictions of policy implementation are exacerbated by the complexity and bottom-heaviness of the system. He draws attention to the incorrect analysis that considers the change in university organizations to be the exclusive product of external forces, disregarding the need to assess the compatibility between the demands for change that come from the environment and the university structure and its performance. Following Clark's approach, we examine whether the influence of the external forces (quality assurance and government research funding) on the university performance vary among private institutions.[3]

Methodology

Our research aims to provide an understanding of how private universities have reacted and adjusted to policy changes in their environment. In particular, we contemplated those quality assurance and government funding policies carried out between 1995 and 2010 that could influence the formulation and implementation of institutional activities in order to develop and consolidate the research activity at these universities. To fulfill this aim the research design combines analysis of public policy documentation, university and R&D indicators, and a case study analysis.

In the data analysis, we collected the following information and indicators: the CONEAU's quality assurance resolutions and results, the evolution of scholars at public and private universities, researchers by maximum academic level achieved, trends in R&D expenditure by public and private sector, and trends in the number of CONICET researchers and doctoral fellows at private universities.

For the case study analysis, we selected two private universities of different size, date of foundation, profile, and geographic location. Table 4.1 shows their general characteristics.

The selected universities have all conducted the quality assurance processes under study: institutional assessment and program accreditation. In each case, we have carried out an in-depth analysis of the CONEAU's assessment reports, the President's letters attached to the report at the conclusion of each process, and medicine and engineering accreditation resolutions. We chose these fields of knowledge as they are considered the two leading programs to be declared of public interest. We conducted 25 semistructured interviews with university authorities.[4] These interviews were analyzed to identify changes (intended and factual changes) in some dimensions of the research function at these private universities and to know the role public policies played to promote them. Documents and the

Table 4.1 Characteristics of the two universities selected (the universities' names are kept anonymous for privacy reasons)

Characteristic	Case 1	Case 2
Size	Small (total enrollment, less than 5,000 students)	Medium-sized (total enrollment, more than 10,000 students)
Founded	1990s	1960s
Profile	Teaching and research (among the five private universities with large proportion of CONICET researchers and fellows)	On demand (core mission: teaching, not research)
Location	Buenos Aires (multicampus)	Mendoza (single-site university)

Source: Table based on Corengia (2010).

interviews were examined following a categorization strategy of thematic analysis (Maxwell 1996).

It is very difficult to connect causes and effects as quality assurance policies, and the government funding of research are merely some of the many factors that can affect changes in the institutional strategies that universities develop. In this research, we believe that these policies could be considered causes or contributing causes of the changes detected, whether the causal nexus is recognized by the authorities interviewed or whether the changes are mentioned as *intended* changes in the self-assessment reports or in the improvement plans that the institutions have agreed to develop once the self-assessment and accreditation processes have been carried out. *Factual* changes refer to those changes effectively accomplished when implementing the institutional assessment (self-assessment and external review) and accreditation policies. Specifically, we examine the observed impact of the quality assurance policies in two dimensions that affect the development of the university research function: *faculty member* and *research activities*. Regarding faculty members, we examined the universities' policies to improve the academic qualifications, to the change in the type of labor contract (to increase the number of full-time faculty), and to new hiring practices and faculty evaluations. Concerning research activities, we studied the academic training of researchers, the creation of R&D departments and groups, and R&D funding (Corengia 2010).

Higher Education Policies

In what follows, we first focus on the impact of the CONEAU's quality assurance policy for the private university sector and then on the influence of the expansion and development of funding instruments to promote research activity at private universities.

The Quality Assurance Policy

The CONEAU is a decentralized organization under the jurisdiction of the Ministry of Education and is responsible for a wide range of tasks. Among the most important responsibilities are the following. First, it possesses legal power to condition the creation of new universities that the Ministry of Education authorizes, ruling on the consistency and viability of the institutional projects so that the Ministry of Education can authorize their creation. In particular, the CONEAU's resolutions are decisive to the authorization of the private universities' provisional functioning. As a result of its control activity, the growth in the number of private institutions has notably decreased. Prior to the CONEAU, in only six years (1989–1995), 24 private universities were founded, doubling the number of universities that existed at that time (Del Bello et al. 2007). From 1996, when the CONEAU was established, to 2006, only 10 of the 96 authorization requests to open new private universities were approved (Del Bello et al. 2007). Until March 2011, out of the 22 projects presented between 2005 and 2010 for provisional authorization, only 7 received a favorable resolution (García de Fanelli 2011). This implies that the CONEAU has raised the quality bar.

Second, the CONEAU oversees the institutional external review of every university. The main purpose of these evaluations is to help institutions improve their proposals for quality upgrading. These analyses take place at least every six years and complement the self-evaluations that universities conduct to assess their achievements and challenges.[5] There is no benefit or penalty associated with their good or bad performance in these procedures.

Third, the CONEAU is also responsible for the accreditation of professional undergraduate programs. The Higher Education Act establishes that those programs that can compromise public interest or directly put at risk the health, security, rights, assets, or training of the citizens be regulated via mandatory accreditation procedures. Accreditation is set to guarantee the fulfillment of minimum quality standards and to promote improvement in courses that do not achieve such standards. The Higher Education Act establishes accreditation as a condition for degree validation and has defined a six-year period for the fulfillment of accreditation procedures. A new resolution was later approved offering a possible three-year accreditation under the condition that the institution commits to improving the course. Those courses that are accredited for only three years must be submitted to a second cycle for accreditation by demonstrating that they have fulfilled the commitments they had undertaken. Of the courses accredited in their first cycle between 2001 and 2010, the private sector has presented a higher number of three-year accredited or nonaccredited courses than the public sector (García de Fanelli 2011).

Finally, graduate courses were subjected to periodic mandatory accreditation. Until March 2011, 35 percent of private graduate courses were not accredited, while public universities registered a lower 24 percent rate for the same type of courses (García de Fanelli 2011).

Like the institutional external review, the accreditation results are public, thus affecting the reputation of undergraduate and graduate programs. However, unlike these institutional assessments (self-assessment and external review) that are voluntary, accreditation procedures are mandatory; private universities cannot grant official degrees unless they have been officially approved. As a result, we hypothesize that accreditation procedures will have a greater influence on universities than the institutional assessment (self-assessment and external review), as we analyze in the case study further.

Another consequence of the CONEAU's performance was the development of an incentive structure for the promotion of quality improvement. To externally evaluate the quality of a public or private university or to accredit an undergraduate or graduate program, the peer-reviewers have to consider the following aspects, among others: (a) it should have a high quality academic staff, particularly professors who both teach and conduct research on a full-time basis; (b) the academic staff should hold a doctoral degree or, at least, a master's degree; (c) universities must demonstrate an adequate development of research activities. These three aspects coincide with the models of research universities in the United States, which, as was stated earlier, were taken as models for the elite private sector.

Since external funding is a key factor to successfully produce research (Del Bello et al. 2007; García de Fanelli and Estébanez 2008), most private universities need to align with government grants. In the following section we deal with this issue and focus on how funding policies have evolved and impacted these universities.

The Government Research Funding Policy

Along with the CONEAU, the creation of the Secretariat of Science and Technology (SECYT: *Secretaría de Ciencia y Tecnología*) in 1996 was the other factor which significantly changed the environment for research activities at public and private universities. In 2007 this SECYT achieved the status of the Ministry of Science, Technology, and Productive Innovation (MINCYT: *Ministerio de Ciencia, Tecnología e Innovación Productiva*). This ministry is responsible for planning and implementing national policies, as well as dealing with issues concerning the coordination, assessment, and promotion of science and technology. The CONICET and ANPCYT, the most important organizations that advance research, are under its jurisdiction.

The CONICET, created in 1958 and inspired in France's National Center for Scientific Research (*Centre National de la Recherche Scientifique*), manages the scientific researcher career and the system of grants for doctoral students. The CONICET's scientific researchers and doctoral fellows carry out their tasks at universities or other public and private entities dedicated to research. The ANPCYT, created in 1996, aims to identify, manage, and assess mechanisms that advance or promote scientific and technological innovations. In particular, this research agency runs two competitive sources of funds: the *Fondo para la Investigación Científica y Tecnológica* (FONCYT: Fund for Scientific and Technological Research) and the *Fondo Tecnológico Argentino* (FONTAR: Argentinian Technological Fund) (García de Fanelli and Estébanez 2008).[6]

As a result of these policies, public and private expenditure on R&D grew in real terms by 64 percent or from 0.45 to 0.67 percent of gross domestic product (GDP) between 1999 and 2009 (MINCYT 2012). The most significant growth in the expenditure on R&D by sector of performance took place in the government sector. This includes wages for researchers and the support of different government entities related to research activities. The second most important sector of R&D expenditures was the public university. Finally, private universities also increased their spending over the same period of time, but quite below those of other public sector bodies (figure 4.1).[7]

Another feature of the 2000s was a significant expansion in the number of scholarships for doctoral studies, along with an increase in researchers who were hired to join the CONICET's scientific researcher career. The number of scholarships for doctoral and postdoctoral studies funded by the CONICET grew from 4,713 in 2006 to 8,801 in 2011. Likewise, the number of researchers appointed to the CONICET's scientific researcher career almost doubled between 2003 and 2011 from 3,677 to 6,939 (CONICET

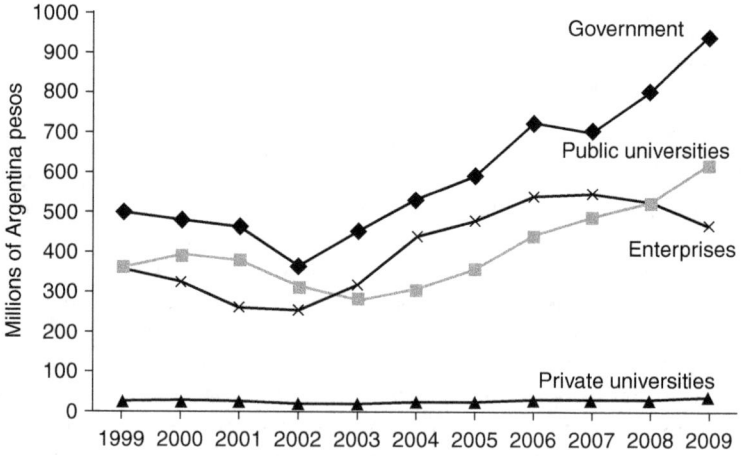

Figure 4.1 Trends in the Argentinian expenditure on R&D by sector (in constant pesos of 1999).

2012). Table 4.2 presents the impact these research funding policies had on human resources devoted to research at private universities.

Table 4.2 shows that the number of CONICET researchers at private universities more than doubled between 2004 and 2012. Even more

Table 4.2 Number of CONICET researchers and doctoral fellows at Argentinian private universities, 2004 and 2012

University*	Researchers		Doctoral fellows	
	2004	2012	2004	2012
Católica Argentina	13	32	2	18
Torcuato Di Tella	8	26	7	9
San Andrés	6	21	3	2
Austral	5	19	3	18
Católica de Córdoba	1	14	0	19
De Belgrano	4	9	0	3
Maimónides	2	7	0	18
Católica de Santa Fe	4	6	0	3
Del Salvador	8	5	4	2
Católica de Salta	1	4	1	2
Argentina de la Empresa	5	3	0	4
De Palermo	0	2	0	1
Abierta Interamericana	0	2	0	0
Atlántida Argentina	0	2	0	0
Del CEMA	0	1	0	11
Fasta	0	1	0	9
Católica de Cuyo	0	1	0	2
CAECE	1	1	0	2
Del Cine	1	1	0	1
Favaloro	1	0	2	4
Juan Agustín Maza	1	0	0	1
John F. Kennedy	4	0	0	0
Católica de Rosario	2	0	1	0
Adventista del Plata	1	0	0	0
Católica de La Plata	1	0	0	0
Centro Educ. Latinoamericano	1	0	0	0
Total	*70*	*157*	*23*	*129*

Source: Based on database supplied by CONICET's human resources management.
*Universities ranked by the number of CONICET researchers in 2012.

telling was the growth in the number of doctoral student grants that rose six times in that period. The table also illustrates that a small group out of the total private universities concentrated researchers and doctoral fellows. This group remains largely stable during the two periods of time. The increase in the number of researchers at these universities is particularly striking since they tripled the number registered in 2004. In addition to the increase in the number of CONICET positions opened to researchers and doctoral fellows, as we have already mentioned, this change can be attributed to the rise in the CONICET's wages between 2004 and 2009.

It is remarkable that three of the top five private universities in terms of the number of CONICET researchers in 2012 (Torcuato Di Tella, San Andres, and Austral) are also among the smallest private universities. While the average enrollment in the largest private universities is between 20,000 and 25,000 students, Di Tella, San Andrés, and Austral have a total enrollment of 2,999, 1,969, and 4,316 students, respectively (Ministerio de Educación 2012). So, these three small private universities have the highest number of researchers per student at private universities. This shows how heterogeneous the private sector is in terms of its institutional mission and the relative weight of research activities. Nonetheless, it is also significant that the number of human resources dedicated to R&D at several of the other private universities grew during the same period.

The data on scholars devoted to R&D as a whole, not solely those belonging to CONICET's research career, confirm that they expanded faster than at public universities. Between 1999 and 2009, the amount of researchers at private universities doubled from 504 to 1,049, while they increased by 50 percent at public institutions, from around 10,000 to 15,000 (MINCYT 2012). Moreover, with reference to academic qualifications, between 2001 and 2009 the proportion of private university researchers that achieved a doctoral degree increased from 18.5 to 26.7 percent. The public sector remained stable, around 23 percent of the total (MINCYT 2012).

Nonetheless, scholars and the amount of funding allocated to R&D in the private sector did not increase at the same rate as the number of scholars. Between 1999 and 2009, the expenditure per researcher at private institutions fell by 37.9 percent. The same indicator was positive in the public university sector (MINCYT 2012).

The Balance of the Changes in the Private University Sector

In sum, we conclude that the CONEAU quality assurance and government research funding policies have influenced private universities in at least three ways. First, as stated earlier, the CONEAU authorized the expansion of new private higher institutions with minimum quality standards and requirements. Second, these policies promoted the development of R&D human resources at private universities. This can be observed both in the growth of researchers and doctoral fellows and in the improvement of the educational profile of the teaching staff. Third, taking into account one of the central objectives of the policies analyzed, to improve research activity, it is possible to predict isomorphic responses at most private universities. As DiMaggio and Powell (1983, p. 150) said, "The greater the extent to which organizations in a field transact with agencies of the State, the greater the extent of isomorphism in the field as a whole." Our case study focused on this issue as well as on the efficacy of the institutional assessment (self-assessment and external review) versus undergraduate accreditation procedures to foster the development of research activities at private universities. Nonetheless, contrary to the isomorphic prediction, table 4.2 shows that only some private institutions, whose institutional features correspond to the elite type analyzed by Levy (1986), concentrate the majority of the scholars devoted to R&D in the private sector. As Clark (1983, 2004) said, not all university organizations respond equally to changes in the external environment. The capacity, as well as the willingness to increase the number of scholars and doctoral fellows, varied greatly according to the relevance research activity has for these organizations.

However, the consolidation of an Argentinian elite private university sector that emulates its US Ivy League counterpart has encountered some restrictions. The main obstacles are in the organizational features and especially in the overall available financial resources for R&D. In terms of enrollment, private institutions face some challenges attracting the best high school graduates who can attend a free of charge, not very selective public university. Moreover, some public universities, like the University of Buenos Aires, enjoy high prestige both among students and employers. This competitive organizational environment, along with the high tuition and fees students are charged at elite private universities, has prevented their enrollment expansion and their institutional consolidation. We should also take into account that despite an increase in resources for research, Argentina's GDP devoted to R&D falls below other Latin American countries, such as Brazil and to a lesser extent Chile (RICyT 2012).

In relation to the other type of higher education institution, the core mission of the demand-absorbing sector is teaching, not research. In these cases, the CONEAU's policies and government research funding may have influenced changes in the structure of the universities via the incorporation of R&D offices and some moderate increases in the number of researchers. However, the research orientations promoted by public policies do not harmonize with their institutional missions that focus primarily on teaching. We hypothesized that it is likely that the observed changes are merely a response to first, coercive isomorphic forces from the enforcement of the new regulations, and second, mimetic isomorphic changes to meet the minimum quality standards set forth by the government and to gain a more solid reputation in the higher education system, defining what a quality university is. To deepen the analysis, the next section analyzes how two private universities reacted to these government policies. We believe these examples can be of help to understand organizational changes that prompted research activity at these types of private organizations.

Case Study Findings

In this section we present a synthesis of the case study results. A comprehensive analysis of the interviews, citations that support each of the conclusions of the case study, consulted documents, and the interview guide can be found in Corengia (2010). This chapter selects only a few quotations from the interviews that illustrate university authority opinions and institutional policies carried out in response to the mechanisms for quality assurance and the government funding of research.

We have organized the presentation of the results by analyzing the impact each quality assurance policy and research funding had on the two cases. As was discussed earlier in the methodology, the case study was conducted taking into account two dimensions of analysis that affect the development of the role of research within universities: faculty members and research activities.

The Institutional Assessment (Self-Assessment and External Review) Policy

Regarding the *faculty members dimension* in Case 1, the documentary analysis and interviews showed that no significant changes occurred as a consequence of institutional assessments. Case 2 revealed some evidence of a formal or cosmetic change that had little impact on deeper academic structures. This is because the CONEAU recommends that the university should include a faculty hiring practice similar to the one established at public universities.[8] However, the authorities considered that the open competitive procedure applied at public universities was ill-suited for the recruitment and promotion of their faculty. At private universities, the decision is generally taken by the governing board upon the recommendation of the faculty staff based on the candidate's academic and professional qualifications and personal contacts (Del Bello et al. 2007).

In the *research activities dimension*, Case 1 evidenced the presence of intended changes but not of real ones. This university carried out some improvements and modifications to advance research, but they did not seem to be related to institutional assessments. In fact, the following quotation asserted that changes were a consequence of R&D policies the Ministry of Education has set for universities through the CONICET:

> Research is an important issue (...). If universities want to do serious research, they have to be assessed by the government research organization, not the CONEAU, but the CONICET and the Ministry of Science and Technology, which have a very strict assessment system carried out by peers who understand their fields of research. We do not rely on the CONEAU, but on the willingness of this university to do serious research. (President of Case 1)

In Case 2, the CONEAU makes numerous recommendations for improving the *research activities dimension*. The President attributed this weakness to budgetary restraints that affect his university. This showed indicators of intended changes to advance research but not of factual ones. Moreover, during the interviews conducted in this case, the lack of steady funding was repeatedly mentioned as a counteracting factor that negatively impacted research activity.

Finally, consider the opinion of this University Academic Affairs Director in Case 2 who concluded that the institutional assessment has not made a significant impact since "it is done and put away."

We concluded that for both case studies the institutional assessment policy did not produce any factual changes to improve the *research function* in the two dimensions: *faculty members* and *research activities*.

The Undergraduate Program's Accreditation Policy: Medicine

For Case 1, the analysis of the accreditation resolutions showed evidence of factual changes in the *faculty member dimension*: through modifications in the number of full-time labor contracts, the increase in faculty with doctoral degrees, and more specialized processes of recruiting new professors. These changes were observed between the first and second accreditation cycle.

The interviews (President, Academic Affairs Directors, and Director of the Medical Education Department of the Biomedical Sciences School) showed that the relationship among variations in the faculty training, the type of labor contract (full or part time), and the accreditation policy was granted as long as this policy helped to reflect, promote, and foster a goal that the university itself had. In other words, there was an external standard that demanded adjustments:

> Accreditation has helped us to think about the type of labor contract, the need to have full-time professors. But we already had this because our university was born with the ideal of full-time professors. This is very helpful for us because we see an external standard that reminds us about its importance and helps us to move forward in the same way. All these procedures have somehow helped the university to put things in order. There comes a time when you wonder to what extent things are mixed up (...) and you don't know what comes first.

Concerning modifications in the procedures for recruiting new professors, the interviews evidenced more formal or cosmetic changes than real ones. The Director of the Medical Education Department from Case 1 regarded them as a typical formal change induced by the CONEAU,

> There was a change; in fact, a Commission for Faculty Recruitment was created. I do not know its name; it was a commission that included the dean, the academic affairs director, myself, and a professor from the area. It is fine, but it was not an important issue; it was more like a cosmetic thing. It is one of the typical formal changes induced by the CONEAU. (...) It helps to organize the structure, but, in fact, it is not a deep or real change.

The documentary analysis of Case 2 showed several intended and factual changes as a consequence of the requirements the CONEAU enforces. These requests were carried out between the first and the second cycle of the accreditation process and they referred to a type of labor contract (full or part time), professors' formal training, and the assessment of the faculty's performance.

Regarding the *research activities dimension*, the findings for Case 1 revealed that the accreditation process did not produce any intended or factual changes. This is due to the fact that both the institution and the CONEAU regarded the research dimension as the strongest asset of the program. The interviewees agreed unanimously on this subject,

> I would say that this is a strong point in our academic unit. (...) We have largely exceeded standards. Such standards have not produced any

significant improvement in our productivity. In our profile, research becomes an important issue; therefore, in this field, we are fine. We have improved according to our own criteria and not because of the accreditation process. (Director of the Department of Medical Education, Case 1)

Unlike Case 1, institutional actors in Case 2 stated that the most significant impact of the accreditation was on the *research activities dimension*. Moreover, Case 2 presented factual changes carried out between the first and the second accreditation cycle as follows: (a) new regulations for the board that controls research; (b) a new center for advanced research; (c) the organization of the first preparatory seminar on health research and a research committee; (d) several agreements with other research institutions to ensure the conclusion of successful projects; (e) the general enhancement of the library with new booths for researchers; and (f) a new research laboratory. These actions were positively assessed by the CONEAU: "The institution has begun to comply, laying the basis to ensure effective improvement continuity."

The following interviews showed factual improvements and how they were closely related to accreditation. Interviewees mentioned that accreditation forced them to redirect resources toward research and to reengineer the entire research system,

> The university has worked hard to meet these internal research standards. It did so incorporating laboratories, hiring highly qualified researchers, and promoting research projects that some students have been working on for their PhDs. Therefore, the university has been forced, in certain way, to redirect its resources to promote research (…). It has been forced to redirect and reengineer our entire research system (…). (Academic Affairs Director, School of Health Sciences, Case 2)
>
> I believe that the issue of research and all the efforts the university has made are very important, because, in fact, it is the work of the whole university and not only of the School of Medicine. The central administration and all the different areas of the university have contributed to the fulfillment of this goal. (Vice dean, School of Health Sciences, Case 2)

We can conclude for Case 1 that the undergraduate program accreditation policy for medicine has made a strong impact, thus producing intended and factual changes toward improving both the *faculty members dimension* (especially in the type of labor contract, qualifications, and faculty evaluation) and the *research activities dimension*. This policy acted as a trigger to improve research in a career that already had high quality standards. A formal or "cosmetic" change in connection with hiring practices was found. For Case 2, this policy produced intended and factual changes toward improving the *faculty members dimension* (especially in connection with the type of labor contract, qualifications, and faculty evaluation) and the *research activities dimension*.

The Undergraduate Program's Accreditation Policy: Engineering

We have found intended and factual changes in Case 1 to improve the *faculty members dimension* with respect to an increase in the number of full-time labor contracts, better academic qualifications, and new hiring practices. The interviews showed a close relationship between these changes and accreditation processes: "These made us realize what we needed, in the first place, more full-time faculty and, second, more qualified professors, and, in fact, this year we have already hired three more PhDs" (Academic Secretary, School of Engineering, Case 1).

As a consequence of the CONEAU's requirements, Case 2 produced a plan to incorporate more full-time professors and fostered a more intensive training strategy for faculty members, especially in the basic sciences. At the same time, the institution made other important changes to meet the requirements.[9] As was mentioned, the institution committed to expanding advanced training for faculty members (intended changes). In addition, interviews (Dean, Academic Affairs Director and Financial Director of the School of Engineering) showed that accreditation compelled administrators to provide opportunities for professors to engage in graduate studies.

Throughout the analysis of the documents, Case 1 evidenced some intended changes in the *research activities dimension*. The institution showed its commitment to fostering new research projects in topics related to industrial engineering and incorporating professors and students.

All the interviewees in Case 1 at the academic unit level mentioned that undergraduate accreditation was very influential in encouraging *research activities*. They saw accreditation as a key factor that initiated thinking processes and agreements with the CONEAU to foster improvements, such as advanced degrees and researchers sponsored by the CONICET, as this dean asserted: "The fact is that when we look at the accreditation process, I think that the CONEAU may have triggered the problem and triggered reflection" (Dean, Engineering Unit, Case 1).

We can infer both from Case 2's documentary analysis and the interviews that several factual and intended changes toward improvement have occurred. The main changes were carried out between the first and the second accreditation cycle to comply with the CONEAU's requirements and recommendations, which can be summarized as: (a) a new set of

Scientific and Technological Research Activities regulations to incorporate new researchers and projects; (b) a gradual increment in the time for professors to conduct research; (c) the reorganization of labs and teaching areas to facilitate research activities; (d) a comprehensive strategic plan to boost research in the basic sciences[10]; and (e) the organization of an area within the engineering department to promote and assess researchers and their projects and undertakings. The institution has also developed an "improvement strategy" that included six select partially funded grants for students who participate in research projects.

Interviews in Case 2 also revealed the impact that accreditation had on the *research activities dimension*. Interviewees stated that research for the university "was something extra, but not an important goal." It is possible to see how research has become a central part of the CONEAU's vision of accreditation. The following supports this point,

> Regarding undergraduate accreditation, I believe that it is research where accreditation has mostly impacted. (...) Yes, I think it did so actually because for us research has always taken second place. It has never been the main focus of the university. The CONEAU mainly has a research-centered vision; they require and demand this aspect more than any other—I do not know whether they can be satisfied with the other aspects—but I feel they mainly focus on research. (...) We have plans to improve; we have many plans, and we have focused on research and made a great deal of efforts. (Dean, School of Engineering, Case 2)

As the Financial Director (School of Engineering, Case 2) asserted, "Research, well, it is an issue; it is a huge challenge for us and for the university." Nonetheless, it is remarkable that another authority of this university (the Academic Affairs Director, School of Engineering, Case 2) revealed a lack of information on the existence of competitive public funds for research,

> We do not receive any funding from any government agency. Our university has always funded research; funds are limited, always meager. (...) Therefore, developing research has always been a problem. In fact, if I have to put it in plain terms, it is very difficult to support research with tuition and fees at a private university, and this has always been a problem.

However, what was true, and made a huge difference in comparison with the public university sector, is what the Dean of the Engineering Faculty in Case 2 mentioned in relation to the lack of public funding to help universities achieve their commitments after the accreditation process. Since 2004 the Ministry of Education has allocated three-year non-competitive funds to public universities (the Project for the Improvement of Teaching Engineering Programs [PROMEI: *Proyecto de Mejoramiento de la Enseñanza de la Ingeniería*]) so that undergraduate courses that had been accredited for three years could meet their commitment to fulfill improvement plans. Private universities have no access to these funds.

We conclude that the impact of accrediting the engineering program was significant for both case studies. The most remarkable factual changes in Case 1 had to do with the faculty's qualifications and their type of labor contract (full or part time). We have also found factual changes in the *research activities dimension*. However, we infer from the interviews in Case 1 that these changes (in the research dimension) were not only a consequence of accreditation, but also of strategic planning to improve the academic unit. This process was generally perceived as "positive," "excellent," and as a "move that helps to improve." In Case 2, the accreditation produced intended and factual changes to advance the *research function* (*faculty members* and *research activities dimensions*). The interviewees acknowledged that the impact would have been higher if they had had access to the funds allocated to public universities through, for example, the PROMEI.

The Government Research Funding Policy

Findings from Case 1 showed that the institution took some actions toward advancing research during the mandatory second institutional self-assessment (2010–2012).[11] This fact revealed how government funding policies have influenced the institutional mission.[12]

During an interview, the President acknowledged the importance of seed money to encourage serious research: "For us, alternative sources of research funding are highly relevant, actually, essential. Either we go after these extra sources of money, or we will never be able to conduct relevant research" (President, Case 1). He also added,

> There is no private university in this world that can continuously carry out research with what it collects from tuition; there is no such institution; really, there isn't. So, either this university provides for its needs through external funding (especially the government, as well as international organizations, foundations, and companies) or it will be extremely difficult to do significant research because research is expensive. (President, Case 1)

A supporting attitude toward research is linked to the type of people appointed to key positions, for instance, the President and the Research

Director belong to the select group of CONICET researchers. This makes a difference, as the President stated, "This fact already defines a profile." The same president expanded his point of view saying that government, through different organizations, such as the CONICET, ANPCYT, FONCYT, and FONTAR, has a key role stimulating research,

> So, we have made several decisions that are critical to developing research at the university, for instance, associating with different government funding organizations. In my opinion, the PICTO is a typical example of a good decision; the co-funded grants with the CONICET are another example; the relationship with the FONTAR for the support of the meteorology laboratory is another example of a governmental agency that advances research funding (...). The challenge is to see whether we will be able to maintain this situation in the future. (President, Case 1)

In this way, administrators are very supportive of government funding to advance research, as the following quotation voices, "I think that the relationship with government funding agencies is good news. And I think this is good because I believe it is happening in a better way, when compared with other Argentinian private universities (...); anyway, nowadays, believe me that this is only a sample, we need to get much more" (President, Case 1). Therefore, we infer that Case 1's positive research performance (research activities) is the result of aligning the university's mission with policies that the country promotes to advance R&D.

Unlike Case 1, we learned that Case 2's university does not receive any government subsidy for research, as a letter from the Dean (School of Engineering, future president) expressed, "Since our budgets are limited, and the university does not receive any government grants, it is not possible to pay professors high fees, keep a high quality library, and achieve significant levels of publications." As quoted before, we also learned that some of the university leaders had a lack of knowledge regarding the possibilities to access government funding for research, "I think that private institutions do not receive the same nationwide consideration as public ones do. When new funds for research projects are available, private universities are generally excluded (...). We are not given the same opportunities and chances; we are completely excluded" (President, Case 2). The two presidents portrayed in Cases 1 and 2 represent two mindsets that also condition external funding and, therefore, research productivity. Whether or not these perceptions reflected real facts, they are still powerful and can potentiate or cripple policy decision-making.

Discussion of the Case Studies

The case studies showed that the institutional assessment of private universities did not generate significant factual changes that would improve the quality of faculty members or the research activity at the two cases analyzed. This could be attributed to the lack of rewards or penalties associated with the results of these evaluations. As a consequence, the institutional assessment (self-assessment and external review) did not produce coercive isomorphism. However, since these assessments were conducted, universities have become more aware of their strengths and weaknesses, and these processes may even foster intended changes in some dimensions, as we observed in our cases.

Instead, as the accreditation of undergraduate programs is mandatory for those universities granting official degrees, the programs must comply with the minimum standards of quality. According to our case studies, the influence of the program accreditation on the faculty member dimension was important in both cases.[13] The impact of accrediting Medicine and Engineering programs on the research activity was more important in the less developed academic units (Engineering in Case 1; Medicine and Engineering in Case 2). These academic units were forced to redirect their missions toward research to meet the accreditation standards and to validate their degrees. This situation illustrates an explicit imposition of a mainstream university model that is reflected in the accreditation standards (coercive isomorphism). These processes regulate "basic curricular contents," "criteria of practical training," "activities reserved exclusively for the degree," and "the accreditation standards" (Art. 43 Higher Education Law No. 24,521). In addition, although the Higher Education Act stipulates that these requisites should be established by the Ministry of Education in line with the University Council, in fact, other organizations comprised by school deans have a significant influence. For instance, the Association of Medical Science Schools of Argentina and the Federal Council of Engineering Deans, groups representing professional fields, are powerful collegial bodies that have a bearing on accreditation (Campos 2007; Corengia 2005). In line with DiMaggio and Powell (1983), professionalization is a collective struggle for some people in the same profession to define the conditions and methods of their work and to control the production of their producers. So, these professional groups, through their participation in defining the accreditation standards, contribute to normative isomorphism.

Beyond the isomorphism that took place among professional programs, the factual changes accomplished in the research dimension of Case 1 (an elite-type university) could also be attributed to internal leadership and institutional strategies. In particular, Case 1 was able to carry out factual changes in both dimensions (faculty members and research activity) and to take advantage of the government's competitive grants in order to foster their research performance. The government's funding policy only impacted Case 1, that is, the university with more research capacity. So, as Clark (1983, 2004) stated, the results of external forces do not produce equal results at all universities. At some institutions, such as Case 2, the quality assurance policies trigger changes (often expressed only as "intended" changes to be accomplished in the future). At others, as in Case 1, these policies accompany changing processes that are based on the organization's internal decisions.

Conclusions

In the first part of this chapter we analyzed some global indicators regarding the results of the CONEAU's policy and the trends in R&D human resources and funding in the higher education sector. From these data we can conclude that the 1990s' and 2000s' regulatory framework (quality assurance) and incentive structure (government research funding policies) have impacted on private universities in the following ways. First, the CONEAU authorized the expansion of private university institutions with minimum quality standards. In particular, to externally review the institutional quality or to accredit a program, the CONEAU's peer-reviewers had to consider, among other aspects, the quality of the faculty members and the development of research activities. Second, R&D expenditure in the private sector grew in real terms but far below that for other public sector bodies. Third, the number of scholars and doctoral fellows devoted to R&D expanded faster in the private university sector than in the public one. Fourth, the proportion of private university researchers that achieved doctoral degrees surpassed the percentage in the public sector. Finally, a few elite-type private universities concentrated the majority of the increased number of CONICET scholars and doctoral fellows. In sum, the main response of private universities to a public policy environment that promoted greater research activity was to improve the quality of their human resources devoted to R&D. Additionally, this improvement in R&D human resources was more relevant to only a few elite-type private universities. Nonetheless, the funding for the R&D at private universities has still not grown with the same momentum as their human resources. The main sources of financing for R&D in the private university sector are, first, the funds internally allocated by the institution to this end and, second, the government's competitive grants. In the first case, the universities face serious limitations to invest as they ultimately depend on tuition and fees. In the second case, a strong academic group is a necessary prerequisite to successfully compete for these funds.

Similarly, the case study reveals that, as a consequence of the undergraduate accreditation processes, both cases selected development strategies to improve the quality of their faculty members, increasing the proportion of full-time contracts, promoting the graduate training of their faculty, installing offices to manage the R&D, and funding some R&D projects. However, as we observed in the analysis of the global indicators, the elite-type university accomplished factual changes in both dimensions (faculty members and research activities), its authorities were more aware of the opportunities of government research funding, and its faculty were more successful at competing for grants and scholarships.

Both macro and micro levels of analysis reveal that the quality assurance policies contributed to guaranteeing a "floor" for quality, not a "ceiling." The private university sector in Argentina is still heterogeneous in terms of, say, the relevance of teaching and research activities at each university. Some institutions have a greater orientation toward teaching while others consider that research is an intrinsic part of the university's mission and thus try to develop strategies to achieve a better position in this field.

If we applied DiMaggio and Powell's (1983) neoinstitutionalist approach to interpreting the findings of our research, we would expect private universities to be more similar as a result of institutional isomorphic processes triggered by the State, via quality assurance and government research funding policies. Indeed, we have noted a consensus in responses with respect to the CONEAU guaranteeing a minimum standard of quality. Nonetheless, the differentiation persists in terms of the weight each university gives, for example, to the role of research. This was expressed in the interviews with the authorities, in the strategies addressed in response to the accreditation procedures and in the ability of teachers to join the CONICET as researchers or to obtain doctoral scholarships, among others.

In line with Clark's (1983, 2004) internal approach, governmental policies are not effective unless organizations and programs have the basic conditions to adopt and benefit from them. Thus, institutional reactions, depending on their mission and market niche, appear to be crucial.

NOTES

1. By organizational field, DiMaggio and Powell (1983, pp. 64–65) mean "those organizations that, in the aggregate, constitute a recognized area of

institutional life: key suppliers, resource and product consumers, regulatory agencies, and other organizations that produce similar services or products." For an analysis of the organizational field of higher education in Argentina, see García de Fanelli (2012).
2. DiMaggio and Powell (1983) distinguish two types of isomorphism: competitive and institutional. The first refers to competition among organizations in an organizational field for resources and customers. We focus on the second type because it is more suitable for analyzing changes and interactions among nonprofit organizations.
3. According to Levy's findings on Argentina, China, and Hungary, private education growth is related to changes in political economy. These changes tend to reduce the centrality of the state and its public institutions and open up possibilities for alternative organizational goals and means of legitimacy. Market interactions like these generate a greater interorganizational distinctiveness (Levy 2004).
4. These include presidents, deans, academic affairs directors, program directors, and institutional leaders in charge of assessment and accreditation.
5. In 2012, 34 private institutions were evaluated and 2 were reevaluated for the second time (CONEAU 2012).
6. The ANPCYT uses the Proyectos de Investigación Científica y Tecnológica (PICT, Scientific and Technological Research Projects) as the main policy tool to promote the generation of new knowledge in areas of public interest. In 2005, PICT approached the Consejo de Rectores de Universidades Privadas (CRUP, Council of Presidents of Private Universities) to promote research activities. This government research-funding agency also awarded grants to groups of researchers at private universities in the fields of social sciences and humanities and biomedical sciences and technology. The call for proposals, issued jointly by the research agency and private universities, was dedicated to supporting research groups to foster their consolidation (ANPCYT 2012).
7. However, the increased spending on R&D at private universities was higher than what these figures reveal. The wages of CONICET researchers with offices at private universities are included in the data on government performance.
8. Faculty members at public universities are usually hired through an open competitive procedure. Academic posts are announced publicly and applicants are evaluated by the "competition jury." Faculty appointed through this modus operandi are called "regular" or "ordinary" faculty. A dismissal proceeding involving a faculty member in a regular position is very rare and is only justified on just and sufficient causes (García de Fanelli 2006).
9. As follows: (a) one professor for every 15 students for the basic sciences; (b) the creation of a Commission for the Assessment and Redistribution of type of labor contract (full or part time) and positions to comply with the received recommendations; and (c) the designation of the basic sciences and full-time specialists to conduct research.
10. For instance, the university hired two prominent researchers to advance research in basic disciplines, such as math and physics.

11. The institutional assessment department of this university provided this information.
12. The following indicators confirm the mentioned statement: (a) the agreement with the ANPCYT for an Oriented Scientific and Technological Research Project (PICTO) benefitted research projects with US $400,000; (b) an agreement with the CONICET for cofunded grants (in the past three years, 15 doctoral and postdoctoral grants were awarded); (c) the decision to hire new researchers; (d) an agreement with FONTAR; (e) other competitive research funds obtained through the ANPCYT; and (f) the President and Director of Research are CONICET researchers.
13. One of the findings of the research on the way quality assurance impacted higher education in Argentina, Chile, Colombia, Costa Rica, Spain, Mexico, and Portugal had to do with faculty management; universities adopted new hiring practices that included open competitive contests and more transparent procedures to appoint the faculty (Lemaitre and Zenteno 2012).

References

Agencia Nacional de Promoción Científica y Tecnológica (ANPCYT) (National Agency for the Promotion of Science and Technology). 2012. *Fund for Scientific and Technological Research*. Buenos Aires, Argentina: ANPCYT. Available online at: http://www.agencia.gov.ar/spip.php?page=convocatorias _articulo&mostrar=741, accessed on September 4, 2012.

Balán, Jorge, and Ana García de Fanelli. 1997. "El Sector Privado de la Educación Superior" ("The Private Sector of Higher Education"). In *Los Temas Críticos de la Educación Superior en América: Los años 90. Expansión Privada, Evaluación y Posgrado* (Critical Themes of Higher Education in the Americas: The 1990s. Private Expansion, Evaluation, and Graduate Programs), volume 2, edited by Rollin Kent (pp. 9–93). Mexico City, Mexico: Fondo de Cultura Económica.

Campos, María Soledad. 2007. *Acreditación de las Carreras de Medicina: Formalismo o Mejora Institucional* (Accreditation of Medical Programs: Formalismo or Institutional Improvement). Master's thesis. San Fernando, Argentina: San Andrés University.

Clark, Burton. 1983. *The Higher Education System. Academic Organization in Cross-National Perspective*. Berkeley, CA: University of California Press.

———. 2004. *Sustaining Change in Universities: Continuities in Case Studies and Concepts*. Maidenhead, Berkshire: The Open University Press-McGraw-Hill.

Comisión Nacional de Evaluación y Acreditación Universitaria (CONEAU) (National Commission for University Evaluation and Accreditation). 2012. *Webpage Home*. Available online at: http://www.coneau.gov.ar, accessed on September 4, 2012.

Consejo Nacional de Investigaciones Científicas y Técnicas (CONICET) (National Council for Scientific and Technological Research). 2012. *CONICET Human Resources*. Available online at: http://www.conicet.gov.ar/web/conicet.acercade .cifras/convocatorias, accessed on July 23, 2012.

Corengia, Angela. 2005. *Estado, Mercado y Universidad en la Génesis de la Política de Evaluación y Acreditación Universitaria Argentina (1990–1995)* (State, Market, and University in the Emergence of the Argentinean University Evaluation and Accreditation Policy [1990–1995]). Master's thesis. San Fernando, Argentina: San Andrés University.

———. 2010. *Impacto de las Políticas de Evaluación y Acreditación en Universidades de la Argentina. Estudios de Caso* (Impact of Evaluation and Accreditation Policies on Argentinean Universities. Case Studies). Doctoral dissertation. San Fernando, Argentina: San Andrés University.

Del Bello, Juan Carlos, Osvaldo Barsky, and Graciela Giménez. 2007. *La Universidad Privada Argentina* (The Argentinean Private University). Buenos Aires, Argentina: Editorial del Zorzal.

DiMaggio, Paul. J., and Walter W. Powell. 1983. "The Iron Cage Revisited: Institutional Isomorphism and Collective Rationality in Organizational Fields." *American Sociological Review* 48 (2): 147–160.

García de Fanelli, Ana. 2005. *Universidad, Organización e Incentivos* (University, Organization, and Incentives). Buenos Aires, Argentina: Miño y Dávila-Fundación OSDE.

———. 2006. "Argentine Higher Education." In *International Handbook of Higher Education*, edited by James Forest, and Philip Altbach (pp. 573–585). Dordrecht, Netherlands: Springer.

———. 2011. "La Educación Superior en Argentina 2005–2009" ("Higher Education in Argentina 2005–2009"). In *Educación Superior en Iberoamérica. Informe 2011* (Higher Education in Iberic-America. 2011 Report), coordinated by José Joaquín Brunner, and Rocío Ferrada Hurtado. Santiago, Chile: Centro Interuniversitario de Desarrollo-UNIVERSIA, The World Bank [CD-ROM].

———. 2012. "State, Market, and Organizational Inertia: Reforms to Argentine University Education between 1990 and 2010." In *State and Market in Higher Education Reform*, edited by Hans G. Schuetze, and Germán Alvarez Mendiola (pp. 97–111). Rotterdam, Netherlands: Sense.

García de Fanelli, Ana, and María Elena Estébanez. 2008. "National Case Studies: Argentina." In *University and Development in Latin America. Successful Experiences of Research Centres*, edited by Simón Schwartzman (pp. 107–144). Rotterdam, Netherlands: Sense.

Lemaitre, María José, and María Elisa Zenteno, editors. 2012. *Aseguramiento de la calidad en Iberoamérica. Educación Superior. Informe 2012* (Quality Assurance in Iberic-America. Higher Education. 2012 Report). Santiago, Chile: European Union-UNIVERSIA, CINDA.

Levy, Daniel. 1986. *Higher Education and the State in Latin America: Private Challenges to Public Dominance*. Chicago, IL: University of Chicago Press.

———. 2004. *The New Institutionalism: Mismatches with Private Higher Education*. PROPHE Working Paper No. 3. Albany: State University of New York (SUNY). Available online at: http://www.albany.edu/dept/eaps/prophe/publication/paper.html, accessed on July 5, 2012

Ley de Educación Superior No. 24,521 (Higher Education Law No. 24,521). 1995. Buenos Aires, Argentina: Consejo Federal de Educación (Federal Council of

Education), Ministry of Education. Available online at: http://www.me.gov.ar /consejo/cf_leysuperior.html#titulo, accessed on August 20, 2012.
Maxwell, Joseph A. 1996. *Qualitative Research Design. An Interactive Approach.* London, UK: Sage.
Ministerio de Ciencia, Tecnología, e Innovación Productiva (MINCYT) (Ministry of Science, Technology, and Productive Innovation). 2012. *The 2009 Indicators' Report.* Buenos Aires, Argentina: MINCYT. Available online at: http://www .mincyt.gov.ar/publicaciones/index.php, accessed on August 20, 2012.
Ministerio de Educación (Ministry of Education). 2012. *2010 Yearly University Statistics Report.* Buenos Aires, Argentina: Ministry of Education. Available online at: http://portal.educacion.gov.ar/universidad/universidad-en-cifras /anuario-2010/, accessed on August 15, 2012.
Rabossi, Marcelo. 2011. "Differences between Public and Private Universities' Fields of Study in Argentina." *Higher Education Management and Policy* 23 (1): 1–20.
Red de Indicadores de Ciencia y Tecnología (RICYT) (Network for Science and Technology Indicators). 2012. *Comparative Indicators.* Buenos Aires, Argentina: RICYT. Available online at: http://www.ricyt.edu.ar/index.php?option=com _content&view=article&id=150&Itemid=20, accessed on August 18, 2012.
Scott, W. Richard. 2003. *Organizations: Rational, Natural, and Open Systems.* 5th edition. Englewood Cliffs, NJ: Prentice-Hall.
Thornton, Patricia H. 2011. "Isomorphism." In *The Palgrave Encyclopedia of Strategic Management*, edited by David J. Teece, and Mie Augier. New York: Palgrave Macmillan.
Van Vught, Frans. 1989. *Governmental Strategies and Innovation in Higher Education.* London, UK: Jessica Kingsley.

Chapter 5

Institutional Frameworks and Scientific Productivity in Chile and Colombia, 1950–2012
Pedro Pineda

Introduction

Should private universities change their traditional teaching mission and engage in generating knowledge? If so, what conditions enable them to accomplish that goal? A mainstream perspective has traditionally explained research productivity through the so-called best practices implemented by university administrators. The classic works of Burton Clark (1998, 2004) on entrepreneurial universities and more recent studies on world-class universities by Philip Altbach and Jamil Salmi and his other colleagues (2007, 2011) represent this approach. These well-known authors in the field of higher education studies identify and recommend administrative practices that are believed to improve financial sustainability and research production of universities around the world.

Research on the topic has therefore tended to focus on the differences between individual universities, rather than the broader institutional frameworks that establish the conditions for the development of their research activities. This alternative approach can be traced to Joseph Ben-David's (1960, 1977; Ben-David and Zloczower 1962) comparative explanation of scientific productivity of universities at developed countries. The analysis of these frameworks, broadly understood as formal regulations, informal procedures, and surrounding ideologies framing social organizations (DiMaggio and Powell 1983; Scott 2007), would most likely allow for a better understanding of the institutionalization of research.

By broadening awareness of these systems of formal laws and informal conventions, this study aims to offer a comprehensive view of the process of institutionalization of research at private universities. In this line of reasoning, I aim to contribute to the discussion held in this book by conducting a detailed comparative analysis of governmental and higher education policies impacting research productivity at private universities of two Latin American countries: Chile and Colombia. Conceptually, this allows me to establish a transversal viewpoint of the conditions related to greater scientific productivity in private universities.

In the first section, I conduct a systematic review of the expansion of scientific activities at universities in Chile and Colombia based on scientometrics. I explain the reasons for similar trends in the enhancement of scientific activities at universities, in order to focus in the second section on the large differences between the private universities of both countries regarding the degree of expansion. In the third section, I compare the differences between the institutional frameworks of the studied countries. These differential conditions, which largely explain the differential levels of scientific infrastructure found in the private higher education, are further discussed in the fourth section. My conclusions provide a general framework to understand the variations found in the countries and universities approached in the book.

My working hypothesis is that scientific productivity is explained through the relationship between the state and higher education, rather than by the supposed autonomy of private universities to become more entrepreneurial and adopt supposed best practices of research governance. It allows acknowledges university administrators' restrained possibilities within the broader political commitment of governments and society to support research. This alternative approach may draw the attention of scholars and practitioners interested in studying the effects of higher education and science policy and can offer conceptual tools for practitioners interested in incentivizing the teaching or research profile of their universities.

Research Strategy and Methods

I approach the institutionalization process through a comparative strategy and use mixed methods to analyze the collected information.

Research productivity is operationalized through published documents in the Science Citation Index (SCI), the Social Science Citation Index (SSCI), the Book Citation Index (BKCI) (ISI Web of Knowledge 2013), and granted patents (World Intellectual Property Organization—WIPO 2013). I also include the h-Index due to its increasing acceptance as an indicator of scientific productivity (Bellis 2009; Jacsó 2009). The webpages of universities were analyzed to comprehend the discursive changes along with universities' scientific activities. This information is complemented with qualitative data collected through semistructured interviews to representatives (presidents, vice-presidents, and directors of research offices) of seven private universities with different levels of research productivity in each country during October 2011 and January 2012.

In my comparative approach, I select Chile and Colombia because they share substantial similarities in the discourse of politicians and university administrators (first section) but nonetheless display different outcomes in research activities at the university level.[1] This approach may yield a positive identification of explanatory factors and conditions for the development of research activities. Both countries are also located in a region where the historical tradition of the Latin American University prevailed, meaning that universities typically integrated teaching-oriented French universities with the socially embedded character imprinted by the Córdoba reform—but not a scientific profile (Bernasconi 2008; Brunner and Uribe 2007). Still, both countries are now in quite different phases in the process of the institutionalization of research, as can be seen in the major differences in the scientific indicators of their private universities (see second section).

Common Patterns in the Institutionalization Process

The increase of research at universities is a global phenomenon, which involves both public and private universities in Chile and Colombia. In this section, I show how both countries share fundamental similarities in the institutional frameworks in which university research has developed. I then argue that a similar discourse presenting research activities as a solution for higher education development is related to common pressures of national and international forces promoting an institutionalization of research practices. I subsequently show that the concentration of basic research activities inside universities and the development of applied research mainly outside higher education is a further common pattern in higher education in both countries.

The Expansion of Research Inquiry

The analysis of key indicators of scientific productivity shows the common increasing participation of private universities in national scientific activity. The indicators found in the SCI (ISI Web of Knowledge 2013) show that the number of published documents from Chilean private universities increased from 330 in 1980 to 3,179 in 2011. Similarly, only 16 articles from Colombian private universities were published in the SCI in 1980, but this number rose to 942 in 2011. Other available indicators of scientific production, such as books and patents, show this positive trend. Chilean private universities count 167 published books in the BKCI and 13 registered patents (WIPO 2013). At the time of writing, Colombian private universities have published 38 books and successfully registered 6 patents.

This increase in research outputs has been accompanied by a rhetoric stressing the importance of developing research. This discursive shift can be tracked through analyzing the changes in university structures and mission statements of 56 and 83 private universities in Chile and Colombia, respectively. Half of the Chilean private universities and more than two-thirds of the Colombian peers had a research mission statement. It is possible to see through webpages that, respectively, private universities have 19 and 23 research vice-presidents and 6 and 1 technology transfer offices.

Internal and External Driving Forces

A second common characteristic that explains the expansion of research activities in private universities of Chile and Colombia can be found in the internal and external actors that locally influence the institutionalization process. Primarily, international agencies (UNESCO, the World Bank, the Organization of American States—OAS, the Inter-American Development Bank—IADB, and the Organisation for Economic Co-operation and Development—OECD) have given both logistical and financial assistance to governments for the institutionalization of research through the creation of governmental bodies (Drori 2003; Rodríguez-Gómez and Alcántara 2001). In the case of Chile and Colombia, this influence is related to the foundation of governmental national science agencies, higher education vice-ministries, and accreditation agencies that incentivized research productivity in universities (Jang 2003).

The recommendations of these international organizations, however, do not focus on some ostensibly neutral idea of research for development, but rather have increasingly favored applied university research. In the case of Latin American countries, an analysis of the main policy documents of these agencies clearly shows a trend toward promoting research directly linked to economic activity (Rodríguez-Gómez and Alcántara 2001; Schwartzman 2008). Their recommendations and discussions have used an economic language, best exemplified by the rhetoric that portrays research as "innovation," as can be seen in policy documents such as OECD's (n.d.) "National Innovation Systems." This intensity in the policy rhetoric favoring innovation, as experts have observed (Etzkowitz and Leydesdorff 2000; Krücken 2003), has taken place since the 1970s in the United States, the 1980s in Europe, and later in Latin America (Puyana and Serrano 2000).

University rankings are another recent external force driving the institutionalization process in Chile and Colombia. Research vice presidents commonly reported during the interviews that close attention is paid to the QS Latin American University Rankings, launched in 2011, and to the regional SCImago Institutions Rankings, available since 2009. In the case of Chile it was also mentioned in the national ranking administered by the journal *El Mercurio* (*The Mercury*). These rankings clearly foster competition between universities for prestige and scientific commitment, which in the long term may be capitalized upon to increase incomes through tuition fees or external funds. The influence of these rankings is increased by a public's lack of awareness as to their methodological validity (Ordorika and Rodríguez 2010; Teichler 2011).

Another common external force promoting the institutionalization of research in private universities in both countries is the funding that comes from local and foreign donors. For instance, since the 1950s, the Rockefeller Foundation has supported research in the fields of medicine and economics at the Pontifical Catholic University of Chile (PUCC: *Pontificia Universidad Católica de Chile*) (Fuenzalida 1984). Similarly, the IADB, the OAS, and the Ford Foundation financially supported the development of research capacities and advanced training at the Colombian University of the Andes (Uniandes: *Universidad de Los Andes*), opening new graduate degrees in engineering and economics (Bell 2008). Some elite Colombian private universities (*Universidad Eafit* [Eafit University] in 1962 and the *Universidad del Norte* [Uninorte: University of the North] in 1966) were created with external support from local and international nongovernmental organizations such as the Whirlpool Foundation and the US Agency for International Development (López 2010; Uninorte 2013).

Foreign-trained graduates returning home is, likewise, one of the strongest internal forces promoting institutionalization of research. The return of scholars from abroad, bringing a conception of research practices and regulation forms from their universities, is part of a general expansion of higher education and scientific infrastructure in all countries around the world (Drori 2003; Fuenzalida 1984; Schwartzman 1993). In this regard, the interviews to both university administrators of Chilean and Colombian universities provided evidence supporting the importance of academics returning from abroad as a fundamental driving force for research institutionalization.

Another important internal force for the widespread adoption of a research function is the isomorphic pressure of accreditation agencies. The monitoring of quality in higher education is a growing worldwide phenomenon (Ramirez 2010) that impacts the *institutional frameworks* on university governance. Both the main accrediting agencies in Chile and Colombia, the Chilean *Comisión Nacional de Acreditación* (National Accreditation Commission) and the Colombian *Consejo Nacional de Acreditación* (National Accreditation Council), refer to flexible definitions of the university. However, isomorphic pressures occur when these agencies evaluate the coherent development of the institutional discourse in university infrastructure (Fernández 2007). Given the broadening rhetoric of scientific inquiry in mission statements, the accreditation process ends up promoting convergence across the different subsectors of higher education.

Low Applied Research and High Basic Research

A third general common characteristic in the expansion of research among private universities of both countries is the low level of technological development at both private and public universities. Studies have also identified that lack of development as an overall regional problem (Fernández 2007; Schwartzman 2008), explaining these limitations by analyzing the economic models of Latin American countries. Their economies are mostly based on the primary sector, not on secondary and tertiary sectors that demand advanced technology for specialized industries and services. Without the demand side of this market, economic support for developing applied research has remained weak.

The aforementioned trends are evidenced by the low number of patents granted to private university faculty. For instance, in 2011, of the total 30 and 4 patents in Chile and Colombia, only 9 and nil, respectively, were produced inside private institutions of higher education (WIPO 2013). The small amount of applied research at these universities does not seem to match the predominant discourse favoring the role of "innovation" in economic growth promoted by international organizations.

On the other hand, publications in scientific databases, better representing basic research activities, mainly occur inside higher education. This common feature of the expansion of research activities can be observed in the low participation in research based outside of universities in 2011 (articles that do not list at least one university academic as an author). Only 210 and 160 publications out of the 5,644 and 3,154 publications in Chile and Colombia (3.7 percent and 5 percent), respectively, were developed outside of universities (ISI Web of Knowledge 2013). Basic research seems to be conducted, for the most part, in universities. By contrast, the same analysis in developed countries such as France, the United States, and Germany shows that research centers contribute independently up to one-fifth (24 percent, 18 percent, and 20 percent) of national publications. They seem to have a tradition of institutionalization of research that strongly involves research centers outside of higher education.

Differences in the Intensity of the Institutionalization Process

Even though Chile and Colombia have similar discourses promoting research at the university level, there are significant variations in the intensity and characteristics of the institutionalization that takes place in both countries. In this chapter, I examine these differences in specific subsectors and argue that the overall differences between the two private higher education sectors of both countries, taken together, are for the most part due to the research productivity of an elite group of private universities that receive direct funding from governments.

Overall, private universities in Chile published 3,179 documents in the SCI in 2011, while in Colombia produced only 889 (table 5.1). These differences cannot be explained by the overall size of the private sectors of higher education. In 2011, private universities in Chile had 450,681 students enrolled at 41 higher education centers, while Colombia had 494,532 students at 47 (Ministry of Education Higher Education Division 2013; National Ministry of Education 2013). A weighted average of publications per professor shows that one academic at a private university in Chile publishes 0.24 articles per year in the SCI. This means that it requires about 4 academics to publish an article a year, while in Colombia it needs 33 academics at private universities to publish a single registered article. Chilean universities also count higher figures in social-science databases and registered books (ISI Web of Knowledge 2013).

Table 5.1 Knowledge production of private universities in Chile and Colombia

Institution	Percentage academics with doctorate academic	Patents 2011	SCI 2011	SSCI 2011	BKCI-S, all years	BKCI-SSH, all years
PUCatólica	42	7	1153	190	59	37
U. Concepción	44	1	648	53	39	8
U. Austral Chile	32	1	358	30	17	1
U. T.F Santa María	20	1	224	11	6	0
U. N. Andrés Bello	16	0	195	9	3	1
U. C. del Norte	33	0	186	29	13	0
U. Diego Portales	21	0	62	67	0	2
U. Los Andes (Chile)	13	0	44	17	4	0
U. del Desarrollo	11	0	43	29	0	3
U. Adolfo Ibáñez	37	0	42	30	14	2
Total selected universities Chile (n = 10)		13	2955	465	155	54
Total universities Chile (n = 58)		30	6038	888	313	118
Catholic Chile (n = 8)		8	1352	240	63	49
Private Chile (n = 41)		9	3179	507	167	70
UniAndes (Colombia)	42	0	375	80	14	26
U. Javeriana	7	0	124	48	17	3
U. del Rosario	12	0	76	24	3	4
U. Antonio Nariño	3	0	64	0	3	2
UniNorte (Colombia)	0	0	42	9	0	0
Total selected universities Colombia (n = 5)		0	681	161	37	35
Total universities Colombia (n = 80)		4	2907	390	85	71
Catholic Colombia (n = 7)		0	158	49	17	15
Private Colombia (n = 47)		0	889	222	38	54

Sources: División de Educación Superior del Ministerio de Educación 2013; ISI Web of Knowledge 2013; Ministerio de Educación Nacional 2013; WIPO 2013.

Percentage patents	Percentage SCI per academic	Percentage SCI, 2011	Percentage SSCI, 2011	Percentage BKCI-S, all years	Percentage BKCI-SSH, all years	Percentage engineering	Percentage natural and computer sciences	Percentage medicine	Percentage agriculture	Percentage soc. sciences. law	Percentage humanities
22	0.64	19	21	19	31	30	23	26	4	27	18
17	0.50	11	6	12	7	13	12	16	0	16	13
17	0.45	6	3	5	1	8	6	1	0	5	1
0	0.44	4	1	2	0	2	3	11	9	19	9
0	0.15	3	1	1	1	2	3	1	0	3	2
0	0.38	3	3	4	0	0	1	0	0	1	0
0	0.14	1	8	0	2	3	4	4	0	3	0
0	0.21	1	2	1	0	0	0	0	0	0	0
0	0.14	1	3	0	3	0	0	0	0	0	0
0	0.16	1	3	4	2	0	0	1	0	0	0
56		50	51	48	47	58	52	60	13	74	43
100	0.30										
22	0.31	22	27	20	42	30	24	28	4	27	18
65	0.27	53	57	53	59	59	53	62	13	74	44
0	0.27	13	21	16	37	27	17	32	33	28	28
0	0.03	4	12	20	4	9	12	4	33	5	5
0	0.06	3	6	4	6	0	4	0	0	1	0
0	0.04	2	0	4	3	0	0	0	0	0	0
0	0.05	1	2	0	0	0	0	0	0	0	0
0	0.45	23	41	44	50	36	33	36	66	34	33
100	0.04										
0	0.02	5	13	20	21	9	12	4	33	5	5
10	0.02	31	57	45	76	36	35	37	67	36	34

These differences seem to be explained by the engagement of universities inside specific subsectors of higher education: elite and demand-absorbing. As identified by Daniel Levy (1986; Kinser and Levy 2006), the elite and demand-absorbing subsectors in Latin America differ primarily, in both their founding and social classes they target. In turn, traditional Catholic universities founded during the colonial period and secular universities founded usually in the mid-twentieth century comprise the elite subsector. Demand-absorbing universities were founded in recent decades.

Research in the private sector in Chile and Colombia is mostly undertaken in the elite subsector. I support this assertion can be supported by the indicators of scientific productivity presented in table 5.1, which show the indicators of scientific production at universities publishing more than 40 publications a year in the SCI. The top universities of each country, the PUCC and the Uniandes, publish 36 and 42 percent of the total number of 3,179 and 889 publications of the private sector. These universities are also the most efficient, as they publish 0.64 and 0.27 publications per scholar in the SCI, respectively. Comparatively, however, these figures clearly represent the overall national differences among private universities in both countries.

Table 5.1 also provides insight into the scientific role of other elite universities in each country. The Chilean *Universidad de Concepción* (University of Conception), the *Universidad Austral de Chile* (Austral University of Chile), the *Universidad Técnica Federico Santa María* (Technical University Federico Santa Maria), and the *Universidad Católica del Norte* (Catholic University of the North) are part of the select group of universities that contribute to the scientific activities of the country. These universities are financially supported by the government and are known as the universities of the Council of Chilean University Presidents (CRUCH: *Consejo de Rectores de las Universidades Chilenas*) because of the collegial body they share. Only two universities from this group, the *Universidad Católica de la Santísima Concepción* (Catholic University of the Holy Conception) and the *Universidad Católica de Temuco* (Catholic University of Temuco), did not publish at least 40 publications in the SCI. Clearly, only private universities with governmental support have developed a virtuous circle, whereby the initial governmental funds have promoted academic quality and furthered academic prestige.

In Colombia also, mostly universities with an elite profile comprise the list of universities that contribute to national science. These include the *Pontificia Universidad Javeriana* (PUJ: Pontifical Javeriana University), the *Universidad del Rosario* (Rosary University), and Uninorte. The compared performance of the PUCC and the PUJ, the two most important

Catholic universities of both countries, the first of which produces almost ten times as many publications as the second, provides further evidence of the differences in the degree of institutionalization of research in private Chilean universities.

Yet, many Colombian private universities with local prestige, such as Eafit, Externado, and Sabana, to name a few, do not show up on the list. This fact may partially challenge the broad statement made on the relationship between the social status of universities and the scientific inquiry in the case of Colombia. Such loose linkages could be interpreted as stemming from a lack of social recognition of the advantages that the Humboldtian principle may bring to the quality of academia. Nevertheless, the growing figures of scientific production driven by the forces identified in the first section seem to imply a slow change in the social value given to research.

Concerning the demand-absorbing sector, two subtypes of universities seem to accomplish some levels of scientific activity. The first subtype is represented by the cases of the *Universidad Diego Portales* (Diego Portales University) and the *Universidad de los Andes* from Chile (University of the Andes Chile). These universities have tried to preserve traditional features of the Latin American university model like academic strength in the liberal arts and a prevailing mission of training future professionals in these areas of studies. They have however, developed some scientific inquiry in disciplines such as law, medicine, and engineering. The Chilean *Universidad Andrés Bello* (Andres Bello University) and the Colombian *Universidad Antonio Nariño* (Antonio Nariño University) represent, in turn, a second subtype. They are cases of demand-absorbing universities that have developed research infrastructure in the natural sciences and engineering. These universities are the fifth and fourth most research-active universities in their respective countries.

Differences in the Institutional Frameworks

The differences in scientific production at private universities—and the systematic variations between subsectors—suggest fundamental disparities in the institutional frameworks of both countries. Given that both countries have been subject to similar global pressures to institutionalize research, it is reasonable to focus here on both the formal governmental regulations incentivizing for university research and the resulting informal conventions shaping scientific activities. In particular, attention will be given to the intervention of governments in creating an artificial market of resources for research and its relation to higher levels of competition and an elitist accumulation of scientific activities at some private universities.

To comprehend the impact of public funding, I follow a similar line of argumentation to the one Joseph Ben-David (1960, 1977; Ben-David and Zloczower 1962) used to understand the differential impact of long-term public funds for research and higher education. The main role governments play through active intervention is conceptualized as an enabling condition for the institutionalization of research. This relationship, I argue, also helps to explain the differential development of scientific activities at private universities in Chile and Colombia.

Ben-David's insightful analysis departs from the historical case of nineteenth-century universities. In this setting, he argues, the central state fostered competition among 30 universities located at the former states that comprised the German empire. This system and its effects on fostering research activities contrasts with the one of neighboring France, which had a central control over the *grandes écoles* (great schools), and the Imperial University, a highly centralized state university founded by Napoleon and existing until 1896. The situation in Germany also differs from the historical trend of England, where higher education had been centralized in major universities such as Cambridge and Oxford (Ben-David and Zloczower 1962).

Ben-David also applied this reasoning to explain the later higher productivity in American universities. He places a key explanatory role in the "decentralized competitive market for academic achievements," which can be traced to the time of the Morrill Land-Grant Act, established in 1862 (Ben-David 1960). In his historical analysis, he highlights the way these established a tradition for the promotion of competition at all levels (i.e., students, academics, and funds) as a means for fostering research. Through the central sponsor of decentralized universities across the nation, he explains (1960; Ben-David and Zloczower 1962) a tradition of competition for resources that would give a distinctive feature for the comparative success of scientific activities of American universities.

Based on the preceding considerations, I describe, in three stages presented in the following subsections, the establishment of different sets of formal policies in Chile and Colombia aimed at promoting competition among universities, including private universities.

Chile

A first stage in which private universities start institutionalizing research can be traced to the 1950s. In 1954, the Chilean government established the *Fondo de Construcción e Investigaciones Universitarias* (FCIU: Fund for Construction and University Research) with Law 11,575 of 1954. This law redirected 0.5 percent of direct and indirect nonmunicipal taxes for the following 20 years. The law makes special emphasis on infrastructure for applied research aiming to improve the country's economy and, in particular, industry and mining. The *Universidad de Chile* (UChi: University of Chile) received 56 percent of these funds, and the rest were distributed to the remaining six universities. In this way, from the earlier stages of Chilean higher education, the government supported both private and public universities in developing research infrastructure.

A second stage of the institutionalization process started in 1981. At this time, neoliberal reforms introduced by the military government framed a new relationship between the state and the society, including changes to the funding regime of higher education. The underlying principle applied to higher education policy was simple: the invisible hand of the market should organize higher education (Espinoza 2008). Based on this ideological framework, the following strategies were undertaken: decentralization of the previously nationwide UChi; expansion of education provision through private institutions; the shift to market-type funding by the state; and diminishment of government funding. These measures would have effects on both promoting further competition between higher education centers and diminishing quality through the disorganized expansion of the demand-absorbing subsector.

The military government pursued the first of these strategies through the implementation of Decree 1 of 1981. This regulation established the division of the UChi and the *Universidad Técnica del Estado* (Technical University of the State) into 14 public universities. This creation of regional universities seemed to follow the political rationale of weakening the politically influential UChi (Bernasconi and Rojas 2003; Mönckeberg 2007). In addition, whether intentionally or incidentally, I maintain that the existence of different regional universities provided the impulse for universities to compete for resources, reorganize, and innovate with the goal of creating more and higher quality research.

The second strategy, the disorganized expansion of private higher education, was undertaken through the allowance of the government for the foundation of new private universities. I showed in the second section that this expansion led to a steep massification of higher education but did not contribute to the institutionalization of university research in a major way. Remarkably, this parallel process of expansion occurred without government oversight, a fact that largely explains the social unrest against higher education policies, decades later.

The third strategy consisted of fundamental changes in the mechanisms of state funding through Decree 4 of 1981. This decree restructured the funding regime of higher education for a group of the public and private universities supported by the government (CRUCH). Since then, government funding has been principally divided into direct and indirect public support (*aporte fiscal directo* and *aporte fiscal indirecto* [direct and indirect fiscal contribution]). Direct support is provided according to the historical allocation in which funds had been steered. The indirect portion of these funds is allotted to universities according to their performance. The provision of these funds depend on indicators such as the number of enrollments with the best results in the new national standardized exam, number of matriculated students, the educational level of the academics, research projects, and publications (Bernasconi 2003). This method of funding is seen rarely across the globe: outside of Chile, only Kazakhstan, Hungary, and Georgia have governmental funding methods linked to the former academic performance of the enrolled students (OECD and World Bank 2009).

In addition to the basic funding of higher education, the military government introduced market-type mechanisms to universities through a competitive fund to support science and technology, the *Fondo Nacional de Desarrollo Científico y Tecnológico* (FONDECYT: National Fund for Scientific and Technological Development) in 1982. This new fund continued to be socially accepted as fundamental for scientific development during the military government and later with the return of democracy. At the same time, however, the military government implemented a fourth strategy of diminishment of funds for higher education. Experts estimate a decrease of funds between 1974 and 1980 between 15 percent and 35 percent (Bernasconi and Rojas 2003).

The funding policy that defined the second stage of the institutionalization process continued during the democratic government after 1991. The Congress did not pass the draft law or modifications to the main regulating principles of higher education in 1992, 1993, or 1996 (Bernasconi and Rojas 2003). Further economic support for universities was, however, provided through alternative laws and instruments that would prompt scientific research. These new funds included initiatives such as Law 19,021 of 1991, which created the *Fondo de Desarrollo Institucional* (Institutional Development Fund) for promoting research infrastructure (Bernasconi and Rojas 2003). The *Programa para el Mejoramiento de la Equidad y Calidad de la Educación Superior* (Program for Higher Education Equity and Quality Improvement) in 1999, covered by funds partially coming from the World Bank, was also directed toward improving infrastructure, promoting postgraduate education, and establishing quality-assurance mechanisms. Moreover, the government has maintained stable scholarships for studying postgraduate studies in Chile since 1988 and, since 2008, for studying abroad (*Becas Bicentenario* and *Becas Conicyt* [Bicentennial and Conicyt Scholarships]). In 2000, almost ten years after the return to democracy, governmental funding gained the level it had had in 1981 (Bernasconi 2007).

Since the second half of the 1990s, Chilean public and private universities seem to have entered a third stage of the institutionalization of research that I label as entrepreneurial. This shift, as I explained in the first section, is part of global policy discourse favoring research activities with economic impact (Etzkowitz and Leydesdorff 2000; Krücken 2003). Such changes in the form of the institutionalization of research are evidenced, at the governmental level, by the orientation of the national scientific agency called National Commission for Scientific and Technological Research—CONICYT in establishing new programs intended to bring universities closer to industrial sectors and regional governments. In addition, the Chilean government started to channel research funds through the *Corporación de Fomento de la Producción* (CORFO: Corporation for Production Improvement), an independent body founded in 1939. This organization has broadened their functions from creating new enterprises and administrating public industry to the direct financial support of technological research. The consulting cluster *Consejo Nacional de Innovación para la Competitividad* (National Council of Innovation for Competitiveness) founded in 2005 is another governmental initiative that focuses on supporting applied research in universities. This group of experts advises the president and guides long-term innovation strategy. The creation, in 2006, of a new tax on the mining industries under the name *Fondo de Innovación para la Competitividad* (Fund for Innovation for Competitiveness) promises to further contribute to the institutionalization of research with an emphasis on technological development.

The entrepreneurial view of research can be observed, at a university level, in the new rhetoric of university administrators who promote applied research with an emphasis on economic outputs. They also manifest an unprecedented administrative emphasis on undertaking accountability measures for monitoring and incentivizing research. Efforts to acquire national and international visibility are promoted by unconventional compensation systems, for example, flexible systems, which are partially calculated according to visibility in international scientific databases. The extension of these practices to demand-absorbing universities that have had a traditional, teaching-oriented mission with the purpose of increasing academic quality and governmental support can be seen as a new and third element that defines this stage of the process.

Recently, in 2012, additional governmental regulations closer to higher education policy placed new available direct funds called the *Fondo Basal por Desempeño* (Performance-Based Fund). These resources are mainly oriented to the 25 public and private universities that belong to CRUCH. They provide additional support based on the accomplishment of goals such as accredited doctorates and publications. They explicitly differentiate universities that are oriented toward teaching, toward teaching and research in certain fields, and toward research more generally. Membership of universities in each of the categories is reviewed every two years. During the entrepreneurial period, and through these new extra available resources, the funding structure of higher education has been maintained. Thus the government's involvement in the promotion of scientific research, starting in the 1950s, facilitated the underlying logic that more funding creates an artificial market to increase research.

Colombia

Colombian universities had their first stage of official research organization during the rectory of José Félix Patiño (1964–1966), at the National University. This was part of a broader restructuring process of higher education known as the *Reforma Patiño* (Patiño Reform) (Puyana and Serrano 2000). This reform built on earlier initiatives, such as the *Instituto de Crédito Educativo y Estudios Técnicos en el Exterior* (Institute for Educational Credit and Technical Studies Abroad), a national agency founded in 1953 to help Colombian nationals study abroad (Levy 1986; Uricoechea 1999). Following the National University, other public universities started to develop a centralized scientific infrastructure. However, the government promoted research through public universities located in the largest cities. The private sector had a secondary participation in research in this first period, even though, by 1975, enrolled 59 percent of student body. Colombia had the strongest development of private universities in Spanish-speaking Latin America (Levy 1986).

A second period of sound policies for the promotion of university research followed at the end of the 1980s. The *Misión de Ciencia y Tecnología* (Science and Technology Mission), a commission that worked from 1988 to 1990 to give a rational for science and higher education reform, helped to further foster the institutionalization process. Law 29 of 1990, framed by the new constitution of 1991, subsequently aimed explicitly at the promotion of scientific research and technological development both inside and outside of universities.

Regulations like this established a set of distinctive characteristics for Colombian higher education policies in research matters. First, discussions about scientific policy strongly involved a democratic steering regarding resources for the different regions of the country. This conception can be observed in the creation of the so-called regional commissions for science and technology (Decree 585 of 1990). This democratic rationale pursuing a balance of opportunities to academic units of universities has lead public attention to focus on the gaps between more and less industrialized regions of the country, rather than the national gaps at a global level. Second, and a related trend, is the notion that science is a national activity for the production of knowledge. This assumption was endorsed through the creation of a nationwide scientific database managed by the Department of Science, Technology, and Innovation (Colciencias) to identify publications with local academic value. A third particularity in the governance of science established since this second period is the exclusive allocation of funds to the so-called *grupos de investigación* (research groups).

After this general regulatory framework for research, at the beginning of the 1990s, there were many other subsequent initiatives that seemed to have a limited effect on promoting scientific activities. However, these seemed to bring little new impulse to the institutionalization process due to their lack of stability. These initiatives included the foundation of research clusters called *Centros de Investigación de Excelencia* (Research Excellence Centers 2004) and the funds for *Cofinanciación de Proyectos* (Project Co-funding) and *Financiación de Proyectos de Innovación y Desarrollo* (Fund for Innovation and Development Projects). Such flux of programs is related to a clearly anti-intellectual profile among several governments (presidents Andrés Pastrana and Álvaro Uribe), according to Gabriel Misas and Mónica Oviedo (2004). The discourses of their officials supporting research did, however, evidence a clear gap between political rhetoric and research productivity in the country.

However, during this second stage, higher education policies made important changes to facilitate research at public universities, a process that would eventually give a symbolic value to research activities in the private sector as well. Decree 1,444 of 1992, followed by Decree 2,912 of 2002 at universities, formally established the academic career and encouraged scientific activities among public university professors through salary increases according to the amount of publications professors produce (Delgado 2011). After this policy, Colombian public publications in the SCI showed an exponential growth.

Again, private universities did not play a major role in this second stage of research institutionalization, and around 80 percent of the research funded by Colciencias during the years that followed this regulation was undertaken in public universities (Uricoechea 1999). In practice, most private universities have not benefited from governmental funds because they have not found stable and visible research groups. The private Uniandes carried out 75 percent of the research projects of private universities and was a notable exception. Although the government did not undertake any parallel initiative to formalize the academic profession in the private sector, the increasing institutionalization process in the public sector, however, may have had a mimetic effect in some private universities. The weight of this effect in the institutionalization process of research inside the private sector is difficult to determine.

In the past few years, government regulations in Colombia seem to have reacted to the global changes pointed out in the first section as well, and Colombia has experienced a third entrepreneurial stage in the institutionalization process. This promotion of applied research in a country that has not yet achieved a stable infrastructure for basic scientific activities highlights a paradox between the convergent rhetoric of scientific development and the divergent scientific infrastructure and intellectual basis of scientific production in Colombian universities. The new Law 1,286 of 2009 on science, following the previous Law 29 of 1990, takes a step further in this direction by transforming Colciencias into an administrative department, thus giving it more autonomy and bringing it closer to national economic planning. The new regulation clearly underlies the shift toward a mission of innovation for the role of the university in the economy at the expense of their scientific role and for a broader definition of development.

Law 1,530 of 2012, the most recent regulation on scientific matters, is representative of the style of scientific policy in Colombia. The law legally assigns 10 percent of incomes from royalties to science and technology. It is expected that scientific research will receive additional incomes that will represent an increase in expenditures on science and technology from 0.19 percent to 0.4 percent as a percentage of the gross domestic product (GDP). The law has a number of particularities. First, funds are restricted to applied research. Second, the fact that governors and not Colciencias establish the criteria to allocate funding causes that the allocation of resources follow a democratic and not a scientific rational. In any event, private universities in Colombia may strive for access to the additional resources offered by Law 1,530 of 2012.

In sum, given the lack of governmental commitment to funding research infrastructure, scientific inquiry in the Colombian private sector has relied on internal resources mostly derived from increased tuition fees. Private universities have, therefore, struggled between a teaching-oriented mission and the illusion of becoming a research university according to international standards. The rhetoric of science for research and the government's lack of a historical and interdisciplinary conception of the governance of research have created the conditions for this contradiction to survive for the past decades.

Discussion

I have examined the trends in the research production of private universities in Chile and Colombia and the degree of commitment of both governments to incentivizing research in the private sector. These common patterns are not explained by deviances in the political rhetoric or by the shared internal and external stakeholders promoting the institutionalization process. Therefore, it is certainly more helpful to search for an explanation in the differences encountered in the establishment of the regulatory frameworks of governments and more specifically in long-term policy instruments (funds for higher education and for basic and applied research, scholarships) that promote a market of academic competition in a select group of private universities. I will now discuss the presence of each of these explanatory elements in more detail for each of the countries in question.

Governmental Funds

First, Chilean higher education and science policy has created a market in which universities compete for the performance-based funds supplied by the government. Both the mechanisms for funding state-supported public and private universities and the competitive funds established by science policy have incentivized university administrators to change university structures and foster an internal culture that allows the competition with universities at the private and public sector. The government directed these resources toward training new professors, establishing research infrastructure, and maintaining research projects. Clearly, Chile introduced a series of funds which were of crucial importance to enhancing scientific inquiry in a time in which the governments of other countries may have seen these initiatives as unnecessary.

Colombian governmental policy statements, on the other hand, promise to involve universities in technological development and in the implementation of new policies. However, this discursive shift has occurred while private universities, with the identified exceptions, have not even consolidated stable scientific activities in basic research. This governmental discourse has been prone to adopt the terminology of new best practices but has been limited in the actual promotion of research activities, thus showing the "artificial character" of Colombian universities already described at the end of the decade of the 1990s (Uricoechea 1999, p. 20).

Furthermore, the lower research outputs of Colombian universities, including those in the private sector, clearly cannot be explained only in terms of resource availability. In fact, the numbers of publications are not proportional to the public expenditures on research and higher education. The broad investment of Chile in research and development (R&D) represents 0.42 percent of GDP, public expenditures in higher education represent 0.7 percent of GDP, and private expenditures represent 1.7 percent (OECD 2013). In Colombia, the broad investment in research and experimental development activities only represents 0.19 percent of GDP. Yet, public expenditures to higher education represent 0.98 percent of GDP for available year 2007 (OECD, IBRD, and World Bank 2013); private expenditures are equivalent to 0.92 percent of GDP. In view of these broad figures, it is reasonable to conclude that Chile does not have particular high governmental expenditures on higher education or science.

Hence, a similar line of reasoning as the one followed by Ben-David (1960, 1977; Ben-David and Zloczower 1962) could be followed to explain scientific productivity in private universities. Private universities require governmental intervention. For the reasons explained in the first section, they may not be capable of acquiring sufficient resources coming from technology ravenous or philanthropic assistances in order to maintain the research enterprise. In economic terms, the Chilean government seems to have more strongly recognized the value of knowledge as a public good (Batina and Ihori 2005). Applied to research activities, this idea seems to fit scientific activities best in the case of research in the social and medical sciences (Fuenzalida 2001), which requires expensive infrastructure and high social, but low economic, profitability. Newfield (2008, p. 214) explains in the same line of reasoning that "many technical reports confirm this analysis, and some universities are honest about this, but most are not clear about the fact that 'all research is subsidized research'".

Elitist Structure

Second, the Chilean government has historically implemented an elitist form of funding by choosing a group of public and private universities to compete for research funds. This strategy has been carried out through governmental support of research at the universities of the CRUCH since 1954. These relationships explain in great part why a select group of 9 private universities (along with the 16 public universities out of 59 universities) has, over the decades, assembled a critical mass of experts capable of carrying out high level scientific inquiry. Government support for the development of research infrastructure at this group of private universities was augmented by a further differentiation of the CRUCH universities for the provision of funds through the Performance-Based Fund in 2012.

Overall, this governmental support has contributed to the elitist character to these private universities, which, according to Levy (2006) is uncommon around the world.

For the most part, the organization of scientific production in Colombia attempts to foster science through promoting the organization of "research groups" described earlier. Although looking forward to incentivize scientific networking, the registration of "research groups" is a common practice for increasing the prestige of universities in different subsectors of public and private higher education. Presenting numbers of research groups to other departments and the authorities lets a given academic community shield itself from directly submitting its publications and evaluations of its academic products by experts of the field.

The strong focus in Colombia on funding research in these "research groups" may itself impede scientific activity in many areas where research is done individually or in small groups. It may hinder national and international academic mobility, overemphasizing the value of local academic networking at the cost of the international level. Furthermore, the extent to which it can promote interdisciplinary work between groups remains unclear. In this regard, the institutionalization process seems, for the case of Colombia, to be better explained by an institutional explanation (Drori et al. 2006; Krücken 2003; Ramirez 2007). This theoretical framework shares the useful insight that administrators of complex social activities such as schooling and science tend to avoid the report of their activities. The creation of mechanisms such as "research groups" as measures of accountability may be interpreted as the attempt of scholars to avoid directly reporting the number or impact of its publications, measures of scientific production considered valid by the international academic community.

Overall, the open accumulation of resources in a selected number of research centers in Chile seems to reinforce the conception of scientific activities as organized in clusters of selected experts. This observation is in the sane line of the work of Robert Merton (1968). This renowned sociologist of science analyzed this tendency in individual researchers, calling this phenomenon the Mathew Effect. However, this argument can be extended to scientific centers in general. Jonathan Cole and Stephen Cole (1967, 1973) examine the underlying mechanisms in more detail and claim that both recognition and scientific productivity increase over time, starting with a slightly different productivity in an initial moment and a further loop that allows the attainment of further fame and resources. Differences in the accumulation of research, as Altbach and Salmi (2011) state, occur in countries located at the center and the periphery.

Policy Stability

Third, a very important feature that emerges from this comparison is the stability of research funds. This feature of Chilean science and higher education policy has allowed universities to plan in the long-term, knowing the conditions under which research would be supported. Government funds directed toward strengthening the scientific activities of public and private universities can be traced to the FCIU in 1954 and continued to be directed by the FONDECYT in 1982 and the subsequent programs in the 1990s. In Chile, the government's relationship to scientific activity has clearly been far from laissez-faire (Bernasconi 2003). Policies focused on incentivizing scientific activity rather than merely regulating it, although this type of relationship does not apply to the private sector overall and excludes the large demand-absorbing subsector. Chilean higher education policy's effectiveness in incentivizing research culture may have had a different interpretation than the one that highlights its negative effects in reproducing social inequality and in lowering academic quality (Espinoza 2008; Mönckeberg 2007).

In Colombia, as I have shown, additional funds for scientific infrastructure have fluctuated historically and have depended on external credits (Jaramillo et al. 2004). The varying funds provided by the Colombian government do not allow universities to count on governmental support for long-term projects with the certainty that conditions will be maintained in the future. Colombian science policy has been highly permeable to the new discourses and policy fads adopted by successive governments.

Neither Chilean nor Colombian private universities, however, have met with remarkable success in developing technological research. Higher education and science policy, by international standards of technological production, have failed to promote applied research in the universities of both countries, largely due to the reasons I point out in the first section. However, recent programs in Chile to promote applied research involving universities may indicate that applied research could become more strongly institutionalized, notwithstanding the limited role that universities may play.

The effects of this long-term policy stability are in line with the work of Douglass North (1990), who argues that permanence of rules and laws is a fundamental element in the development of markets. I claim that this insightful principle for explaining economic development can be extended to scientific production to explain the effects of the Chilean government's adoption of long-term rules of the game. This stability has allowed the emergence of internal formal and informal rules for encouraging scientific research inside universities. Universities need stable long-term policies because the production of new and original ideas requires a research program that can take years, sometimes even decades, to establish.

Concluding Thoughts

In this chapter I have argued that the state's long-term promotion of science in the private sector through directing competitive funds to an elite group of private universities is a fundamental condition for the development of scientific inquiry in private universities. Using this proposition, I explain the fundamental differences in the institutionalization process in a select group of Chilean private universities. My approach offers a perspective critical of mainstream explanations of scientific inquiry. It allows for reflection on the relationship between the state and higher education in order to explain research practices in higher education, rather than assuming that private universities should develop a research mission by becoming more entrepreneurial and adopting supposed best-practices of research governance (Altbach 2007; Clark 1998).

A comparative perspective on Chile and Colombia shows that the most relevant difference between universities of both countries is the role that governments play actively, and not merely discursively, supporting the involvement of the private sector in the formalization of research activities. In this regard, the insights of neoinstitutional theory led to a recognition of the limitations of rhetoric that overemphasizes the administrative capacity of private universities and helped to explain the differences in the scientific productivity of various universities (Drori et al. 2006; Ramirez 2007).

The findings of this study clearly imply that science and higher education policy should take into account stability and a combination of focused, performance-based funds for basic and applied projects and competitive funds for research infrastructure that do not disperse funds into peripheral research centers. By highlighting the historical development of scientific inquiry in higher education in Chile and Colombia, I also show the consequences of governments' lack of commitment to research. Also, I provided evidence that science and scholarship tend to couple to an elite organization and supported theoretically my observations on the pivotal works of sociology of science (Cole and Cole 1967; Merton 1968).

Further research might investigate whether the conditions I have identified for the development of scientific inquiry have been met in other geographic areas. Through a more detailed analysis of the subsectors of private higher education, it might be possible to locate exceptions to my analysis. Furthermore, critical analysis of the risks of planning higher education development based exclusively on market-type mechanisms and of the myths of its supposedly unlimited benefits (Dill 2007; Pineda 2013) may enrich future inquiry.

Nevertheless, it would be desirable in future studies to provide a historical analysis on a broader scope, based on indicators of scientific production. By doing so, one might counterbalance the empty rhetoric surrounding the supposed need for the institutionalization of research in the private sector. Moreover, one could provide further insight into the intrinsic limitations of the development of scientific infrastructure at private universities and critically identify the conditions under which it might be socially desirable to cultivate well-defined subsectors of higher education.

Note

1. For a more detail description of this approach, see Ebbinghaus (2009) and Tilly (1984).

References

Altbach, Philip G. 2007. *World Class Worldwide: Transforming Research Universities in Asia and Latin America*. Baltimore, MD: Johns Hopkins University Press.

Altbach, Philip G., and Jamil Salmi. 2011. *The Road to Academic Excellence: The Making of World-Class Research Universities*. Washington, DC: World Bank Publications.

Batina, Raymond G., and Toshihiro Ihori. 2005. *Public Goods: Theories and Evidence*. Berlin, Heidelberg, Germany: Springer-Verlag Berlin Heidelberg.

Bell, Gustavo. 2008. *Historia de la Universidad de los Andes* [History of the University of the Andes]. Bogotá, Colombia: Universidad de los Andes.

Bellis, Nicola de. 2009. *Bibliometrics and Citation Analysis: From the Science Citation Index to Cybermetrics*. Lanham, MD: Scarecrow Press.

Ben-David, Joseph. 1960. "Scientific Productivity and Academic Organization in Nineteenth-Century Medicine." *American Sociological Review* 25 (6): 828–843.

———. *Centers of Learning: Britain, France, Germany, United States*. Sponsored research studies by the Carnegie Commission on Higher Education. New York,: McGraw-Hill.

Ben-David, Joseph, and Awraham Zloczower. 1962. "Universities and Academic Systems in Modern Societies." *European Journal of Sociology* 3 (1): 828–843.

Bernasconi, Andres. 2003. *Organizational Diversity in Chilean Higher Education: Faculty Regimes in Private Higher Education*. Boston, MA: Boston University.

———. 2008. "Are there Research Universities in Chile?" In *World Class Worldwide: Transforming Research Universities in Asia and Latin America*, edited by Philip G. Altbach and Jorge Balán. Baltimore, MD: Johns Hopkins University Press.

Bernasconi, Andrés, and Fernando Rojas. 2003. *Informe sobre la Educación Superior en Chile: 1980–2003* (Report on Higher Education in Chile: 1980–2003). Caracas, Venezuela: Instituto Internacional para la Educación Superior en América Latina y el Caribe de la UNESCO (ESALC: UNESCO International Institute for Higher Education in Latin America and the Caribbean).

Brunner, José Joaquín, and Daniel Uribe. 2007. *Mercados Universitarios: El Nuevo Escenario de la Educación Superior* (University Merkets: New Scenario of Higher Education). Santiago, Chile: Ediciones Universedad Diego Portales.

Clark, Burton R. 1998. *Creating Entrepreneurial Universities: Organizational Pathways of Transformation*. Oxford, UK: Pergamon Press.

———. *Sustaining Change in Universities: Continuities in Case Studies and Concepts*. Maidenhead, England: Society for Research into Higher Education, Open University Press.

Cole, Jonathan, and Stephen Cole. 1967. "Scientific Output and Recognition: A Study in the Operation of the Reward System in Science." *American Sociological Review* 32 (3): 377–90.

———. 1973. *Social Stratification in Science*. Chicago, IL: University of Chicago Press.

Delgado, Jorge. 2011. "Journal Publication in Chile, Colombia, and Venezuela: University Responses to Global, Regional, and National Pressures and Trends." Doctoral dissertation. Pittsburgh, PA: University of Pittsburgh, School of Education.

Dill, David D. 2007. "Will Market Competition Assure Academic Quality? An Analysis of the UK and US Experience." In *Quality Assurance in Higher Education*, edited by Peter Maassen, Johan Muller, Don F. Westerheijden, Bjørn Stensaker, and Maria J. Rosa (pp. 47–72). Dordrecht, Netherlands: Springer.

DiMaggio, Paul J., and Walter W. Powell. 1983. "The Iron Cage Revisited: Institutional Isomorphism and Collective Rationality in Organizational Fields." *American Sociological Review* 48 (2): 147–160.

División de Educación Superior del Ministerio de Educación (Ministry of Education Higher Education Division). (2013). *Sistema Nacional de Información de la Educación Superior: Académicos e Investigadores* (National Information System of Higher Education: Academics and Researchers). Santiago, Chile: Ministry of Education. Available online at: http://www.mifuturo.cl/index.php/academicos-einvestigadores, accessed on February 1, 2013.

Drori, Gili S. 2003. *Science in the Modern World Polity: Institutionalization and Globalization*. Stanford, CA: Stanford University Press.

Drori, Gili S., John W. Meyer, and Hokyu Hwang, editors. 2006. *Globalization and Organization: World Society and Organizational Change*. Oxford, UK: Oxford University Press.

Ebbinghaus, Bernhard. 2009. "Vergleichende Politische Soziologie: Quantitative Analyse- oder qualitative Fallstudiendesigns?" ("Comparative Political

Sociology: Quantitative Analysis and Qualitative Case Study Design?") In *Politische Soziologie (Political Sociology)*, edited by Viktoria Kaina and Andrea Römmele (pp. 481–501). Wiesbaden, Germany: VS Verlag für Sozialwissenschaften.

Espinoza, Oscar. 2008. "Creating (in) Equalities in Access to Higher Education in the Context of Structural Adjustment And Post-Adjustment Policies: The Case of Chile." *Higher Education* 55 (3): 269–84.

Etzkowitz, Henry, and Loet Leydesdorff. 2000. "The Dynamics of Innovation: From National Systems and 'Mode 2' to a Triple Helix of University-Industry-Government Relations." *Research Policy* 29 (2): 109–123.

Fernández, Enrique. 2007. "Universidad y Reconcentración de la Investigación Científica en Chile, 1982–2005" ("University and Reconcentration of Scientific Research in Chile"). *Persona y Sociedad (Person and Society)* 21 (3): 31–57.

Fuenzalida, Edmundo. 1984. "Institutionalisation of Research in Chile's Universities." In *Education and Development*, edited by Roger M. Garrett. London, UK: Croom Helm.

———. "Fin y Principio: La Transición en la Cultura Chilena" ("End and Beginning: Transition in Chilean Culture"). *Universum* (16): 101–113.

ISI Web of Knowledge. 2013. *Journal Citation Reports*. Philadephia, PA: Thomson Reuters. Available online at: http://wokinfo.com/, accessed on February 1, 2013.

Jacsó, Péter. 2009. "The h-Index for Countries in Web of Science and Scopus." *Online Information Review* 33 (4): 831–837.

Jang, Yong S. 2003. "The Global Diffusion of Ministries of Science and Technology." In *Science in the Modern World Polity: Institutionalization and Globalization*, edited by Gili S. Drori, John W. Meyer, Francisco O. Ramirez, and Evan Schofer. Stanford, CA: Stanford University Press.

Jaramillo, Hernán, María Alejandra Botiva, and Andrés Zambrano. 2004. *Políticas y resultados de ciencia y tecnología en Colombia* (Policies and results of science and technology in Colombia). Borradores de investigación. Bogotá, Colombia: Universidad del Rosario.

Kinser, Kevin, and Daniel C. Levy. 2006. "For-profit Higher Education: U.S. Tendencies, International Echoes." In *International Handbook of Higher Education*, edited by James Forest and Philip G. Altbach. Dordrecht, Netherlands: Springer.

Krücken, Georg. 2003. "Learning the 'New, New Thing': On the Role of Path Dependency in University Structures." *Higher Education* 46 (3): 315–339.

Levy, Daniel C. 1986. *Higher Education and the State in Latin America: Private Challenges to Public Dominance*. Chicago, IL: University of Chicago Press.

———, editor. 2006. "Intersectoral Interfaces in Higher Education Development: Private and Public in Sync?" Washington, DC: The World Bank.

López, Juan C. 2010. *Universidad Eafit 20 Años* (Eafit University 20 Years). Medellín, Colombia: Eafit University.

Merton, Robert K. 1968. "The Matthew Effect in Science." *Science* 159 (3810): 56–63.

Ministerio de Educación Nacional (MEN) (National Ministry of Education). 2013. *Sistema Nacional de Información de Educación Superior* (National Information System of Higher Education). Bogotá, Colombia: MEN. Available online at: http://www.mineducacion.gov.co/snies/, accessed on February 1, 2013.

Misas, Gabriel, and Mónica Oviedo. 2004. *La Educación Superior en Colombia: Análisis y Estrategias para su Desarrollo* (Higher Education in Colombia: Analysis and Strategies for Its Development). Bogotá, Colombia: National University of Colombia.

Mönckeberg, María O. 2007. *El Negocio de las Universidades en Chile* (University Business in Chile). Santiago, Chile: Debate.

Newfield, Christopher. 2008. *Unmaking the Public University: The Forty-Year Assault on the Middle Class*. Cambridge, MA: Harvard University Press.

North, Douglass C. 1990. *Institutions, Institutional Change, and Economic Performance. The Political Economy of Institutions and Decisions*. Cambridge, UK: Cambridge University Press.

Organisation for Economic Co-operation and Development (OECD). N.d. *National Innovation Systems*. Paris, France: OECD.

OECD. 2013. *Education at a Glance: 2013*. Paris, France: OECD.

OECD, International Bank for Reconstruction and Development, World Bank. 2013. *Evaluaciones de Políticas Nacionales de Educación: La Educación Superior en Colombia* (Evaluations of National Education Policies: Higher Education in Colombia). Paris, France: OECD.

OECD, and World Bank. 2009. *Tertiary Education in Chile. Reviews of National Policies for Education*. Paris, France: OECD.

Ordorika, Imanol, and Roberto Rodríguez. 2010. "El Ranking Times en el Mercado del Prestigio Universitario" ("Times Ranking in the University Prestige Market"). *Perfiles Educativos (Education Profiles)* XXXII (129): 8–29.

Pineda, Pedro. 2013. "Between Myth and Rationality: University Models and the Institutionalization of Research in Chile and Colombia 1950–2012." Doctoral dissertation. Berlin, Germany: Humboldt-Universität zu.

Puyana, Aura M., and Mariana Serrano. 2000. *Reforma o Inercia en la Universidad Latinoamericana: La Universidad Nacional de Colombia y la Universidad Nacional Autónoma de México* (Reform or Inertia in Latin American University: National University of Colombia and National Autonomous University of Mexico). Bogotá, Colombia: TM Editores.

Ramirez, Francisco O. 2007. *Growing Commonalities and Persistent Differences in Higher Education: Universities between Global Models and National Legacies. New Institutionalism in Education*. Albany: State University of New York Press.

———. "Accounting for Excellence: Transforming Universities into Organizational Actors." In *Higher Education, Policy, and the Global Competition Phenomenon. International and Development Education*, edited by Laura M. Portnoi, Sylvia S. Bagley, and Val D. Rust. New York: Palgrave Macmillan.

Rodríguez-Gómez, Roberto, and Armando Alcántara. 2001. "Multilateral Agencies and Higher Education Reform in Latin America." *Journal of Education Policy* 16 (6): 507–525.

Schwartzman, Simon. 1993. "Policies for Higher Education in Latin America: The Context." *Higher Education* 25 (1): 9–20.

———. 2008. *Universidad y Desarrollo en Latinoamérica: Experiencias Exitosas de Centros de Investigación* (University and Development in Latin America: Successful Experiences of Research Centers). Caracas, Venezuela: IESALC.

Scott, W. R. 2007. "Institutional Theory: Contributing to a Theoretical Research Program." In *Great Minds in Management: The Process of Theory Development*, edited by W. R. Scott, Ken G. Smith, and Michael A. Hitt. Oxford, UK: Oxford University Press.

Teichler, Ulrich. 2011. "Social Contexts and Systemic Consequence of University Rankings: A Meta-Analysis of the Ranking Literature." In *University Rankings: Theoretical Basis, Methodology and Impacts on Global Higher Education*, edited by Jung C. Shin and Robert K. Toutkoushian. Dordrecht, Netherlands: Springer.

Tilly, Charles. 1984. *Big Structures, Large Processes, Huge Comparisons*. New York, NY: Russell Sage Foundation.

Universidad del Norte (Uninorte) (University of the North). 2013. *Sobre Nosotros* (About Us). Barranquilla, Colombia: Uninorte. Available online at: http://www.uninorte.edu.co, accessed on December 15, 2013.

Uricoechea, Fernando, editor. 1999. *La Profesionalización Académica en Colombia: Historia, Estructura y Procesos* (Academic Professionalization in Colombia: History, Structure, and Processes). Bogotá, Colombia: Tercer Mundo Editores.

World Intellectual Property Organization. 2013. *Patentscope: Search International and National Patent Collections*. Available online at: http://patentscope.wipo.int/search/en/search.jsf, accessed on December 15, 2013.

Part II

Successful Cases of Research Productivity at Private Universities

Chapter 6

A Research and Innovation Ecosystem Model for Private Universities

The Monterrey Institute of Technology Experience

Francisco J. Cantú-Ortiz

Introduction

European universities are centennial organizations with a well-established tradition for the generation and transmission of knowledge that goes back to, at least, the tenth century when the first universities appeared in Europe, evolving from medieval monasteries in cities like Bologna, Paris, Salamanca, and Oxford. Prior to the European-type university, even before the Christian era, other centers of studies existed in ancient Greece, China, India, Arabia, and Mesoamerica (Perkin 2006).

The word *university* comes from the Latin *universitas*, which means the gathering of masters (*magistorum*) and scholars (*scholarium*) to study, discuss, and advance knowledge in a given subject matter. The *studium generale* were monastic centers devoted to inquiry in the fields of theology, philosophy, medicine, and other disciplines known as *Trivium* (grammar, rhetoric, and dialectic) and *Cuadrivium* (arithmetic, geometry, astronomy, and music). Scholasticism, a dominant school of thought led by Thomas Aquinas (1225–1274) in the thirteenth century, emerged from those centers (Schmitt 1998). Likewise, under the influence of the philosophical movements of nominalism and voluntarism, developed by Duns Scotus (1266–1308) and William of Ockham (1285–1349), the *stadium generale* focused on the tension between the "contingent and temporary" and the "permanent and eternal." These philosophical foundations were key for the emergence of experimental discoveries during the fifteenth and sixteenth centuries, along with the empiricism of the British philosophers Francis Bacon (1561–1626), John Locke (1632–1704), and David Hume (1711–1776), with the contributions of scientists such as Nickolas Copernicus (1473–1543), Johan Kepler (1571–1630), Galileo Galilei (1564–1642), Rene Descartes (1596–1650), and Isaac Newton (1642–1727). These scientists and philosophers used a scientific hypothetical-deductive method of inquiry aimed at predicting and controlling nature. The industrial revolution of the eighteenth century was, to a great extent, a result of this paradigm shift. In that context, universities adapted to the new circumstances by establishing colleges of natural science, technology and engineering, and building laboratories (Cantú Ortiz 2011, pp. 51–57).

During the twentieth century, universities assumed a new role in society that added to the generation of fundamental theoretical knowledge for the advancement of sciences. They became engines of economic development by inserting themselves into what is called "Ecosystems of Innovation" (Etzkowitz 2001). The word ecosystem is taken from environmental and natural sciences to denote a set of individuals and groups interacting to preserve themselves using limited resources without altering their surrounding environment. An example would be a forest with trees that take rain to yield fruits that feed animals like squirrels, rabbits, or birds, which at the same time are food for predators such as wolves or eagles. In the same way, an "Innovation Ecosystem" is an analogy for natural resources that include persons, groups of people (a city, country, or world region), and economic resources in constant interactions looking for balance. Thus, an innovation ecosystem is defined as "the people, institutions, policies and resources that promote the translation of new ideas into products, processes, and services" (National Science Foundation—NSF 2013). Within the context of an innovation ecosystem, the term "Triple Helix" was coined to establish a model of interaction between universities, industry, and government to foster innovation, regional development, and competitiveness in cities, countries, and even regions (Leydesdorff 2012; Etzkowitz and Leydesdorff 1997, 2000). Universities have been forced to play an active role in this new setting by contributing with new models of knowledge and management to train professionals. Consequently, professors are constantly challenged to collaborate not just in the generation of knowledge and scientific models, but in their transference to economic and social sectors. In addition, they have to take care of intellectual property regulations through patents, brands, utility models, and other forms of copyright. This way, professors are becoming entrepreneurial researchers, a role that is actually reshaping academia (Etzkowitz 2001).

Another aspect of innovation ecosystems is their dependency on products and services designed for specific markets that result from the intersection of technological and scientific research. This way, "Technoscience" is a concept that expresses this new connection between science and technology. French philosopher Gaston Bachelard coined the term in 1953, and it was later used by Belgian philosopher Gilbert Hottois in the 1970s and popularized by various English and Spanish scholars in the 2000s and beyond. Technoscience is a type of innovation ecosystem and triple helix model. It fosters the interdisciplinary and collaborative work of industry, government, and academia to undertake multimillion dollar research and technology efforts toward national and strategic interest related to security, health, and competitiveness, among others. Technoscience also refers to social contexts and historical consensus for scientific knowledge and how it has been generated throughout the past centuries (Sismondo 2010).

At this point, it is important to pinpoint some issues about the distinction usually made between public and private universities, which are relevant in governmental and academic sectors because of the role they play in modern society and from a funding standpoint (Hegde 2005). Since their creation, especially in continental Europe, major universities have been mainly funded with public monies (from emperors, kings, governments, etc.). The United States has the strongest private higher education system in the world, which can be attributed to a combination of smaller governmental structures and religious and philosophical ideologies that fueled capitalism and utilitarianism from the very beginning. Currently, both public and private universities compete for federal research funding on the basis of academic performance and scientific credentials (Levy 1986). This is not necessarily the case among Latin American higher education systems. The present chapter addresses the issue of developing research in private universities when federal funding is mainly allocated to public institutions.

Public and private universities are essential institutions for innovation ecosystems and the development of the triple helix model. In this context, the concept of world-class universities has developed to identify universities that are research-oriented, handle multibillion dollar endowments, and attract the best students and professors from around the world. These institutions are engines of technological, economic, and social development that are reflected in world university rankings, such as the Shanghai

Academic Ranking of World Universities (ARWU), the US News & World Report's Best World Universities, the QS World University Rankings, and the TIMES Higher Education World University Rankings. Those rankings include both public and private universities. As rankings categorize institutions, they play an important role in university strategies to compete for the highest ranks (Salmi 2009).

In order to explain the interconnection among the concepts of innovation ecosystems, triple helix, and world-class universities, the following sections introduce key elements of an original type of research and innovation ecosystem (RIE) geared toward private universities that consider both the context and situation of Latin American countries. The model is represented with the case study of a university that implemented an institutional strategy to develop research capabilities in a teaching-oriented private university from Mexico, the *Instituto Tecnológico y de Estudios Superiores de Monterrey* (ITESM: Monterrey Institute of Technology and Higher Education) (Cantú-Ortiz et al. 2009, pp. 155–156).

In the pages to come, this chapter is structured in four sections. Section one presents the key elements of an RIE for private universities. Section two introduces the ITESM case, where an institutional RIE has been in operation during the past decade. Section three describes how management supports research at ITESM. Section four discusses experiences and lessons learned from developing research strategies at the ITESM. Finally, section five presents some conclusions from this analysis.

A Research and Innovation Ecosystem for Private Universities

In this chapter, the word "research" is placed before "innovation ecosystem" to emphasize the scientific and technological knowledge coming from university research teams, industrial research centers, and alliances among them. Thus, in this section, the RIE is described as part of a strategy to foster research, particularly in private universities. It describes the challenges that Latin American universities currently face and the central features of RIEs.

Private Universities in Latin America

During the past two decades, there have been concerns about the quality of private universities and governments not implementing enough and adequate quality assurance systems to monitor these institutions. Private universities compete against each other mostly to attract students developing strategies that help them stand out as leading institutions (Byrne and O'Leary 2012). In pursuing these goals, private universities implement innovative initiatives such as student-centered learning, learning by doing, constructivist approaches, and learning technologies. Other efforts include online education, flexible class schedules, experience-oriented internships, opportunities to take courses abroad, and other internationalization strategies. Nonetheless, institutional advantages do not last long as competitors quickly imitate others' strategies.

Generating knowledge is not a priority among most private universities, as their focus is mainly teaching either through traditional or innovative programs. Many private universities are more concerned about developing competencies and skills to make students competent in different fields than developing their research capacity (Marmolejo 2009). However, private universities that are interested in the scientific enterprise struggle to make research programs sustainable due to the lack of a culture of science, institutional commitment, and/or government support (Levy 1986; Sowter 2013). The availability of funding and support for research is often limited, which is a challenge when considering that some types of projects are quite expensive and demand highly qualified human resources and sophisticated facilities. Several authors have analyzed some of the issues that universities experience to produce relevant research in Latin America (Altbach and Salmi 2011; Enriquez 2008; Gregorutti 2011a; Marmolejo 2009). Some private universities have incorporated research as a distinctive characteristic of their institutional models and seek to gain prestige by increasing faculty research productivity (Bustani et al. 2006; Gregorutti 2010). There are private universities in Latin America that have been able to overcome the barriers and even to be included in major international academic rankings (Sowter 2013). In one of the contextual chapters of this book, Jorge Enrique Delgado (2014a) identifies universities included in the main academic rankings and suggests characteristics that make private universities competitive and successful.

The next section outlines the main features of a RIE that can serve as a framework for those private universities that aspire to be successful in producing and disseminating research.

Research Innovation Ecosystems

There are several terms used to denote innovation ecosystems, including knowledge cities, technology parks, and techno poles. These terms emphasize interactions in the context of the triple helix model. This section shows how a university took the steps to become a productive innovation ecosystem and passed from being a mainly teaching-focused institution to become more research oriented. This case hopefully can serve as a model for other private universities in Latin America. Even though several elite universities in the region have embraced the challenge of becoming world-class universities through aggressive strategies and important investments, this is not an easy and simple goal to achieve. It requires the decided commitment of high-level administrators to developing and implementing successful strategies to produce relevant research that can impact and be transferred to the productive sector and the society in general (Salmi 2009).

For several years, colleagues from the ITESM and I have designed and developed a model that we consider fundamental to create an innovation ecosystem in Mexico (Cantú-Ortiz et al. 2009). An innovation ecosystem that develops research can be represented through the following characteristics: The *basics*, which include (a) full-time faculty, (b) professors with doctoral degrees, and (c) time dedicated to research; the *work force* that consists of (d) doctoral programs in selected fields with talented students, (e) postdoctoral positions, (f) research infrastructure, and (g) international collaboration (including student and faculty mobility); *knowledge generation*, which refers to (h) scientific publications and (i) innovation and entrepreneurship; and *management* that is determined by (j) research evaluation, (k) funding for research, and (l) research administration and support offices.

The Basics

Having full-time faculty with competitive salaries is a central starting point to develop research within a private institution. However, many productive institutions also rely upon the services of part-time professors who have full-time jobs in industries or specialized government agencies. Those professors are important to develop relationships with sectors other than the government and that can be sources of funding for research. On the other hand, in order to engage in research activities, professors should not use more than 50 percent of their workload to teaching and have no more than 10 students per course. Full-time professors should not be overloaded with teaching because they need time to conduct research in their fields, which can be varied out through research groups, publications in prestigious journals, and presenting their research in prestigious forums and conferences. In addition to having a majority of full-time professors, it is necessary that they hold doctoral degrees, hopefully obtained from a variety of local and international institutions. It is important to avoid inbreeding (Horta et al. 2010). According to Jay Liebowitz (2004), it is highly desirable that at least 20–30 percent of the faculty body consists of national and international professors who represent the increasingly globalized networks of researchers who have access to resources worldwide.

The Workforce

To develop research-oriented curricula, it is important to have a set of doctoral programs in several well-defined areas of study. Administrators and decision-makers need to identify specific areas of knowledge to focus on through strategic planning. Institutional resources should be committed only to those areas of research defined as a priority, since universities cannot excel in all the fields. Also, attracting talented students to graduate programs provides additional human resources and the workforce professors need to advance their projects. In order to have them more involved in research, graduate students need to be granted some kind of internal or external financial aid (e.g., research grants, work-study modalities, scholarships from foundations or industries) because they help their professors. Budgets of private universities typically rely on tuition as the main source of revenue. However, usually doctoral students do not pay for their studies because graduate schools invest much more than what is collected through tuition. The factors mentioned earlier plus national and international accreditations, the capacity to attract the most talented students, and the support for research productivity contribute to build the prestige of an institution.

Another way to expand research in private universities is establishing postdoctoral programs to attract young researchers who have obtained their doctoral degrees within the past five years. Postdoctoral scholars work full time as part of research groups on specific projects. Ideally, these researchers do not have teaching responsibilities, although they may participate in theses/dissertation committees. Typically, postdocs are appointed for one or two years. Their positions may be funded by science and technology governmental agencies, projects with the productive sector, or special funds within the university. Salaries should cover the researchers' living expenses. Postdocs should not be alumni from the same institution and it is desirable they obtained their doctoral degrees from foreign universities. It is expected that while these researchers publish their own journal articles, they can also collaborate with professors to improve manuscripts that contribute to advance disciplinary knowledge and career appointments.

Research infrastructure is necessary to develop research projects. Setting up laboratories requires an investment that has to be planned carefully. This is particularly important in experimental sciences that demand expensive equipment, such as reactors, particle accelerators, microscopies, and sequencers, as well as materials that may require special handling and storage, such as nanomaterials, biological reagents, and medicaments. Collaborative work is an effective way to increase and improve research in private institutions. Universities share facilities, degree-granting programs, and carry out complex studies with other national/international universities or research centers. Collaborations may include faculty and student exchange and participation in joint research projects and publications. In this context, mobility does not involve undergraduate students, but faculty and doctoral students who can visit partner institutions for one or more semesters. Several Latin American universities have been successful in increasing their faculty publications in high-impact journals by developing partnerships with well-established universities in other cities and countries. The University of the Andes (Uniandes) in Colombia is an example that has followed this approach.[1]

Knowledge Generation

Peer-reviewed presentations in international conferences and publications in indexed journals are some of the outcomes of research. Publication in prestigious high-impact (based on citations) journals is greatly valued among academic communities. Indexes such as those included in the Thomson Reuters' Web of Science and Scopus of Elsevier are in general the main referents used worldwide to determine the value of a publication. The popular saying "publish or perish" is an imperative for professors, researchers, and students. However, what, where, and when to publish require a careful consideration because new discoveries are subject to intellectual property. In this regard, universities create intellectual property offices to monitor copyright of publications and patents, mainly when research outcomes are transferred to the productive sector and the society. Successful research-oriented universities must develop policies to promote high-level publication and monitor copyright (Delgado 2011, 2014b; Delgado and Weidman 2012).

A further step that private universities can take in the transfer of knowledge is the creation of spin-off companies by professors and students. This is an example of institutional ecosystems for innovation and entrepreneurship. Results of such systems include creating jobs, generating revenues for professors and students, and producing royalties for universities through licenses and patents.

Management

Assessing the quality of research outcomes is a key factor at any institution of higher education. In addition to publications and their scientific impact, there are other metrics that are used to assess research outcomes, for example, number of doctoral graduates, number of postdoctoral positions, awards and prizes received by faculty members, and external funding (in the form of grants and contracts), patent licensing, royalties, and technical services and training (Cantú-Ortiz et al. 2009). Private universities should develop strategies to provide faculty members with information and even training on these indictors of productivity.

Research funding is required to develop research in private universities. As it has been pointed out, tuition fees are the main source of revenue in most private universities, which does not necessarily leave much room to invest on research facilities and fund projects. The question is how to diversify the sources of revenue to depend less on tuition income. Most successful universities generating several sources of funding have established endowments with alumni donations and extension programs and search for different types of grants and contacts, international foundations, and, in some cases, even lottery systems. Ideally, tuition fees should not represent more than 50 percent of the operating budget, and the other 50 percent should come from alternative sources to strengthen and diversify university portfolios (Lombardi et al. 2011).

Finally, universities need to create specific units to support researchers. They are crucial to assist them when writing articles, grant proposals, or contracts, so researchers meet legal requirements and comply with university policies. These specialized offices can also help manage intellectual property, generate and monitor activities and the use of funding granted to research projects and programs.

Figure 6.1 summarizes the 12 features described earlier to develop research through an innovation ecosystem. These elements combined should help private universities creating a research culture, establishing the organizational arrangements and providing the physical infrastructure necessary to consolidate the scientific work.

The 12 categories of the RIE model can be applied to both public and private universities. Perhaps, the main difference between public and private universities in Latin America could be associated with category 11, funding for research. A great portion of public university budgets in most higher education systems in the region comes from government funding. On the contrary, as it was mentioned earlier, the main source of revenue in most private universities is tuition. Public funding for research is usually available for public universities (where most research is originated) and a

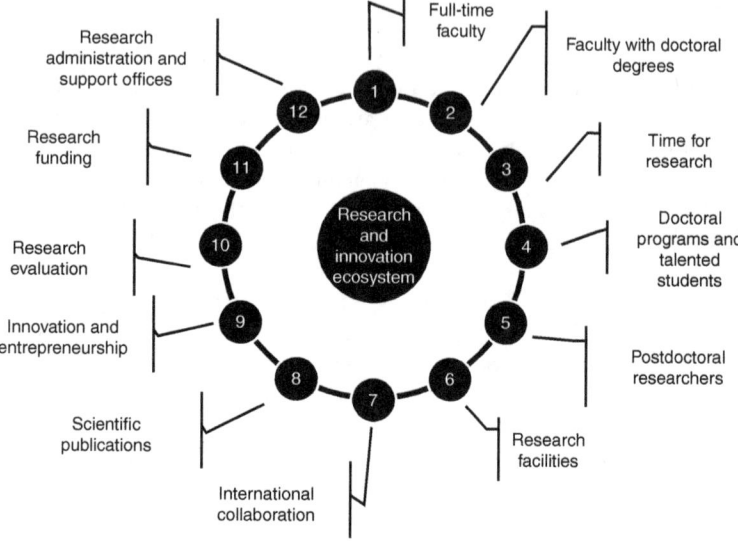

Figure 6.1 Components of a research and innovation ecosystem for private universities.

few elite universities. However, there is so much variation throughout the region that even public universities are pressed to broaden their sources of revenue to develop the research enterprise (Bernasconi 2007; Riveros et al. 2008).

In the following section, the ITESM is used to illustrate how the RIE model can be successfully used in a private institution. In 2002, the ITESM started a transformation where research has a central role in the institution's mission in order to become a world-class university.

A Case Study: The Instituto Tecnológico de Monterrey

The ITESM is a private, multicampus university headquartered in the city of Monterrey, Mexico. A group of entrepreneurs led by the MIT graduate Eugenio Garza Sada founded the ITESM in 1943. This institution was aimed at preparing professionals with the highest standards for the growing industry in Mexico. The ITESM is a comprehensive university with a flagship campus in Monterrey, where most of the research is conducted. Having undergraduate and graduate programs, enrollment at the Monterrey campus consists of about 15,000 undergraduate students and more than 3,500 graduate students, including 673 doctoral students and 50 postdoctoral positions. This university also has research groups in Mexico City, Puebla, and Guadalajara campuses that constitute what is called the *TEC Research Group*. The Monterrey campus includes schools of engineering, information technology, biotechnology and food sciences, architecture, business, social sciences, the humanities, and medicine. The ITESM is proud of having 31 campuses throughout the country that enroll more than 100,000 students. The ITESM system also comprises a second university called *TEC Milenio* (Millennium), which is a teaching-oriented university with 35 campuses countrywide with nearly 50,000 students. The *TEC Milenio* is set to provide regional industries and businesses with well-trained practitioners.

The ITESM developed a successful undergraduate education system that gained international recognition. As part of its innovative leadership, the ITESM Management created in 2002 a unique program to advance research; it was called Research Chairs. Its objective is to strengthen research and development as a way to achieve the institutional goal of becoming a world-class university. Cantú-Ortiz et al. (2009) described extensively the chair model. This program is structured to provide seed money to a principal researcher who works in association with adjunct faculty, postdoctoral researchers, and graduate students to conduct research within a specific field, creating a cluster. As a distinctive feature, Research Chairs also seeks to identify potential researchers among undergraduate students who become involved through internships that emphasize research skill development (Galeano Morales-Menendez, and Cantú-Ortiz 2012). Seed money is guaranteed to each Research Chair for at least five years and it can be renewed after a cyclical assessment method that considers quantitative indicators and a qualitative peer-evaluation. This rigorous assessment system has been applied to all Research Chairs and is a main procedure to advance research among those chairs (Cantú and Moreira 2009; Gregorutti 2011b).

The 12-category RIE Model was built based on experiences learned from designing and implementing the Research Chair Program. The following sections show the main results of this program for the 2003–2013 year interval.

The Basics

The ITESM has approximately 3,200 full-time faculty members in all the schools, of which nearly 1,000 hold doctoral degrees. The following indicators represent research outcomes of *TEC Research* (Monterrey Campus and the research groups in other campus). The number of professors accredited by the *Consejo Nacional de Ciencia y Tecnología* (CONACYT: National Council for Science and Technology) through the *Sistema Nacional de Investigadores* (SNI, National Researcher System) grew from 72 in 2002 to 257 in 2013. The number of Research Chairs in the 2003–2013 year period increased from 22 in 2003 to 144 in 2013. The areas of knowledge and the number of Research Chairs per area in 2014 are:

- Engineering: 36.
- Social sciences: 33.
- Business: 30.
- Information technologies: 22.
- Life sciences: 10.
- Humanities: 8.
- Medicine: 5.

It is important to note that faculty members can use a chair's budget to reduce their teaching load up to 50 percent of the required teaching in order to conduct more research. The same budget can be used to support postdoctoral scholars, graduate and undergraduate students, some travel and operating expenses.

The Workforce

The doctoral programs offered at the ITESM are discipline oriented and had in 2012 the following indicators, totaling an enrollment of 673 students:

- Science of engineering: 170.
- Management science: 115.
- Information and communication technologies: 113.
- Humanities: 95.
- Public policy and management: 80.
- Biotechnology: 55.
- Social sciences: 38.
- Clinical sciences: 7.

All these programs have been accredited by CONACYT through the *Programa Nacional de Programas de Calidad* (PNPC: National Program of Quality Programs). The only exception is the PhD in clinical science, which is a brand new program currently under evaluation for PNPC accreditation. This certification qualifies students to receive federal scholarship for living and traveling expenses throughout their doctoral studies, even if they need to visit a research center for a whole year. As a consequence of this extra funding, the number of doctoral students grew from 265 in 2002 to 673 in 2012.

The number of postdoctoral researcher positions has grown steadily since 2005. Most of these positions have been funded by CONACYT through the postdoctoral scholarship program, which is open annually. The number of doctoral positions in Research Chairs is about 50, and this number will grow to about 10 new doctoral positions per year in the next five years, using other sources of funding.

International collaboration is also important for scholars to gain research and publication experience by working with well-established research groups at partner universities. The ITESM partners include the following universities in the United States and Canada: Texas at Austin, Texas A&M, Carnegie Mellon, Cornell, Johns Hopkins, Houston, British Columbia, and Toronto. There are also university partners in Europe and Asia.[2]

As a result of strategic facility development, professors and students have access to an improved environment to carry out complex projects. For instance, in the past years, research infrastructure has grown in areas such as biotechnology, manufacturing, mechatronics and robotics, optics, information technologies, electronics, industrial engineering, sustainable development, including laboratories for solar energy, water studies, construction, and civil engineering. In order to increase sources of income, the university created endowments, increased donations, implemented lotteries, and expanded consulting services. Even though alumni donations are not yet significant when compared with US standards, contributions have become more regular. This is an important breakthrough for this institution.

Knowledge Generation

As a result of the Research Chair Program, publications and citations have changed drastically. For instance, the Scopus database shows how publications, citations, and citations per article have increased since 2002 (table 6.1).

In addition, the ITESM has developed an innovation program through a network of patents and technology transfer offices to help

Table 6.1 ITESM publications and citations in Scopus since 2002

Year	Articles	Citations	Cites/articles
2002	63	334	5.3
2003	95	385	4.1
2004	190	572	3.0
2005	247	748	3.0
2006	245	923	3.8
2007	260	1000	3.8
2008	265	1336	5.0
2009	285	1481	5.2
2010	295	2005	6.8
2011	279	2233	8.0
2012	318	2580	8.1

researchers protect discoveries and engage in commercialization initiatives. For instance, in 2004, the ITESM signed an agreement with the *Instituto Mexicano de la Propiedad Intelectual* (Mexican Institute for Industrial Property) to conduct workshops intended to raise awareness among professors and students regarding patents and industrial property practices. These workshops concluded with annual certification equivalent to patent experts. More than 200 scholars have been trained in the past few years. As a result, a culture of invention, patenting, and intellectual property has helped propel a growing number of patent registrations. For instance, in 2002, professors reported zero patents, whereas in 2012 this number rose to 61, for a total portfolio of 342 patents in the ten-year period, in Mexico and abroad, in areas such as biotechnology, engineering, medicine, and informational technology. Some of these patents have been licensed to companies and government agencies, generating incipient royalties to professors and the institution. Regarding entrepreneurship, some of those patents have been licensed to professors to start spin-off companies. Between 2005 and 2009 there were about 10 companies founded by professors. In 2010, the strategic leadership started the Incubation Cell Program to help doctoral students develop technology-based spin-off companies from their own research. Between 2010 and 2012, graduate students created close to 50 of those companies, of which 35 were still active in 2013. The university provides doctoral students with services that include incubation, access to funding, angel capital, investor networks, and legal, fiscal, and financial counseling to set up companies.[3]

Management

The support offices at the ITESM offer a set of services that address three important issues to facilitate research: evaluation, funding, and administration.

Research evaluation considers both a quantitative and a qualitative assessment. The first one is based on a set of indicators and a grading system that assigns scores for publications, impact factor, SNI recognition and prizes, graduated doctoral students, postdoctoral positions, external funding, undergraduate teaching, and consulting and academic service (e.g., being part of editorial boards, special program committees, and organizing conferences or workshops). As part of the quantitative assessment, a Research Chair Group must obtain at least 1,000 points per year to be able to maintain steady funding from the university. In addition, a committee made up of internal and external members assesses activities and projects based on qualitative indicators. The principal investigator, or leader of the Research Chair, gives an oral presentation about the group's achievements and answers questions from the referees. Finally, the quantitative and qualitative scores are combined to yield a final evaluation that may recommend continuation, cancellation, or the need to implement improvements in weak areas. Over the past ten years, more than one hundred Research Chairs have been assessed in three- to five-year periods. About 20 percent of them were canceled for not achieving the expected performance.

Through this methodology, a private university can obtain sustainable research funding. To do so, this institution has set apart a certain percentage of tuition income, as seed money, to support Research Chairs. Chairs, for instance, use seed money to attract external funding. For instance, they have been successful to attract US$ 1.3 for each seed dollar. In addition to encouraging research with new sources of money, external funding has been used to upgrade facilities and research equipment, a factor that is essential to continue starting new projects. Also, the ITESM has established a research endowment that grows through consulting services, continuing education, and strategic alumni and companies' donations. This endowment is still in an embryonic stage and it has not contributed significantly to the advancement of complex projects. In 2012, the total income for research, including internal and external sources, reached US$ 50 million. This is a significant landmark for a private university in Latin America.

Finally, research administration and support offices are important units that make things happen. Thus, as a strategic move to support and guide researchers, the following offices were created to leave scholars with more time to conduct research:

- writing articles, revising style and grammar, and selecting conferences and journals to communicate and publish research;
- grant and contract writing for external funding that meets legal and university policy requirements;
- managing intellectual property when there are paper presentations in conferences or/and publication of journal articles;
- generating and auditing financial statements for externally funded projects.

In short, this case study illustrates how a private university like the ITESM is transforming with the purpose of joining the select group of world-class universities. This is the result of a clear leadership combined with a system that supports research and innovation as part of its educational model.

Discussion

With about 15 percent of the world population, Latin America accounts for less than 2.5 percent of scientific publications, according to the SCImago 2013 ranking of research universities. The region also has less that 2 percent of the world's 500 best universities, as reported by US News & World Report in 2012 (Marginson 2012; Sowter 2013). The latter percentage corresponds to 10 Latin American universities in Brazil, Chile, Colombia, and Mexico. Out of the 10, 3 universities can be regarded as private research universities, namely, Pontificia Universidad Católica de Chile (PUCC), Uniandes from Colombia, and ITESM. A close analysis of their profiles reveals that these three institutions meet the 12 characteristics of the RIE in various degrees of development. For instance, PUCC has close ties with the central government, receiving grants and important state support for their research program in a competitive basis. Uniandes has developed international collaborations with scholars from top-ranked European and North American universities, in order to boost research outcomes such as coauthorship of scholarly publications. The ITESM is known for its close linkages with industries and the private sector that sponsor applied research programs with active student participation. Employers worldwide consider graduates from the ITESM among the best in Latin America (Sowter 2013). These three institutions have demonstrated a clear strategy with abundant results.

The whole concept of innovation ecosystem, the ITESM has implemented to convey the triple helix interaction in a real and practical way, is resulting in sustained advancement of research in multiple forms. This also means that a private university, very much oriented to teaching and training professionals, can redirect resources and institutional missions to make it happen. Although this complex system has shown a very positive impact, it has come through many adjustments over the years, since its initial launch in 2002. Moreover, the system still faces important challenges to reach full potential. One of them is related to people and their culture, motivation, expectations, and leadership. In other words, everything boils down to people, so the ITESM requires better scholar recruitment selection methods to guarantee new academics fit the institutional mission to develop high productivity research. In addition, this university, like most private universities in Mexico, faces challenges to partner with the government to strengthen a type of relationship that is promoted through the triple helix model. Mechanisms of public funding do not tend to promote entrepreneurial venture with private education; actually, the government spends most resources on public universities that already have productive scholars.

Considering research productivity alone, ten years ago, the ITESM was not even ranked among the top 100 universities in the region. The fact that the institution is now ranked among the top 10 in Latin America is a direct consequence of the policies implemented with the RIE program. This growth is the result of the combination of internal and external factors within the ecosystem. The teaching load is one of the most crucial components of the RIE program, since it constitutes the biggest obstacle for professors to engage in research. This, in turn, is related to university financial constraints and mainly strategic decisions by upper level administrators to establish and support research tracks for professors pursuing research careers in their home institutions. Even though the publications; outcome has improved in the past ten years as a consequence of the Research Chairs model (from 30 to 300 indexed publications approximately), publications need to grow from 300 to around 3,000 in the next few years in order to reach the level of leading public universities in Latin America. This requires a critical mass of researchers including professors, graduate students, and postdoctoral researchers.

A second strategy to improve research performance is focusing research on few disciplines and subjects, so the resources available are invested wisely. Having too many areas of research leads to dispersed efforts and results. The ITESM has chosen to concentrate on information technologies, mechatronics and robotics, biotechnology, and sustainable technologies to increase its research performance.

A third factor is attracting the best possible talent to research programs, particularly doctoral students and postdoctoral fellows in selected disciplines and research subjects. Talent should be organized in research groups specialized in particular subjects and be provided access to the infrastructure and facilities necessary to develop the research enterprise. This also demands a strong commitment from administrators to provide funding to support and expand research capacity. In order to do so, the ITESM created an endowment to sponsor research that feeds from alumni donations, industrial partner funding, local government projects, and continuing education programs.

A fourth strategy is the incubation of technology-based companies to commercialize research and innovation outcomes by students, professors, and industrial partners that license university technologies. In the past three years, more than 50 spin-out companies have been established and this number is expected to grow in the near future. Key elements of this aspect are the commercialization of value-added products and services and the creation of better-paid jobs.

Keeping an international competitive level for universities is especially difficult in the social, political, and economic instability Mexico has been immersed over the past years. Those problems also create a very unpredictable future that threatens stability and the probability of success in the long term. However, there are signs of positive regaining that allow optimism in the near future and Mexico can regain some momentum. In short, important challenges still remain, particularly those that have to do with cultural issues within institutions of higher education and their sustainability in a global context of rapid technological change and academic competitiveness and collaboration worldwide. Private institutions that will implement the strategies presented here may be more successful to compete for more resources.

Conclusion

This chapter has described a RIE model that could be used to develop research among private universities in Latin America. This model has been developed over the past ten years by observation, benchmarking, and experimentation, but also as a direct result of strategies implemented to transform a teaching-oriented university into one that would be among the best institutions in the region. The RIE includes 12 parameters that are grouped in four categories (basics, workforce, knowledge generation, and management) and has been instrumental to make the dream of having a world-class university a reality. Faculty members and their qualifications constitute the basics; the workforce is made up of graduate students, postdoctoral researchers, and outstanding professors; knowledge generation is the core of all this process of knowledge creation and transfer; and management is necessary to successfully implement strategies that would lead to continuous and improved productivity.

This model of research productivity has shown that private universities can compete globally to attract the best talent (professors and students) to play a relevant role worldwide. Successful research and innovation programs seem to be a magnet to attract key human resources. Perhaps, this is one of the main reasons why world-class universities have embraced a strong leadership to consolidate ecosystems. In this context, collaboration among institutions and researchers has become essential for growth. For the ITESM, this is also an important factor that has contributed to link research productivity with indicators of successful economic and social impact (Lancho et al. 2012).

In short, the RIE model described here may be implemented and helpful for similar institutions elsewhere. Even though the model needs to continue evolving, it can be used as a roadmap and checklist to start research and innovation programs in Latin American private universities. This model is useful to be competitive in the globally growing higher education.

Notes

1. Times Higher Education. 2013. Top 400—The Times Higher Education World University Rankings 2013–2014. Retrieved: October 3, 2013.
2. For further details, see a book chapter published by Cantú-Ortiz and Ceballos (2012) on the patterns of international collaboration within Research Chairs.
3. There is a description of the incubation cell model for technology-based entrepreneurship by Cantú-Ortiz et al. (2013).

References

Altbach, Philip, and Jamil Salmi, editors. 2011. *The Road to Academic Excellence: The Making of World-Class Research Universities*. Washington, DC: The World Bank.

Bernasconi, Andrés. 2007. "Is There a Latin American Model of University?" *Comparative Education Review* 52 (1): 27–52.

Bustani, Alberto, Eugenio Garcia, and Francisco Cantú-Ortiz. 2006. "Strategies for Moving from a Teaching University towards a Teaching, Research and Entrepreneurial University: The Tecnológico de Monterrey Experience."

Proceedings of the Ethiopia Triple Helix Conference, Addis Ababa, Ethiopia: Triple Helix Association.

Byrne, Danny, and John O'Leary. 2012. *The QS World University Ranking Report 2012–2013*. London, UK: QS Intelligence Unit.

Cantú-Ortiz, Francisco. 2011. "Conciliando Ciencia y Religión: La Cuarta Misión de la Universidad del Siglo XXI" ("Reconciling Science and Religion: Fourth Mission of the XXI Century University"). *Revista Liber Annuus* 5 (1): 47–70.

Cantú-Ortiz, Francisco, Alberto Bustani, Nathalie Galeano, and Patricia Mora. 2013. "Incubation Cells: A Technology-Based Entrepreneurial Spin-Out Program for University Research Students and Professors." Technical Report ITESM-ORE-001–13. Monterrey, Mexico: Monterrey Institute of Technology.

Cantú-Ortiz, Francisco, Alberto Bustani, Arturo Molina, and Hector Moreira. 2009. "A Knowledge-Based Development Model: The Research Chairs Strategy." *Journal of Knowledge Management* 13 (1): 154–170.

Cantú-Ortiz, Francisco J., and Hector Ceballos. 2012. "A Framework for Fostering Multidisciplinary Research Collaboration and Scientific Networking within University Environs." In *Knowledge Management Handbook: Collaboration and Social Networking* (2nd edition), edited by Jay Liebowitz (pp. 207–217). Boca Raton, FL: CRC Press.

Cantú-Ortiz, Francisco, and Héctor Moreira. 2009. *La Investigación en el Tecnológico de Monterrey* (Research at the Tecnológico de Monterrey). Monterrey, Mexico: Tecnológico de Monterrey Press.

Delgado, Jorge Enrique. 2011. *Journal Publication in Chile, Colombia, and Venezuela: University Responses to Global, Regional, and National Pressures and Trends*. Doctoral dissertation. Pittsburgh, PA: University of Pittsburgh. Available online at: http://d-scholarship.pitt.edu/9049/.

———. 2014a. "Latin American Private Universities in the Context of Competition and Research Productivity." In *Private Universities in Latin America: Research and Innovation in the Knowledge Economy*, edited by Gustavo Gregorutti and Jorge Enrique Delgado. New York: Palgrave Macmillan.

———. 2014b. "Scientific Journals of Universities of Chile, Colombia, and Venezuela: Actors and Roles." *Education Policy Analysis Archives* 22 (34, Special issue: The Future of Educational Research Journals). Available online at: http://dx.doi.org/10.14507/epaa.v22n34.2014, accessed on February 20, 2014.

Delgado, Jorge Enrique, and John C. Weidman. 2012. "Latin American and Caribbean Countries in the Global Quest for World Class Academic Recognition: An Analysis of Publications in Scopus and the Science Citation Index between 1990 and 2010." *Excellence in Higher Education* 3 (2): 111–121.

Enriquez, Juan C. 2008. *In the Pursuit of Becoming a Research University*. Doctoral dissertation. Tucson: University of Arizona. Proquest UMI Microform 3303759.

Etzkowitz, Henry. 2001. "The Second Academic Revolution and the Rise of the Entrepreneurial Science." *IEEE Technology and Society* 20 (2): 18–29.

Etzkowitz, Henry, and Loet Leydesdorff. 1997. *Universities and the Global Knowledge Economy: A Triple-Helix of University—Industry—Government Relations*. London, UK: Cassell Academic.

———. 2000. "The Dynamics of Innovation: From National Systems and 'Mode 2' to a Triple Helix of University—Industry—Government Relations." *Research Policy* 29 (2): 109–123.

Galeano, Nathalie, Morales-Menendez, Ruben, and Francisco Cantú-Ortiz, 2012. "Developing Research Skills in Undergraduate Students through an Internship Program in Research and Innovation." *International Journal of Engineering Education* 28 (1): 48–56.

Gregorutti, Gustavo. 2010. "Moving from a Predominantly Teaching Oriented Culture to a Research Productivity Mission: The Case of Mexico and the United States." *Excellence in Higher Education* 1 (1–2): 69–83.

———. 2011a. "Commercialization of Higher Education in Latin America: The Case of Mexico." *Comparative & International Higher Education* 3 (1): 11–14.

———. 2011b. "La Producción de Investigación en las Universidades Privadas: Estudio de un Caso" ("Research Production in Private Universities: A Case Study"). *Enfoques XIII* (Approaches XIII) (2): 5–20.

Hegde, Deepak. 2005. "Public and Private Universities: Unequal Sources of Regional Innovation?" *Economic Development Quarterly* 19 (4): 373–386.

Horta, Hugo, Francisco M. Veloso, and Rócio Grediaga. 2010. "Navel Gazing: Academic Inbreeding and Scientific Productivity." *Management Science* 56 (3): 414–429.

Lancho Barrantes, Bárbara, Vicente Guerrero Bote, Zaida Rodríguez, and Félix de Moya Anegón. 2012. "Citation Flows in the Zones of Influence of Scientific Collaborations." *Journal of the American Society for Information Science and Technology* 63 (3): 481–489.

Levy, Daniel. 1986. *Higher Education and the State in Latin America: Private Challenges to Public Dominance*. Chicago, IL: The University of University Press.

Leydesdorff, Loet. 2012. "The Triple Helix of University-Industry-Government Relations." In *Encyclopedia of Creativity, Innovation, and Entrepreneurship*, edited by Elias Carayannis and David Campbell. New York: Springer.

Liebowitz, Jay. 2004. *Addressing the Human Capital Crisis in the Federal Government: A Knowledge Management Perspective*. Burlington, MA: Elsevier Butterworth-Heinemenn.

Lombardi, John, Elizabeth Phillips, Craig Abbey, and Diane Craig. 2011. *The Top American Research Universities. 2011 Annual Report*. Amherst, MA: The Center for Measuring University Performance.

Marginson, Simon. 2012. *Global University Rankings: The Strategic Issues*. Proceedings of the Conference "Las Universidades Latinoamericanas ante los Rankings Internacionales: Impactos, Alcances y Límites." México City, Mexico: National Autonomous University of Mexico.

Marmolejo, Francisco. 2009. "The Long Road toward Excellence in Mexico: The Monterrey Institute of Technology." In *The Road to Academic Excellence: The Making of World-Class Research Universities*, edited by Philip Altbach and Jamil Salmi (pp. 261–290). Washington, DC: The World Bank.

National Science Foundation (NSF). 2013. *The Innovation Ecosystem*. Arlington, VA: NSF. Available online at: http://www.nsf.gov/news/special_reports/i-corps/ecosystem.jsp, accessed on March 12, 2013.

Perkin, Harold. 2006. "History of Universities." In *International Handbook of Higher Education*, edited by James Forest and Philip Altbach (pp. 159–205). Dordrecht, Netherlands: Springer.

Riveros, Luís A., Carlos Cáceres, Efraín Medina, and Jacques Schwartzman. 2008. "Challenges and Dilemmas of the Financing of Higher Education in Latin America and the Caribbean." In *Trends in Higher Education in Latin America and the Caribbean*, edited by Ana Lúcia Gazzola and Axel Didriksson (pp. 367–389). Caracas, Venezuela: UNESCO International Institute for Higher Education in Latin America and the Caribbean.

Salmi, Jamil. 2009. *The Challenge of Establishing World-Class Universities*. Washington, DC: The World Bank.

Schmitt, Charles, editor. 1998. *History of Universities*. Oxford, UK: Oxford University Press.

SCImago Lab. 2013. *SCImago Institution Rankings*. Madrid, Spain: SCImago Group. Available online at: http://www.scimagoir.com/pdf/SIR%20Iber%20 2013.pdf, accessed on March 12, 2013.

Sismondo, Sergio. 2010. *An Introduction to Science and Technology Studies* (2nd edition). Oxford, UK: Willey-Blackwell.

Sowter, Ben. 2013. *The QS University Rankings: Latin America TM Report 2013*. London, UK: QS Intelligence Unit.

Chapter 7

The Emergence of the Puebla State Popular Autonomous University as a Successful Mexican Research University

Stephen P. Wanger and Édgar Apanecatl-Ibarra

Introduction

This chapter explores the strategies that a private Catholic Mexican university employed to incorporate research into its institutional mission. Over the past two decades the Puebla State Popular Autonomous University (UPAEP: *Universidad Popular Autónoma del Estado de Puebla*) has strived, while maintaining its traditional teaching mission, to respond to the regional and global influences on higher education that increasingly emphasize research and the transfer of knowledge for economic purposes (Chen et al. 2005; Stromquist and Monkman 2000). The intent was to preserve within the university the human and spiritual dimensions of education while simultaneously leveraging research capacity. The collaborative efforts of UPAEP administrators, faculty, staff, and students represent innovative approaches to this endeavor, not only within the context of Mexican higher education but also in Latin America. Their efforts are enabling UPAEP to become an example of a successful twenty-first-century Latin American university in which teaching, learning, research, and the transfer of knowledge are concurrently paramount. The focus of this chapter is accordingly on the strategies pursued and the resulting actions and initiatives that enabled the transition in institutional mission from teaching to research and knowledge production.

For much of the past 50 years, the literature on higher education in Latin America focused on public universities, particularly on their social, cultural, and political roles (Arnove 1967; Bernasconi 2008; Jaksic 1985; NACLA 2000; Petersen 1970; Stavenhagen et al. 1964; Waggoner 1970). Recently, however, literature began to address the evolving Latin American university. Whether seen as an emulation of the US model of the research university (Bernasconi 2008), or as the transplantation of the Bologna Process (Aboites 2010; Arocena and Sutz 2005), a central focus of the emerging university is responding not only to globalization, but also to the growing internationalization of higher education and the pivotal roles that higher education plays within the knowledge-based economy. Not surprisingly, the former model of the public Latin American university as a nation-state university—in essence, the state's educational arm—that emphasized public funding, free tuition, and professional training is increasingly questioned (Bernasconi 2008). Multiple factors contribute to this evolution, including: massification, perceived deterioration of quality, politicization, the decreased social influence that public universities experienced during the 1960s and the 1970s (Carvalho de Mello and Etzkowitz 2008; Jaksic 1985; NACLA 2000), and the burgeoning influence of regional and international organizations such as Economic Commission for Latin America and the Caribbean, the World Bank, and the Organisation for Economic Co-operation and Development. Consequently, the dominant model of higher education that is emerging emphasizes knowledge production as a key element for economic development (Jiménez-Ortiz 2011).

Public universities may be particularly well positioned to navigate this model. Throughout Latin America, public universities employ more than 60 percent of all researchers (Thorn and Soo 2006). In Mexico, the percentage is even higher; public universities employ 66 percent of the researchers in the National Researcher System (SNI: *Sistema Nacional de Investigadores*). One university alone, the National Autonomous University of Mexico (UNAM: *Universidad Nacional Autónoma de México*), employs over 22 percent of the researchers within Mexican higher education; consequently, more than half of the total research conducted in the country is produced through UNAM (Ordorika Sacristán et al. 2009). For private universities, therefore, transitioning to the new model of higher education may be especially challenging.

Some scholars suggest, however, that private universities in Latin America may possess characteristics that better enable them to respond to the global emphasis on research and the production and dissemination of knowledge (Bernasconi 2008; Carvalho de Mello and Etzkowitz

2008). According to the literature, these advantages are associated with the origins, missions, and structures of private universities. They include, for example, nimble, streamlined bureaucracies and founding missions that often are directly connected to economic development.

The case study reported in the following pages—the case of UPAEP—includes some (but not all) of these advantages. The case highlights potential strategies that universities may adapt to enhance research capacity while maintaining their teaching and learning missions. The case study suggests that the strategies are especially effective when they are linked to effective leadership and the spirit of collaboration. This chapter begins with a brief history of the university, followed by an overview of the theoretical framework and the methodology employed for the research study. It then presents the findings of the research study and concludes with a discussion of the relevance of the findings for theory, research, and practice.

The University

UPAEP is located in the capital of the State of Puebla, Puebla City, which is 110 kilometers south of Mexico City. According to the most recent national census, the population of the city is nearly two million people. UPAEP is a Catholic Mexican private university that was founded in 1973 in response to the ideological and political university movements of the 1960s and 1970s in Mexico (UPAEP, *General Information*). In short, the university was created as an alternative to local and national public institutions that were perceived to be in ideological and political crisis. The founding of the university was an initiative of a diverse group of citizens who saw the need for an institution that would be especially responsive to the local community. Its initial purpose was "to create schools of thought and train leaders who would change society" (UPAEP, *Mission*). Specifically, the mission of the university states that

> we can define our mission in the light of a catholic inspiration, as the creation of schools of thought and the formation of leaders that will transform our society, that respect the dignity and freedom of human beings, that are responsible, whose thoughts, words and actions agree with each other and that believe in values such as truth, solidarity, honesty, love, freedom and justice and live them in a transcendent way.

Although the university was founded to serve the local community, it has experienced exponential growth during its four decades and currently enrolls over 15,000 undergraduate and graduate students from most states in Mexico and numerous countries across the globe (UPAEP 2012). In addition, UPAEP's accreditations in Mexico include those of the National Association of Universities and Higher Education Institutions (*Asociación Nacional de Universidades e Instituciones de Educación Superior*), the Mexican Federation of Private Higher Education Institutions (*Federación de Instituciones Mexicanas Particulares de Educación Superior*), the National Council for Science and Technology (CONACYT: *Consejo Nacional de Ciencia y Tecnología*), and a host of other Mexican agencies that certify the majority of its graduate and undergraduate programs (UPAEP, *Accredited Quality*). The university has several dual degree programs and academic agreements with American and European universities that not only facilitate extensive faculty and student mobility, but also increase its international visibility.

Over the past decade the number of available graduate academic programs increased significantly, from less than 12 to currently 33 master's and 13 doctoral programs; the current 46 programs do not include online professional programs. The majority of graduate programs belong to the Registry of Quality Graduate Programs (*Programa Nacional de Posgrados de Calidad*). The UPAEP System, as the university is now called, includes 10 campuses that offer programs throughout the State of Puebla, online graduate programs that enroll national and international students, and high schools in diverse regions of the State of Puebla and in the neighboring State of Tlaxcala (UPAEP 2012).

Faculty participation in research likewise has grown substantially in recent years. In 2007, UPAEP was 1 of only 15 private universities in Mexico included in a comparative study on the performance of Mexican universities with regard to research production. By 2009, however, 10 percent of all SNI researchers who were employed by private universities in Mexico worked at UPAEP (Ordorika Sacristán et al. 2009), giving the university significant access to research funding (UPAEP 2012). Currently, 89 percent of faculty members hold graduate degrees from national and international institutions, which potentially contributes to the growing emphasis on research not only by faculty but also by graduate students. Both faculty and graduate students have recently won awards at international competitions organized, for example, by prestigious universities in the United States.

After brief sections that address the theoretical framework and the methodology, the chapter addresses the processes utilized to achieve these outcomes. It reveals a university that not only embraced the inclusion of research within its mission but also achieved noteworthy outcomes as the result of that inclusion. The chapter indicates that the outcomes are attributable to the strategies that were proactively and collaboratively selected by the UPAEP community, a community that included faculty, administrators, staff, and students.

Theoretical Framework

The process described in this chapter is a blend of both planned and emergent change. Bess and Dee (2008, p. 797) define "planned change" as "an intentional effort to improve organizational processes through the implementation of new ideas based on scientific knowledge." Conversely, they define "emergent change" as "decentralized local adaptation" to external situations (p. 798). Whereas planned change is implemented "top down" by senior administrators, emergent change typically begins "bottom up" and reflects the actions and participation of individuals at all levels of the organization. As Bess and Dee note, in emergent change "the role of leadership shifts from directing and controlling change to facilitating creativity and experimentation among others" (p. 809).

Although planned and emergent change may appear to be mutually exclusive, they accurately reflect the process that was intentionally utilized at UPAEP; senior administrators initiated and managed the process (planned change), but the process featured the active participation of numerous individuals from every area and level of the university who worked together to position UPAEP to respond to external situations (emergent change). This was achieved through an effective merger—subsequently examined in this chapter—of strategic planning and appreciative inquiry (AI).

The framework employed to analyze this blend of planned and emergent change is Edgar H. Schein's model of cultural change. Schein (1985, p. 9) defines "culture" as

> *a pattern of basic assumptions—invented, discovered, or developed by a given group as it learns to cope with its problems of external adaptation and internal integration—that has worked well enough to be considered valid and, therefore, to be taught to new members as the correct way to perceive, think, and feel in relation to those problems.* (Italics in the original)

Culture is accordingly evinced in three levels of the organization: artifacts, espoused beliefs and values, and basic underlying assumptions (Schein 2010). Artifacts are visible phenomena that include divergent considerations such as the language, rituals, ceremonies, and technologies of the organization. Espoused beliefs and values "provide meaning and comfort to group members" (p. 26) and are the conscious articulations of the organization's ideologies and philosophies. Basic underlying assumptions are those beliefs and values that have been so readily tested, practiced, and accepted by the group that they move from the conscious to the unconscious. As such, they are the deepest level of culture, normalize both group and individual behavior, and are the most challenging level of culture to change. According to Schein, understanding basic underlying assumptions is difficult to achieve; they require methodologies beyond the scope of this case study, which, as discussed here, employs interviews and document analysis to assess meaning. Consequently, to understand how UPAEP made significant research improvement, the case study focuses on Schein's first two levels of culture: artifacts and espoused beliefs and values.

Methodology

A case study research design was employed to examine the strategies that UPAEP observed. This allowed in-depth exploration—through multiple data sources—of the sequence of strategies that the university used during the pivotal years of institutional transition. Data collection included on-site interviews and document analysis of relevant internal and external documents. For the former, criterion sampling (Patton 2002) was utilized to select participants who were knowledgeable of the strategies developed during the change process. This restricted participant selection only to current faculty and administrators at UPAEP who either led or participated in the process of transformation. To ensure their confidentiality, participant identities are not revealed in this chapter. Extensive, audiotaped interviews were conducted with four participants using a 24-question semistructured interview protocol. Interviews typically lasted two hours. The interview protocol allowed both uniform data collection and the ability to ask clarifying or follow-up questions. The interviews focused on four key considerations: (a) the internal and external factors and motivations that influenced UPAEP to move toward greater emphasis on research productivity, (b) the strategies that were used to achieve the transition, (c) the steps the university took to position itself within both Mexican and international higher education, and (d) the impact of the change on the university and its stakeholders. Document analysis included analysis of university documents, government documents, and data found on the university web site. When combined with the interviews, document analysis of these sources facilitated triangulation of the data. Three steps were followed throughout the study to ensure trustworthiness. First, data were collected from multiple sources; as indicated earlier, these included interviews, university and government documents, and the university web site. Second, participants were interviewed from different levels of the university; their roles and perceptions of the change process varied. Third, when possible, member checking was utilized.

Although multiple data sources were examined, the research design contains limitations. First, because we used a case study design, the research study is not generalizable to other universities. The findings—and consequently all conclusions that are drawn from them—are limited to this particular case at this particular time. This means that some of the strategies that were useful for UPAEP may not work at other universities. Second, although the study included participants whose roles and perceptions of the change process varied, not all voices at the university were heard. Like in most case study designs, the inclusion of full representation across the university was not feasible. However, despite these limitations, the researchers proffer that the findings of the case study, to which we now turn, may inform the leaders of other Latin American universities as they seek to better incorporate research into institutional missions.

Findings

The primary themes that emerged in the findings are associated with the change process that occurred at UPAEP over the past two decades. They are framed by historic change that transpired across institutional, national, and international contexts, and, as such, reflect both internal and external factors that shaped the university. In response to and in anticipation of these factors individuals within the university—including administrators, faculty, staff, and even students—collectively utilized a series of strategies to navigate change and to better position the university for increasing success. Their strategies are the themes that emerged in this study. They are: (a) the incorporation of strategic planning into the institution's planning cycles, (b) the development of the Interdisciplinary Center of Graduate Programs (CIP: *Centro Interdisciplinario de Posgrados*), (c) the merger of AI with strategic planning, and (d) the launch of the institution's vision 2015 plan.

Strategic Planning

Starting in the 1980s, approximately a decade after the founding of UPAEP in 1973, institutional leaders began to position the university by using what they considered to be strategic planning. The process was characterized by a top-down approach in which senior administrators set short-term and long-term goals; other than senior administrators, few individuals participated in the setting of goals. The goals were typically specific in nature and included steps with which they would be achieved. Objectives were often time-based and phrased quantitatively, for example, the university will hire five additional faculty members with PhDs within the next three years. Rowley et al. (1997), however, characterize this type of approach not as strategic planning but as conventional planning. They note that universities in the 1980s and 1990s often considered conventional planning as strategic planning, but the two are substantially different. Conventional planning: (a) reflects an inside-out mindset, (b) lays emphasis on the creation of goals and steps to achieve them, (c) involves planning that is done on a cyclical basis with specified dates for the completion or achievement of goals, and (d) promotes an operational focus that stresses quantification. Conversely, strategic planning: (a) reflects an outside-in mindset (institutional leaders assess and incorporate the multiple external environments surrounding the institution), (b) lays emphasis on aligning the institution with its external environments, (c) involves planning that is done on an ongoing, iterative basis, and (d) promotes a long-term focus that stresses sustainability (pp. 35–38).

Throughout the 1980s, 1990s, and into the early years of the 2000s, the university engaged in multiple cycles of what it considered to be strategic planning. According to a current university official, these cycles "were only moderately successful." During the academic year of 2002–2003, however, the university employed strategic planning as described earlier by Rowley et al. (1997). When coupled with the strategies described in subsequent pages, the results are noteworthy.

Table 7.1 highlights these results and illustrates dramatic institutional transformation at UPAEP over the past two decades. Displaying key performance indicators often associated with research productivity, the table reveals accelerated transition since the academic year of 2004–2005. For example, the number of full-time faculty with PhD degrees grew by 320 percent in the ten-year period between the 1994–1995 and 2004–2005 academic years, but by 675 percent in the eight-year period between 2004–2005 and 2012–2013. Similarly, the number of graduate students more than doubled between the 1994–1995 and 2004–2005 academic years, but increased eightfold between 2004–2005 and 2012–2013. The number of peer reviewed publications nearly tripled over the past eight years, while the number of external grants doubled. During the past eight years the number of collaborations with business and industry expanded by 1,263 percent. In addition, the number of CONACYT projects

Table 7.1 Key performance indicators

Indicator	1994–1995	2004–2005	2012–2013
Full-time faculty with PhD	5	16	108
Number of graduate students	185	441	3,531
Peer-reviewed publications	57	76	221
External grants	0	15	30
Business-industry collaborations	N/A	8	101
CONACYT projects	N/A	2	11
Initial value of CONACYT projects (in Mexican pesos)	NA	0	84,000,000
Patents	0	1	2*
Royalties	0	0	1**
Trademarks	0	1	10

*Eight additional patents in process.
**In process.
N/A No data.

increased fivefold, and the income from these projects grew to 84 million pesos (approximately US$ 6.5 million). UPAEP also began to pursue patents, royalties, and trademarks, all of which represent additional sources of income to the university. Collectively, the key performance indicators reflect solid gains in research production during the ten-year period from 1994–1995 to 2004–2005, but these gains are minor in comparison to the significant increases between 2004–2005 and 2012–2013.

Interdisciplinary Center of Graduate Programs

A key to the emergence of UPAEP as a successful research university was the launch in 2003 of CIP. The university officials interviewed for this study uniformly indicated that CIP was pivotal to recent institutional success. CIP is housed within the Graduate College of the university and includes every graduate program. It has become the heart of how UPAEP not only educates graduate students but also produces and transfers knowledge.

The focus of CIP is interdisciplinarity. It allows graduate students to create their plans of study by incorporating relevant courses from multiple academic disciplines. Plans submitted to CIP often reflect significant interdisciplinary coursework. One administrator said, "We decided to create flexible programs, with a high level of flexibility. So the student basically creates the plan of study along with the advisor." Up to 80 percent of a student's plan of study may be interdisciplinary. This is the opposite of traditional plans of study that are completely tied to a single disciple. Even academic advising in CIP goes beyond disciplinary boundaries because advisors for PhD students may come from a discipline other than the primary discipline of the student.

UPAEP administrators cite several benefits of interdisciplinarity. First, students are more motivated to learn. A long-term faculty member and administrator offered this scenario: "Since you are studying what you would like to, you decide your plan. And the plan can change. Maybe this semester I am getting an offer in international logistics and before I was just doing the purchasing part of logistics. Now maybe you can include international logistics in your plan of study." He also connected student motivation to graduation rates. The administrator declared that interdisciplinary courses in CIP are the reason that "the completion rate is very high compared to other universities."

A second benefit of interdisciplinarity is that students learn from each other. One participant stated: "Instead of having a class by department we decided to have interdisciplinary groups so that our students will learn from... others. Instead of having students [study in] only one field we decided that it was time to have students from different fields approach an opportunity or a problem from different perspectives." The latter part of this statement reflects a third benefit, namely, the ability to analyze problems from multiple perspectives. The same administrator stated:

> What we are doing here right now is trying to approach problems from different angles, from different perspectives in different disciplines in order to solve the problem in an integral manner. You don't just need... specialization; you also need to understand other fields. So, in terms of knowledge creation and research, we found... that you need to have interdisciplinary teams. And that is what we have in classes. We have interdisciplinary people analyzing cases, concepts, and technologies from different angles. And students get enriched from that vision, from different people.

Thus the interdisciplinary approach ensures that graduate students learn across the disciplines and are educated to analyze problems from multiple perspectives. They develop a diverse set of skills that may be applied to global issues that are no longer responsive to limited or singular answers. In addition, the process generates broad-based knowledge that includes extensive intercultural awareness. According to one participant in the study, UPAEP faculty and administrators are convinced that "CIP ultimately facilitates the most effective preparation for leaders that must navigate the complexities of the twenty-first century."

CIP is also closely connected to the production and transfer of knowledge at UPAEP. Multiple research centers are housed within CIP, and each center is connected to a specific industry or set of industries within the region. This structure is patterned after Michael Porter's (1990) concept of the business cluster, a closely connected hub of interrelated businesses, suppliers, and institutions in a particular field. Porter's concept emphasizes the regional development of clusters that assess and focus on the unique resources and competencies within the region. In the case of CIP, industry and education are tightly linked, and the research centers are used to advise industry. Conversely, the clusters enable the university to develop and offer educational programs and the exact courses that are needed by the citizens of the region. A participant stated: "We have a cluster map and based on that cluster map we can say [for example] if Puebla is going to excel in car manufacturing or in textiles or in food processing. Then we know that the careers in engineering and so forth are very important, so we are doing that linkage." Speaking about a specific project associated with a cluster, another participant stated that "we had people not only from the university just talking about these issues but people from society, people from business and government, telling us if this idea was important or not, and so in a way they validated the idea." To ensure that clusters are built on vital, responsive relationships, meetings are held every week. UPAEP participates in four clusters; on Monday, UPAEP representatives meet with the members of two clusters, and on Thursday they meet with the members of the other two. This is a deliberative, ongoing, reciprocal collaboration that UPAEP administrators and faculty see as essential.

UPAEP launched CIP in response to the convergence of multiple internal and external drivers. These included rapid globalization, the increasing internationalization of higher education, escalating emphasis on the knowledge economy and the central role played by higher education within this trend, the growth in demand for graduate programs in Mexico, the need to increase at UPAEP both the number of faculty with PhD degrees and the number of graduate students, and the institutional desire to contribute to the elevation of educational levels in Puebla and Mexico. Prior to establishing CIP university officials conducted extensive interviews across Mexico and other countries, engaging leaders in education, business, and industry. They became convinced that the interdisciplinary approach would increasingly become the norm of the future. They affirm this perspective even more today. An administrator declared: "We decided that the interdisciplinary approach was going to prevail in the future and also the flexible approach in the design of the programs of study. And I will state that is still valid because we are right now in the design of the undergrad programs of study, which is following a flexible and interdisciplinary approach." The university accordingly now expects that faculty and students within CIP will engage in research. Faculty members are expected to publish both individually and with graduate students. As much as possible, interdisciplinary research is encouraged; however, researchers are also expected to pursue disciplinary interests.

At the core of CIP is what university officials term "the human aspect." In keeping with its Catholic heritage the university emphasizes the value and needs of humans throughout all graduate programs and centers associated with CIP. The human aspect is a distinguishing feature of the center and the larger university. All graduate students, regardless of their individual programs, for example, must take a required seminar on ethics. Every person interviewed for this study, as well as every institutional document that we analyzed, in some way cites the human aspect as the heart of CIP. The following comments highlight the centrality of the human aspect:

> The human aspect is the core subject in our grad programs and also at the engineering and the undergrad level. We stress the importance of the human being, and of values, and ethics, and that is a core class [for every student]. People from different fields come and talk at the graduate level in this seminar, and students from all different fields have this class.

And,

> The human and the spiritual side...I would say that is the most important part, and it shows, for example, at the dissertation level. All dissertations have to have a social impact component. For example, in terms of education, what is going to be the social impact of your work? Even in engineering, what is going to be the social impact of your work? And that is...infused in the classes.

CIP began in 2003 with 19 dual degree graduate programs; a decade later the number stands at 61, representing not only a 321 percent growth but also the growing opportunity for graduate students to pursue education that is interdisciplinary, interinstitutional, and international. Today, 2,500 of the 3,500 graduate students at UPAEP pursue their education through the center.

The Merger of Appreciative Inquiry and Strategic Planning

In 2004, shortly after the creation of CIP, the university significantly altered the way it managed change. Senior administrators realized that how the university navigated change during the 1980s and 1990s was only marginally effective. They began to look for a way to leverage the existing strengths of the university while including the voices of the university community in the change management process. What they found was AI. A senior administrator commented:

> [The former president of the university] thought that it was time to start a new and different planning process. We wanted a more participative process, including the whole community. I was part of that decision at the time. We decided to use a new methodology...that was called Appreciative Inquiry. Now it is in the books of organizational development but at that time it was just a PhD thesis. We began a long nine-month process of planning, and we spent a lot of time interviewing people of the university, making everybody available [for] the opportunity to really discuss what he or she was thinking of the future of the university. I can say now that it was really successful.

According to Watkins and Mohr (2001, p. 14), "Appreciative Inquiry is a collaborative and highly participative, system-wide approach to seeking, identifying, and enhancing the 'life-giving forces' that are present when a system is performing optimally in human, economic, and organizational terms." The process emphasizes the discovery of an organization's or a system's tacit strengths. This is done through the inclusive participation of all, or nearly all, of an organization's members, and the extensive use of questions by facilitators to achieve organizational understanding. The AI process is guided by five core principles (pp. 36–39):

1. The Constructionist Principle holds that how organizational members construct beliefs about the organization impacts the future of the organization.
2. The Principle of Simultaneity states that inquiry (into the nature of the organization) and organizational change occur at the same time.
3. The Anticipatory Principle proffers that "the image of the future...guides the current behavior of any person or organization" (p. 38).
4. The Poetic Principle suggests that "an organization's story is continually being co-authored by the people within the organization as well as by those outside who interact with it" (p. 38).

5. The Positive Principle indicates that effective, long-lasting change is best accomplished by employing positive questions during the inquiry process.

These principles steer the five specific steps in the AI process, which are described by Watkins and Mohr (2001, p. 39) as: "1. Choose the positive as the focus of inquiry; 2. Inquire into stories of life-giving forces; 3. Locate themes that appear in the stories and select topics for further inquiry; 4. Create shared images for a preferred future; and 5. Find innovative ways to create that future." Throughout the 2004–2005 academic year, UPAEP employed AI system-wide to discover its institutional strengths. Seven separate groups were created for the planning process, with each group reporting monthly to the collective university. The primary question asked during the nearly year-long process was simply, "How can we make this a university of quality?" In keeping with the tenets of AI, the word "we" was employed to acknowledge and emphasize the importance of participation by everyone associated with the university; all staff, students, faculty, and administrators participated in the endeavor. At one point during the nine-month learning process, the university closed for a two-day period to engage in a system-wide, AI conversation that included all participants.[1]

In addition, and again reflecting the tenets of AI, in 2005 the president began a monthly open-agenda meeting known as "Dialog with the President." The tradition continues today, with monthly meetings typically lasting one–two hours and affording every member of the university community the opportunity to engage the president in open dialog. Broad-based participation is encouraged and welcomed, and meetings are still well attended.

The result during the academic year of 2004–2005 was the merger of AI processes with the strategic planning processes described by Rowley et al. (1997). The merger created an innovative, effective model for navigating organizational change. The combined model produced substantial capabilities, including: (a) procedures to assess accurately both internal and external environments; (b) alignment of institutional strengths with the needs of the external environment; (c) ongoing, iterative planning; (d) inclusion of all or nearly all voices within the community; and, consequently, (e) greater participation in efforts to improve the institution; (f) reduced resistance to change; and (g) the laying of a secure foundation for sustained success. The model created by the merger of the AI and strategic planning processes, coupled with Centro Interdisciplinario de Posgrados, appear to be the twin pillars upon which UPAEP is building a Latin American university that maintains its historic emphasis on teaching while successfully incorporating research into the institutional mission.

Vision 2015

In 2004, UPAEP also began a major institutional transition with the creation of Vision 2015 (UPAEP, *Vision 2015*). Maintaining and emphasizing the core institutional values that the university discovered in the AI process, the new vision allowed UPAEP to focus both on continual institutional improvement and better positioning itself within local, national, and international environments. A single overarching goal framed every aspect and strategy of the new vision, namely, to foster a mentality of leadership and entrepreneurship within students while developing their spiritual and human qualities. To develop Vision 2015 the university employed AI processes and both qualitative and quantitative research methodologies. For the qualitative portion of the planning process, eight teams—comprised of 97 total members representing all areas of the university—interviewed 350 people throughout the UPAEP community (Miranda-López 2005). Interviewees included administrators, faculty, staff, and undergraduate and graduate students. For the quantitative portion, the university surveyed an additional 301 people that included 205 faculty members (with proportional representation of full-time and part-time faculty), 81 staff members, and 15 administrators. The vision that was produced thus represented the collective input of the entire university. Not surprisingly, 63.9 percent of the university community fully agreed with every strategy and 97 percent indicated that they were committed to achieving Vision 2015 (Miranda-López 2005). One of the participants described the process in the following words:

> Vision 2015 involved people from undergrad programs and grad programs, administrators, everybody in the university. But in a way, just to summarize, I would say that the spearhead or the driver was the creation of [the previous] interdisciplinary programs and flexible programs which, at the end, are just very clear in this Vision 2015 in one of the five strategies, in terms of the *innovación en el proceso de enseñanza-aprendizaje*, innovation in the process of education and all the learning.

The vision statement for Vision 2015 (UPAEP, *Vision 2015*) declares:

> We are committed to provide timely and in depth responses to the needs of the environment in congruity with our core values. We will be recognized as a prestigious University in Puebla, in Mexico and in the World which is:
> - engaged in the social environment and the development of proposals;
> - a meeting place for dialogue and investigation in the fields of scientific and prudential knowledge;

- inspired by our catholic and cultural heritage to continually search for sound proposals to current issues;
- dedicated to continuous improvement and the practice of self-evaluation and measurement.

The planning process generated a set of guiding strategies, including: (a) the preservation of a humanistic approach to education, (b) the incorporation within this approach of a focus on knowledge production, (c) continuous internal evaluation, (d) continual strengthening of the institutional culture of trust and collaboration, and (e) promoting the internationalization of the university. The vision emphasized the creation of new undergraduate, graduate, and nondegree programs specifically targeted to address the social and economic needs of the local, national, and global communities. In addition, it accentuated the development and implementation of social research projects (UPAEP, Vision 2015).

Within these guiding strategies Vision 2015 included focused strategies to increase national and international student mobility, strategic alliances, networking and dual degree agreements with foreign universities, and the international positioning of UPAEP. The new vision underscored the use of technology to increase the online presence and impact of UPAEP throughout Mexico and beyond borders (UPAEP, *Vision 2015*). Additional focused strategies included the improvement of teaching, learning, and administrative processes; increasing outreach with businesses, government agencies, universities, and other educational organizations; and the expansion of the university.

A particularly noteworthy emphasis of the vision is the full implementation of a flexible educational model that better responds to the personal needs of students and that promotes both intra- and interdisciplinary work (UPAEP, *Vision 2015*). UPAEP is a leading university in this area and has received substantial positive recognition from other universities, the Mexican secretary of education, and noneducational organizations. As one of the participants asserted, "The main guides of the strategic planning that you can see now in Vision 2015 is…how we are going to make this university a university of academic excellence."

Discussion

The findings that emerged in this study hold meaning for multiple perspectives. The paragraphs that follow explore these meanings in relation to theory, research, and practice. This section begins with an analysis of the findings through the lens of the theoretical framework.

Theory

Schein's (1985, 2010) model of cultural change posits that culture within an organization is revealed in three levels of the organization: artifacts, espoused beliefs and values, and basic underlying assumptions. Artifacts are the visible phenomena that occur within an organization. Espoused beliefs and values are the ways in which an organization's philosophies and ideologies are expressed; they give meaning to its members. And basic underlying assumptions are unconscious manifestations of an organization's core long-term beliefs and values.[2]

The artifacts that emerged in this study are associated with the change management process. In essence, they are the distinguishing features of the process, and they have come to symbolize the culture of the university. The first of these is the inclusive, collaborative nature of the process that the university utilized after it merged strategic planning with AI. The words "inclusive" and "collaborative" consistently appear throughout the interviews and the documents analyzed in this study. They represent a visible phenomenon, namely, how UPAEP stakeholders have seen that they are welcome to participate in and contribute to the life of the university. The nature of the change management process is thus more than how the university transitions toward the inclusion of research in its mission; it is how the university now defines itself. This in turn shapes what UPAEP is becoming and provides meaning for those associated with the university. In short, this frames the internal narrative of the university. Miranda-López (2005, p. 232) poetically summarizes this artifact by stating that there is great value in

> the positive impact of the application of the principles and beliefs of appreciative inquiry in the identification of the forces that give life and the originating causes, in the construction of the long term vision of the organization and in the formulation of strategies to achieve it, all in an atmosphere of trust and clear and ample communication, freedom and commitment, involving the holistic view of the organization, carried out in a systematic and dynamic manner, taking advantage of the opportunities offered by new information and communication technologies.

His words also demonstrate the second artifact discovered in this study, the type of leadership utilized to navigate change. Initially, as previously noted, senior leaders of the university observed a top-down approach during the 1980s and 1990s. This resulted in restricted involvement in the change process, superimposed goals, marginally effective strategies, limited buy-in among administration, faculty, and staff, and increased resistance to change. With the merger of the strategic planning and AI processes, however, leaders espoused a "holistic view of the organization" that fostered not only "an atmosphere of trust" but also "clear and ample communication." A current administrator who participated in the merged process stated: "In order to feed back the strategic planning we created seven groups. These groups were feeding the planning process. In fact, they were reporting each month to the full group. It was about 250 people [that participated in the process], half of the community at that time." With half of the university involved in the planning process, it is not surprising that the results in recent years have been greater than those of the 1980s and 1990s.

James Macgregor Burns (1978), the father of modern leadership studies, characterizes this type of leadership as transformational leadership. He states that leadership of this type "occurs when one or more persons *engage* with others in such a way that leaders and followers raise one another to higher levels of motivation and morality.... Their purposes, which might have started out as separate but related...become fused. Power bases are linked not as counterweights but as mutual support for common purpose" (p. 20). Leadership is thus based on the relationships between leaders and followers, relationships that are mutually beneficial and that propel all persons involved toward common goals. Such leadership is juxtaposed to transactional leadership in which individuals trade one commodity (votes, money, psychological support, etc.) for another; after the exchange is made both parties go their separate ways and are not bound "together in a mutual and continuing pursuit of a higher purpose" (p. 20). The higher purpose at UPAEP, of course, was the ongoing positioning of the university within local, national, and international environments through sustained, inclusive collaboration.

Espoused beliefs and values, according to Schein, represent the second level of an organization where culture is evidenced. The espoused beliefs and values discovered in this study represent a relatively unique blend among Latin American universities. They reflect an amalgamation of values that include emphases on the human condition, the importance of research, extensive industry and business collaborations, and continual efforts to position the university. Concerning the first of these humanistic values, a senior administrator stated:

> UPAEP believes that the main problems in the world are human and spiritual. One of the main reasons that students, faculty, staff and even administrators choose UPAEP is the support they know they will receive in this area. It is no accident that at the very center of CIP is the human and the spiritual. They inform everything that we do through the Center.

Similar comments were made by every person interviewed and appear throughout written and online university documents.[3]

At the same time that UPAEP accentuates humanistic values it places substantial emphasis on increasing research productivity among its faculty and graduate students. The importance of research is the second espoused belief and value. One administrator indicated that "the university uses a litany of methods to instill a culture of research that will lead to greater research productivity." These include: the prior creation of the graduate college and CIP, launching multiple research centers, paying for faculty to earn a PhD, hiring proven researchers, allowing faculty to negotiate their productivity, requiring researchers to pursue membership in the national research system (a type of certification), reducing course loads, encouraging faculty to conduct research with UPAEP students and intra- and interinstitutional colleagues, and working to establish in the near future a financial incentive system for research productivity (with awards going, e.g., to faculty for the best manuscript, the most cited manuscript, etc.).

The third espoused belief and value relates to the importance of collaboration with business and industry. Table 7.1 clearly demonstrates this. Whereas the university was involved in 8 such collaborations during the 2004–2005 academic year, by the 2012–2013 academic year the number exploded to 101. This dramatic growth is a reflection not only on a thoughtful, ongoing analysis of the needs of the region but also on the interests and capabilities of individuals and teams within the university. Ultimately, it is an indication that the culture of the university sees as meritorious a multifaceted response to human needs, a response that goes beyond the proverbial ivory towers of higher education to engage the larger community of external environments.

The fourth espoused belief and value is the continual effort by university stakeholders to better position the university. From one perspective this may be seen as a value that springs from the merger of the strategic planning and AI processes. From another perspective it is this value that actually drives the merged processes, and thus the change management process itself. From yet another it may be seen as an outcome of the first three espoused beliefs and values. As Schein indicates, to determine the root of this or any other espoused belief and value necessitates analysis of the third level of an organization—basic underlying assumptions—which is beyond the methodology of this study. Regardless of the perspective, however, sustained consistent endeavors to strengthen the position of the university are indicative of the core culture of UPAEP.

Research

As they do for theory, the findings of this study hold meaning for research. They suggest potential lines of inquiry that warrant further attention. The following paragraphs highlight six lines of inquiry that are relevant not only for UPAEP but also for Latin American higher education: evolving curricula, organizational culture, leadership development, regional clusters, student and faculty mobility, and the nature of a university's presence.

The creation of flexible programs that allow students to personalize their plans of study and reflect their individual academic interests, coupled with institutional emphases on interdisciplinarity and graduate student research, signifies that UPAEP recognizes the importance of addressing the curricular needs of students. As warranted, changes are made at UPAEP because the university continually assesses its local, national, and global environments, all of which indicate that the curricular needs of students are in flux. In the context of the transplant of the Bologna Process and the Tuning Project (Aboites 2010) to Latin America, and the push toward the standardization of professional competencies, it is significant that UPAEP navigates these trends while maintaining a steady focus on students. As higher education in Latin America and across the globe continues to evolve, the curricular needs of students will likely metamorphose for the foreseeable future. Ongoing research will be needed to determine how the external environments of higher education—in particular, global trends—intersect with and potentially impact curricula in Mexico and throughout Latin America.

According to Waggoner (1970), Latin American universities were traditionally characterized by departmentalization, nonunified campuses, and the absence of liberal education. UPAEP challenges that paradigm. Vision 2015 is the antithesis of Waggoner's characterization. It indicates that the organizational culture—again, out of necessity due to perpetual changes in the external environments—is one of cooperation and smaller disciplinary fences. Binding all of this together, and reducing the traditional silo mentality within higher education, is liberal education and its emphasis on humanistic perspectives.

To develop future UPAEP leaders the university is focusing on both the development of internal personnel and the recruitment of external talents. The university provides financial resources for faculty and staff development, and the sense of community within the university is appealing to potential recruits. Both of these facilitate the retention of personnel, all of whom are encouraged to pursue further education and assume greater leadership within the university. A senior administrator said, "We established a very strong scholarship program to make that happen." Accordingly, it is likely that the number of UPAEP faculty with doctoral degrees and the number of faculty that belong to Sistema Nacional de Investigadores will continue to grow, which in turn should burgeon research productivity. The potential links between faculty/staff development and research productivity are worthy of further examination.

Due to the North American Free Trade Agreement (NAFTA) and the massive privatization of public companies, most industrial activity in Mexico, and throughout Latin America, is run by foreign companies (Aboites 2010; Arocena and Sutz 2001). This often diminishes reliance on local knowledge. Consequently, the push toward building and maintaining institutional relationships with the private sector is essential for higher education institutions. UPAEP effectively champions these relationships. Emphasis on regional clusters, as previously addressed, insures that the future production of knowledge will focus on the needs of the local community and local industry. Unfortunately, the literature is limited regarding the role of Latin American higher education in regional clusters.

UPAEP administrators envision that student and faculty mobility will continue to increase. They also foresee ongoing expansion of knowledge production through the growing number of dual degree programs and the research projects that are conducted by UPAEP students with international higher education institutions. Tierney and Findlay (2009) indicate that these are key strategies of the second wave of globalization. Again, although internationally the literature related to student and faculty mobility is expanding, greater knowledge is needed about the topic as it relates to Latin America.

The physical and virtual expansions of UPAEP also foreshadow the future. Responding to international trends, the university is addressing cross-border education as a strategic strength; this will likely further enhance the international presence of the institution. In addition, through the construction of new campuses throughout the state, and a growing number of online programs that enroll an increasing number of national and international students, the university continues to extend its local, national, and international presence. Given escalating competition among higher education institutions, there is a need for extensive, multifaceted research into the nature and impacts of university presence.

Practice

The focus of this chapter is the processes that UPAEP observed to emerge as a successful research university. Although the case study design negates generalization to other universities, the focus on the processes, rather than the minutia of the decade's long evolution, allows practical conclusions to be drawn that may inform the leaders and stakeholders of other Latin American universities. However, the researchers encourage every leader to assess carefully the unique internal and external environments of the institution before attempting to duplicate or adapt the strategies that are working at UPAEP. Clearly, what is effective at one university may be disastrous at another due to different strengths, weaknesses, opportunities, or challenges. With these caveats in mind, the following paragraphs offer six considerations that emerge from the findings of this study.

First, throughout the change management process, particularly after the infusion of AI with strategic planning, UPAEP emphasized its strengths. Rather than spending large amounts of time and resources to develop marginal programs, or to duplicate those offered by other universities in the region, the university logically and systematically identified programs for which it had strength or through which it possessed competitive advantage. This was done through a sustained conversation that included every voice within the university. UPAEP then championed these programs in multiple ways, including infusing financial resources, providing physical resources, hiring and retaining key faculty, recruiting students, pursuing requisite accreditations, forming collaborations with business and industry, and engaging in marketing and public relations.

Second, university leaders were cognizant of and responded to internal resistance. Embracing the use of AI, with its accent on the inclusion of all stakeholders, proactively and effectively addressed and reduced resistance. The monthly open dialogs with the president further diminished voices of dissent. Both endeavors dampened resistance by affording participation, ownership, and identification with the university and its initiatives.

Third, UPAEP recognized the reality of internationalization. This was manifested in a host of university initiatives, including but not limited to CIP, dual degree programs, the development of online programs, emphasis on research productivity and knowledge transfer, the formation of regional clusters, and the establishment of relationships with local businesses and industries, some of which are divisions of large international corporations.

Fourth, while recognizing internationalization the university focused on the local. This was visibly achieved both through the AI process and the regional clusters. It was evidenced as well in the focus on the needs of students, faculty, and the Puebla community.

Fifth, in response to balancing the global with the local, UPAEP emphasized interdisciplinary education. The creative approach through CIP engendered the development of multiple skills and cognizance among students. This well positioned not only recent and immanent students of the university but also the university itself for the foreseeable decades ahead. It enabled the university to achieve an additional balance between the globalizing trends that push the unquestionable adoption of the business model and the core values that characterized the university from its creation.

Sixth, as a result, the growing emphasis on the production of knowledge and on the preparation of students for the global market remained coupled with the human and spiritual dimensions of education. This differentiated UPAEP from other higher education institutions in Mexico. This balance, as well as the previously noted balances achieved by UPAEP, likely contributed to its emergence as a successful research university and, if retained, will sustain its success well into the future.

Conclusion

This chapter examines the processes that a private Catholic Mexican university employed to incorporate research into its mission. It uncovers more though than the effectiveness of particular processes, steps, or strategies; it highlights nothing less than the transformation of a university's DNA. Once a reactive organization, UPAEP is now a focused, proactive, invigorated university. Stakeholders embrace and embody the collaboratively determined values of the organization, the university community consistently assesses its internal strengths and employs those strengths to respond to the needs of its multiple external environments, and the concept of research is increasingly embedded in the mission and vision of the university while teaching and learning are still emphasized as crucial for the human situation. This still evolving DNA fuses the best of historic and emerging university missions and positions UPAEP well for the inevitable changes that are yet to come.

Notes

1. It should be noted that the AI process was utilized by other universities in Mexico during the same time period. However, other universities typically used the process within single academic programs, whereas UPAEP employed it across the entire university system.
2. As noted earlier in the chapter, examining the basic underlying assumptions of an organization requires methodologies that were not employed in this study. Accordingly, they are not included in the analysis of the findings.

3. See, for example: http://www.upaep.mx/index.php?option=com_content&view =article&id=3212&Itemid1560 and http://www.upaep.mx/index.php?option =com_content&view=article&id=395&Itemid=4.

References

Aboites, Hugo. 2010. "Latin American Universities and the Bologna Process: From Commercialization to the Tuning Competencies Project." *Globalization, Societies and Education* 8 (3): 443–455.
Arnove, Robert F. 1967. "A Survey of Literature and Research on Latin American Universities." *Latin American Research Review* 3 (1): 45–62.
Arocena, Rodrigo, and Judith Sutz. 2001. "Changing Knowledge Production and Latin American Universities." *Research Policy* 30: 1221–1234.
———. 2005. "Latin American Universities: From an Original Revolution to an Uncertain Transition." *Higher Education* 50 (4): 573–592.
Bernasconi, Andrés. 2008. "Is There a Latin American Model of the University?" *Comparative Education Review* 52 (1): 27–52.
Bess, James L., and Jay R. Dee. 2008. *Understanding College and University Organization: Theories for Effective Policy and Practice*. Sterling, VA: Stylus.
Burns, James MacGregor. 1978. *Leadership*. New York, NY: Harper & Row.
Carvalho de Mello, José Manoel, and Henry Etzkowitz. 2008. "New Directions in Latin American University-Industry-Government Interactions." *International Journal of Technology Management and Sustainable Development* 7 (3): 193–204.
Chen, Derek, Hung Chiat, and Carl Johan Dahlman. 2005, October. *The Knowledge Economy, the KAM Methodology and World Bank Operations*. World Bank Institute Working, paper no. 37256. Washington, DC: The World Bank.
Jaksic, Ivan. 1985. "The Politics of Higher Education in Latin America." *Latin American Research Review* 20 (1): 209–221.
Jiménez-Ortiz, M. 2011. "Worldwide Discourse on Educational Modernization: The Evaluation of Quality and Reform in Latin American Universities." *Espacio Abierto* 20 (2): 219–238.
Miranda-López, José Alfredo. 2005. *Valoración de los Principios de la Indagación Apreciativa en la Identificación de las Fuerzas que dan Vida a las Organizaciones, la Construcción de la Visión de Futuro y en la Elección de las Estrategias para Alcanzarla: Un Estudio del Caso en la UPAEP* (Assessment of Appreciative Inquiry Principles to Identify Forces That Give Life to Organizations, Construction of a Vision of Future to Reach It: A Case Study). Doctoral dissertation. Puebla, Mexico: Puebla State Popular Autonomous University.
North American Congress on Latin America (NACLA). 2000. "The Crisis of the Latin American University." *NACLA Report on the Americas* 33 (4): 1–11.
Ordorika Sacristán, Imanol, Roberto Rodríguez Gómez, Francisco Javier Lozano Espinosa, Alejandro Márquez-Jiménez, Jorge Martínez Stack, Martha Montes de Oca Cáliz, Pilar López Martínez, and Gabriela Olguín Carro. 2009.

"Desempeño de Universidades Mexicanas en la Función de Investigación: Estudio Comparativo" ("Performance of Mexican Universities Regarding the Research Function: Comparative Study"). *Cuadernos de Trabajo de la Dirección General de Evaluación Institucional* (Work Notebooks of the General Direction for Institutional Assessment) 1 (2). Available online at: http://www.dgei.unam.mx/cuaderno2.pdf, accessed March 12, 2014. rof Futurens, Construction of a aVesioo Institutional Assessmentive Study give life to als center.)

Patton, Michael Quinn. 2002. *Qualitative Research and Evaluation Methods* (3rd edition). Newbury Park, CA: Sage.

Petersen, John H. 1970. "Recent Research on Latin American University Students." *Journal of Studies in International Education* 5 (1): 37–58.

Porter, Michael E. 1990. *The Competitive Advantage of Nations.* New York, NY: The Free Press.

Rowley, Daniel James, Herman D. Lujan, and Michael G. Dolence. 1997. *Strategic Change in Colleges and Universities: Planning to Survive and Prosper.* San Francisco, CA: Jossey-Bass.

Schein, Edgar H. 1985. *Organizational Culture and Leadership: A Dynamic View.* San Francisco, CA: Jossey-Bass.

———. 2010. *Organizational Culture and Leadership: A Dynamic View* (4th edition). San Francisco, CA: Jossey-Bass.

Stavenhagen, Rodolfo, E. Arriaga, R. Freedman, N. Keyfitz, J. V. Grauman, and R. R. Puffer. 1964. "Social and Demographic Research in Latin American Universities." *The Milbank Memorial Fund Quarterly* 42 (2): 148–174.

Stromquist, Nelly P., and K. Karen Monkman. 2000. "Defining Globalization and Assessing Its Implications on Knowledge and Education." In *Globalization and Education: Integration and Contestation across Cultures*, edited by N. Stromquist and K. Monkman (pp. 3–26). Lanham, MD: Rowman & Littlefield.

Thorn, Kristian, and Maarja Shoo. 2006. "Latin American Universities and the Third Mission: Trends, Challenges and Policy Options." World Bank Policy Research Working Paper 4002. Washington, DC: The World Bank.

Tierney, William G., and Christopher C. Findlay. 2009. *The Globalization of Education: The Next Wave.* Singapore: PECC, APRU.

Universidad Popular Autónoma del Estado de Puebla (UPAEP: Puebla State Popular Autonomous University) N.d. *Accredited Quality.* Puebla, Mexico: UPAEP. Available online at: http://www.upaep.mx/index.php?option=com _content&view=article&id=3215&Itemid=1558, accessed on February 12, 2014.

———. N.d. *General Information.* Puebla, Mexico: UPAEP. Available online at: http://www.upaep.mx/index.php?option=com_content&view=article&id=32 09&Itemid=1559, accessed March 12, 2014

———. N.d. *Mission.* Puebla, Mexico: UPAEP. Available online at: http://www .upaep.mx/index.php?option=com_content&view=article&id=3212&Itemid1 560, accessed on March 12, 2014.

———. N.d. *Vision 2015.* Puebla: UPAEP. Available online at: http://www .upaep.mx/index.php?option=com_content&view=article&id=274&Itemid =8, accessed March 12, 2014.

———. 2012. *Informe del Rector 2012* (President's 2012 report). Puebla, Mexico: UPAEP.

Waggoner George R. 1970. "Latin American Universities." *The Journal of Higher Education* 41 (9): 740.

Watkins, Jane Magruder, and Bernard J. Mohr. 2001. *Appreciative Inquiry: Change at the Speed of Imagination*. San Francisco, CA: Jossey-Bass, Pfeiffer.

Chapter 8

Central American Outliers
Leveraging International Cooperation for Research Productivity

Nanette Svenson

Introduction

Latin America tends to attract little attention for its higher education and research capacity; Central America tends to be forgotten altogether. This is not surprising since statistics for the subregion in these areas are not impressive. None of Central America's universities appear in the international rankings; few of its university professors hold accredited PhDs; and Central America accounts for less than 0.05 percent of global research and development (R&D) expenditures and only 0.07 of all Science Citation Index publications (Svenson 2012). In spite of these figures, however, there are pockets of dynamic academic activity and collections of institutions that are consistently producing valuable research, especially applied research in areas critical for national and regional development. These outliers are worthy of more in-depth study as they may serve as useful examples for other countries in Latin America, as well as for small developing countries in other regions. This is particularly true given that strategic investment in key areas of applied research is becoming increasingly important for small emerging nations, individually and collectively, as a means to maximizing their limited resources and setting their own development agendas (Holm-Nielsen et al. 2005; Svenson 2012).

This chapter concentrates on these Central American exceptions and highlights some of the factors contributing to their success, which include internal academic and administrative decisions along with external conditions related to national and international policy. Because little has been written about these institutions to date, input to the chapter relies considerably on information culled from key informant interviews as well as from these schools' internal files and public web sites.

Regional Context

Geographically, Central America is the southernmost isthmus section of North America that connects the continent with South America. It consists of seven countries, Belize, Costa Rica, El Salvador, Guatemala, Honduras, Nicaragua, and Panama, which cover roughly 300,000 miles of territory and house a population of around 42 million. Central America is usually placed within Latin America for investigative purposes and is considered a somewhat more conflictive, less productive subregion. There are a number of reasons, however, for examining Central America on its own as the subcontinent incorporates various geographic and demographic characteristics that are distinct from those found in the larger Latin American region.[1]

Like Latin America, Central America has established increasingly stable democratic governance structures over the past several decades, uses Spanish as the predominant language (everywhere except Belize, where English is the official language and Spanish is the second language), and still relies heavily on commodities and resource extraction for much of its economic activity, particularly as demand from China for raw materials continues to grow. Unlike most of the rest of Latin America, the countries of Central America tend to be smaller in terms of land mass and population, less economically productive, and ranked collectively lower on the human development index (United Nations Development Programme [UNDP] 2012).[2] These scale and fiscal limitations make it harder to generate internally the kind of scientific growth necessary for advancing development. Also important to note is that all the countries of Central America fall into the World Bank's "middle-income" category of developing countries (World Bank 2012a). This means that despite the "developing" classification and a 40 percent overall poverty rate, most of these countries are not poor enough to qualify for significant donor aid.

These circumstances have implications for educational performance at all levels. Except for Costa Rica, Central American public spending on education is well below the Organisation for Economic Cooperation and Development (OECD) annual average of about 5 percent of gross domestic product (GDP) (OECD 2012) and, in some cases, even below the Latin American average of 4 percent of GDP (OECD and Economic Commission for Latin America and the Caribbean 2011). So while primary education coverage and literacy rates have improved significantly over the past decades and primary completion is now at or above 90 percent for most of the subregion, there are still large gaps in the system. Secondary enrollment is only around 75 percent, for example, with completion rates far lower than that. And while tertiary enrollment has reached an average of 25 percent of the age cohort, completion rates are much lower here as well. Added to this, quality is a critical issue for every level of education. Reports from multiple sources point to serious problems across Central America with inadequate and outdated teacher training, curriculum development, standards and assessment mechanisms, and accountability systems (Partnership for Educational Revitalization in the Americas 2007; UNESCO 2007; World Bank 2005).

Central America's higher education has undergone radical changes in the past couple of decades, particularly in the private sector, but these changes have not necessarily been beneficial for promoting R&D. Traditionally, the countries of Central America could each count on a single public university, or a few at most, with little or no private contribution to the sector. Today there is a much more complex and diversified system. Higher education institutions with a single urban campus have expanded into multibranched, nationwide public universities; technical and vocational schools have evolved into polytechnic and technical institutes; and private schools now dominate in many countries (UNESCO 2012).

At present, the countries of Central America have more universities than ever before and in relatively high proportion to their respective populations (table 8.1). This institutional proliferation of the past 20 years, along with increased primary and secondary education coverage and a range of labor market financial incentives, has fueled the increasing tertiary enrollment. Most of the new private institutions are for-profit ventures and often criticized for their extreme commercialization of the higher education sector (UNESCO-IESALC 2010; World Bank 2005). The vast majority of the programs offered through these schools concentrate on teaching for professional productive sector job preparation; little if any funding is dedicated to research.

Added to this, the severe reduction of governmental financial resources allocated to higher education throughout the region has meant less university funding across the board. Unlike the situation in industrialized countries, Central American R&D is principally funded (nearly 70 percent) by government and some international sources (roughly 20 percent),

Table 8.1 Central American public and private universities by country, 2012 (the designation of "university" is used here as defined by the respective Ministry of Education of each country)

Country	Total universities	Public universities	Private universities	Population (millions)
Belize	1	1	0	0.36
Costa Rica	56	5	51	4.73
El Salvador	41	1	40	6.23
Guatemala	14	1	13	14.76
Honduras	10	2	8	7.76
Nicaragua	42	4	38	5.87
Panama	37	5	32	3.57

Sources: Jain 2011; CEPS (Guatemala) 2012; MINED (El Salvador) 2012; MEDUCA (Panama) 2012; World Bank (population data).

as opposed to business. This presents a harsh limitation as most Central American governments find it difficult to budget adequately for infrastructure and many of the basic public services, much less for scientific research, which is often viewed as a luxury. At the same time, there is no established tradition or precedent for corporate or private sector contribution to the financing of research. This doubly negative scenario makes investment in scientific research activity extremely difficult (Svenson 2012).

In this general overview of Central America, it is important to acknowledge the extent of diversity between the countries of the subcontinent. Collective Central American averages mask underlying inequalities. While similar in many ways, the seven countries exhibit considerable divergence on a number of development statistics (table 8.2). Costa Rica and Panama are the more advanced with higher GDP per capita, lower poverty rates, higher government effectiveness, broader educational coverage, and higher general human development figures. Conversely, Nicaragua, Honduras, and Guatemala appear at the opposite end of the same statistics. These figures are relevant because they determine much of the fundamental base necessary for propelling education and scientific advancement.

Another influencing factor is the degree of inequity within each country. Central America, like the rest of Latin America, suffers from extreme income inequality. Most countries post Gini indices above 50 (table 8.2), indicating an acute concentration of resources in a disproportionately small percentage of the population.[3] This also negatively affects the

Table 8.2 Central America: select development statistics, 2012

Country	GDP per capita (US$)	Poverty (% of pop.)	Gini index	Human development ranking (out of 187)	Government effectiveness (percentile)	Literacy (% of adults)	Secondary enrollment (% gross)
Belize	4,064	33.5	59.6	93	39.7	70	75
Costa Rica	7,691	24.2	50.3	69	64.6	96	100
El Salvador	3,426	37.8	46.9	105	56.0	84	63
Guatemala	2,862	51.0	53.7	131	28.2	74	59
Honduras	2,026	60.0	57.7	121	30.1	84	73
Nicaragua	1,132	46.2	52.3	129	15.8	78	69
Panama	7,589	32.7	52.3	58	60.3	94	74
Region's average	*4,113*	*40.8*	*53.3*	*101*	*42.1*	*83*	*73*

Sources: World Bank 2012b; UNDP 2012 (Human Development and Gini indices).

capacity for educational attainment and scientific research, particularly given the historical tendency for the private sector's lack of investment in R&D.

Based on the information presented in table 8.2, the developmental, educational, and scientific scenario for Central America appears rather bleak. Nevertheless, there are private higher education institutions that have managed to beat these odds and produce consistently over time with regard to national and regional applied research. A few of these institutions fall into the category of "traditional" private universities, that is, nonstate, nonprofit higher education institutions established by religious or other philanthropic organizations.

Exemplary in this regard are some of the private universities of Guatemala, which have a longer history than the private universities of most other Central American countries and have been strongly supported by the professionals produced in the public University of San Carlos (*Universidad de San Carlos*), the oldest, most historic university in Central America founded originally in 1562. Most notable of these Guatemalan private universities in terms of its research capacity is the University of the Valley of Guatemala (UVG: *Universidad del Valle de Guatemala*), a nonprofit, secular institution established in 1966 by a private foundation associated with the American School of Guatemala. UVG was the first Guatemalan private university to invest in research and technology and in 1977 established its own research institute, which is now comprised of 8 independent centers and 17 laboratories. The UVG Research Institute concentrates on applied research in key areas required for national development—environmental studies, agriculture and forestry, food science, information technology, health, archaeology and anthropology, civil engineering and earth sciences, and education—and has produced extensive results over the past three decades (UGV 2012). It is the most prolific researcher of the private universities in Guatemala, even though others such as the Rafael Landívar, Mariano Gálvez, and Galileo are now beginning to follow in its footsteps.

More of the Central American private university outliers, however, fall into a different, nontraditional, more ambiguous category of international, nonstate, nonprofit learning institution. These examples will form the basis for the focus of this chapter since it is with this genre of university that more of the applied research directly associated with regional and global development objectives is being produced. Accordingly, it is this model that appears to offer some of the most useful and potentially replicable lessons for developing country higher education and research.

International Cooperation and R&D: A Nontraditional Private University Model

Examples of this less traditional type of international nonstate university can be found in several countries of Central America and demonstrate a range of different administrative structures and academic concentrations. What they all have in common is they are not public institutions and with regard to their research capacity, they share two essential characteristics: (a) focus on a specific thematic area of regional importance for development, and (b) the leveraging of international cooperation as a means to achieving and maintaining their scientific research productivity. Their success illustrates how local academics have been able to come together with international partners—multilateral and bilateral organizations, along with recognized universities and private sector actors from both OECD and emerging Latin American economies—to provide an applied, practice-oriented type of higher education and research in Central America that propels critical aspects of development. The resulting institutions are not stereotypically "private" in the traditional sense of the term, but they all operate outside the bounds of the public university sphere and are nonprofit, secular, sector-specific, research intensive, and oriented toward established international standards for instruction, research, and publication. More of these universities are found in Costa Rica, where consistent national policy and investment have been aimed at advancing educational achievement at all levels and human development, but other countries in Central America also host programs of this nature. These schools typically offer a limited range of degrees—some only at the graduate or undergraduate level and in a single academic discipline—and devote considerable resources to applied research, project development, and consulting. The majority of these institutions are not new but rather were established decades ago and have been steadily productive over time—some of them for half a century or more. Most operate bilingually, in Spanish and English, and attract distinctly international faculty and student bodies. They are also internationally, as well as nationally or regionally accredited, which is unusual in the region and represents a clear competitive advantage (Jain 2011).

Examples of this type of higher education and research institution include the Center for Tropical Agricultural Research and Education (CATIE: *Centro Agronómico Tropical de Investigación y Enseñanza*); the School of Tropical Agriculture (EARTH University: *Escuela de Agricultura de la Región Tropical Húmeda*); the Zamorano Pan-American Agricultural School (*Escuela Agrícola Panamericana Zamorano*); the Latin American

School of Social Sciences (FLACSO: *Facultad Latinoamericana de Ciencias Sociales*); the INCAE Business School (*Instituto Centroamericano de Administración de Empresas*); and the University for Peace (UPEACE: *Universidad de la Paz*). Of these, CATIE, EARTH, INCAE, and UPEACE are based in Costa Rica; FLACSO is in Costa Rica and Guatemala (with a lesser program presence in El Salvador); and Zamorano is in Honduras. All have a regional Central and Latin American focus for research objectives as opposed to a purely national orientation and relatively narrow thematic concentrations. The scientific research and the publications produced by these institutions fall into two broad categories: (a) earth and environmental sciences, and (a) social sciences, both of which are integral to Central American development across countries.

Institutional Profiles

The CATIE, EARTH, and Zamorano programs focus exclusively on earth and environmental sciences, particularly with regard to agriculture and natural resource management. The FLACSO, INCAE, and UPEACE programs relate to different areas of the social sciences. FLACSO is broader in its application across the discipline, whereas INCAE focuses on business administration and sustainable economic development, and UPEACE concentrates on issues pertaining to peace, security, governance, and international development. The following sections offer brief organizational and academic overviews for each of these institutions.

CATIE

CATIE is the region's oldest tropical agricultural school. It grew out of early efforts initiated by the United States and Latin America that led to the1942 Pan-American Union establishment of the Inter-American Institute of Cooperation on Agriculture (IICA) in Costa Rica. Over 30 years later, in 1973, CATIE broke away from IICA as an independent higher education and research institution, through an agreement between IICA and the Costa Rican government, and established its headquarters in Turrialba, just outside of Costa Rica's capital, San José. Its clearly defined goal is to bring together the three functions of scientific research, graduate education, and technical cooperation to better integrate agricultural and natural resource management in Latin America and the Caribbean, and thereby reduce poverty in the region (CATIE 2012).

CATIE is a nonprofit institution that receives income allocations from IICA and its member countries (Belize, Bolivia, Colombia, Costa Rica, the Dominican Republic, El Salvador, Guatemala, Honduras, Mexico, Nicaragua, Panama, Paraguay, and Venezuela), which serve to partially finance its activities. CATIE also benefits from an affiliate nonprofit, The Tropics Foundation, which was established in 1999 in Atlanta, Georgia, to support CATIE's work in sustainable rural development and environmental conservation in the American tropics. This link with the foundation enhances support from individual donors and helps foster alliances and partnerships between CATIE and US-based businesses, academic institutions, and scientific research centers (CATIE 2012).

CATIE offers eight master's programs related to tropical agriculture and development, along with several doctoral programs. It structures its investigative and project efforts around six research programs: agro-forestry and sustainable agriculture; livestock and environmental management; forest production and conservation; climate change and watersheds; governance and socioeconomics of environmental goods and services; and competitiveness and value chains. These thematic areas form the basis for both the research and technical cooperation project work undertaken by CATIE. This work is also a critical source of income for the institution: the university's annual core budget is relatively low at US$ 5–6 million, but it raises five–six times that amount in project revenue. The interdisciplinary research and technical cooperation initiatives also constitute an important complement for practical education. CATIE attributes the fact that nearly half of its graduates go on to work in R&D in the academic, public, or private sectors to the university's unique integration of educational, research, and technical cooperation perspectives and its range of continuous, ongoing project work. At present, for example, CATIE is engaged in over 100 research and sustainable development projects in 17 countries. Results from this work provide the data and input for CATIE's extensive publishing, as well, in both English- and Spanish-language academic and professional journals.

EARTH University

EARTH was established in 1986 as a private, nonprofit, international university with support from the Costa Rican government, the US Agency for International Development (USAID), and the W. K. Kellogg Foundation. It offers a four-year undergraduate program in agricultural sciences and natural resource management along with a research facility dedicated to scientific exploration in the same thematic areas. Its primary campus is in Guácimo, located within the tropical rainforest of the Costa Rican Caribbean lowlands. The Guácimo campus houses classrooms, laboratories, academic farms, student and faculty residences, a commercial banana plantation, reforested areas, and a forest reserve. A second campus is located in the dry tropics of Costa Rica's Guanacaste province. On both campuses, EARTH strives to combine theoretical and practical learning by orchestrating proximity of classrooms to ongoing research initiatives and sustainable development projects in the local communities. Both campuses also offer additional seminars and training programs open to the public on topics such as renewable energy, environmentally sound entrepreneurship, and sustainable agriculture practice, as well as study-abroad programs for students from around the world (EARTH University 2012).

Like CATIE, EARTH offers a dynamic, experiential teaching and learning process that is intrinsically linked to its research and development project efforts. All EARTH research is applied and focuses on generating solutions to challenges presented in the areas of sustainable agriculture, environmental conservation, and natural resource management. EARTH conducts much of its research in collaboration with other institutions such as the University of Florida, the US National Aeronautics and Space Administration, and the National Biodiversity Institute of Costa Rica. Examples of specific topics explored in some of these initiatives include cures for the regionally prevalent Chagas disease, agricultural uses for ethanol production by-products, and development of bioindicator field guides for on-site water quality assessments. Also like CATIE, EARTH has a nonprofit EARTH University Foundation established in Atlanta, Georgia, to facilitate fundraising for EARTH in the United States as well as the broadening and strengthening of its US institutional network (EARTH University 2012).

EARTH's Community Development Program and commercial activities are closely linked to its research agenda as well. With the surrounding agricultural community and throughout Costa Rica, EARTH has installed close to 1,000 bio-digesters to help farmers convert organic waste into methane gas and launched several other broad-based agricultural waste management projects. EARTH's commercial banana operation employs more than 600 individuals and supplies both Costa Rican and US markets. Other EARTH operations produce natural yogurt, cleaning products, and biological agricultural inputs, along with a range of products including sustainably grown pineapple, tropical flowers, frozen fruit, and coffee for Whole Foods Market in the United States (EARTH University 2012).

EARTH has 11 countries of the Americas currently represented in its student population, but also important to the university's identity is its intercontinental educational perspective. A full 15 percent of the entire student body is from Africa, which signifies considerable opportunity for knowledge transfer. These students take back with them to their home countries significant learning on agricultural exports, sustainable farming, and natural resources management—knowledge that is often beyond what might be available to them from institutions in their nations of origin. In this way, EARTH engages in an interesting and progressive chain of developmental cooperation that spans various countries and continents.

Zamorano

The Zamorano Pan-American Agricultural School, better known as Zamorano, was founded in 1942 and is registered as a nonprofit university in the state of Delaware in the United States. It is located on an expanse of property in the Yeguare River valley of Honduras and began as a vision of US philanthropist and former president of the United Fruit Company, Samuel Zemurray. After spending years working in the region, Zemurray set out to establish a first-class, university-level tropical agricultural school to develop exceptional scholars and professionals from all socioeconomic backgrounds. He recruited Dr. Wilson Popenoe, a recognized botanist and horticulturalist from the US Department of Agriculture and the United Fruit Company, to help found and run this school. Dr. Popenoe is credited with instilling the work-based educational methodology that has characterized the institution from its inception (Zamorano 2012).

Zamorano is now an independent, international university that concentrates on undergraduate education and applied research in areas related to agronomy. It offers degrees in agricultural science and production, food science and technology, agribusiness management, and environmental sciences. Its board of trustees is composed of internationally renowned scholars and professionals and is responsible for most major decisions related to university management. Supervision of all academic programs and responsibility for compliance with board objectives correspond to the rector and the dean of Academic Affairs. Zamorano also has international representatives in some of the countries it serves—Bolivia, Costa Rica, United States, Guatemala, Panama, Ecuador, and Peru—which facilitate recruitment of students and institutional partnership development (Zamorano 2012).

Because of its origins, focus, and physical location, Zamorano is also home to one of the largest herbaria in Latin America. The Paul Standley Herbarium boasts almost 300,000 classified specimens from Meso-America, one of the largest collections of its kind, along with a similar collection of 200,000 insect species. The Zamorano Wilson Popenoe Library is another regional research resource with over 18,000 specialized volumes, 6,500 technical journals, and access to numerous global databases and digital publications. Research has always been an integral part of Zamorano work, and its faculty and students produce over 200 research projects annually on issues related to rural development, forest and watershed management, agricultural enterprises and agribusinesses, and regional and global agriculture markets, among other topics. Since 1950, Zamorano has published *Ceiba*, a scientific and technical agricultural journal, in both English and Spanish, to capture much of its most important R&D work (Zamorano 2012).

It is only in the past decade, however, that the institute has established four permanent R&D centers for study in biodiversity, renewable energy, rural entrepreneurship, and e-learning—a move that has fostered more longer-term, interdisciplinary projects. An example of one such project is linked to the research trials Zamorano has been conducting on *Jatropha curcas*, a species of flowering plant, the seeds of which produce an oil suitable for biodiesel applications. In partnership with the Syngenta Foundation for Sustainable Agriculture, Zamorano is evaluating economic prospects for jatropha production in the region and the use of such biofuels in other developing countries as well (Zamorano 2012).

FLACSO

FLACSO describes itself as an autonomous intergovernmental institution with a regional focus and mission to promote research, teaching, and cooperation in the field of social sciences throughout Latin America and the Caribbean. It was founded in 1957 through an initiative of the United Nations Educational, Scientific and Cultural Organization (UNESCO) with support from the Organization of American States and is comprised of the countries in the region that entered into its founding agreement: Argentina, Bolivia, Brazil, Costa Rica, Cuba, Chile, Ecuador, Honduras, Guatemala, Mexico, Nicaragua, Panama, Paraguay, Dominican Republic, Suriname, and Uruguay. Because of its intergovernmental structure, FLACSO is perhaps the most ambiguous of the nontraditional entities included in this chapter regarding its classification as "private," and the balancing of its academic autonomy within this structure is of constant concern. Nevertheless, it is not a public institution in any of the countries where it has established programs; its funding is almost entirely nongovernmental; and its collective research agenda reflects a more private entity appearance and feel, particularly in its Central American operations (Levy

1996).[4] Thus, its inclusion here is relevant given its mission, connection to international cooperation, and investigative model.

FLACSO offers graduate (master's and doctoral level) degree programs in various areas of the social sciences. With regard to research, its objectives are: (a) to promote critical analysis of Latin American social problems and processes; (b) to provide research and consulting services to governments, research institutions, and educational centers of the region; and (c) to generate collaboration and exchange in the study of the social sciences among international, regional, and national universities, research institutions, governments and private sector entities (FLACSO 2012).

The FLACSO academic headquarters is located in Argentina and its general secretariat is located in Costa Rica. In 1975, FLACSO began to open academic branches in different countries throughout Latin America as a means to expanding its instruction and research activity. Though these branches also focus on certain areas of national interest, most maintain a distinctly regional and subregional orientation with regard to instruction, research, faculty, and student bodies. In Central America, academic branches opened in Costa Rica in 1997 and in Guatemala in 1998. Thematic areas for research concentration include social development and public policy; migration; local economic development; decentralization and municipal administration; democratic governance and political institutions; sustainable tourism; social movements; globalization, markets, and inequality; and citizen security.

Since its inception, FLACSO has published thousands of books along with countless reports and papers and several regional journals; hundreds of these have come directly from the Costa Rica and Guatemala campuses. Costa Rica, in conjunction with the National University of Costa Rica and the University of El Salvador, is responsible for publishing semiannually the *Revista Centroamericana de Ciencias Sociales* (*Central American Journal of Social Sciences*), with support from the Swedish International Development Agency. FLACSO Costa Rica also publishes a series of thematically focused social science "notebooks." Both of these publications serve to showcase social science research results from FLACSO projects as well as those from the projects of other universities in the region. Both Central American FLACSO branches also house extensive digital social science libraries through a project called the Central American Academic Link (*Enlace Académico Centroamericano*), funded by the Ford Foundation and supported by the participation of all Central American countries. In addition to sponsoring projects for research publication and dissemination, the Ford Foundation also funds specific areas of FLACSO research in subject areas such as labor rights and migration in the region (FLACSO 2012).

Almost from the moment of its foundation, FLACSO has engaged in widespread social science research, publishing, and consulting activity—all directed to a range of highly visible social issues central to Latin American development. As a result, FLACSO is now a highly respected academic partner throughout the Americas and has been for several decades.

INCAE

INCAE began as an initiative within US president John F. Kennedy's plans for strengthening development assistance to Central America in the 1960s. He enlisted the support of Harvard Business School for developing a new program and the first private INCAE Business School campus was inaugurated in 1969 in Nicaragua with financing from the Central American Bank for Economic Integration (BCIE) and backing from USAID and the regional business community. In 1983, INCAE opened a second campus in Costa Rica, largely because of the ongoing conflict in Nicaragua and Costa Rica's history of stability and development. Though Nicaragua still hosts an INCAE MBA program, Costa Rica is now the main INCAE campus, offering master's, doctoral, and executive degrees along with significant research capacity and professional consulting services. Throughout the years, INCAE has graduated over 13,000 professionals from countries around the world, and its faculty has published and developed over 300 case studies, 450 articles, 150 papers, 58 books, close to 100 research studies and nearly 200 consultancies (INCAE 2012a).

The major research arm of INCAE is its Latin American Center for Competitiveness and Sustainable Development (CLACDS: *Centro Latinoamericano para la Competitividad y el Desarrollo Sostenible*). CLACDS was founded in 1996, also with financing from the BCIE and support from the AVINA Foundation, and from the outset established itself as a regional leader in applied research for business policy and strategy. By concentrating on both competitive business practice and sustainable development, CLACDS positioned itself to address some of Latin America's most critical development issues—productivity, climate change, and energy sourcing, among others—and also serve private, public, and civil society sector organizations across the region. The center's activity includes a range of applied research, consulting, and customized training projects, all of which is directed at improving economic, social, and environmental development over the medium to long term. CLACDS works with an extensive list of international partners that provide access to necessary funding as well as collaborative learning and networking opportunities. This list includes governments throughout Latin America; development agencies such as the German Organization for Technical Cooperation and USAID; academic institutions like York University and Florida International University; national and multinational corporations (many of which are led by INCAE alumni); and international organizations such as the World Economic Forum (WEF) and the AVINA Foundation (INCAE and CLACDS 2012b).

CLACDS is also involved in launching activities and events to bring economic researchers and corporate actors together for examining and developing sustainable business solutions. It hosts the annual Latin America Forum, which assembles global experts on strategy, sustainability, and Latin America, INCAE faculty, and leaders of local corporations and nonprofit organization to utilize and discuss strategic management concepts and address the challenges of organizations operating in Latin America (INCAE and CLACDS 2012b).

UPEACE

UPEACE is an independent, international UN-mandated university headquartered in Costa Rica. It was established in December 1980 as a Treaty Organization by the UN General Assembly

> to provide humanity with an international institution of higher education for peace with the aim of promoting among all human beings the spirit of understanding, tolerance and peaceful coexistence, to stimulate cooperation among peoples and to help lessen obstacles and threats to world peace and progress, in keeping with the noble aspirations proclaimed in the Charter of the United Nations. (UPEACE 2012)

Though the secretary-general of the United Nations is the honorary president of the university and its mission was conceived of within the context of global UN peace and security objectives, UPEACE was established independently under its own charter as a means of guaranteeing its academic autonomy and now relies completely on private funding. It is directed by an international academic council of experts on peace and security issues and is not subject to UN regulation. This governing council is composed of 17 members, ten of which are appointed by the UN secretary-general in consultation with the director-general of UNESCO. This administrative structure has helped the university maintain its UN connection and at the same time pursue an innovative, multicultural, interdisciplinary academic program that revolves around the central subjects of conflict-prevention, human security, human rights, environmental security, and postconflict rehabilitation. The university's charter also calls upon the institution to engage in teaching, research, postgraduate training, and dissemination of knowledge. It officially collaborates with nearly 100 partner institutions worldwide, primarily other universities, institutes, and nongovernmental organizations, on education and research for peace. Its funding comes from a number of donor governments, foundations, and institutions (UPEACE 2012).

UPEACE offers a range of graduate degree curricula along with shorter courses on topics related to peace, security, governance, and sustainable development. Thousands of individuals representing almost every country in the world have graduated from UPEACE programs over the years and alumni are now working in government agencies, international and nongovernmental organizations, research institutes, and private sector entities worldwide. UPEACE also houses the United Nations Human Rights Centre (HRC), which drives its research and publishing efforts. The HRC mission within the university is to promote respect for and understanding and protection of human rights throughout the world. The mission is manifested through human rights education, research, consultancies, awareness raising activity, and training and capacity building initiatives, all of which are integrally connected through a multidisciplinary practice-based approach that blends theory and application. Research is ongoing, conducted by especially dedicated faculty with assistance from graduate students and partner institutions.

HRC research feeds into UPEACE publication, as does the investigative work of other organizations pursuing similar studies. UPEACE publishes two fully peer-reviewed journals: *The Peace and Conflict Review* and the *Africa Peace and Conflict Journal*. UPEACE-HRC is also currently pursuing a book project, entitled *Human Rights Linkages: Implications for the Globalizing World*, which is soon to be released. In addition, UPEACE sponsors the Peace and Conflict Monitor, an online forum for informed debate and peace journalism, and the Open Knowledge Network, which serves as an online platform for dissemination of relevant research, teaching materials, and other learning resources (UPEACE 2012).

Keys to Success

In spite of these highlighted institutions' range of academic pursuits and thematic concentrations, they share a number of common, critical features that can be identified as key to their success, particularly as it relates to research activity. These features have to do with characteristics that are both internationally and internally organizational in nature. With regard to the international orientation, all of these institutions are registered as international organizations, some with established US or cross-border foundations as supporting counterparts, which are dedicated to higher education and research. The international mission status makes them independent from individual government or intergovernmental control and establishes an autonomy that extends even beyond national and regional borders. Additionally, these institutions all started with the financial and academic support of influential international backers and have had throughout their histories executive boards composed of eminent international scholars and professionals. This represents a breadth of expertise and experience that, again, transcends geographical region or focus. Most of these boards are also interdisciplinary in their composition, further broadening the vision of the universities' governing bodies. This, in turn, has led to and supported the attraction of international faculty and student bodies, which creates a vibrant diversity within the institutions and includes a range of nationalities, socioeconomic backgrounds, experience, and academic orientation. It also means that professors are internationally trained and credentialed, which generally portends a higher level of academic achievement—particularly with regard to training in research methods—than is typically available in the region. This ensures a more stable human resource base for the formulation and implementation of research projects and for bilingual (English and Spanish) communications. The international composition of board and faculty, in addition to contributing to the foundation of international standard setting for these Central American institutions' research agendas, propels the establishment of international academic standards for curricula and for publishing. Adherence to globally accepted standards and methods is essential as internationally compatible curricula and guidelines are what allow for student transferability, and international peer-reviewed publishing is what allows for academic exchange, dissemination of research findings, and collegiate cooperation.

The international orientation of these nontraditional universities helps them to develop another valuable asset: their extensive global networks. These networks manage relationships with local, regional, and international alumni, faculty, board members, partner institutions, clients, and other affiliates. They also lead to potential new partners and associates, which can be beneficial for expanding research and consulting options, faculty and student bodies, and funding mechanisms. As an example, CATIE claims that it has created a network of alliances with over 400 strategic partners whose contributions are key to the success of its mission and that this network is made up of universities, research institutes, development centers, government agencies, nongovernmental organizations, cooperatives, small and medium-sized businesses, and corporations, all of which facilitate dissemination of scientific knowledge and practical experience in order to further public and private sector development (CATIE 2011a). Similarly, INCAE's CLACDS counts among its critical worldwide network most of the governments of Latin America; the major Central American integration organizations (such as the Central American Integration System, Central American Tourism Integration System, and Central American Tourism Council); bilateral organizations of the United States, Germany, and Scandinavia; multilateral development organizations such as the World Bank, the International Finance Corporation, the WEF, the Inter-American Development Bank, the Central American Bank for Economic Integration, and multiple agencies of the United Nations; global foundations like AVINA, Soros, the Inter-American Foundation, and Ford; and dozens of the region's business associations. These partnerships contribute directly to CLACDS R&D collaborations as exemplified by those developed with the WEF *Global Enabling Trade Report*, the longstanding United Nations Environmental Programme Financial Initiative (UNEP-FI) Ecobanking Project, established to assist the Latin American financial sector develop better environmental analysis and management mechanisms, and the Sustainable Markets Intelligence Center that focuses on creating more sustainable and profitable agricultural value chains (INCAE 2012a).

International affiliation also drives institutional accreditation processes, which further enhance global academic reputations and possibilities for exchange. Accreditation, as opposed to simple recognition from a national Ministry of Education, is what allows for better cross-border assurance of educational and investigative rigor. It enables international comparison, the transfer of credits between institutions, and improved research collaboration. Accreditation also serves as an impetus for institutions to maintain and expand their research activity in an effort to retain their standing. Almost all of the Central American outlier universities are accredited, some by multiple institutions, in spite of the lack of accreditation culture in the region. Zamorano is the only institution not yet officially accredited, and it is currently undergoing the process with the Southern Association of Colleges and Schools (SACS) in the United States. INCAE is accredited by SACS in the United States, the European Quality Improvement System, and by the Association to Advance Collegiate Schools of Business. It is also affiliated with various business school associations and councils inside and outside of Costa Rica, such as the National Association of Schools of Public Affairs and Administration, the Business Association of Latin American Studies, and the Latin American Business School Council

(INCAE 2012a). The US Department of Education even recognizes INCAE for eligibility for federal student aid as a result of its SACS accreditation. UPEACE, EARTH University, and CATIE are all accredited by SINEAS, the official Costa Rican accrediting body. In addition, UPEACE is also accredited by the Central American Higher Education Accreditation Council and EARTH has had its academic program certified regionally as part of the Iberic-American Network of Accreditation Agencies (RAICES, for its acronym in Spanish). FLACSO has received accreditation from the national accrediting agencies of Argentina and Ecuador.

Apart from these universities' international affiliations that enhance their boards, networks, faculty and student bodies, and accreditation standing, several aspects of their internal organization contribute significantly to their successful research trajectories. First and foremost, they are all organized as nonprofit institutions, which allows for reinvestment of any and all revenue generated beyond their ongoing expenditures. This is critical as research is expensive and requires continuous investment. Second, these universities have finance structures that are supported by multiple national and international funding sources. Student fees, alumni and organizational donations, national and international development and consulting projects, research funding, and entrepreneurial enterprises all contribute to these institutions' independent financing. This diversifies their risk and broadens their revenue generating opportunities. Third, each of these institutions has a relatively narrow thematic focus and in an academic area closely linked to development. This promotes strengthening of niche expertise and avoidance of overextension at the same time as it opens these institutions to technical cooperation benefits. Last, these universities have all developed in-house capacity for producing internationally competitive project proposals and academic journal publications—in English and Spanish. These abilities broaden the institutions' fundraising and knowledge generation reach and serve to strengthen their academic reputations as well as their international recognition and branding power. All of these institutions, like universities and research centers everywhere, struggle constantly to maintain the levels of financial and human resources necessary for generating high-quality, international standard research. Nevertheless, the combination of international and internal factors reviewed here appreciably aids their efforts and distinguishes these institutions from their counterparts in the region.

In addition to the international and internal organizational characteristics of these institutions that contribute to their research success, another element that has provided them (with the exception of Zamorano) with a comparative and competitive advantage is their clustered location within the host country of Costa Rica. Costa Rica is a strategic geographical choice as the country has a history of stability and peace within a region often plagued with violence and unrest. As early as 1865, Costa Rica began to offer asylum to those facing political persecution elsewhere. It went on to abolish the death penalty in 1882 and its army in 1948, more firmly establishing itself as country dedicated to peaceful ideals and means of development. From 1907 to 1918, Costa Rica was the seat of the Central American Court of Justice, the first permanent international tribunal where individuals could instigate legal action against states on issues related to international law and human rights (UPEACE 2012). Costa Rica was one of the first countries to establish legislation on mandatory education and sustainable environmental practice. In line with this commitment, the country has dedicated significant portions of its national budget toward these ends, considerably above the averages cited for other countries in the region and similar to those of OECD countries. Perhaps as a result, Costa Rica also has the most developed Ministry of Science and Technology in Central America and one of the more sophisticated in all of Latin America.

These national characteristics have helped Costa Rica create a favorable environment for development-oriented R&D in terms of fundamental legislative framework and human resource base. The government has also been receptive over the years to assisting these international universities establish themselves in Costa Rica and, in some instances, has been forthcoming with provision of land and facilities. The de facto hubbing of these international development-oriented universities in Costa Rica has propelled the assemblage of a critical mass of development scholars and professionals, which has led to the creation of important synergies among these institutions. Most have official agreements with each other to stimulate academic collaboration; faculty is often exchanged formally and informally between the various institutions; and joint programs and research projects are common. Examples of such activity include the recent INCAE-CATIE launch of a new combined master's in Agribusiness Management; INCAE and EARTH teamwork on the production of the 2010 International Labor Organization report, *Skills for Green Jobs in Costa Rica*; and FLACSO and UPEACE collaboration with the Organization of American States on design of educational programs for hemispheric security (Daley et al. 2010).

Knowledge Hub Potential

Perhaps among the most interesting of these collaborations is the current CATIE-EARTH-INCAE-UPEACE bid, in conjunction with other interested parties, to launch a consortium that would work to establish Costa Rica as a world-class, global knowledge hub for R&D, technology, and innovation related to sustainable human development (UPEACE 2011). While still in the initial stages, this idea builds off Costa Rica's history of investing in education and the environment, working to develop its human capital base, and establishing a reputation for concern with conservation and sustainable progress. It aims to leverage some of the advantages the country has to offer such as its political, social, and economic stability; its established base of recognized higher education and research institutions; and its well-constructed national strategies for carbon neutrality, sustainable tourism, and technological development.

CATIE has taken the lead with this proposal and presented to government officials the framework of a roadmap detailing the development of a national strategy to embody this objective. The view is one of a public-private alliance, with stakeholders representing: (a) the government and its various institutions, (b) the public and private entities dedicated to the pursuit of higher education and research, and (c) other affiliate organizations with interests linked to sustainable development. This alliance, or consortium, would be responsible for developing the cluster and detailing, implementing, and promoting the concept over time (CATIE 2011b). Costa Rican government representatives have acknowledged and spoken positively about this proposal in the press (RTN 2012), but it has not yet been operationally incorporated into national planning or officially launched.

Costa Rica would benefit from embracing the knowledge hub plan. It is a logical next step for expanding upon the research and higher education capacity already based there and has the potential to take the country from being a regional knowledge hub to a global one. The concept is not original. Many other countries around the world are actively engaged in trying to build their own research, teaching, and innovation hubs. Singapore, Hong Kong, Malaysia, Korea, the United Arab Emirates, and Qatar are among the biggest players and have invested heavily in trying to realize such visions over the past decade. These plans are generally tied to both national development strategies and government funding, and they typically depend on attracting programs or branch campuses from established, recognized US or European universities (Global Higher Education 2012; Knight 2011). Even Costa Rica's neighboring Panama is attempting something similar with its City of Knowledge built on the former US military base of Fort Clayton. Panama's effort has been less successful than those of its Asian and Middle Eastern counterparts, however, largely because the endeavor is not tied to either national development strategy or government financing (Svenson and Montoto 2012).

Costa Rica has a unique advantage for implementing this scheme. Through CATIE, EARTH, INCAE, FLACSO, and UPEACE, it already has a base of internationally recognized research and teaching institutions successfully established in the country, something none of the hubs in Asia or the Middle East had to start with. Additionally, these institutions come with extensive, prestigious academic, development, and professional networks, along with a series of ongoing collaborative agreements with global partners. Thus, the cost to Costa Rica of taking the knowledge hub concept to the next level is far less than it is for other countries pursuing the same dream. It is a timely opportunity the country cannot afford to pass up, for the sake of its own academic community and for the sake of the entire region.

Conclusion

As noted at the outset, Central America is not renowned for research or educational productivity. Nevertheless, the region does host pockets of dynamic and innovative activity in these areas, much of which comes from the nontraditional, private international centers described in this chapter. This nonstate, nonprofit international university model, as implemented in Central America over the past several decades with a consistent focus on sustainable development objectives and learning, has made a significant contribution to research productivity in the region. While this is true more in terms of quality than quantity of research and publications produced, the institutions described in this chapter have played—and continue to play—an important, well-documented role in the development efforts of Central (and even Latin) America. Their contribution has been further augmented by the fact that they have been able to build off each other's efforts as a result of their geographical proximity.

This model has benefitted, in all of the cases presented, from its international mission status and the connections established with high-profile academic, professional, and development organizations worldwide. It has also benefitted from an approach that links applied research with teaching, outreach, and technical cooperation and that focuses on singular thematic concentrations closely linked with regional development objectives. Additionally, this model appears to have been successful in Central America, at least in part, due to the national regulatory environment and sociopolitical conditions found in Costa Rica, host country to all but one of the institutions examined here.

The private, nonprofit international university concept is also important with regard to its potential as an international development tool, one that benefits both industrialized and developing countries. The type of collaborative educational research center that combines the strengths and resources of international organizations, universities, and scholars with those of multiple local and regional actors may offer an effective instrument that can be employed in other developing regions as well. Especially because of the success achieved in Central America, a region not known for the strength of either its university systems or its research capacity, there is reason to believe the model could also flourish elsewhere.

Zaglul and Sherrard (2005), both of EARTH University, explore the potential of this concept for the developing world emphasizing: (a) the need for emerging regions' universities to be more engaged in the training and research necessary to promote development; (b) the power of combining teaching, applied research, and hands-on development outreach in a symbiotic educational approach; and (c) the importance of the role of the international community in leveraging support for the range of capacity development required to propel this kind of university initiative. Zaglul and Sherrard, claiming that "every society creates the university it needs; and universities in turn help to shape the character of the society in which they are located" (p. 35), help to illustrate how this nontraditional, private international university model has emerged in response to conditions that are different from those in which most of the traditional, industrialized country private universities have evolved. Through addressing a different set of societal needs, this type of university has also created a different approach to applied research, one that is tied more intrinsically to both teaching and the university's "third mission."

In addition to the traditionally accepted responsibilities of universities to teach and produce research, a third obligation or mission has been contemplated of late that conceptualizes and reflects upon the involvement of universities with society as a whole. This is often described as "outreach" or "extension," which may be characterized as either entrepreneurial or developmental in nature—or both. A fair amount has been written about this third mission, especially in the past decade, though most of it relates to industrialized countries and private sector commercialization, focusing on research and training related to the entrepreneurial knowledge needed for today's markets. More recently, however, certain authors and scholars (Arocena and Sutz 2005; Culum et al. 2013; Reimers 2012; Thorn and Soo 2006) have begun to look at the issue as it relates to Latin America and other developing regions. The collective conclusions are that universities in developing regions must become more responsive to the contexts in which they operate and begin to migrate toward more socially relevant agendas that propel applied research linked to sustainable human development objectives and initiatives. There is also a call for more pragmatic teaching and learning that is integrated with the research and development goals. These are the same conclusions that Zaglul and Sherrard (2005) and others heading the private international institutions cited here arrived at years ago and have been acting upon ever since.

Even with the growing consensus of objective, however, numerous obstacles internal and external to the universities stand in the way of actual achievement of this mission. That is why the international community can provide such a necessary and possibly pivotal partnership at this juncture—in Latin America and in other developing regions. International cooperation can assist with supplemental knowledge, human and financial resourcing, as well as with redirection of research agendas and incentives toward development goals. When combined with local and regional intellectual capacity and insight, international cooperation works to its greatest potential. Under these circumstances, external support shifts from being a conditioned, unsustainable imposition and becomes an integrated collegial partner contributing to practical, sustainable, knowledge-generating solutions. Ironically, in this regard, the Central American experience with private, international institutions' applied research may have some valuable lessons to offer to the rest of the developing, and developed, world.

Notes

Grateful appreciation is extended to the following individuals for their time and invaluable contribution to the preparation of this chapter: Jose Joaquin Campos (executive director, CATIE); Ronnie de Camino (deputy director, CATIE); Adriana Sanchez (head of Communications, CATIE); Luis Pocasangre (director of Research, EARTH University); Ana Maria Majano (associate director, Latin American Center for Competitiveness and Sustainable Development [CLACDS] at INCAE); Victor Valle (vice rector, UPEACE); Doris Martinez (deputy director, Center for Environmental Studies at the Universidad del Valle de Guatemala); and Mario Mancilla (former professor, Universidad Mariano Galvez de Guatemala).

1. Hemispheric geographical division and denomination are open to much debate. The Americas as a whole are generally separated into two continents, North and South, though the subdivisions for Latin America and the Caribbean vary depending upon the particular context or reference. Since this chapter focuses on Central America, the subcontinental parameters reflect this concentration.
2. According to the UNDP, the human development index (HDI) average for Latin America and the Caribbean is 0.731, whereas for Central America the HDI average is only 0.586.

3. The Gini index (or coefficient) is a measure of statistical dispersion developed by the Italian statistician Corrado Gini and is generally used to quantify inequality of income. A low Gini coefficient indicates more equal distribution, with 0 equivalent to perfect equality, while a higher Gini coefficient indicates more unequal distribution, with 1 equivalent to perfect inequality.
4. Daniel C. Levy includes FLACSO in his *Building the Third Sector: Latin America's Private Research Centers and Nonprofit Development* (1996) in spite of its intergovernmental structure because of the nature of its research and its international development orientation. He does note that its status is special and that in extreme and exceptional situations where national public funding has taken over—namely, in Mexico—there is a tendency to view FLACSO as more of a public entity. He also notes that in Central America the opposite has tended to be the case and that FLACSO has maintained a distinctly private research center philosophy and image.

References

Arocena, Rodrigo, and Judith Sutz. 2005. "Latin American Universities: From an Original Revolution to an Uncertain Transition." *Higher Education* 50 (4): 573–592.

Centro Agronómico Tropical de Investigación y Enseñanza (CATIE: Center for Tropical Agricultural Research and Education). 2012. 2011a. *Biennial Report 2010–2011*. Turrialba, Costa Rica: CATIE.

———. 2011b. *Iniciativa: Costa Rica País del Conocimiento* (Initiative: Costa Rica, Country of Knowledge). Presentation at Initiative Meeting I, June 28, 2011, Holiday Inn Hotel, Escazu, Costa Rica: CATIE.

———. *Acerca de Nosotros* (About us). Turrialba, Costa Rica: CATIE. Available online at: http://catieeducacion-web.sharepoint.com/Pages/aboutus.aspx, accessed on January 20, 2014.

Consejo de la Enseñanza Privada Superior (CEPS: Council of Private Higher Education). 2012. *Acerca de CEPS* (About CEPS). Guatemala City, Guatemala: CEPS. Available online at: http://www.ceps.edu.gt, accessed on January 20, 2014.

Culum, Bojana, Nena Roncevic, and Jasminka Ledic. 2013. "Facing New Expectations. Integrating Third Mission Activities into the University." In *The Changing Academy. The Changing Academic Profession in International Perspective*, volume 5, edited by Barbara M. Kehm and Ulrich Teichler. London, UK: Springer.

Daley, Sanola, Luis Reyes, Edwin Vega, and Wendy Alfaro. 2010. *Skills for Green Jobs in Costa Rica*. Geneva, Switzerland: International Labour Organisation.

EARTH University. 2012. *About EARTH*. San José, Costa Rica: EARTH University. Available online at: http://www.earth.ac.cr/?lang=en, accessed on January 20, 2014.

Facultad Latinoamericana de Ciencias Sociales Costa Rica (FLACSO: Latin American School of Social Sciences Costa Rica). 2012. *Acerca de…* (About…).

Curridabat, Costa Rica: FLACSO Costa Rica. Available online at: http://www.flacso.or.cr, accessed on January 20, 2014.
Global Higher Education. 2012. *Educational Hubs*. Cross-Border Education Research Team (C-BERT). Albany, NY: State University of New York at Albany. Available online at: http://www.globalhighered.org/edhubs.php, accessed on January 20, 2013.
Holm-Nielsen, Lauritz B., Kristian Thorn, José Joaquín Brunner, and Jorge Balán. 2005. *Regional and International Challenges to Higher Education in Latin America*. Washington, DC: World Bank.
INCAE Business School. 2012a. *About Us*. Available online at: http://www.incae.edu/en/master-programs/mba-costa-rica.php, accessed on January 20, 2013.
———. 2012b. *Centro Latinoamericano para la Competitividad y el Desarrollo Sostenible (CLACDS)*. Available online at: http://www.incae.edu/es/clacds/, accessed on January 20, 2013.
Jain, Adishwar Kumar. 2011. "Calidad y Acreditación en la Educación Superior en Centroamérica" (Quality and Accreditation in the Higher Education of Central America). *ICAP-Revista Centroamericana de Administración Pública* (ICAP-Central American Journal of Public Administration) (60–61): 29–57.
Knight, Jane. 2011. "Education Hubs: A Fad, a Brand, an Innovation?" *Journal of Studies in International Education* 15 (3): 221–240.
Levy, Daniel C. 1996. *Building the Third Sector: Latin America's Private Research Centers and Nonprofit Development*. Pittsburgh, PA: University of Pittsburgh Press.
Ministerio de Educación (MEDUCA: Ministry of Education). 2012. *Centros Educativos* (Education centers). Panamá: MEDUCA. Available online at: http://www.meduca.gob.pa, accessed on January 20, 2013.
Ministerio de Educación (MINED: Ministry of Education). 2012. *Centros Educativos*. San Salvador, El Salvador: MINED. Available online at: https://www.mined.gob.sv, accessed on January 20, 2013.
Organisation for Economic Cooperation and Development (OECD), Economic Commission for Latin America and the Caribbean (ECLAC). 2011. *Latin American Economic Outlook 2012: Transforming the State for Development*. Paris: OECD Publishing. Available online at: http://dx.doi.org/10.1787/leo-2012-en, accessed on January 20, 2013.
OECD. 2012. *OECD Family Database*. Paris: France: OECD. Available online at: http://www.oecd.org/social/family/database, accessed on January 20, 2013.
Partnership for Educational Revitalization in the Americas (PREAL). 2007. *A Lot to Do: A Report Card on Education in Central America and the Dominican Republic*. Washington, DC: PREAL, Task Force on Education Reform in Central America.
Reimers, Fernando. 2012. "Innovating Universities." *ReVista Harvard Review of Latin America* (Fall). Available online at: http://drclas.harvard.edu/publications/revistaonline/fall-2012/innovating-universities, accessed on January 20, 2013.
RTN Noticias. 2012. "CATIE Propone a Costa Rica como Destino del Conocimiento" (CATIE Proposes Costa Rica as a Knowledge Destination). Available online at: http://www.sinart.go.cr, accessed on January 20, 2013.

Svenson, Nanette. 2012. "R&D in Central America: Panorama and Prospects for International Cooperation." *Higher Education* 23 (September): 1–16.
Svenson, Nanette, and Lisette Montoto. 2012. "Universities and the Knowledge Hubs of the Developing World: An In-Depth Look at the City of Knowledge in the Republic of Panama." *Educación Global* 16 (63): 53–69.
Thorn, Kristian, and Maarja Soo. 2006. "Latin American Universities and the Third Mission: Trends, Challenges and Policy Options." World Bank Policy Research Working Paper 4002. Washington, DC: Word Bank. Pp. 1–23.
United Nations Development Programme (UNDP). 2012. *UNDP Human Development Reports. International Human Development Indicators.* http://hdr.undp.org/en/statistics/.
United Nations Educational, Scientific and Cultural Organisation (UNESCO). 2007. *The State of Education in Latin America and the Caribbean: Guaranteeing Quality Education for All.* Santiago, Chile: UNESCO Regional Bureau of Education for Latin America and the Caribbean.
UNESCO Institute for Statistics. 2012. *Data Centre.* http://www.uis.unesco.org/.
UNESCO International Institute for Higher Education in Latin America and the Caribbean (UNESCO-IESALC). 2010. *La Universidad Latinoamercana en Discusión* (Discussion of the Latin American University). Caracas, Venezuela: UNESCO-IESALC.
Universidad del Valle de Guatemala (University of the Valley of Guatemala). 2012. *Investigación.* Guatemala City, Guatemala: University of the Valley of Guatemala. Available online at: http://www.uvg.edu.gt, accessed on January 20, 2013.
Universidad para la Paz (UPEACE) (University for Peace). 2012. *About UPEACE.* Ciudad Colón, Costa Rica: UPEACE. Available online at: http://www.upeace.org/about/, accessed on January 20, 2013.
UPEACE. 2011. The Hon. Ruth Dreifuss at UPEACE. *UPEACE News Flash* (October 11). Available online at: http://www.upeace.org/news/newsflash/2011/NFOctober2011.pdf, accessed on January 20, 2013.
World Bank. 2012a. *Data—World Development Indicators.* Washington, DC: World Bank. Available online at: http://data.worldbank.org/indicator, accessed on January 20, 2013.
———. 2012b. *Worldwide Governance Indicators. Government Effectiveness.* Washington, DC: World Bank. Available online at: http://info.worldbank.org/governance/wgi/index.asp, accessed on January 20, 2013.
———. 2005. *Central American Education Strategy: An Agenda for Action.* Washington, DC: World Bank.
Zaglul, Jose, and Daniel Sherrard. 2005. "Higher Education in Economic Transformation." In *Going for Growth: Science, Technology and Innovation in Africa*, edited by Calestous Juma (pp. 34–44). London, UK: The Smith Institute.
Zamorano. 2012. *Explore Zamorano.* http://www.zamorano.edu/english/, accessed on January 20, 2013.

Chapter 9

Research and Knowledge Production in the Private Sector
The Brazilian Experience
Elizabeth Balbachevsky and Antonio José Botelho

Brazilian Private Sector: An Overview

Brazilian higher education is a well-known case of a multisector system with a predominance of the private sector. The 2011 census of the higher education system shows that the private sector covers 73.7 percent of the total undergraduate enrollments in Brazil. The federal government, state governments, and local municipalities own public institutions, while local and foreign private equity funds, multinational educational groups, local communities, churches, and family groups own private institutions. The dominant institutional format in the public sector is the comprehensive university. In the private sector, there is a myriad of institutional types that range from small isolated professional schools (or faculties, as they are called in the Latin American region) to mega for-profit universities. On the one hand, the professional faculties are small tertiary education institutions that offer just a few bachelor programs, all leading to professional degrees (usually in law, business, or accounting).[1] They employ a few instructors, all through part-time or per-hour contracts. On the other hand, the mega for-profit universities are enormous teaching-only organizations that offer bachelor's programs in dozens of professional tracks, professional graduate programs (known in Brazil as specialization programs), and usually a small number of academic graduate programs, mostly at the master's level. They employ hundreds of mostly part-time or per-hour professors. Some of those universities are family-owned businesses and some are corporations with shares in the stock market.

In the private sector, diversity in ownership and institutional format do imply there are differences in institutional profiles. However, the most relevant differences are produced by the characteristics of the educational market target. The great majority of the Brazilian private institutions are confined to what could be described as a commodity market. Their students usually come from low-income families with no access to good primary and secondary schools. Because of that, they could not do well in the competitive entrance examinations that give access to tuition-free public universities (Balbachevsky et al. 2010; Schwartzman 1992). For these institutions, the main issue is to provide education at the lowest possible price. Even the largest universities working within this market have to follow the same iron rule: they profit with scale, grow when the country's economy expands, and retract in harsh times. This condition does not provide an environment conductive to support more sophisticated academic activities, like research and knowledge production. In spite of all these negative issues, the demand-driven institutions have experienced significant changes over the past 15 years. These changes are a response to the pressures posed by Federal regulations,[2] which imposed a minimum qualification over the academic staff employed by all tertiary institutions in the country. Responding to these pressures, the demand driven institutions started to hire young academics coming from the ever-expanding and mostly public graduate education in the country. This new professional profile has brought new tensions creating new dynamics inside all private institutions (Sampaio 1999, 2011; Schwartzman and Balbachevsky 2013).

The past two decades have also witnessed strong processes of differentiation and stratification within the private sector, with the growth of a segment of elite institutions that targets students from affluent families. Among these institutions, there are denominational and independent private institutions. Some are universities, others are not. All of them target a highly selective market that consists of children from high-income families in search of good qualifications for the job-market. These institutions build up their prestige over the ability to offer high quality programs with a focus on the new skills that selective companies and businesses look for. They are mainly undergraduate-oriented institutions, but also provide MBAs and other graduate programs. These institutions value their academic staff's degrees and research reputation because these are quality indicators in the market they operate. They tend to be highly innovative both in teaching, by adopting new learning technologies and innovative problem-solving oriented programs, and in exploring their staff's competence to offer good quality consulting services. Examples include the Getulio Vargas Foundation (FGV: *Fundação Getulio Vargas*) in Rio de Janeiro and São Paulo; the Catholic Universities of Rio de Janeiro, Porto Alegre, and, to a lesser extent, Belo Horizonte and São Paulo; the Brazilian Institute of Capital Market (*Instituto Brasileiro de Mercado de Capitais*) in Rio de Janeiro and São Paulo; and the Insper Institute for Teaching and Research (*Insper Instituto de Ensino e Perquisa*) in São Paulo.

This chapter discusses the conditions for research and knowledge creation in the Brazilian private higher education sector. Research and knowledge generation are highly demanding and resource-intensive activities (Bonaccorsi and Dario 2007; Clark 1983, 1995; Geiger 1993). If someone is interested in the roles Brazilian private institutions play in the country's research system, the main focus should be on elite-oriented institutions. These highly active institutions offer the best conditions to support research. However, even within elite-oriented private institutions, developing research is not an easy task. Most of the research activities in Brazil are supported through public funding. While official statistics estimate that public and private companies contribute 45.1 percent of research and development (R&D) funding in Brazil, most resources are used to acquire equipment and technology from abroad (Brazilian Ministry of Science Technology and Innovation 2014). Access to public funding for research is not granted for academics in the private sector. Brazilian legislation forbids public support for for-profit institutions and some institutions in the elite private subsector are for-profit institutions (Castro, 2015). Even not-for-profit private institutions face some challenges due to a heavy dependence on tuition and the restrictions imposed by the country's rules for spending public resources (Castro, 2015), which makes impossible charging institutional overhead costs that could cover institutional expenses to support research-related activities.

Research Questions and Design

In spite of the barriers and difficulties, research and knowledge creation count on relevant institutional commitment among some private institutions in Brazil. This chapter explores how research is organized in the elite-oriented private sector in Brazil. The main questions the chapter addresses are: (a) To what extent is commitment to research and relevant knowledge production possible in the Brazilian private sector, considering the restrictions pointed earlier? (b) What are the specificities of institutional arrangements to support research and knowledge creation in the private sector?

In order to answer these questions, this chapter explores two sources of information. Quantitative data originate from a national survey on the Brazilian academic profession, and qualitative data come from two case studies. The survey is part of the international network called the Changing Academic Profession (Teichler et al. 2013). It was conducted in 2007 with a sample of 1,200 academics from the public and private sectors. The sampling procedure assured representativeness of the entire Brazilian higher education sector and includes research- and teaching-intensive institutions. We use the data from this sample to answer the first research question, which is to provide a general picture of the research activities performed by academics in the private sector.

The two case studies focus on the microenvironment of well-regarded research units inside two private elite institutions, the School of Economics of the FGV in Rio de Janeiro and the Department of Computer Science of the Pontifical Catholic University of Rio de Janeiro (PUCRJ: *Pontifícia Universidade Católica do Rio de Janeiro*). These case studies were carried out in 2006 under the general framework proposed by the project titled, "The Leading Latin American Universities and their Contribution to Sustainable Development in the Region," funded by the Ford Foundation (Schwartzman 2008). We use the data from the case studies to answer the second research question. Both cases represent highly successful examples of the contribution of the Brazilian private sector to the country's body of knowledge and innovation. However, the two cases differ in almost all other dimensions. The first case, the FGV's School of Economics, is a graduate school at a secular nonuniversity institution that focuses on economics and administrative sciences. The second is a department of a comprehensive Catholic university with teaching responsibilities at the undergraduate and graduate levels. Comparing these two experiences enables us to identify common challenges faced by all Brazilian private institutions in the attempt to support research and knowledge production.

Even though data for this chapter come from a project whose results were published elsewhere, the analysis presented here is original. Its design is called the "most different system" (Blatter and Haverland 2012; Przeworski and Teune 1970). As mentioned earlier, the cases selected have a similar outcome, both are highly active players in the Brazilian context for knowledge production, but differ in other major dimensions. The rationale for this design is to compare these different experiences in order to highlight the commonalities, which could be identified as the general conditions supporting the outcome of interest. In our study, by comparing the path followed by these two highly successful and yet very different institutions, we are able to point out some relevant conditionalities and challenges faced by the Brazilian private institutions in order to successfully develop an active research environment.

Conditions for Research and Knowledge Production in the Private Sector

As noted earlier, demand absorbing institutions are strongly oriented to undergraduate education and provide little support for faculty to engage in any other academic activity. Elite-oriented institutions have a more complex institutional environment. Thus, they support scholars' commitments to other activities besides undergraduate teaching. In the 2007 CAP survey, 80 percent academicians working in elite-oriented private institutions reported to hold academic commitments with just one institution, 60 percent of them also reported links with graduate education, and 27 percent of them declared to have access to external support for research and to hold some kind of collaboration with peers from abroad.

Academic careers in the Brazilian private sector show a higher degree of permeability to the signals from the nonacademic market than the public sector. In fact, 35 percent of the academics employed at elite private institutions also reported having work responsibilities outside the academic market, while 42 percent of the scholars employed at demand-absorbing institutions gave the same answer. Most important, when asked if these commitments outside the academic market were relevant for their practice inside their higher education institutions, most academics of the private sector, both at elite and demand-absorbing institutions, gave a positive answer. At the same time, 42 percent agreed with the statement that the working experience outside the academic market is a relevant and positive signal for personnel decisions and for resource allocation inside their institutions.

As it is acknowledged in the literature, in order to be a full-fledged researcher, besides doing research with some regularity, scholars should be able to bring research findings to the attention of their peers, that is, to publish research findings. Another dimension that distinguishes a highly successful researcher is the ability to maintain regular exchanges with peers abroad. These traits define the profile of a highly successful researcher (Fulton and Trow 1975; Musselin and Enders 2008; Polanyi 1962; Scott 2003). In the Brazilian context, researchers should also have the skills to compete for external support, since it is unusual for universities, even public ones, to set aside their own resources for support research activities (Balbachevsky and Schwartzman 2011).

In the 2007 survey, a number of questions provided independent information on these four dimensions: doing research, publishing research results, accessing external funds, and networking with peers domestically and abroad. When combined, these dimensions are relevant to construct a scale to measure scholars' level of commitment to research-related activities. This scale ranks academics from a nonactive role through a full-fledged researcher, that is, an academician who is successful in doing research regularly, publishing research results, assuring external support, and sustaining regular contacts with a network of peers.

As is common in other developing countries, higher education in Brazil has always been strongly oriented toward undergraduate education and teaching tends to be the most salient output, both in the perception of the society and the government (Balbachevsky 2013). Nevertheless, research and graduate education have grown in mutual reenforcing movements (Balbachevsky 2013),[3] in public and private institutions. Table 9.1 provides elements to understand the strength of the link between graduate education and commitment to research. As it can be observed, in all kind of institutions, as the level of teaching responsibilities increase, so does the academic's commitment to research. Among the elite-oriented institutions, 44 percent of the academics with teaching responsibilities at the doctoral level also reported a fully fledged research profile with active connections with colleagues abroad. Among the academics with teaching responsibilities at the master's level, the most usual profile is the domestic researcher with some publishing activity. Finally, among academics with teaching responsibilities at the undergraduate level, 40 percent are not active as researchers, and 17 percent declared doing some research and no publishing at all. Teaching loads of 93 percent of faculty members who work in demand-absorbing private institutions are limited to the undergraduate level. Most of those professors do not conduct any research. Among the academics working in demand absorbing private institutions, 93 percent have their teaching responsibilities confined to the undergraduate level. Almost all are also inactive researchers.

The more relevant feature of education provided by the private sector is employability. Offering tailor-made undergraduate and graduate programs to respond to specific demands of the job-market is central to the marketing strategies of private institutions, especially the elite-oriented ones. As noted earlier, many scholars in the private sector are aware of the fact that, for them, the work experience outside the academic market is valued by their institutions and creates career opportunities in the private academic market. One should expect that this kind of experience would also affect

Table 9.1 Highest teaching level and degree of commitment with the research by subsector*

		Highest teaching level				Total
		Doctoral programs	Master's programs	Undergraduate programs		
Private elite institutions	Fully fledged researcher with international connection	43.8	18.5	6.7		15.9
	Fully fledged researcher with only domestic connections	9.4	18.5	6.7		9.1
	Doing research and publishing without external support	37.5	44.4	30.5		34.1
	Doing research without publishing and external support	3.1	7.4	16.2		12.2
	Not active as researcher	6.3	11.1	40.0		28.7
Total		*32.0*	*27.0*	*105.0*		*164.0*
Demand absorbing private institutions	Fully fledged researcher with international connection	22.2	4.2	1.8		2.4
	Fully fledged researcher with only domestic connections	11.1	12.5	3.7		4.3
	Doing research and publishing without external support	44.4	70.8	35.4		37.4
	Doing research without publishing and external support	11.1	12.5	16.8		16.5
	Not active as researcher	11.1	0.0%	42.3		39.5
Total		*9.0*	*24.0*	*435.0*		*468.0*

Source: CAP—Brazil, Brazilian National file, 2008.
*Data in percentages.

academicians' research performance in the private sector. Nevertheless, the data from the CAP survey refute this assumption. In fact, inside the elite private institutions, research commitment tend to be stronger among those who are able to fully concentrate their professional lives to academy and have commitments just with one institution.

The findings show that research and knowledge production in the private sector are connected to graduate education, particularly to the doctoral level, and to a professional who is completely absorbed by the academic life. In this sense, research and knowledge generation in the private sector is not substantially different from the public sector (Balbachevsky 2013). The institutional commitment to graduate education explains the degree to which institutionalization of research are related within institutions (Balbachevsky and Schwartzman 2010). It seems that the entrepreneurial profile boasted by elite-oriented private institutions has no impact over research. Nevertheless, as the case studies that follow show, this conclusion must be rephrased in more relevant ways. In fact, contrary to what happens in the public sector, research and knowledge production in the private sector maintain relevant links with the demands from the market. Being able to build up relevant connections with the needs and demands of companies and the general society is central for a successful strategy to sustain an internal environment that is supportive of research in the private sector.

Strategic Differentiation to Couple Research Production in the Private Sector

This section is based on two case studies carried out in 2007. The two cases provide good examples of the major dilemmas that elite private institutions face when they commit resources and efforts to developing research capabilities in a domestic environment that is strongly geared toward supporting knowledge creation activities solely in the public sector. The two cases cover different fields: computer science and economics. The two institutions also differ in the nature of their interactions with the market and their institutional frameworks. The first case is a graduate program in economics (master's and doctoral levels) of a nonuniversity private institution, the FGV. Founded on December 20, 1944, FGV's initial purpose was to train qualified personnel in public administration. It has a strong reputation of quality that is supported by its interaction with the market and commitment to generating public goods that are useful to the society and consulting activities for public and private enterprises and the government.

The graduate program in economics is placed among the best in its field by the Brazilian federal agency in charge of evaluating the country's graduate programs (Coordination for Improvement of Higher Education Personnel [CAPES: *Coordenação de Aperfeiçoamento de Pessoal de Nível Superior*]). The second case is the Department of Computer Science of PUCRJ, a traditional and prestigious Catholic university in Brazil. The case studies were conveyed through the review of secondary literature and analysis of primary documental sources and information collected through semi-structured interviews that were carried out with institutional leaders and senior scholars.

The Graduate School of Economics at FGV

As mentioned earlier, FGV was founded in 1944 as a think tank with the goal of contributing to the discussion of the country's economic development. During the past six decades, FGV expanded its scope and developed expertise in areas such as economics and public administration. Its intellectual history is intertwined with the analytical and operational frameworks developed through the Brazilian economic policy. FGV is also known for its contribution to building and sustaining some of the country's more relevant economic indexes since the mid-1950s. More recently, the institution has become a national reference in executive education.

Currently, FGV comprises two campuses, one in Rio de Janeiro and one in São Paulo. The Rio de Janeiro campus includes the Brazilian School of Public Administration, the Program on Business Administration, the Law School of Rio de Janeiro, the Institute of Economics (IBRE), the Center for Research and Documentation on Contemporary History, the Getulio Vargas Foundation Press, the Institute for Educational Development, and an integrated advisory unity that serves all schools and institutes (*FGV Projects*). The Graduate School of Economics (EPGE) is nested in the Institute of Economics and is the only graduate program of economics in Brazil with the maximum score (7) in the country's evaluation of all graduate programs. CAPES conducts this evaluation every three years.

The FGV's main source of revenue is *FGV Management*, a continuing education unit that offers training alternatives and executive programs developed by FGV's schools and institutes. The unit has teaching centers in all major Brazilian cities and supports a network of 30 partner institutions in other 80 cities. Curricula and content of the courses as well as the faculty's training and quality control are the responsibility of FGV's faculty. *FGV Management* also organizes in-company programs that are very prestigious among the major Brazilian companies. *FGV Projects* is another source of revenue. This business unit is in charge of organizing consulting, training, certification, procurement services, and executive seminars.

Since its foundation and until the 1990s, the main EPGE's source of income was public funding from the federal and regional governments. This started to change in the late-1990s with the opening of Brazil's economy and the changes in the policy framework related to private higher education. The new policy framework created access restrictions to public funding to research in private institutions and imposed constraints for the use of public monies for different cross-subsidy activities (for an overview, see Castro, 2015). The new environment posed big challenges to the institution's mode of expansion that was heavily dependent on public support. In the new scenario, as the costs of teaching and research increased, assuring quality became more problematic. At that time, many scholars sought consultancy as a way to increase their income and to face the high increase in the cost of living in an economy marked by high inflation at the beginning of the 1990s. Nevertheless, the time consumed in consulting activities restricted the amount and quality of academic outputs, something that could jeopardize the institution's academic prestige. On the other hand, the many academic commitments assumed by the faculty in some cases compromised the quality of services and consulting work done by these scholars. Reacting to this situation, FGV underwent reorganization, assigning different missions to several units within the institution.

The institution's reform created special units that are responsible for consulting and developing innovative learning programs to improve professionals' skills and attend corporations' special needs. As a result, FGV experienced a major strategic reorientation at the beginning of the twenty-first century. The restructuring reinforced the division of tasks between revenue generating and research producing units. While the former takes advantage of FGV's prestige and social capital to offer educational and consulting services in the market, the latter contributes to FGV's reputation by producing knowledge highly valued by the academic community and the society. In the new structure, the role of EPGE is to produce good quality academic research, which in turn supports the reputation and the FGV's brand.

The reform had a great impact on the institution's academic career. With the new framework, access to a tenure position with a full-time commitment to research and teaching depends on the publication outcomes of faculty members. According to the interviewees, the quality criteria adopted by FGV to evaluate scholars' performance are more stringent and demanding than the ones from CAPES. FGV rewards publications by paying high bonuses for articles published in outstanding international journals (e.g., US$ 25,000 for an article published in a high-impact journal, such as the

American Economic Review). EPGE also has special arrangements to support academics' attendance to seminars and conferences, which include funding for work travel intended to develop collaborative projects with other national and international institutions.

Also, as a result of the reform, the institution created conditions for sustainable growth in the new highly competitive environment. The reform clearly differentiated roles of revenue-generating units (FGV Consult, FGV courses), a social prestige- and market legitimacy-generating unit (EPGE), and a public good producing unit (IBRE). The latter is responsible for conducting applied research and producing some of the more relevant indexes in the Brazilian economy, for example, the General Price Index, which is one of the most accurate indexes to access the country's inflation rates.

Thus, in the FGV experience, sustaining the costly activities of knowledge production is possible because of the strong division of responsibilities and tasks between different units. The generation of academically relevant products is in the hands of part of the academic personnel dedicated to graduate education and academic research. Nevertheless, support for these activities comes from other units dedicated to revenue generating, which are also in charge of supporting the activities related to the production of the major economic indexes of the Brazilian economy. However, as noted earlier, all these initiatives are interconnected. All academic personnel are mobilized to ensure high quality and prestige attached to the consulting and teaching activities developed by the institution as a whole. In this way, research and knowledge creation in the FGV experience is strongly connected by the channels linking the institution to the corporate world.

Department of Computer Science at PUCRJ

The Department of Computer Science (DI: *Departamento de Informática*) at PUCRJ has played a prominent role in the Brazilian higher education and research landscape for more than 30 years. Over the past 15 years, the DI has also developed an intense activity of cooperation with public and private companies, generating spinoffs and producing a new stream of resources to sustain research activities within the department. The graduate program (master's and doctorate) attached to the DI is the only one in the area of computer science that received the highest evaluation score (seven out of seven points) in the national evaluation of graduate education conducted by CAPES.

PUCRJ is the oldest and leading private research university in the country. It was founded in 1946. PUCRJ has a strong tradition of pioneering and excellence in engineering. Throughout the 1970s and 1980s, it received strong financial and institutional support from the federal government for its graduate programs in engineering and science. However, in the late 1990s the public support for graduate and research activities in the private sector started to thin out until its total extinction in 1994. The university still has access to public scholarships and public resources for specific research projects, but there is not institutional support that could pay for the collective costs of research infrastructure and services. Due to the new policies adopted by the federal government, the institution cannot charge for overhead costs. Therefore, the public funds do not generate enough resources for maintaining and upgrading PUCRJ's infrastructure.

In reaction to this situation, the DI created the Institute of Software Technology (ITS: *Instituto de Tecnologia de Software*) in 1994. The ITS environment brings together several laboratories devoted to developing cutting-edge technology projects in partnership with businesses. It aims at providing organizational support for a better integration between the DI and its industrial partners. In 1997, the DI also launched a preincubator initiative in computer science named InfoGene, which offers three entrepreneurship disciplines in the areas of behavior, finance, and business planning that target computing science students. During recent years, the preincubator evolved into the Genesis Technology Incubator with capacity for 20 resident companies and the three entrepreneurship disciplines became the Entrepreneur Training Program (ETP) open to all PUCRJ students. At the beginning of the 2000s, the Genesis Incubator and the ETP were incorporated into the Genesis Institute for Entrepreneurship and Innovation.

The Department of Computer Science is responsible for two undergraduate programs, as well as a master's and a doctoral program in computer science. DI's academic staff consists of 26 academics hired with full-time contracts, 66 academics with part-time contracts, 4 technicians, and 14 staff members in charge of administrative tasks. The DI also comprises a total of 13 laboratories, 11 of which are highly specialized and committed to advanced and contracted research. The other laboratories are general and used for teaching and research activities.

According to the DI's policy, the specialized laboratories should be self-sustaining. The only inputs provided by the DI are physical space, network connectivity, and electricity. Other inputs should be paid through partnerships with companies or public funds for research. The general laboratories used for teaching are supported by the DI's common funds, coming from an overhead imposed on contracted projects, consultancy, and life-learning courses.

There is an informal internal agreement among the DI's scholars that collaborative and contracted projects should also have a strong academic component (i.e., providing inputs for papers, monographs, thesis, dissertations, etc.). The DI systematically rejected projects that were perceived as mere provision of services. In the following paragraphs we will provide an overview of the profile of two specialized laboratories relevant for the DI trajectory. The Laboratory of Graphic Computing (TecGraf), selected considering its size and the strength of the partnership with large companies, especially the Brazilian Oil Company (Petrobras), and the Laboratory of Software Engineering (LES), because of its academic program and role in generating spinoffs.

TecGraf's mission is to investigate and develop tools, mathematical modeling, data structures, algorithms, and design processes that support technical and interactive scientific graphic systems. Today, TecGraf employs around 230 people, most of them with bachelor's degrees, and a large number with master's and doctorates. Besides serving the needs of large companies, research at TecGraf is tightly integrated with the DI's academic production in the generation of thesis, dissertations, and articles published in the most relevant journals in the field.

TecGraf's main client is Petrobras, which is responsible for the laboratory's first endowment and is still the most important client. TecGraf also has contracts with many other companies and branches of the government.

LES's goals are to promote open platforms (e.g., Eclipse Process Framework IBM) and to provide infrastructure for applied research and the development of tools and experimental teaching in software engineering. Some of the main partners of LES are BRQ, IBM, MSP Association, Microsoft, Motorola, Solectron, the National Court of Audit, and the Superior Electoral Court.

The LES has developed a model for the creation of spin-offs. A number of factors contribute to its success in this area. First, all students linked to the LES are encouraged to attend entrepreneurship courses offered by the Genesis Institute for Innovation and Entrepreneurship. Second, the LES deliberately incorporates its spin-offs in most contracts as partners. Third, all spin-offs have the status of associate companies. As such, they have access to LES's research facilities.

In short, the experience of both laboratories provides important clues to understand how relevant the interaction between the academic environment and companies is for the academic success of the DI. In their interviews, academics from the DI pointed out many aspects where academic research benefits from this interaction. The aspects more frequently mentioned in these interviews were: (a) contribution to the emergence of new research questions; (b) cross-fertilization between different laboratories that is generated by business demand; (c) the possibility of attracting top students in search for updated training that is fitted for the demands of the market; (d) opening opportunities for a larger number of students to have research experience with a large number of assistantships; and (e) improvement of the quality of courses, adding real-life experiences that come from applied research programs.

Currently, the main challenges that the DI and its laboratories face are linked to the efforts to expand the support for start-ups and the high level of overhead charged by the university to all contracts. The high level of overhead weakens the competitiveness of the laboratories and, at the same time, restricts their impact over small and medium companies, which makes the laboratories too dependent on a small number of old partnerships.

Once again, it is possible to see how important the interface between the academic and the corporate world is for sustaining the dynamics of knowledge creation in this experience. As in the FGV experience, a degree of division of tasks has occurred between some scholars devoted to academic research and others more involved with applied and contracted research. But in this experience the strain is much less pronounced due to the decision of imposing a degree of academic relevance to all contracts accepted by the department's laboratories. The achievements of the DI are impressive, both in research-related activities, as well as in training opportunities created by the hybrid environment produced by the strong exchange channels between the academic world and corporate needs.

Comparing the Cases

The two cases presented here provide some elements to understand the role of the Brazilian private sector in the country's knowledge production dynamics. In both cases, public support played a relevant role in the first years, when research and academic life were being built and the rules organizing the internal environment were being established. Supporting the findings from the survey, the cases also show how strategic graduate education, in particular doctoral training, is to establish a strong research profile within an institution. In the Brazilian experience, graduate programs offer the main site for institutionalizing research and create a space for peer control, which is essential to strengthen the academic authority inside the institution.

Both institutions also experienced diminishing access to public funding in the 1990s. This situation was widespread at that time for all Brazilian higher education institutions, both in the public and private sectors. The Brazilian debt crisis in the late 1980s and the fight against high inflation rates in the early 1990s were the main causes of this situation. When in the 2000s new public resources became available to support research and graduate education, the new policy framework adopted by the federal government limited the access to the private sector. The new strict rules that regulate spending with public money strongly restricted the possibility of cross-subsidy between different projects and activities. In both institutions, the response to this situation was to reinforce links with the productive sector by selling knowledge and services to public and private enterprises. At first, this move happened at the individual level: facing diminishing resources for research, some academics started to explore the possibility of developing partnerships with businesses. While at the beginning these initiatives were only tolerated, they are currently downright encouraged.

However, success in this endeavor creates new tensions within the institutions. Most of the tensions come from differences in goals, research agendas, and the time horizon of research that serves a client and research that is supposed to be uninteresting and academically oriented. The way each institution responded to this challenge was totally different. While the DI opted to restrict the interface by selecting only demands that could support strong interaction with the academic life, the FGV opted for exploring all alternatives existing in the market. This option produced a clear division of tasks inside the institution, with some units and professionals specializing in services and outreach activities and others specializing in producing academically valued products. As one would expect, these differences also have consequences for the academic life. At the DI, academic life preserved a high level of homogeneity, while at the FGV there is a much more segmented environment.

Concluding Remarks

As presented in the first part of this chapter, most of the private institutions in Brazil are confined to a kind of commodity-like market, where charging the lowest price for education is the main differential. In such an environment, research and knowledge production are unaffordable luxuries. As such, the majority of the private sector in Brazil is almost inactive in research- and knowledge production-related tasks. Nevertheless, there are a few private institutions with strong commitments to research. These institutions explore a growing market of upper-middle class children in search for good quality undergraduate programs, tailor-fitted to the new demands of the labor market.

Two emerging trends are creating incentives for more private institutions to widen their scope and deepen the content of their strategic differentiation toward research and knowledge generation in the coming years. First, the expansion of new federal entitlement admission programs for low-income students and ethnic minorities. These programs reserve quotas for children from low-income and minority families in the public sector. They respond to some deep-rooted demands for access equity in the Brazilian society (Balbachevsky, 2015). Nevertheless, since the number of entry places at public universities is fixed, these programs restrict the access for middle-class students to the tuition-free public universities. This reality is creating a new middle-class market for the private sector in Brazil.

Second, long-term changes in the structure of the academic profession in Brazil further reinforce the incentives mentioned earlier. In the past, institutions from the public and private sectors used to recruit their academics in segregate markets. Public universities had the public graduate system to train their scholars, while the private sector recruited faculty members among its alumni in a market where academic credentials had no importance. This picture is not true anymore. Since 1997, with the new Education Law,[4] private institutions have been constrained to search for scholars with graduate degrees. Since faculty academic credentials are relevant both for the popular institutional assessment and for the evaluation criteria adopted by the federal government, private institutions catering to the new market outlined earlier are pushed to search for better qualified academic personnel, creating a new market for young scholars formed by the mostly public graduate system.

The new profile of academicians hired by private institutions brings new tensions and demands but also creates new opportunities. Among elite-oriented institutions, freed from the iron law of the commodity market, the new generation of scholars poses an opportunity for expanding research and knowledge creation-related roles.

Nevertheless, strengthening knowledge production demands academic autonomy because it critically requires initiative from academics. Mass private sector institutions focused on providing training at a large scale have little room for academic autonomy. On the other hand, institutions that recently have had access to the elite subsector are characterized by strong vertical management structures and routines that jeopardize academic initiative and independence. In order to increase the dynamism and expand the research-related roles, these institutions need to evolve to a more complex mode of governance, which makes possible academic autonomy.

The cases presented here show that research and knowledge production are not opposed to a search of profit. On the contrary, the evidence provided from the two institutions shows that a profit-seeking behavior may be, in fact, a key component of a successful strategy for knowledge generation in the private sector. Notwithstanding, it needs to be balanced with the institutional willingness to subsidize at least part of the research activity with resources created in other activities, such as lifelong learning programs and consulting.

Given the demands for financial sustainability, private elite institutions tend to develop more strategic-oriented research, focusing on the resolution of problems that come from external partners. In a few cases, cross-fertilization can occur and academic units acquire a competitive edge in research productivity due to their unique access to a differentiated set of research problems raised by partners' demands. However, the most usual response is to evolve into a kind of division of tasks inside the institution, where some units specialize in income generation activities, while others specialize in creating academic products. Balancing the needs and the prestige between these two professional branches is a relevant issue in the institution's governance.

Thus, future growth and consolidation of research and knowledge production in the private sector depends on how the dynamics between the state and the market will play out. State activity and agencies constrain the diffusion of the models here discussed and market forces generating incentives for a continuing expansion of research and knowledge creation among private sector universities through a widening and deepening strategic differentiation.

Although the gap remains large, there are sustained trends toward the expansion of research and knowledge production in the private sector in Brazil. A number of private institutions have already made strides in the direction to consolidating research. They will see the new environment as a unique opportunity for continued expansion outside the competitive race to bottom-rock prices that has in recent years characterized the demand-absorbing private subsector. The challenge for these institutions is to develop a modern and dynamic professional culture. In the two cases examined, the academia-market tension found a positive solution, which makes room for the production of synergies between these two contrasting rationalities. It is interesting to note that, in both cases, this process underwent a transformation of the very definition of the activity of knowledge generation, where it is revitalized by the interaction with the needs and challenges of the real world.

One of the challenges faced by the Brazilian research is the fact that the country's success in developing a solid base for academic research has had no impact on the country's innovative performance. While the number of Brazilian papers published in high impact journals have increased substantially in the past decade, the number of patents generated from these efforts stayed low and experienced just a small increase in the same period. It is possible that the small number of well-succeeded experiences of building up a research environment inside the Brazilian private sector provides some relevant clues for initiatives directed to overcome this gap.

Notes

1. Brazil adopted the old Continent's model of higher education where every bachelor's degree is a professional degree in the sense that it recognizes specific professional competences.
2. The Education Act of 1997 required the private sector to improve the academic staff credentials in order to qualify for university autonomy and other privileges granted by the new legislation. The Ministry of Education also exerted some pressure through institutional evaluations by demanding professors with doctoral degrees even in institutions not classified as universities.
3. Central to explaining this process was the institutionalization of procedures related to graduate programs' evaluation since the early 1970s (Balbachevsky 2013; Balbachevsky and Schwartzman 2010).
4. The 1997 Education Law (*Lei de Diretrizes e Bases da Educação*, LDB) imposes that at least one-third of all academics should have at least a master's degree. Since then, the new regulations and evaluation procedures reinforce this demand to all institutions and are mandatory for universities.

References

Balbachevsky, Elizabeth. 2013. "Academic Research and Advanced Training: Building up Research Universities in Brazil. In *Latin's America's new Knowledge Economy: Higher Education, Government and International Collaboration*, edited by Jorge Balán (pp. 113–133). New York, NY: AIFS Foundation and Institute of International Education.

———. 2015. "The Role of Internal and External Stakeholders in the Brazilian Higher Education Policy Dynamics." In *Higher Education in the BRIC Countries*, edited by Simon Schwartzman, Pundy Pillay, and Romulo Pinheiro. Dordrecht, Netherlands: Springer.

Balbachevsky, Elizabeth, and Simon Schwartzman. 2010. "The Graduate Foundations of Brazilian Research." *Higher Education Forum* 7 (1): 85–100.

———. 2011. "Brazil: Diverse Experience in Institutional Governance in the Public and Private Sectors." In *Changing Governance and Management in Higher Education: The Perspectives of Academy*, edited by William Locke, William Cummings, and Donald Fisher (pp. 35–56). Dordrecht, Netherlands: Springer.

Balbachevsky, Elizabeth, Maria Teresa Miceli Kerbauy, and Vanessa Santos. 2010. "Brazil." In *Getting into Varsity: Comparability, Convergence and Congruence*, organized by Barend Vlaardingerbroek and Neil Taylor (pp. 253–270). Amherst, MA: Cambria Press.

Blatter, Joachim, and Markus Haverland. 2012. *Designing Case Studies: Explanatory Approaches in Small-N Research*. New York, NY: Palgrave Macmillan.

Bonaccorsi, Andrea, and Cinzia Dario. 2007. *Universities and Strategic Knowledge: Specialization and Performance in Europe*. Cheltenham, UK: Edward Elgar.

Brazilian Ministry of Science Technology and Innovation. 2014. "Main Figures of S&T Sector." Retrieved February 5, 2014. Available online at: http://www.mcti.gov.br/index.php/content/view/300803/Brasil_Dispendio_nacional_em_pesquisa_e_desenvolvimento_P_D_por_setor_em_paridade_de_poder_de_compra_PPC.html, accessed on February 2, 2014.

Castro, Maria Helena de Magalhães. 2015. "Higher Education Policies in Brazil: A Case of Failure in Market Regulation. In *Higher Education in the BRIC Countries*, edited by Simon Schwartzman, Pundy Pillay, and Romulo Pinheiro. Dordrecht, Netherlands: Springer.

Clark, Burton R. 1983. *The Higher Education Systems: Academic Organization in Cross National Perspective*. Berkley, CA: University of California Press.

———. 1995. *Places of Inquiry: Research and Advanced Education in Modern Universities*. Berkeley, CA: University of California Press.

Fulton, Oliver, and Martin A. Trow. 1975. "Research Activity in American Higher Education." In *Teachers and Students: Aspects of American Higher Education*, edited by Martin A. Trow (pp. 39–63). New York, NY: McGraw-Hill.

Geiger, Roger L. 1993. *Research and Relevant Knowledge: American Research Universities since World War II*. Oxford, UK: Oxford University Press.

Musselin, Christine, and Jürgen Enders. 2008. "Back to the Future: Academic Professions in the 21st Century." In *Higher Education to 2030*, Volume 1: Demography. Paris, France: Organisation for Economic Co-operation and Development.

Polanyi, Michael. 1962. "The Republic of Science. Its Political and Economic Economy." *Minerva* 1 (1): 54–73. (reedited by Minerva, 2000).

Przeworski, Adam, and Henry Teune. 1970. *The Logic of Comparative Social Inquiry*. Malabar, FL: Krieger Publishing Co.

Sampaio, Helena. 1999. *Ensino Superior no Brasil: o Setor Privado* (Higher Education in Brazil: The Private Sector). São Paulo, Brazil: FAPESP/HUCITEC.

———. 2011. "O Setor Privado de Ensino Superior no Brasil: Continuidades e Transformações" ("The Private Sector in Brazilian Higher Education: Continuities and Change"). *Revista Ensino Superior* 2 (4): 28–43.

Schwartzman, Simon. 1992. "Brazil." In *The Encyclopedia of Higher Education*, organized by B. R. Clark and G. Neave (pp. 82–92). Oxford, UK: Pergamon Press.

———. 2008. *University and Development in Latin America: Successful Experiences of Research Centers*. Rotterdam, Netherlands: Sense Books.

Schwartzman, Simon, and Elizabeth Balbachevsky. 2013. "Research and Teaching in a Diverse Institutional Environment: Converging Values and Diverging Practices in Brazil." In *Teaching and Research in Contemporary Higher Education*, edited by Jung Cheol Shin, Akira Arimoto, William K. Cummings, and Ulrich Teichler (pp. 221–235). Dordrecht, Netherlands: Springer.

Scott, Peter. 2003. "Challenges to Academic Values and the Organization of Academic Work in a Time of Globalization." *Higher Education in Europe* 28 (3): 295–306.

Teichler, Ulrich, Akina Arimoto, and Williams K. Cummings. 2013. *The Changing Academic Profession: Major Findings of a Comparative Survey.* Dordrecht, Netherlands: Springer.

Chapter 10

Contributions from a Private University in Peru
The Case of the Cayetano Heredia Peruvian University

José Anicama and José Livia

Knowledge Society and the University

The relationship between progress in the modern society and scientific and technological development has been and will be an issue of constant interest among policymakers and researchers. It is remarkable how research and research products generate changes that transform people's lives. Nuclear energy, laparoscopic surgery, and man walking on the moon are a few examples of technological breakthrough. At the same time, discoveries have prompted new ideas to the point of transforming industrialized societies into knowledge-based economies. Change continues to happen at a fast pace. In this context, the most important factor to progress is no longer the availability of capital, labor, raw materials, or energy, but the information and knowledge that people can generate (Tünnermann and de Souza 2003).

According to an early report of the World Bank (1999), the difference between the poor and the rich, at the individual and country levels, is not only that poor people have fewer resources but less information. In present times, knowledge enlightens and drives all human transactions (Abello et al. 2001). Hence, generating ideas is necessary in the society where universities play a central role. As the *World Declaration on Higher Education* (UNESCO 1998) noted, higher education should develop its mission in three dimensions: training, service, and research. In this context, the university becomes a powerful institution that provides services and contributes to the cultural, social, and economic development of society toward new models of growth.

The information society is an economic and social system where knowledge is the primary production factor and fundamental source of well-being and development (UNESCO, 2003). Under this premise, building policies that endorse research, innovation, and technology transfer is needed. As Iván De la Vega (2009) indicated, the promotion of scientific and technological advancement is the key to navigate the twenty-first century in the current knowledge-based society. However, universities face many economic and organizational difficulties in generating knowledge. In the Peruvian context, institutions are forced to develop strategies to organize and fund their resources efficiently. It is crucial for them to work with innovative models that include high-performance researchers and structures that facilitate the advancement of new ideas (Trujillo et al. 2010).

This chapter is a case study that examines how the Cayetano Heredia Peruvian University (UPCH: *Universidad Peruana Cayetano Heredia*) has been successful, as a private institution, in the production of scientific knowledge in Peru. This chapter begins by describing how the university has evolved to promote scientific research within a context of political instability in Peru. In particular, it highlights the structural, organizational, and management changes that the university has undergone to produce knowledge. The study also shows how the academic leadership has been able to place the institution at the top of Peruvian academic rankings. The discussion section provides insights for policy and implementation of similar cases in Latin America.

Peruvian Universities and Research

Peruvian university began with the foundation of the National University of San Marcos (*Universidad Nacional de San Marcos*) by Royal Proclamation on May 12, 1551. The initial institution had the schools (named faculties or *facultades*) of Theology and Arts that were followed by the creation of the faculties of Law and Medicine, where philosophy teaching was the basis for any professional career. After San Marcos, the Catholic Church continued creating other institutions that became very important to the country. By the time of the independence of Peru from Spain, higher education was in private hands. According to Jorge Basadre (1968), the independence revolution unfavorably influenced professional and university education because the state allocated most resources to war, leaving culture aside.

On the other hand, as José Ignacio López Soria (2004, p. 88) notes, "In the early decades of the Republic of Peru, universities reduced law and legal disciplines...in manifest detriment of the disciplines that have to do with the world of objectivity and related to the spheres of representation." Basadre (1968) also explains that "the university is faced with multiple aspects: growth crisis, a crisis related to social background of students, the crisis with regard to infrastructure and equipment, the economic crisis, the crisis of the organization, the crisis that reflects the political compromises which has been happening over the country and the world, and the crisis of educational philosophy" (p. 165). This problematic situation remains at the present day in different ways and has stimulated only a few Peruvian universities to produce scientific knowledge. Instead, they have spent more time on training technicians and professionals. Inherited from Spain, the undergraduate education model in Peru focuses on preparing practitioners in the professions.

In 1920, Law 4,004 recognized main student demands and created, with the leadership of Haya de la Torre, the Federation of Students of Peru. Universities became the focus of political and intellectual turmoil with opposing views between progressive students and civilian academics. In general, the Cordoba University movement that led to university reform in Argentina in 1918 hit Peru. The Cordoba reform includes the principles of university autonomy, joint government, university extension, periodicity of the chairs, and competitive examinations and background (Tünnermann 2008). The conceptual framework of the reform manifesto was powerful and nurtured successive laws that regulated and still rule university life in Peru, including the current Law 23,733. The university reform with its challenging approaches encouraged academics to innovate in science and technology. It was the first major stimulus from within the university for the development of scientific research in Peru.

In 1968, the democratic government was overthrown through a coup d'état by a military junta, which also modified the University Law of 1960. A second university reform that departed from the 1918 Cordoba's ideas was attempted. Leading intellectuals and academics were convened to develop a new standard that was enacted through the Organic Law of Peruvian Universities-Decree 17,437 (*Ley Orgánica de la Universidad Peruana-Decreto de Ley* 17,437) in 1969, which consists of the following features: (a) The introduction of the system concept; the Peruvian university system is the group of all state and private universities, officially recognizing 22 national universities and 12 private universities; (b) the creation of the National Peruvian University Council (CONUP: *Consejo Nacional de la Universidad Peruana*) that was defined as the most representative agency and management system; (c) the establishment of University Regional Councils as intermediate bodies between universities and the CONUP; (d) the creation of academic programs and departments replacing faculties. Academic departments were defined as operational centers for research, teaching, and program outreach that bring together related disciplines. Programs are entities that arise from the functional curriculum structure of the various departments to coordinate specific formative, academic, or professional aspects of education (Ongaro 2002; Sota 2002).

This reform attempt pursued, from a nationalist point of view, modernizing the university to make it functionally appropriate for a self-managed economy, which would propel Peruvian industrial production and boost research to generate the scientific and technological knowledge that the society demanded. The aspiration was that universities would be able to support national and regional development. Law-Decree 17,437 was followed by Law-Decree 19,326 in 1972, which further developed the concept of Peruvian university by granting institutions policy, academic, economic, and administrative autonomy, in order to foster a high level of scientific and technical advancement. The legislation had positive characteristics that still remain, such as flexible curriculum and credit system. It had a bigger impact on public than private universities because some of them had already initiated such changes (Guerra 2006).

Democracy returned in 1980 and in 1983 the University Law 23,733 (*Ley Universitaria* 23,733), granting more autonomy to universities and restoring the former academic organization by faculties, was enacted and is still in place. Between 1980 and 1990, 18 universities were founded, 3 public and 15 private (Guerra 2006). During the first Alberto Fujimori's presidency (1990–1995), the number of institutions of higher education was 60 and the National Council for Operation Authorization of Universities (*Consejo Nacional para la Autorización y Funcionamiento de Universidades*) was created as a modality to regulate and rule private universities. Several low-quality institutions were opened, encouraged by the Law for Investment Promotion in Education (*Decreto Ley 882-Ley de Promoción de Inversión de la Educación*) that prompted an uncontrolled increase of the universities in the country. In this scenario, basic and applied research were very limited (Burga 2005). According to Oswaldo Zegarra (2005), characteristics of private universities are lack of research development with small scientific production and a more academic approach (teaching focus) to business, which makes some universities a good business venture. In this line of thought, the National Assembly of Rectors (ANR: *Asamblea Nacional de Rectores*) (2012a, b) warned about the disproportioned growth of private higher education institutions within the purview of Decreto Ley 882.

An important event of the past decade was the creation of the National Evaluation, Accreditation, and Quality Assurance in Education System (SINEACE: *Sistema Nacional de Evaluación, Acreditación y Certificación de la Calidad de la Educación*). Luis Piscoya (2007) describes how Peru was the only South American country that lacked an accreditation system. In July 2006, Law 28,740 created the SINEACE, aimed at ensuring that public and private institutions offer quality services and conduct scientific research to provide solutions to the country's problems. To achieve this, students are required to write a research thesis for graduation (theses were eliminated in the 1990s). It also asks academics to allocate time and resources for research.

It has only been in recent decades that the interest and support for scientific research at the university level became a policy priority among universities to conduct basic and applied research. Peru faces a challenging development process at both public and private universities, which are realizing that the reason of a real university is the production of knowledge through research. Otherwise, they are just preparing professional technicians. The organization of scientific research in Peru is described in the next section.

Organization of Scientific Research in Peru

To promote scientific research, the Peruvian government created the National Council of Researchers (CONI: *Consejo Nacional de Investigadores*) in 1968. In 1981, CONI became, through Decree DL 112, the National Council for Science and Technology (CONCYTEC: *Consejo Nacional de Ciencia y Tecnología*), which in 2005 was determined as the governing body of the National System of Science, Technology, and Technological Innovation (*Sistema Nacional de Ciencia, Tecnología e Innovación Tecnológica*) in order to regulate, direct, encourage, and evaluate science, technology, and technological innovation, through programs and projects of public, academic, business, and social institutions in Peru. However, the leadership of CONCYTEC was not enough to increase national research, because it cannot meet funding and other needs of researchers. CONCYTEC's efforts are oriented mainly to subsidize some graduate studies in Peruvian universities and annual research competitions for a small group of projects (Burga 2005).

Zegarra (2005) analyzes the research crisis of Peruvian universities, pointing out that its backwardness is amplified with the changes in the ways to do science in the late twentieth century. The massification of higher education is an expression of a specific idea of the university, but it has generated negative attitudes toward research, poor professional researchers, emigration abroad of locally trained scientists, lack of continuity of journals, and government indifference. The Peruvian government needs to make some decisions regarding: (a) increasing the number of fellowships in science and technology abroad; (b) funding research and technology through partnerships between private companies and the government; (c) enhancing international collaborative programs; and (d) developing programs to repatriate Peruvian researchers trained and living abroad. This is essential to develop the science and technology system because, as Jayme Ávalos (2006) states, most research in Peru is conducted in universities. Also, in order to produce good research, it is a prerequisite to have well-trained and high-quality researchers. That is why it is important to implement scientist repatriation policy and fellowship programs.

Peru is one of the Latin American countries with the lowest investment in research and development (R&D), which is only higher than Ecuador and Paraguay. Peru's investment on R&D represents 0.15 percent of the gross domestic product (GDP), while Brazil, leader in the region, spends 1.16 percent GDP. Other countries such as Chile and Colombia invest 0.42 percent and 0.18 percent on R&D (Moreno-Brid and Ruiz-Nápoles 2009; World Bank 2014). Indicators like this are important to understand why some countries are improving their research outcomes and how they should result in benefit, development, and socioeconomic progress (Quispe 2012).

However, despite the lack of policies and programs to stimulate research, according to Samaly Santa and Víctor Herrero (2010), the Peruvian intellectual production has been improving in rankings such as those developed by the SCImago Group based on information from Scopus. There are some institutions that have made major contributions in terms of research products. In the next section, we present the case of a private university that has learned how to stimulate and develop research as a central element of its educational project. We reviewed various authors who have studied that institution as well as the university databases that depict its institutional evolution.

Cayetano Heredia Peruvian University

Located in Lima, UPCH was created through Peruvian Government Presidential Decree No. 18, on September 22, 1961. This university focuses mainly on health sciences. It is organized in the following faculties: (a) medicine, which offers majors in medicine and medical technologies in hearing, speech and language therapy, clinical laboratory, disasters and emergencies, and radiology; (b) dentistry; (c) science, including majors in biology, chemistry, nutrition, pharmacy, and biochemistry; (d) public health and health care administration, with majors in health management, public health, and global health; (e) nursing; (f) psychology; (g) education; (h) veterinary medicine and animal husbandry.

UPCH has a current enrollment of around 8,500 students and a total of 1,190 academics. Table 10.1 shows the number of academics with PhD, master's, and professional degrees by faculty. It is based on data from the Office of Human Resources and the Vice Chancellor for Research (VRI: *Vicerrectorado de Investigación*). It is evident that due to the nature of this university doctors and teachers devote a significant portion of their workload to research and show the latest findings in class.

Table 10.1 shows the number of faculty members by academic degree and degree level attained. The Faculty of Medicine, the largest academic unit within UPCH, and the Faculty of Sciences and Philosophy have the highest number of professors with doctoral degrees. Most basic research is carried out at both faculties. Likewise, the majority of articles published in international journals originate in those faculties.

Table 10.1 Academics by faculty with PhD, master's, and professional degrees

Academic degree	Faculty		
	Doctorate	Master's	Professional
Medicine	62	122	369
Sciences and philosophy	42	64	86
Stomatology (dental medicine)	13	58	124
Public health and administration	13	49	56
Psychology	9	10	16
Veterinary medicine	3	7	18
Education	2	7	16
Nursing	1	15	28
Total	*145*	*332*	*713*

In the SCImago Institution Rankings (SCImago Research Group, 2011, 2012), UPCH is the top Peruvian university given its scientific production as measured through the Scopus database. It is ranked 158 in Iberic-America and 88 in Latin America. On the other side, the University Ranking in Peru developed by Piscoya (2007) ranks National University of San Marcos first, the Pontifical Catholic University of Peru second, and UPCH third. These rankings emphasize knowledge generation and UPCH stands out as a private institution. Raúl Cuevas et al. (2002) analyzed Peruvian publications by institution in the Science Citation Index (SCI) in 2002. They identified 244 articles published by Peruvian researchers, which represented 0.02 percent of the world total. UPCH had a prominent role in that inventory. Many of the projects were carried out with strong support from the international community that contributed up to 60 percent of research funding. The main area of production was medicine with 41 percent. Later, Ciro Maguiña (2013) analyzed the International Scientific Index 2000–2009 and concluded that 45 percent of Peru's scientific production has been carried out by the UPCH. Awards and prizes received by its students show the high quality of its teaching, research, and entire institutional life. In sum, this university contributes to the scientific development of Peru with international-class research.

Research Development Fields at UPCH

UPCH has excelled in health science fields in the institutes of tropical medicine, gerontology, and research on altitude. The institutes are described here.

Institute of Tropical Medicine

Created in 1968, the Institute of Tropical Medicine (IMT: Instituto de Medicina Tropical Alexander Von Humboldt) is one of the most important centers in Peru and Latin America for research and teaching. It has been expanding since 1977 and currently consists of the Clinical Unit of Infectious and Tropical Diseases and the Department of Infectious, Tropical, and Dermatologic Diseases. Both are located at the Cayetano Heredia National Hospital. The IMT also has an independent laboratory that is managed by the faculty and offers testing, diagnostics, and other advanced studies of different types of infectious diseases. The approach to the study of diseases such as malaria, bartonellosis, HIV, and tuberculosis (TBC) is multidisciplinary, including clinical specialties, immunology, genetic epidemiology, and even molecular biology and microbiology.

According to Humberto Guerra and Luis Varela (2011), during its 43 years of existence, the IMT has conducted epidemiological basic research and laboratory analysis (especially molecular diagnostics) to improve or develop new forms of treatment and control for all types of tropical infectious diseases. Thus, by studying the human T-lymphotropic virus (HTLV-1), the IMT turned Peru into one of the two Latin American countries with a system for early identification of HTLV-1 and preventing its spread in the population. Similarly, studies on HIV and TBC, including TBC-XDR, make this institute a leader in the most advanced research in all components of study for these diseases with differential diagnosis and new treatment options. This research made possible the development of high-quality postgraduate and doctoral programs.

Furthermore, the IMT has contributed to international scientific scholarship. Every year, there are between 15 and 20 journal publications and numerous book chapters from the IMT that are published in the United States, Spain, England, Mexico, and Brazil. These publications are possible through funding from various organizations, such as the World Health Organization, the European Union, the Belgian Development Agency, and the Bill Gates Foundation.

The basic idea of these efforts is that from collaborations with, for example, the Institute of Tropical Medicine in Antwerp (Belgium), the IMT has become a center of excellence in clinical research of infectious and tropical diseases. It allows the IMT to contribute to a better control and clinical management of those kinds of illnesses in Peru and Latin America.

Gerontology Institute

The Gerontology Institute (IGERO: Instituto de Gerontología) was created in 1989. It is a multidisciplinary unit that brings together academics from different faculties who are interested in the study of various aspects of gerontology. The IGERO promotes, develops, and disseminates research on geriatrics and gerontology. At the same time, it trains human resources and provides specialized services targeting the elder. IGERO's more remarkable research areas are diabetes mellitus, cardiovascular risk factors, and morbidity among the elders. Its vision is to become the main center of research, the reference center for teaching, and a specialist advisor on gerontology through multidisciplinary work (Guerra and Varela 2011).

Members of the IGERO have received important scientific awards. According to Valera and Chavez (as cited in Guerra and Varela 2011), this institute has produced numerous studies: assessment of depression, motor functional status in elderly population, sleep, oral health, morbidity, and patient mortality. It also participated in the international research project titled Health, Wellness and Aging SABE 2011, which found information about the health status and social determinants of the elder in Peru. Likewise, the project optimized the Comprehensive Geriatric Rating, a multidimensional and interdisciplinary diagnostic process designed to identify and quantify physical, functional, psychological, and social problems, in order to develop a better plan of treatment and follow-up, while optimizing available resources.

Research Institute on Altitude

This institute was created the same year the university was founded (1961) with funding from the National Institutes of Health of the United States. The Research Institute on Altitude conducts research programs at the sea level and in various cities in the Peruvian highlands, particularly, in Cerro de Pasco at an altitude of 4,330 meters. The Institute on Altitude has the following operational units: Endocrinology, Breathing, Internal Environment, Nephrology, Physiology to the Adaptation to Altitude, and Reproduction and Comparative Physiology. According to the National Institute of Statistics and Informatics, 25 percent of the population in Peru lives at high altitudes (above 3,000 meters), which indicates that about 7,500,000 people live in areas dedicated mainly to mining. Peru is an Andean country, and as such it constitutes a natural laboratory of the chronic effect of altitude on the human body. This institute has been recognized for research on increased respiratory and pulmonary blood pressure in subjects living at high altitude due to chronic hypoxia, human reproduction and its alterations produced by altitude, upper gastrointestinal bleeding in the Andes, kidney disease, leprosy, chronic mountain disease, Monge's disease, and others.

In short, research in this field is rich in variety, production of basic and applied knowledge, and publications. The leadership of this institution has also attracted academic exchanges with the international community. Thus, of the eight world congresses of medicine and physiology on altitude, two were hosted by the Institute on Altitude, the second in Cusco in 1996 and the eighth in Arequipa in 2010.

Other faculties at the UPCH also perform important research tasks. The Faculties of Stomatology and Public Health, for instance, have important publications of journal articles. In sum, from its founding to the present time, the UPCH has shown through its various organizational units or structures, a strong commitment to the generation of scientific research at both the undergraduate and graduate levels.

Research Promotion Policy

The UPCH has been, since its creation, an important research center in the health sciences. The interest in promoting research was evident with the creation of a Department of Scientific Research (DSR) in 1961, whose purpose was to motivate and manage the search for funding for research. As Guerra and Varela (2011) point out, the university began to promote and support research through the Office of Scientific Research, later called University Research, Science, and Technology Office (DUICT: *Dirección Universitaria de Investigación, Ciencia y Tecnología*), in order to ensure continued scientific development and promoting ethical aspects of human experimentation. Thus, the Institutional Ethics Committee was installed in 1992.

Aimed at implementing research promotion policies, there have been several meetings to review university achievements in teaching and research. As part of the policy, every three years assessments are conducted with three qualified professionals from outside the university (foreign peers), who have analyzed achievements, weaknesses, and development plans. Academics and students take part in this process as a qualitative follow-up of the recommendations by the external peers and the policy. In short, the UPCH implemented a research policy that includes a budget for research.

In 1999, the emphasis on research moved forward with the creation of the VRI, which implemented strategies to provide a better support for researchers and continue developing a culture of research at the institutional level, in order to position the UPCH at the forefront of national and international science. Thus, research was prioritized via institutional support and strategies to obtain local and international funding for research. As a result, a new cadre of researchers at the new faculties and institutes, multidisciplinary approaches, working groups, and a diversity of topics emerged.

The DUICT and the VRI have promoted scientific communication through social networks, which allows the dissemination of funding opportunities and the achievements of researchers, academics, and students. A *Sistema Descentralizado de Información y Seguimiento a la Investigación* (SIDISI, Decentralized Research Monitoring and Information System) was created to systematize and manage research at the UPCH. Currently, the university has an advanced version of the system called SIDISI 3.0. This tool has incorporated the concept of research management, which differs from previous versions that only emphasized projects recording and tracking. This new development includes useful processes and workflows to promote academic and multidisciplinary research of high complexity.

The UPCH established and still maintains a series of stimuli for researchers that include:

1. Awards for best postgraduate research in the health sciences, in coordination with the Hipólito Unanue Foundation
2. Monetary incentives for academics through research grants that are managed by the university
3. Publication of best articles in the medical journal *Revista Médica Herediana*, the official medical journal of the UPCH that is included in several bibliographic databases
4. Annual research project competition for students

Moreover, according to Guerra and Varela (2011), there is since 2003 additional funding to support research. The university has the following programs:

1. Fellowship for Returning Researchers: It is used to maintain economically Peruvian researchers who return to the country with PhD degrees. This scholarship initiative is open every two years in order to initiate or to promote research in a field that is relevant for faculties and institutes. Researchers are chosen based on their academic portfolios and potential and work exclusively on research.
2. Support Fund for the Researcher and Academic: This is another program funded by the VRI that, since 2004, has supported teaching of several academics and researchers. Both modalities have been successful in number of publications and funding for research mainly from foreign sources. In this respect, the Faculty of Sciences and Philosophy has also a research fund financed by the Cobián Foundation, which is similar to the Fellowship for Returning Researchers and is granted for one-year periods. Between 2009 and 2010, 29 external researchers joined the UPCH in the three existing categories, that is, research assistant professors, research associate professors, and research professors.
3. UPCH Competitive Funds: These funds are directed to fund research projects for professors and students, benefitting 61 and 26, respectively.

Moreover, the UPCH participates and has implemented several activities where researchers can get involved and build networks within the scientific community. Some of them are listed here:

1. Scientific Conferences: They are performed biennially in order to present research progress reports and the work of investigations to the university community and scientific institutions.
2. The Annual Researchers' Conference: This is another event that brings UPCH researchers together. In its latest versions, the conference has promoted the dialogue among academia, businesses, and government. It seeks to provide an effective interaction and to collaborate in the generation of knowledge for national development, either by public policies or by technological transfer (Guerra and Varela 2011).
3. Technological Transfer Office: The Innovation, Management and Technological Transfer Area was created in 2007 and later became the Technological Transfer and Intellectual Property Office of the DUICT. This office plays a central role in the transfer of knowledge to the society in an orderly manner and ensures the protection of UPCH professors, researchers, and students' copyright.
4. Peruvian Academic Network: This network was created in 2003 with the goal of promoting scientific and technological research. The initiative seeks to build and manage a transportation, service, and information systems network based on advanced communication technologies to interconnect all regions in Peru. In this way, it is also integrated to the institutions of education or research in a high-performance advanced network to enhance the research work. This network consists of five Peruvian universities, leaders in science and technology, which have come together to form a Research, Development and Innovation Network with the purpose of developing enterprise technological innovation, bringing together unions, companies, the government, and international partners.
5. Peruvian Network of Universities: Created in 2007 with 13 universities, its aim is to promote scientific research.

In other words, the creation of VRI allowed the UPCH to pursue an academic goal by implementing research policy and defining strategies to stimulate and support the production of scientific knowledge and to publish it. This decisions and initiatives help to generate scientific and technological knowledge to turn the UPCH into one of the leading universities in Peru.

Discussion

As noted by several authors (Burga 2005; Guerra 2006; Zegarra 2005), scientific research and production of basic and applied knowledge in Peru has been very limited. The absence of a direct and effective public policy to encourage and support the production of scientific knowledge through research, through various government agencies and private institutions that could guide this process, is evident.

Likewise, the National Accord on Development Priority Policies (2014) in its Article 20 states:

> Strengthening the country's capacity to generate and use scientific and technological knowledge, to develop human resources and improve the management of natural resources and the competitiveness of enterprises. Similarly, it is committed to increase the research and the control of the achieved results, evaluating them properly and promptly. We also commit to allocate more financial resources through public competitive merits leading to the selection of the best researchers and projects as well as to protect intellectual property.

This policy is a priority. However, it is not being continuously implemented by the different Peruvian governments. With this objective, the government will: (a) allocate greater resources, apply tax rules, and promote other funding options for human capital formation, scientific research, and the improvement of research infrastructure and technological innovation; (b) establish mechanisms to raise the level of scientific research and technological development of universities, research institutes, and enterprises; (c) provide funding to train highly qualified human resources in the most promising productive sectors to the national economy; (d) develop national and regional programs with productive, social, and environmental impact; and (e) promote in the entire population, particularly the youth, creativity, research methodology, critical and logical reasoning, and love for nature and society through the media (National Agreement 2014).

Various public and private institutions as well as representatives of the civil society coincide in the need of making agreements to ensure stable development lines, in order to give continuity to government policies and programs. However, policies have not been adequately implemented and resources have not been allocated to support science and technology development to reach a competitive level.

With the exception of a few private and public universities, most private universities have focused on teaching and lack research programs and funding. The result is a modest scientific production. In addition, CONCYTEC has not promoted enough research work to generate substantial contributions to science and technology. It has only supported some fields with grants for a small group of research projects. There is a link in public policies in terms of education and science and technology. It results in lack of adequate financial resources for agencies like the CONCYTEC, which is responsible for promoting, encouraging, and financing research and training new generations of researchers. This situation is even more critical for private universities that receive less funding for research than their public counterparts (CONCYTEC 2013).

The UPCH, as an exception to the mainstream in Peru, has emphasized research from its inception in 1961 by creating a DSR. However, major changes occurred around 1999 when there was even a greater support for research with the creation of the VRI. In this sense, the university established a number of awards and incentives for academics and students, especially graduate ones, to engage in research. It sought to promote the publication of their work with annual research contests for students, which creates a climate of searching for new knowledge and strengthens research work. Thus, it is important to note that the achievements of the UPCH have been due to the combination of two main factors: (a) The definition of an academic policy that promoted research as a core activity and creating management structures like the VRI and assuming that the reason of a university is the production of knowledge through scientific research; and (b) the implementation of specific budgetary strategies to encourage scientific research with institutional and external funding and promoting multidisciplinary and international projects. Without specific research funds, an institution cannot do research and the UPCH has become a model of funding allocation and funding search nationally and internationally.

Compared to other private universities in Peru, the UPCH obtains greater financial support from foreign and private institutions, which places it as the first Peruvian university regarding scientific production, according SCImago (SIR 2011, 2012). This funding improvement is also observed specifically when the administrative costs that burden the university to the fund obtained for a research is very low, facilitating the goals of specific research. These policies are consistent with the proposal made by the ANR (2013). Moreover, the UPCH uses those funds not only to equip laboratories and improve library resources, but also to significantly increase researchers' grants, so they can spend with confidence to the task of knowledge production.

These policies and key strategies for intellectual production have been achieved in the context of a flow of interactions between various administrative levels and the professors who conduct research projects. There are commissions involved in deliberations with the University Council and the University Assembly. These events did not happen in isolation from the concerns of academic leaders from other institutions. The ANR (2013) has recommended encouraging other universities to create structures and processes to facilitate research. This assembly promoted the creation of VRIs in Peruvian universities, in order to assume "the task of making the university community to participate in the activity of creating new knowledge, and to promote, encourage, manage, coordinate, support and broadcast the efforts and results of research carried out at university" (p. 11). This statement of the ANR, however, requires a practical and concrete implementation of policies to stimulate research, awards for the best research thesis, supporting projects, publishing research, and training professors in research design and execution, among many other aspects. This has only been implemented and strengthened since 2012 when there was a significant change in the direction of the research-related agencies in the ANR.

In short, the key to success of the university has been to align the private endeavor with the essence of the university, that is, the generation of scientific knowledge through research. This alignment will impact the country positively by increasing its international competitiveness and improving its productive structure to solve the most pressing problems with human resources and more efficient and relevant technology. The UPCH is a good example of how scientific knowledge generation is possible when there are appropriate policies and resources.

Universities have the challenge to define policies. Implementing policies involves specific agreements between the different actors of a society who demand professional services produced by university. In all cases, research must be a primary endeavor for every academic manager who aspires that the university stand out and have a presence in the national and international stage. Without research, we insist, there is no production of knowledge, and without it, society loses the competitiveness that today's world requires for survival, growth, and development.

References

Abello, Raimundo, Javier Páez, and Claudia Dacunha. 2001. "¿Son la Ciencia y Tecnología un Instrumento de Desarrollo? Un Análisis de Caso para América Latina" ("Are Science and Technology an Instrument for Development? A Case Analysis for Latin America"). *Investigación y Desarrollo* [*Research and Development*] 9 (Julio): 382–397.

Acuerdo Nacional (National Agreement). 2014. *Políticas de Estado* (State Policies). Lima, Peru: Government of Peru, Office of the First Minister.

ANR. 2012b. *Panorama de la Investigación en la Universidad Peruana* (Research Panorama in the Peruvian University). Lima, Peru: General Research Office, ANR.

———. 2013. *Propuestas para la Creación de Vicerrectorados de Investigación* (Proposals for the Creation of Research Vice-Rectorships). Lima, Peru: General Research Office, ANR.

Asamblea Nacional de Rectores (ANR: National Assembly of Rectors). 2012a. *Censo Nacional Universitario* (National University Census). Lima, Peru: ANR.

Ávalos Jayme. 2006. *Ciencia y Tecnología en el Perú* (Science and Technology in Peru). Lima, Peru: National Council for Science and Technology (CONCYTEC: Consejo Nacional de Ciencia, Tecnología y de Innovación Tecnológica). Available online at: http://www.upch.edu.pe/Tropicales/ti /TICS2006/PRESENTACIONES/jaimeavalos.ppt, accessed on January 15, 2014.

Basadre, Jorge. 1968. *Historia de la República del Perú: 1822–1933* (History of the Republic of Peru: 1822–1933). Lima, Peru: Universitaria.

Burga, Manuel. 2005. "¿Nueva Reforma Universitaria o Nuevo Modelo de Universidad? Universidad Pública: Financiamiento, Calidad y Gobierno Eficiente" ("New University Reform or New University Model? Public University: Financing, Quality, and Efficient Government"). In *Temas de Reflexión en Torno a la Universidad Peruana: Vol. 10. Documentos de Trabajo* (Topics for Reflection about the Peruvian University), edited by Manuel Burga, Oswaldo Zegarra, and Salomón Lerner. Lima, Peru: Commission for the Coordination of University Reform.

CONCYTEC. 2013. *Presupuesto Institucional Anual* (Annual Institutional Budget). Lima, Peru: CONCYTEC.

Cuevas, Raúl, María Mestanza, and Ana García. 2002. *Indicadores Bibliométricos de la Producción Científica Peruana en el Año 2002* (Bibliometric Indicators of Peruvian Scientific Production in 2002). Available online at: https:// espanol.groups.yahoo.com/neo/groups/RMCP-org/conversations/topics/8469, accessed on March 13, 2013.

De La Vega, Iván. 2009. *Módulo de Capacitación para la Recolección y el Análisis de Indicadores de Investigación y Desarrollo* (Training Module for Collection and Analysis of Research and Development Indicators). Washington, DC: Inter-American Development Bank.

Guerra, Humberto, and Luis Varela. 2011. *La Investigación y el Aporte al Conocimiento. Universidad Peruana Cayetano Heredia: 50 años* (Research and Contribution to Knowledge: Cayetano Heredia Peruvian University: 50 Years). Lima, Peru: Centro Editorial UPCH.

Guerra, Roger. 2006. *50 años de las Universidades Peruanas* (50 Years of Peruvian Universities). Lima, Peru: National Academy of Medicine.

López Soria, Jose Ignacio. 2004. "La Acreditación Universitaria en el Perú" ("University Accreditation in Peru"). *Revista Iberoamericana de Educación* (Iberic-American Journal of Education) (35): 113–132.

Maguiña, Ciro. 2013. "¿Por qué Investigar en el Perú?" ("Why to do Research in Peru?"). *Revista del Cuerpo Médico del Hospital Nacional Almanzor Aguinaga Asenjo* (Medical Journal of the Almanzor Aguinaga Asenjo National Hospital) 6 (3): 6–8.

Moreno-Brid, Juan Carlos, and Pablo Ruiz-Nápoles. 2009. *La Educación Superior y el Desarrollo Económico en América Latina* (Higher Education and Economic Development in Latin America). México City, Mexico: ECLALC.

Ongaro, Andrés. 2002. *La Legislación sobre Educación Superior en el Perú: Antecedentes, Evolución y Tendencias* (Higher Education Legislation in Peru: Antecedents, Evolution, and Trends). Lima, Peru: Cartolan.

Piscoya, Luis. 2007. *Ranking Universitario en el Perú* (University Ranking in Peru). Lima, Peru: Asamblea Nacional de Rectores.

Quispe, Luis. 2012. *El Uso de Indicadores Bibliométricos en la PUCP* (Use of Bibliometric Indicators at the PUCP). Lima, Peru: Pontifical Catholic University of Peru.

Santa, Samaly, and Víctor Herrero. 2010. "Producción Científica de América Latina y el Caribe: Una Aproximación A través de los Datos de Scopus (1996–2007)" ("Scientific Production in Latin America and the Caribbean: Analysis through Scopus Data (1996–2007)"). *Revista Interamericana de Bibliotecología* (Inter-American Journal of Library Science) (33): 379–400.

SCImago Research Group 2011. *SCImago Institution Rankings. SIR Iber 2011*. Madrid, Spain: SCImago Group. Available online at: http://www.scimagoir.com/pdf/iber/SIR%20Iber%202011%20HE.pdf, accessed on November 20, 2013.

———. 2012. *SCImago Institution Rankings. SIR Iber 2012*. Madrid, Spain: SCImago Group. Available online at: http://www.scimagoir.com/pdf/iber/SIR%20Iber%202012%20HE.pdf, accessed on November 20, 2013.

Sota, Javier. 2002. *Diagnóstico de la Universidad Peruana: Razones para una Nueva Reforma Universitaria. Comisión Nacional por la Segunda Reforma Universitaria* (Diagnostics of the Peruvian University: Reasons for a New University Reform. National Commission for a Second University Reform). Lima, Peru: Congress of the Nation.

Trujillo, Elvira, Modesta Jiménez, and Ángel Rivera. 2010. "Sociedad del Conocimiento y Universidad Pública" ("Knowledge Society and Public University"). *Pampedia* 6: 43–54.

Tünnermann, Carlos. 2008. *Noventa Años de la Reforma Universitaria de Córdoba: 1918–2008* (Ninety Years after the University of Cordoba Reform: 1918–2008) (1st edition). Buenos Aires, Argentina: Latin American Council of Social Sciences.

Tünnermann, Carlos, and Marilena de Souza. 2003. *Desafíos de la Universidad en la Sociedad del Conocimiento. Cinco Años Después de la Conferencia Mundial Sobre Educación Superior* (University Challenges in the Knowledge Society. Five Years after the World Conference on Higher Education). Paris, France: UNESCO.

UNESCO. 1998. *La Educación Superior en el Siglo XXI. Conferencia Mundial sobre la Educación Superior* (Higher Education in the Twenty-First Century. World Conference on Higher Education). París, France: UNESCO.

———. 2003. *Contribución de la UNESCO a la Cumbre Mundial sobre la Sociedad de la Información. Consejo Ejecutivo 166° Reunión* (UNESCO Contribution to the World Summit on the Information Society. 166th Meeting of the Executive Board). París, France: UNESCO.

World Bank. 1999. *El Conocimiento al Servicio del Desarrollo* (Knowledge for Development). Washington, DC: The World Bank.

———. 2014. *Gasto en Investigación y Desarrollo* (Expenditure on Research and Development). Washington, DC: The World Bank. Available online at: http://datos.bancomundial.org/indicador/gb.xpd.rsdv.gd.zs.

Zegarra, Oswaldo. 2005. "La Investigación Científica y la Universidad" ("Scientific Research and University"). In *Temas de Reflexión en Torno a la Universidad Peruana: Vol. 10. Documentos de Trabajo* (Topics for Reflection around the Peruvian University: Volume 10. Work Documents), edited by Manuel Burga, Oswaldo Zegarra, and Salomón Lerner. Lima, Peru: Commission for Coordination of University Reform.

Chapter 11

Research and Incentives
The Case of Two Private Universities in Argentina
Marcelo Rabossi

Introduction

Over the past decades, research-driven universities have been positioning themselves as central players of an economy that has proven to be increasingly dependent on the creation and dissemination of knowledge for the advancement of human progress. Those institutions frequently receive high rankings and boast their prestige (Salmi 2009). Thus, in higher education research has become a critical function that impacts not only society, but also the institutions that carry it out.

Even though there are several research universities in Latin America that have proven to be competitive, this type of institution is largely relegated to the developed world. Latin America has shown different levels of productivity, since not all its countries have managed to redirect its universities from teaching to the production of findings.[1] Insufficient funding, lack of a critical mass of well-trained researchers, divergent priorities, or simply the indifference of governments explain why some universities are not performing significant research. On the other hand, it is also true that not all universities can be expected to produce research with an economic impact. In the United States, for example, no more than 5 percent of all universities produce economically relevant discoveries; this is happening in a context of global "elite institutions." The same occurs in Great Britain, where only around 20 institutions conduct cutting-edge research (Altbach 2007). Building world-class universities is not easy task, as it involves copious resources. In 1998, the "985 project" entailed the allocation of a vast amount of funds to create elite institutions in China. Similar programs in Asia and Europe, like the 2002 Center of Excellence in Japan, confirm that creating competitive research institutions is reserved for a handful of countries and that only a selected minority of universities will benefit from such policies (Shin 2009). This is a real fact that must be taken into consideration when policymakers seek ways to transform their institutions.

In the Latin America context, pursuing external funding to cultivate research is one of the problems many private universities must face. Most of public research funds tend to go directly to public universities, since they have better facilities and human resources to perform relevant research (Gregorutti 2012). In this way, private higher education is forced to exhaust its creativity in order to attract even a portion of the available funding, thereby making the task more complicated. In these circumstances, few institutions dare face the challenge of becoming research oriented.

Purpose of the Study

Considering that most of the research discoveries occur in public universities that receive government funding, this chapter analyzes how some private universities in Argentina organize their administration and resources in order to produce knowledge. Specifically, two private Argentine universities are examined to identify the primary mechanisms employed to generate the "correct" incentive to stimulate their faculty body to perform research. To that end, the new institutional economic (NIE) theory has been selected as the framework in which we explore the internal labor market of these two universities.[2] The NIE is an unorthodox economic frame that helps to answer questions such as: What are organizations and why do they differ? This theoretical approach is designed to explain organizations and human behavior from an economic perspective (Alchian and Demsetz 1972; Williamson 1996) and, more precisely, to shed light on which mechanisms these universities brought to bear in order to select their best human resources, that is, the potentially most productive candidates.

The NIE helps show how universities address selection problems and what incentive mechanisms they develop to animate less motivated workers, by proposing a model in which the traditional economic analysis is complemented by ideas and concepts drawn from organizational theory and the analysis of law. This study wants to know how these two institutions deal with what the NIE calls "agency costs" (Alchian and Demsetz 1972; Eisenhardt 1989; Jensen and Meckling 1976). These costs can be seen as implicit financial burdens borne as a result of adverse selection (i.e., when employers misjudge good or bad candidates due to informational asymmetries) and moral hazard situations (i.e., when employees underperform due to high performance assessment costs). These organizational anomalies impede institutions from reaching their capacity, in this case, the research potential of two private universities.

In addition to the NIE approach, this chapter studies the tacit rules that condition human interaction and relationships, such as the level of satisfaction and recognition among researchers. These rules are an element essential to unveiling the organizational climate that fosters cooperation among employees. They also represent mechanisms that enable the alignment of personal and organizational needs in order to increase research outputs at these two institutions. This sociological approach complements the economic vision described earlier.

The first section of this chapter recounts a period of history in the higher education of Argentina and the general environment where the two universities in question produce their research. The second part describes the theoretical framework that is used to interpret the findings. The third section introduces the two cases and the methodology that is followed to carry out this study. The fourth section presents the main results of this research. Section five compares the two cases. Conclusions close the study.

University and Market for Research in Argentina

In an environment unfavorable for private alternatives, the first nonpublic university in Argentina opened its doors in the late 1950s. After 140 years of the public university's reign as the only type of higher education institution in the country, the Catholic University of Buenos Aires was founded in 1958 (del Bello, Barsky and Giménez 2007).[3] By the early 1970s, private universities accounted for almost 18 percent of university enrollment in the country (Levy 1986). However, from the mid-1970s to the late 1980s, the national government was especially opposed to new private institutions, even though some private proposals were actively seeking authorization to operate as legally recognized universities.

Throughout the 1990s, the government promoted policies that support all kinds of private investments in tertiary education. In fact, during the first half of that decade, 23 new institutions entered the market, diversifying a system dominated by the public university. After a 16-year period that saw no new private institutions enter the market, this decade witnessed the emergence of several new universities touting research as their new mission,[4] one of which forms part of this study. However, since university accreditation requires the production or increased production of outputs to legitimize an institution's presence, they began to allot more room for research projects.[5] The second university studied here, a traditionally teaching-oriented institution, fits within this latter paradigm.

Nowadays, there are 60 private universities and they have managed to outpace their 55 public counterparts; however, public institutions still keep the lead in student enrollment. In 2010, from a total of 1,718,507 students, 79.5 percent attended public universities—a figure not too far from what was happening in the 1970s (Rabossi 2012).

Let us put Argentina in geographical perspective. The number of faculty members in Latin America has been growing steadily since the end of World War II. Between 1950 and 1990, the academic market grew from 25,000 to more than 600,000 docents. As was to be expected, this phenomenal increase entailed greater heterogeneity in academic profiles, which in turn led to a sort of job stratification. In the case of Argentina, approximately 16,000 faculty members belong to private universities, which is to say 12 percent of the Argentine higher education system (del Bello, Barsky, and Giménez 2007). According to Marquis (2002), as many as 90 percent of professors in the country hold part-time contracts. Thus, universities face strong limitations in their attempt to reach a critical mass of professors who would be able to conduct significant research. Due to this situation, it is likely that no more than 10 percent of all faculty members have the time and resources to publish in international peer-reviewed journals and books (Brunner 1995).

Even though private institutions can now compete for public research funds, most of the government budget is channeled directly to public universities and research-intensive institutions. The National Commission for Atomic Energy, the National Institute for Agricultural Technology, the National Council for Science and Research, and the National Institute for Industrial Technology are all public centers in charge of vast research programs and exist for the most part independent of universities. In addition to this, some productive private research institutes, such as the Leloir Institute Foundation, the Center for the Study of the State and Society, and the Foundation for Latin American Economic Research[6] are also independent of private universities. This trend is a natural consequence of a traditional division between training and research, not only in Argentina but also across Latin America. The first one, teaching, has been conceived as a dominant university task while top-quality research is mainly carried out outside universities.

To put things into perspective, in 2011 almost 44 percent of all funds invested in research and development (R&D) went to public research centers, whereas public universities invested 27 percent and private universities only 1.5 percent. The rest was invested by private enterprises and non-for-profit private centers (Ministry of Science, Technology, and Productive Innovation 2011). Moreover, between 2003 and 2009, public research centers and universities received larger public research funding, which had a negative impact on the private sector. For every Argentine peso public institutions received for R&D in 2003, only seven cents reached private universities. This difference was even larger in 2009 (six cents on the peso). However, both sectors increased the amount of funds they received during the same period. In terms of gross domestic product, total public spending in R&D grew from 0.46 percent (2003) to 0.67 percent (2009) (National Agency for Scientific and technological Promotion [ANPCYT: *Agencia Nacional de Promoción Científica y Tecnológica*] 2011).

To understand research activities at private universities in Argentina, it may be helpful to assess the number of scholars at each sector. For instance, for approximately ten researchers working in the public institution, there is only one in the private university (ANPCYT 2011). It is evident that R&D is mainly relegated to the public domain. Additionally, the amount of time that researchers devote to their scholarly work can be another indicator of public-private research imbalances. By adjusting the number of scholars according to full-time-equivalent contracts, one can measure the real time dedicated to research. This is relevant since full-time faculty members enjoy more time to conduct research than professors holding part-time contracts. For instance, in 2003, for each hour private university researchers invested in R&D, professors at public institutions allocated 15 hours. This situation did not substantially change in 2009 (1:14). However, between 2005 and 2009 the number of hours devoted to research increased 30 percent overall, that is, 41 percent in private institutions and 31 percent among public universities (ANPCYT 2011).

Regarding fields of specialization, a clear differentiation is visible between the two types of universities. Although social sciences prevail in both, the private devote almost half of its research to this field of study, while its public counterpart invests only a quarter of its resources to this area. Public universities allocate 24 percent of their human resources to math and natural sciences, disciplines that require many resources and are generally offered by public universities. The private sector invests merely 9 percent in that field (ANPCYT 2011). On the other hand, the private sector has 20 percent of faculty members in the health sciences while public universities just 13 percent. This fact comes as no surprise, considering that during the past 15 years, health disciplines have been the fastest growing programs in the private market. Almost 60 percent of new private institutions created after 1996 offered courses in health sciences (7 of 13 institutions), and five of them started as health university institutes (Rabossi 2011).

Even though private universities were historically excluded from obtaining public funding for research, since the mid-1990s—and after the creation of the ANPCYT—nonpublic tertiary institutions are now eligible for public money. Following the logic of contracts, private and public universities compete under the same rules for federal funding. However, public support for research does not actually help private institutions increase research outputs. To better understand the diminishing impact these public resources have had on the private sector, suffice it to note that, between 2008 and 2009, only 25 of the 1,264 awarded contracts went to private hands (ANPCYT 2011), which is to say, less than 2 percent of the total for institutions that enroll 20 percent of students. Undoubtedly, public funding for private research is highly underrepresented, which forces these universities to find alternative funding systems to produce knowledge.

Theoretical Approach

Agency Costs: The Economic Side

The NIE has been selected, in part, because there are a few, if any, analyses on the academic labor market that take advantage of the theoretical tools this conceptual framework offers. The NIE is an alternative model used to study and explain interorganizational and human interactions. In order to assess how organizations structure their internal activities with the aim of influencing human behavior, this study applies the NIE framework at a micro-level in order to explore the dynamics that deal with issues of governance (Eggertsson 1990).

One central issue in NIE theory (fundamental to my analysis) is agency costs. If the organization faces contradicting objectives between the principal (the employer) and the agent (employee), along with informational asymmetries between them, the situation may give rise to increases in the costs of monitoring the agent's performance and two common anomalies, or agency costs, namely: adverse selection situations and moral hazard risks. An adverse selection situation is a precontractual fact. From Akerlof's

(1970) theoretical explanation, the problem of adverse selection always entails an inefficiency of market allocation. It is a condition in which organizations are forced to think that all applicants are average. Due to information asymmetries, the employer (university) will be unable to distinguish between a good and a bad candidate (professor's future research productivity). This anomaly may lead to the selection of a poor candidate. On the other hand, moral hazard risks are triggered when informational asymmetries are present; but, contrary to adverse selection problems, they arise in a postcontractual situation. If the interest of the employer (in this case, the university) is to differ from the wishes or preferences of the employee (professor or researcher), the latter may choose to work below his or her potential productivity, avoid responsibilities, or even seek personal benefit, adverse to the well-being of the organization. Due to high monitoring cost or difficulties in assessing employees' actions, the organization is likely to underperform.

Since human behavior and actions are also ruled by legal agreements, labor contracts can be designed to reduce agency costs. Any written document that specifies rules and determines behaviors can be interpreted as an explicit agreement, through a contract, between the employer (in this case, the university) and the employee (faculty). As such, contracts prove to be a key mechanism for the management of human behaviors that impact the microeconomic environment of an organization (Dechenaux et al. 2011). Through contracts, parties stipulate the terms of an arrangement, either temporarily or permanently, along with the rights and conditions of the agreement.

The analysis of contracts is central to NIE theory. By analyzing the employment practices and policies of remuneration and promotion at each institution, which are usually laid out in explicit contracts (such as faculty handbooks), in order to assess how they attempt to boost faculty member research output, we see how these two private universities channel resources to reduce informational asymmetries and align the preferences of the principal (employer) with those of agents (employees). In short, these two institutions take measures to reduce their agency costs in order to increase faculty research productivity, and it is essential for us to know how.

Organizational Climate: A Sociological Complement

Implicit contracts can be described as a set of tacit rules that guide human relationships and shape the organizational climate. In this context, *climate* is defined as unspoken and assumed perceptions as well as behavior patterns that condition actions. Kilman et al. (1985) assert that institutional culture is a social energy that drives individuals to act in a specific way, and in it the challenge is to encourage people to behave according to the needs of an institution that promotes certain cultural patterns. By analyzing the cultural climate at these two universities, I aim to understand the rewards that these organizations implicitly implement to shape the behavior of a given agent (researcher) in order to align it with the needs of the principal (university). If an organization fosters a work environment that mitigates unpleasant tasks, individuals can modify their behaviors (Milgrom and Roberts 1992). In other words, through the establishment of a responsive work environment, agency costs accrued by dissatisfied workers can be reduced.

Climate, as described by Denison (1990), can be understood as features of the institutional environment that are consciously perceived by the members of the organization—individuals' perception of the implicit and/or explicit institutional rules and norms that determine employees' practices. Several studies have shown a positive correlation between certain dimensions of the organizational climate and workers' output (Bartram et al. 2002; Gordon and Di Tomaso 1992). A better working climate, with higher levels of workers' satisfaction, increases productivity. In other words, satisfaction is seen as a mediator that fosters the agent's productivity (Kopelman et al. 1990; Patterson et al. 2004). Satisfaction is also related to questions of motivation and performance (Ostroff 1992). In addition, employers can use recognition as a tool to reinforce a desired behavior or performance—an instrument and motivational factor that can take the form of monetary or nonmonetary compensation. Thus, when agents (employees) are repeatedly recognized, their behaviors are reinforced as a pattern of actions, matching the main purpose that the principal (employer) wishes to keep. Research shows that intrinsic rewards, such as nonmonetary compensation, have positive effects on professors' attitudes and bear an even greater impact than extrinsic rewards do (Frase 1989; Sergiovanni 1967). Aligned with these findings, Feistritzer (1986) reports that, for teachers, recognition for a *job well-done* ranks above other extrinsic motivators, such as their salaries, which, on the other hand, are important for retaining the best human resources (Sykes 1983).

Method and Case Studies

Here I have studied two different private universities in Argentina and compared how they have reacted to the increasing pressure to conduct research. I compared two institutions that, at the outset, had already presented different organizational features. The objective to evaluate dissimilar organizational contexts required a systematic collection of the same information among the units of analysis and the guidance of a theoretical framework to support the main findings (George and McKewon 1985; King et al. 1994). The method used for this research is the case study, as it proves useful in describing intricate events or complex phenomena (Krathwohl 1993). Also, when the focus is centered on only a small number of observations, an intentional selection must be followed, and this selection has to be aligned with the research goals (King et al. 1994). I analyzed regulatory documents and institutional and faculty bylaws. The objective was to evaluate how these two universities select their faculty members and how they promote and remunerate their researchers. I also developed a questionnaire to understand faculty members' points of view about their research activities, working conditions, and the level of satisfaction and recognition they receive for performing such activity (see the appendix). A total of eight questions were asked to faculty members, including the type of contract they held (full-time and part-time), with a Likert scale ranking for each question. A Chi-Square test for independence was used to identify the presence or absence of a relationship between variables and the type of labor agreement (full- or part-time). In other words, the purpose was to detect any significant correlation between professors' research and their labor situation and, in this way, this study is both quantitative and qualitative.

Regarding the cases, for reasons of confidentiality, I used pseudonyms for the two institutions studied, namely, Beta University (BU) and Gamma University (GU).[7] When choosing BU and GU as the private cases in the sample, I first took into account that these institutions shared some central common features. Both opened in the early 1990s. Located in city of Buenos Aires, these universities are geographically close enough for us to assume that they can recruit professors and students from a similar pool of candidates. However, to deepen the analysis, there are also some differences to ensure variation in some of the variables of this study. BU is a small institution with around 3,000 students; whereas GU is large, enrolling more than 15,000 learners. To put things in perspective, the average private institution in Argentina enrolls around 7,500 undergraduate students (*Secretariado de Políticas Universitarias* [SPU: Secretariat of University Policy] 2010). On the other hand, BU possesses a heavy concentration of graduate programs. In fact, more than half of its students are enrolled in graduate courses. This stands in stark contrast to GU, which has only 2 percent of its total enrollment at the graduate level. In this way, GU offers a better portrayal of the actual student-graduate programs ratio within universities, since in Argentina graduate students represent only 5 percent of total enrollment (SPU 2010).

Another difference is that BU can be categorized as an elite institution, belonging to the second wave, according to Levy's (1986) private development model; GU, in contrast, can be placed in the third wave or demand-absorbing institutions. The second and third waves refer to Levy's classification for the historical development of the private sector in Latin America. The second wave, the so-called Secular Elite Expansion, was the private elite's response to massive public enrollment and its attempt to reestablish itself in new exclusive institutions. The third wave, or Non-elite Private Alternatives, describes secular private development as a response to the failure of the public sector (Levy 1986). Thus, BU tends to enroll middle-upper- and upper-class students, whereas the average GU student comes from a middle-class family. Mirroring these social differences, BU tuition is almost three times more expensive than tuition at GU.

Regarding faculty members, BU has always emphasized full-time contracts and sought professors with doctoral degrees, enabling it to generate greater research outputs. This university was modeled after the US elite model[8] and requires professors to have master's and doctoral degrees—more than 90 percent of the faculty has at least a master's and a high percentage of them have earned a doctoral degree. This fact, along with policies to promote research, helps explain why knowledge production is such a high priority for BU faculty.

In the case of GU, enrollment expanded rapidly right from its beginning in the mid-1990s. A combination of affordable tuition fees and diverse curricula with market oriented programs has contributed to an increase in enrollment. These and other characteristics reveal GU as a teaching-oriented institution, like most private universities in Argentina and Latin America (Bernasconi 2007). Although certain research activity in some academic units is present, the main emphasis promotes teaching quality.

As a way of confirming the fact that BU is a more research-intensive institution than GU, I also compared research productivity of both universities. To identify and evaluate differences in the research productivity of each faculty member at both institutions, I used the Iberic-American Ranking SIR 2012. For example, during the 2005–2010 period, BU produced almost 150 peer-reviewed journal articles, while GU had less than 60. When this number is standardized and account for the number of students, the difference is even bigger. While BU generates one scholarly paper for every 22 students, GU produces only 1 for every 400.[9]

Empirical Evidence: The Cases

Selection, Promotion, and Salary Policy

Beta University

The more research-oriented of the two case studies, BU follows strict procedures during the hiring process, particularly when the university needs a candidate to fill a research position. These full-time professors dedicated to scholarly work, who represent nearly 25 percent of the faculty, are selected by each school or department and presented to the president, according to the needs and budget of each academic unit. Some of the central requirements that Faculty Counsel members take into account when hiring are a doctoral degree, potential to complete research projects, and teaching skill, although this last one is not as important as the previous two. On the other hand, there are no general or specific requirements that the university or academic units apply to meet part-time needs. Research for this group of faculty members is not a prerequisite. Experience at public and international organisms or at well-recognized enterprises is preferred for both groups.

At BU, there are two main academic tracks for full-time positions: the teaching track, in which ordinary professors are not required to produce scholarly work and they teach six courses per year; and the research track, in which professors teach three courses per year, investing the rest of their time in research and, in some cases, consultancy. Within the research track, where the rules of promotion are similar to those of the US system, faculty members remain assistant professors for seven consecutive semesters before they are assessed by the Faculty Council. At the end of the sixth year, a second evaluation is carried out and, if the candidate is successful, the council will propose a promotion to the associate professor status. Academic standards for promotion to the top of the hierarchical pyramid (full professor) are strict and demand excellence in research. The aspiring professor must have already gained international repute for his or her academic contributions.

Regarding salaries, university policy informs us that part-time professors are hired through hourly-based contracts, whereas full-time positions depend on professors' track and research productivity—a situation that generates a wide range of salaries for this group. Research productivity is evidently the dominant variable that determines salary variation from one year to the next, although academic units do follow different procedures to remunerate productivity. In other words, deans or directors use their personal criteria to measure professorial activities within the limits of university policies.

Gamma University

Deans at each academic unit are in charge of identifying candidates according to requirements. Contrary to the BU case, neither graduate education nor research publication counts as prerequisites for professors to compete for a position. Although general research activities are given consideration when an applicant is hired, internal procedures and bylaws place teaching skills front and center in the selection process. However, since GU has started to showcase investigation, the research profile of a candidate has also started to weigh in. Nonetheless, this is a small group of professors (merely 2 percent of the whole faculty body), who are not necessarily under full-time contracts.

In terms of promotion, decisions are based on competitive procedures and in accordance with preestablished rules. Although the academic degree and relevant research productivity bear certain weight on the determination of a promotion, teaching performance plays a stronger role. Even though GU salaries are based on rank, seniority, and workload, in 1999 this institution developed an incentive program to reward faculty members for teaching and research productivity each semester. This option is not mandatory, however, and professor may forgo it. In a kind of internal competition, faculty members who were more productive receive the highest rewards. All qualifying candidates are evaluated in four different areas in which institutional commitment and pedagogical issues are of primary importance. In other words, research is undervalued. This process occurs twice per year, and only the top 50 percent of the faculty body receives this extra monetary compensation. That being said, things seem to be changing. In 2013, the university offered a similar incentive to increase research productivity. Professors willing to breach this research track must present a research plan that covers a three-year span. Although requirements are not difficult to meet, in comparison to international standards (during the period, professors must present at least one paper at a seminar or conference and publish another in a peer-review journal), this policy counts as a first step toward a paradigm shift for an institution that has focused primarily on teaching.

Organizational Climate at Beta and Gamma Universities

I developed a questionnaire to capture the organizational climate (see appendix), evaluating faculty *satisfaction* and *recognition* in relation to their research activities. As for satisfaction, four questions were posed: satisfaction with the kind of research they are involved in (*kindrese*), the time to perform this activity (*timerese*), library space and quality (*library*), and satisfaction with their salary.[10] With regards to recognition, it is important to remember that they are nonmaterial inducements to acknowledge professors activities. According to Barnard (1938), nonmaterialistic rewards are of great importance to achieve cooperative behaviors. Money without distinction or recognition proves ineffective. In other words, recognition refers to any kind of extra nonmonetary reward given to faculty members. I tested four variables of recognition: first, whether faculty members felt rewarded and recognized by the research they did (*rewresea*); second, whether or not they felt supported and aided in obtaining internal and external grants (*assifund*); third, whether or not institutional efforts to provide faculty members with travel funds was adequate (*travfund*); and fourth, how they considered the existing policies for sabbatical leaves (*sabbatic*).

At BU, the instrument was applied to 140 professors representing those who teach at least one undergraduate course and have no administrative appointment. The response rates were 59 percent for full-time professors (31 professors) and 48 percent for part-timers (42 responses). At GU, the same questionnaire was handed out to all faculty members at both the Business School and the Informational Technology School. I collected 90 surveys from the latter academic unit, which represented 68 percent of their entire faculty body. A total of 30 questionnaires were completed at the Business School, which represented 24 percent of all professors.

Satisfaction at BU: table 11.1 illustrates the level of satisfaction regarding research activities at BU. It shows that some significant differences were present in terms of research activity and the type of contract under which the faculty member is working. Not surprisingly, while part-timers are dissatisfied with the time they have for research, full-time academics are very pleased. A similar pattern was found in terms of the kind of research in which they were involved (*kindrese*). In other words, they like what they do. On the other hand, while 43 percent of full-time professors manifested their dissatisfaction with library availability, only 13 percent of part-timers expressed the same response. In addition, both full- and part-timers believe that salaries are inadequate, yet dissatisfaction was partial.

When each of these four variables was tested (chi-square $p<0.05$), I found that three of them were related to the contract type (full- or part-time). An association between satisfaction and the kind of contract is present in *kindrese, timerese, and library*. One can infer that satisfaction with research activities at BU mainly depends on the kind of contractual agreement under which the professor was hired. Thus, I reject the null

Table 11.1 BU: faculty body satisfaction with research activities according to type of contract in percentage of responses

Variable	Very satisfied		Somewhat satisfied		Neither satisfied nor dissatisfied		Somewhat dissatisfied		Very dissatisfied	
Contract	Full	Part	Full	Part	Full	Part	Full	Part	Full	Part
Kindrese*	72	0	20	43	4	57	0	0	4	0
Timerese*	64	11	24	11	4	0	4	67	4	11
Library*	4	43	46	30	8	15	35	13	8	0
Salary	11	5	37	33	26	30	11	23	15	10

*There is an association between satisfaction and the full- or part-time status of faculty members at p<0.05.

Table 11.2 GU: satisfaction with research activities to the faculty body according to type of contract in percentage of responses

Variable	Very satisfied		Somewhat satisfied		Neither satisfied nor dissatisfied		Somewhat dissatisfied		Very dissatisfied	
Contract	Full	Part	Full	Part	Full	Part	Full	Part	Full	Part
Kindrese	17	24	67	36	0	27	17	9	0	3
Timerese	14	12	14	24	43	36	0	12	29	15
Library	33	23	33	29	17	26	17	17	0	6

hypothesis that states that both variables are independent. Only salary was not statistically significant.

Satisfaction at GU: table 11.2 shows the level of satisfaction at GU. To detect differences in satisfaction between faculty members, the three variables were crossed with the two types of contracts (full- or part-time). There were some differences. Full-timers were more satisfied with the kind of research in which they were involved than part-timers were, but they were also more dissatisfied regarding the time they have for research (29 percent of full-timers and 15 percent of part-time professors were very dissatisfied with the time available for research). Although not extremely considerable, percentages show that full-timers felt more satisfied regarding library availability than their counterparts. In comparison to BU, here professors are less satisfied in terms of the kind of research in which they are involved and the time they invest in this activity. Also, the difference in terms of general satisfaction between full- and part-timers at GU is less evident than it is at BU.

When the three variables were tested, no significant (chi-square $p<0.05$) relationship between the level of satisfaction and the part-time and full-time status of faculty members was found for this sample. In other words, the null hypothesis was true, which means that the type of contract and the level of satisfaction with the research job were not significantly correlated for the sample at GU.

Recognition at BU: table 11.3 presents how BU faculty members felt recognized for their research involvement.

There were some differences between full- and part-time professors. Results reflected the logic of an organization that honors full-timers over part-timers, particularly when a research reward is at stake. In this sense, 64 percent of full-time professors felt recognized in comparison to 22 percent of their counterparts (*rewresea*). This comes as no surprise, given that research is generally a full-time activity. In this sense, there is a "natural" or systemic discrimination against part-timers. This differentiation is high in the dimension of institutional effort for funding travel and sabbatical policies (*travfund*; *sabbatic*). For example, 41 percent of full-time scholars strongly or somewhat agree with what funding they receive to travel to present papers while only 4 percent of part-timers share that sentiment. Again, full-timers felt more recognized than part-time professors.

When I tested the four variables (Chi-square $p<0.05$), two of them yielded a significant association with the type of contract. Both related to the institutional effort category of research recognition (*travfund*; *sabbatic*). The other two variables (*assifund*; *rewresea*) were not significantly correlated to the full- or part-time status of faculty members. It can, thus,

Table 11.3 BU: recognition of faculty body research activities according to type of contract in percentage of responses

Variable	Strongly agree		Somewhat agree		Neither agree nor disagree		Somewhat disagree		Strongly disagree	
Contract	Full	Part	Full	Part	Full	Part	Full	Part	Full	Part
Assifund	4	0	24	33	24	44	24	11	24	11
Rewresea	24	0	40	22	16	33	12	33	8	11
Travfund*	22	0	19	4	37	33	0	4	22	59
Sabbatic*	33	0	48	16	15	53	0	5	4	26

*There is an association between satisfaction and the full- or part-time status of faculty members at $p<0.05$.

Table 11.4 GU: recognition of faculty body research activities according to type of contract in percentage of responses

Variable	Strongly agree		Somewhat agree		Neither agree nor disagree		Somewhat disagree		Strongly disagree	
Contract	Full	Part	Full	Part	Full	Part	Full	Part	Full	Part
Assifund	29	24	29	12	29	33	14	21	0	9

be inferred that only the explicit institutional effort (money and extra time) to recognize research activities was related to the type of contract.

Recognition at GU: table 11.4 presents the results for GU. Only *assifund* was tested, since the institution did not allow me to ask the other three questions.

Again I found similar differences according to the type of contract (full- vs. part-time). Full time professors felt that they received better assistance to obtain internal and external grants to carry out research (*assifund*). However, after testing the variable (Chi-Square $p<0.05$), there was no significant relationship between the level of satisfaction in terms of research funding, and their appointment status (part- or full-time). The null hypothesis was accepted. There was no association between the type of contract under which faculty members are working and the variable under analysis (*assifund*).

Comparative Approach to the Main Findings

The National Commission for University Evaluation and Accreditation (CONEAU: *Comisión Nacional de Evaluación y Acreditación Universitaria*)[11] has highlighted research as a central activity for university quality and, at the same time, maintained that the rate of productivity in the nonpublic sector has been insufficient. This accrediting agency has been functioning as an exogenous force that pushes universities to increase its research activities. However, there are also some internal factors that lead institutions to organize their efforts so that they produce more research-oriented outputs. At the micro level, each institution's board of trustees plays an even more important role than the CONEAU in defining the type of university it wanted to create at its foundation, but also throughout governance activities. From the very beginning, given the presence of distinctive missions, one can infer that research-producing incentives wielded varying degrees of power between these two institutions. For example, the research profile of the board at BU was decisive in the definition of its mission: research as a fundamental objective was determined from its inception. On the other hand, with a board more concerned with teaching than research activities, the production of new academic knowledge at GU does not find the most fertile ground. In short, the mission of the university (be it research- or teaching-oriented) ends up defining organizational practices. Thus, when the time comes to hire new faculty members, promote them, and pay for academic work, each university follows its own mission pattern.

In order to understand how each institution's faculty research productivity evolved, I compare several dimensions of their strategies. The first, for example, is the way that they each select new professors. When both universities have tenure track openings (mainly full-time positions), they showed sophisticated procedures for hiring the most potentially productive candidates, be it for teaching or for research. In both cases, practices were carefully described through well-written bylaws, a committee assesses candidates, and open competition is generally promoted. However, certain differences arise between these universities, since they are responding to their own specific academic needs. For example, BU has prioritized research leading full-time professors to be hired based largely on their potential to conduct this kind of academic work. On the other hand, GU is a teaching-oriented institution and, as such, teaching skills are highly regarded, while research potential does not make a candidate more competitive, which helps explain why full-time professors are highly underrepresented.

Within this context, to reduce situations of adverse selection, BU uses signaling mechanisms.[12] For this institution publications and a doctoral degree, particularly from a US institution, are highly important for a tenure track position. In the case of GU, the use of screening methods to reduce adverse selection is a common practice.[13] This procedure follows the logic of an institution that considers teaching skills at the core of a professor's excellence. The data also showed that a large percentage of GU professors did not have real chances of receiving tenure. In other words, faculty members may stay as nontenured for a long time, working under renewable short-term contracts. This limits the development of faculty members who can devote time to scholarly work.

The remuneration system in both cases presented relevant disparities. The central role of research at BU heavily determines how that university remunerates scholars. Thus, salary becomes an important explicit variable that the university uses to increase research outputs. In this more competitive context, moral hazard situations in the production of research output are mainly mitigated through monetary compensations. On the other hand, the salary scheme at GU follows different logic. Both tenure and nontenured professors are paid according to what Hansen (1988) describes as an equal percentage increase, plus a small portion of the total salary designed to reward merit. Given the emphasis on training people for the labor market, the institution especially rewards teaching skills. In other words, faculty research productivity is practically absent when the time comes to decide who receives extra pay. In addition, salaries at GU tend to be set according to seniority, avoiding problems of fairness. However, GU is trying to change its teaching-oriented profile, by making available monetary incentives for professors who voluntarily decide to increase their research productivity. Research goals are clearly set beforehand, and faculty members who attain them (i.e., two or more publications over the past three years, paper presentation in conferences, etc.) receive a bonus. Although not as competitive as in the BU case, this institution is trying to decrease moral hazard situations in the production of research by offering monetary incentives, whether or not one ventures into the research track to compete for this extra money is a decision to be made by the faculty.

Regarding organizational climate as a function that impacts faculty research productivity, two aspects of satisfaction were studied: the extrinsic (pay and job security) and the intrinsic (learning and using working skills). Although both have real effects on overall satisfaction, extrinsic satisfaction is perceived to have a stronger impact on satisfaction of semiskilled workers, whereas intrinsic satisfaction has a greater influence over skilled employees (Blauner 1964; Gruenberg 1980). In this way, professors at BU appear to be driven by intrinsic motivations, since they are trained to produce complex research reports that demand highly developed skills. On the other hand, the GU case showed a large proportion of part-time professor with hardly any time to get involved in research activity. In addition to this, more than 65 percent of the entire faculty body has an undergraduate education, and less than 10 percent has received doctoral training. Within this context, I find no clear intrinsic motivators within this group of professors to produce relevant research work. Extrinsic motivators, such as pay increases, must be in place at GU to boost faculty research productivity.

Although both faculty groups showed high levels of satisfaction with their current research studies, at BU this was more closely associated with the type of contract they held. As shown in table 11.1, full-time professors were more satisfied with the type of research they conducted than part-time employees. In the case of GU, job appointment did not show significant differences. This is probably a natural result of its not taking research outputs as a central variable to assess professional activities. In fact, part-time professors and also some full-timers arrive to teach a class and then they leave the institution; they don't have personal offices to meet with students or conduct projects. Therefore, and beyond the type of contract, it is not surprising to find some degree of dissatisfaction among those who conduct research at GU.

When it comes to recognition of faculty research productivity, I must first highlight that many studies show professors to perceive that universities undervalue their teaching engagement in relation to research involvement (de Rome et al. 1985; Gregorutti 2010; Halsey and Trow 1971; Young 2006). However, at neither institution was there strong tension in terms of recognizing teaching over research, and vice versa. This is an interesting finding that puts in question the general assumption that professors prioritize research over instruction, and it may show that private universities seek ways to carry out teaching and research as much as possible. Sometimes research is seen as the only activity to produce knowledge and teaching, as the vehicle to transmit it. Their interrelationship is virtually nonexistent. However, according to Griffiths (2004), research can be teaching-oriented and the opposite is also true: teaching can be research-based. In this sense, universities should develop their curricula around inquiry-based activities, rather than on the simple acquisition of preestablished knowledge, no matter how much this decision may undermine the elite group of highly productive professors who consider teaching a second-tier activity.

Conclusions

Since the creation of CONEAU, private universities have been compelled to improve their research performance. In the case studies, CONEAU operated as an extrinsic motivator, especially for GU, a teaching-oriented university. GU represents core values related to training students for the labor market. The organizational model and teaching style have been imported from secondary education and, with a few exceptions, its faculty members have not been trained to carry out research. Also, given its larger number of students, one may assume that GU has more available internal funding to conduct research than BU,[14] but research productivity remains higher at this latter institution. On the other hand, BU followed the research tradition that was at the heart of its founders. Given that professors are mainly selected based on their findings, it is not surprising to see that the goal of producing relevant research was determined well before the creation of CONEAU.

In sum, the CONEAU has played a more decisive role at GU than at BU, redefining part of the founding objectives of this institution. The evaluation and accreditation agency has clearly operated as an extrinsic motivator, but more importantly, beyond CONEAU we can infer that certain intrinsic incentives inside GU have also contributed to its revamped mission. The intergenerational change taking place on the GU board, where some teaching-oriented members have been replaced by younger trustees who are more prone to developing research activities, may well be giving this institution its new profile. Extrinsic and intrinsic factors are reshaping GU and producing new dynamics in this university. Research, although still incipient, is becoming an added value and is finding its way into a predominantly teaching-oriented entity. Internal rewards, other than a political or accreditation pressure, or the lack of public funding, appeared as a necessary condition to define a stronger research agenda for these two private universities. Thus, these two cases show how both external and internal pressures can impact university missions, although decisions surging from inside the institution appear to be more effective.

A last comment that I find fundamental if the objective is to boost research productivity, not only in the private sector but in the public as well, is the academic training of faculty members. Although there is no reliable data for private universities, less than 9 percent of all professors at the public institution hold a doctoral degree (SPU 2010). This can be a barrier that prevents greater dynamism from producing more discoveries. It is not surprising that the highest degree of faculty research productivity in the country comes from the natural and hard sciences, such as physics, biology, and chemistry, for example, in which most researchers hold doctoral degrees—many more, for example, than researchers in the social sciences or humanities (SPU 2010). Moreover, it is possible to speculate that there will be greater interest in conducting research inside the private sector, as the number of faculty members with graduate degrees grows. This can be seen as an opportunity for GU, if its goal is to increase research output. BU, on the other hand, has the largest proportion of doctors in the country. So, it comes as no surprise that (through a student/faculty productivity ratio) professors are 18 times more productive than their colleagues at GU.

Within a national context that does not actively promote research outside the main public universities and certain national research centers, the private sector must break those (internal and external) barriers to produce relevant research. Thus, university administrators need to be aware that both explicit (promotion and salary policies for rewarding research) and implicit (working environment that encourages researchers) incentives must be consistent, since they support each other in the final goal of reducing agency costs with a view toward greater productivity. In other words, intrinsic motivation is a more efficient way to promote research than extrinsic pressure derived from CONEAU.

This study has aimed to identify some of the rewards—be they extrinsic (coming through market competition among universities or through well-designed public policies that reward relevant research) or intrinsic (increasing the number of doctors at each institution and offering more space to produce significant investigation)—which may trigger greater faculty research productivity. In a diverse higher education demand, some institutions may decide to allocate their resources to strengthen their research potential, while others may feel more comfortable fulfilling a teaching- or professional-oriented market. This means that the same prescription for all institutions or their faculty members to increase research productivity is, to say the least, inefficient. However, as I already mentioned, even among public flagship institutions in Argentina, the percentage of professors who have completed graduate studies remains minute. These organizational weaknesses for building a competitive research system must be addressed by encouraging highly trained human resources.

Finally, an ideal higher education system should satisfy a wide set of social and economic needs. It is ever more difficult to find universities with full-time professors, who hold doctoral degrees and are very much committed to producing significant research. Actually, part-time positions might not be questioned if professors were to bring practical experience to their teaching, but in the end it seems to come down to an option of missions.

Notes

1. Most scientific research in Latin America is not historically rooted within the university, but in association with private research centers created outside academia during European immigration at the turn of the twentieth century (Levy 1996).
2. In contrast to external labor markets, where salaries and the distribution of workers among diverse jobs are competitively determined by the forces of supply and demand, in internal labor markets workers are hired into entry-level jobs, and promotion is hierarchically decided. Also, wages are determined internally, without market pressure.
3. Even though there were some tertiary institutions well before 1958, none of them had university status.
4. In 1973, the government implemented a policy that banned new private universities. That law was changed in 1989, making way for a new wave of private higher education in Argentina.
5. To a certain extent, the opening of the National Council of University Accreditation (CONEAU) in 1996 added pressure to the private sector to allocate more resources for research projects.
6. Funding for private research centers in Argentina comes primarily from foreign donors, such as US foundations, where Ford is a leading supporter (Levy 1996).
7. Although both institutions were open to all my inquiries, they preferred to remain anonymous.
8. In this chapter, the term "US elite model" is used to describe a group of universities dominated by full-time researchers with doctoral degrees. According to the Carnegie Foundations, it comprises those institutions categorized as doctorate-granting universities. Of course, given its scale, BU does not meet all the criteria for this category, but it is very close to the original concept.

9. I used the ratio students per paper as a proxy instead of paper per faculty given that there are no official statistics regarding the number of faculty members at private universities and their contractual situation.
10. GU did not allow me to ask how satisfied faculty members were with their salary.
11. Created in 1996, the CONEAU is an independent public organization that operates under the Ministry of Education. It is in charge of preparing reports for private universities to attain provisory authorization. In addition to this, CONEAU conducts external evaluations every six years to check if institutions comply with teaching, research, and extension goals. Both public and private universities are evaluated.
12. In higher education, *signaling* implies that a candidate presents his or her academic degrees, seminars, conferences, research activity, publications, and characteristics of previous jobs in an effort to convince the employer of his or her abilities. Previous screening can reduce problems of adverse selection by tracking personal references and, for instance, administering aptitude tests.
13. References from previous employers and teaching observation are common practices at GU.
14. On average, private universities receive nearly 90 percent of their funds through tuition fees (del Bello, Barsy, and Giménez 2007). Many private universities financed their research work with internal funds. That being said, GU ranks among the top five private universities in terms of financial income while BU is closer to the fifteenth place (del Bello, Barsky, and Giménez 2007). On the other hand, academic salaries, which for the private system represent more than 50 percent of their expenditures, are higher at BU than at GU. So we can assume there are more potentially available internal financial resources for research in the latter.

References

Agencia Nacional de Promoción Científica y Tecnológica (ANPCYT: National Agency for the Promotion of Science and Technology). 2011. *Gestión 0809010: Informe de Actividades Generales* (Management 0809010: Report of General Activities). Buenos Aires, Argentina: ANPCYT. Available online at: http://www.agencia.mincyt.gob.ar/frontend/agencia/post/561, accessed on November 30, 2013.

Akerlof, George. 1970. "The Market for Lemons." *Quarterly Journal of Economics* 84 (3): 488–500.

Alchian, Armen, and Harold Demsetz. 1972. "Production, Information Costs, and Economic Organization." *American Economic Review* 62 (5): 777–795.

Altbach, Philip. 2007. "Peripheries and Centers: Research Universities in Developing Countries." *Higher Education Management and Policy* 19 (2): 111–134.

Barnard, Chester I. 1938. *The Functions of the Executive*. Cambridge, MA: Harvard University Press.

Bartram, Dave, Ivan Robertson, and Militza Callinan. 2002. "A Framework for Examining Organizational Effectiveness." In *Organizational Effectiveness: The Role of Psychology, 1–10*, edited by Ivan Robertson, Militza Callinan, and Dave Bartram. Chichester, England: Wiley.

Bernasconi, Andrés. 2007. "Is There a Latin American Model of the University?" *Comparative Education Review* 52 (1): 27–52.

Blauner, Robert. 1964. *Alienation and Freedom*. Chicago, IL: University of Chicago Press.

Brunner, José Joaquín, coordinator. 1995. *Educación Superior en América Latina: Una Agenda de Problemas, Políticas y Debates en el Umbral del Año 2000* (Higher Education in Latin America: Agenda of Problems, Policies, and Debates toward Year 2000). Bogotá, Colombia: National University of Colombia.

de Rome, Elizabeth, David Boud, and John M. Genn. 1985. "Changes in Academic Staff Perceptions of the Status of Teaching and Research." *Higher Education Research and Development* 4 (2): 131–143.

Dechenaux, Emmanuel, Jerry Thursby, and Marie Thursb. 2011. "Inventor Moral Hazard in University Licensing: The Role of Contracts." *Research Policy* 40 (1): 94–104.

Del Bello, Juan Carlos, Osvaldo Barsy, and Graciela Giménez. 2007. *La universidad privada argentina* (Argenitean private university). Buenos Aires, Argentina: Libros del Zorzal.

Denison, Daniel. 1990. *Corporate Culture and Organizational Effectiveness*. New York, NY: John Wiley & Sons.

Eggertsson, Thráinn. 1990. *Economic Behavior and Institutions*. Cambridge, UK: Cambridge University Press.

Eisenhardt, Katheleen. 1989. "Agency Theory: An Assessment and Review." *Academy of Management Review* 14 (1): 57–74.

Feistritzer, C. Emily. 1986. *Profile of Teachers in the U.S.* Washington, DC: National Center for Education Information.

Frase, Larry. 1989. "Effects of Teacher Rewards on Recognition and Job Enrichment. *Journal of Educational Research* 83 (1): 52–57.

George, Alexander, and Timothy McKeown. 1985. "Case Studies and Theories of Organizational Decision Making." In *Advances in Information Processing in Organizations 2*, edited by Robert Coulam and Richard Smith (pp. 21–58). Greenwich, CT: JAI Press.

Gordon, George, and Nancy Di Tomaso. 1992. "Predicting Corporate Performance from Organizational Culture." *Journal of Management Studies* 29 (6): 783–798.

Gregorutti, Gustavo. 2010. "Moving from a Predominantly Teaching Oriented Culture to a Research Productivity Mission: The Case of Mexico and the United States." *Excellence in Higher Education* 1 (1&2): 69–83.

———. 2012. "Impact of Neoliberal Policies: The Cases of Chile and Mexico." *Comparative & International Higher Education* 4 (1): 9–13.

Griffiths, Ron. 2004. "Knowledge Production and the Research-Teaching Nexus: The Case of the Built Environment Disciplines." *Studies in Higher Education* 29 (6): 709–726.

Gruenberg, Barry. 1980. "The Happy Worker: An Analysis of Educational and Occupational Differences in Determinants of Job Satisfaction." *The American Journal of Sociology* 86 (2): 247–271.

Halsey, Albert, and Martin Trow. 1971. *The British Academics*. Cambridge, MA: Harvard University Press.

Hansen, Lee. 1988. "Merit Pay in Higher Education." In *Academic Labor Markets and Careers*, edited by David Breneman and Ted Youn (pp. 114–137). New York, NY: The Falmer Press.

Jensen, Michael, and William Meckling. 1976. "Theory of the Firm: Managerial Behavior, Agency Costs, and Capital Structure." *Journal of Financial Economics* 3 (4): 305–360.

Kilman, Roy, Mary Saxton, and Roy Serpa.1985. *Gaining Control of the Corporate Culture*. San Francisco, CA: Jossey-Bass.

King, Gary, Robert Keohane, and Sidney Verba. 1994. *Designing Social Inquiry: Scientific Inference in Qualitative Research*. Princeton, NJ: Princeton University Press.

Kopelman, Richard, Arthur Brief, and Richard Guzzo. 1990. "The Role of Climate and Culture in Productivity." In *Organizational Climate and Culture*, edited by Benjamin Schneider (pp. 282–318). San Francisco, CA: Jossey-Bass.

Krathwohl, David. 1993. *Methods of Educational and Social Science Research: An Integrated Approach*. New York, NY: Longman Press.

Levy, Daniel. 1986. *Higher Education and the State in Latin America: Private Challenges to Public Dominance*. Chicago, IL: University of Chicago Press.

———. 1996. *Latin America's Private Research Centers and Nonprofit Development: Building the Third Sector*. Pittsburgh, PA: University of Pittsburgh Press.

Marquis, Carlos. 2002. "Universities and Professors in Argentina: Changes and Challenges." In *The Decline of the Guru: The Academic Profession in Developing and Middle-Income Countries*, edited by Philip Altbach (pp. 53–76). Boston, MA: Center for International Higher Education.

Milgrom, Paul, and John Roberts. 1992. *Economics, Organization and Management*. Upper Saddle River, NJ: Prentice Hall.

Ministry of Science, Technology, and Productive Innovation (MINCYT: Ministerio de Ciencia, Tecnología e Innovación Productiva). 2011. *Indicadores de Ciencia y Tecnologia. Argentina*. Buenos Aires: MINCYT. Available online at: http://www.mincyt.gob.ar/tag/Indicadores, accessed on November 15, 2013.

Ostroff, Cheri. 1992. "The Relationship between Satisfaction, Attitudes, and Performance: An Organizational Level Analysis." *Journal of Applied Psychology* 77 (6): 963–974.

Patterson, Malcolm, Peter Warr, and Michael West. 2004. *Organizational Climate and Company Productivity: The Role of Employee Affect and Employee Level*. Discussion Paper No. 626. London, UK: London School of Economics, Center for Economic Performance.

Rabossi, Marcelo. 2011. "The Private Sector in Argentina: A Limited and Selective Expansion." *Excellence in Higher Education* 2 (1): 42–50.

———. 2012. "Why the Argentina Private University Sector Continues to Lag Latin American Counterparts." *International Higher Education* 22 (Winter): 29–30.

Salmi, Jamil. 2009. *The Challenge of Establishing World-Class Universities.* Washington, DC: The World Bank.
Secretariado de Políticas Universitarias (SPU: Secretariat of University Policy). 2010. *Estadísticas* (Statistics). Buenos Aires, Argentina: SPU. Available online at: http://portales.educacion.gov.ar/spu/investigacion-y-estadisticas/anuarios/, accessed on November 15, 2013.
Sergiovanni, Thomas. 1967. "Factors which Affect Satisfaction and Dissatisfaction of Teachers." *The Journal of Educational Administration* 5 (1): 66–82.
Shin, Jung Cheol. 2009. "Building World-Class Research University: The Brain Korea 21 Project." *Higher Education* 58 (5): 669–688.
Sykes, Gary. 1983. "Public Policy and the Problem of Teacher Quality: The Need for Screens and Magnets?" In *Handbook of Teaching and Policy*, edited by Lee Schulman and Gary Sykes (pp. 97–125). New York, NY: Longman.
Williamson, Oliver. 1996. *The Mechanisms of Governance.* Oxford, UK: Oxford University Press.
Young, Pat. 2006. "Out of Balance: Lecturers' Perceptions of Differential Status and Rewards in Relation to Teaching and Research." *Teaching in Higher Education* 11 (2): 191–202.

Chapter 12

Private University Strategies to Promote Knowledge Production
Development of a Graduate Program in Biotechnology in Uruguay

*Enrique Martínez Larrechea and
Adriana Chiancone*

Introduction

Private higher education in Uruguay has its roots in the preparatory courses or middle-school education existing in the country since the nineteenth century. The first private institutions for advanced studies were created in the second half of the twentieth century. The Institute of Higher Studies (*Instituto de Estudios Superiores*) and the Institute of Philosophy, Science, Literature, and Linguistics (*Instituto de Filosofía, Ciencia y Letras*) are two examples. The latter was the center around which the Catholic University of Uruguay was established.

The military government (1973–1984) recognized private studies and diplomas with the enactment of Decree-Law 15,661 of 1984, which determined that diplomas would have the same value and standing as those awarded by the University of the Republic (UR: *Universidad de La República*). This piece of legislation allowed the activities of the Catholic University of Uruguay (UCUDAL: *Universidad Católica del Uruguay "Dámaso Antonio Larrañaga"*), the first private university in Uruguay.

Before the institutional expansion of 1973, it was unthinkable that higher education services could be formally offered by providers other than the government. However, with the end of the dictatorship in 1985, private institutions emerged, although the UCUDAL was the only existing private university for a while.

In 1985, a number of legislative acts continued to open the doors to private education. For instance, the parliament that was elected democratically a year earlier ratified Decree-Law 15,661 through Law 15,738 of March 6, 1985. However, the Ministry of Education and Culture (MEC) maintained an administrative approach that would grant "tertiary" level status only to certain programs from private technical institutions. The environment lacked a regulation that would make possible the recognition of the private subsector of education. Finally, in 1995, the government of President Julio Sanguinetti, whose Minister of Education Samuel Lichtensztejn had been rector of the UR before and after the military dictatorship, enacted Decree 308 to authorize new institutions and recognize degrees granted by private universities.

In the field of science, technology, and innovation (STI), research and development (R&D) in Uruguay is undertaken mainly in the public sector where the UR concentrates approximately 70 percent of human resources in research. There are other public institutions, particularly the National Research Institute of Farming (INIA: *Instituto Nacional de Investigaciones Agropecuarias*) and the Clemente Estable Institute of Biology Research (*Instituto de Investigaciones Biológicas Clemente Estable*), that also have an important participation.

The new government elected in March 2005 found that there was limited funding for R&D, a lack of coherent funding mechanisms to promote STI, little scientific production, a weak culture of innovation, and a modest engagement with stakeholders. There was also a high degree of fragmentation of the national innovation system, a weak supply-and-demand relationship for scientific-technical knowledge (with the exception of the farming sector), and little demand for locally generated knowledge as a result, to some degree, of inexistent public policies in STI.

In this situation, the government proposed to develop the necessary policies and expressed a special interest in the generation of strategies to promote technological development. The goal would be to take advantage of the national innovation potential to strengthen productive competitiveness and improve the capacity for scientific-technological development (Program for Technological Development, and MEC n. d). To that end, in 2005, a pool of priority areas was defined: agro-industrial networks, tourist complexes, biotechnology and pharmaceuticals, alternative energies, information and communication technologies (ICTs), and natural resources and environment. Four years later, with the introduction of the National STI Strategic Plan (*Plan Estratégico Nacional de Ciencia, Tecnología e Innovación*), biotechnology was defined as a priority area cutting across other thematic areas, such as ICTs, transportation and logistics, environment, and environmental technologies, and nanotechnologies. In addition, various initiatives for the promotion of research, technological development, and innovation in the priority areas were implemented (Gabinete Ministerial de la Innovación 2010). This was clearly a new phase of STI public policy that, in principle, was accompanied by an increase in spending from approximately 0.25 percent to 0.50 percent of the gross domestic product.

The emergence of private universities is a relatively new topic of study. This is not surprising since only in the 1980s and 1990s comparative policies of higher education began to address significant transformations and consolidated this subsector as an interdisciplinary field of knowledge. There are important studies[1] in the field of comparative education policies, but they are dispersed and fragmented. Burton R. Clark (1991), in his book on higher education systems, introduced the model of higher education coordination. Also important are the publications of Edward Shills (1997), Joseph Ben-David (1968, 1971), and Joseph Ben-David and Awraham Zloczower (1962). In addition, Pierre Bourdieu (2008) contributed to this field with a critical perspective.

According to Ben-David and Zloczower (1962), the *illuminists* (exponents of the French Enlightenment) considered universities as relics of the past and that it would be better to replace them with professional schools and academies. Despite losing their central position, universities survived skepticism when the German model of university emerged as a "novelty" in the early nineteenth century. Contemporary universities maintain teaching and research missions. However, differences exist in the weight each university gives to these two functions.

In the first half of the 1970s, Mark Trow (1974) identified the trend of making university education accessible to the masses, which he saw as critical. Later, Clark (1991) drew attention primarily to the expansion of academic subjects and the structure of organizations and academic disciplines. In addition, Daniel Levy (1995) studied the various waves of the private challenge to the dominant public and developed a chronology and typology of higher education privatization. In the twenty-first century, researchers such as Philip Altbach (1999, 2001), Altbach and McGill (2000), José Joaquín Brunner (2007), Brunner and Uribe (2007), Levy (1985), Guy Neave (2001), and Trow (2000) and, even more recently, Juan Carlos Del Bello and Osvaldo Barsky (2007), Gustavo Gregorutti (2011), and Claudio Rama (2012a,b), among others, have introduced new interpretations to the growth and characteristics of private higher education. These authors described and, to a certain extension, explained the new phenomena as massification and substantial growth of the fields of knowledge (Clark 1991; Trow 2000). They developed theoretical models about how higher education systems work and highlighted relevant problems related to changes in the higher education political economy, as well as emerging trends as internationalization (Altbach and Peterson 2000), privatization (Del Bello and Barsky 2007; Gregorutti 2011), and virtualization (Rama 2012b).

Clark (2004b) identified five characteristics of "enterprising universities," which comprise a set of features that lead to transformations of conventional universities into the new institutional model:

1. Consolidation of a strong governing nucleus, the center of the networks of power within the institution
2. A periphery of wide-ranging development, which implies a process of creation and maintenance of diverse institutional procedures for the circulation of demands and resources among the university and its environment
3. Stimuli from a motivated academic core in such a way that innovation, flexibility, and capabilities of the institution can rapidly respond to the demands of the society
4. Diversification of the financial base to overcome dependency on a single source
5. Driving force of an entrepreneurial university culture and staff with a proactive culture in relation to the environment

The private sector responds to the current challenges and societal context through institutional differentiation. Private universities, as part of higher education subsystems but different from the traditional and the new public sector, appear to respond to an external logic. They are also different from the vast market of nonuniversity higher education institutions. They represent the most important institutional providers in many Latin American countries. The newly arrived for-profit providers (Didou 2004; Knight 2002, 2003) are frequently established as *holdings* (García Guadilla 2002) and face the challenges of finding funding opportunities in the STI systems. Hence, private universities have arrived at a crossroads. There is a deep differentiation between segments of institutions focused on local commitments, vis à vis large-scale universities that are linked to global capital.

In this context, we analyze the opportunities for Latin American private universities to overcome the conceptual and organizational teaching-centered model toward a culture of research and innovation that requires generating transformative strategies. In this study, we examine the links between public policies in R&D and institutional strategies for the development of STI. We asked the questions: In what ways and through which paths is knowledge produced in private universities? How do they struggle with the restrictions from the local context in order to develop new science and technology fields? To answer these questions, we analyze the strategies developed by a private university in Uruguay in the field of biotechnology.

Methodology

The study assumes that in a particularly inertial[2] (Martínez Larrechea and Chiancone 2011) context, like the Uruguayan higher education, entrepreneurial and innovative institutions struggle amid strong restrictive factors that prioritize teaching over research. Inertia is seen in the tardy adoption or reaction to regional and international trends; in the slowness of debates on necessary reforms within institutions; and the delayed introduction of innovations in the system. Likewise, this work assumes that external factors, such as state regulation, other universities' competitiveness, existence of new providers, and contextual opportunities, act first as driving or restricting elements, that is, as confounding variables, before they become central and critical issues.

We chose to study the program in biotechnology of the ORT University (ORT) from Uruguay. ORT is strongly oriented toward the development of training and technological knowledge. The Uruguayan higher education system is still being developed as an "isomorphic" reproduction of the traditional characteristics of the only public university, the UR. The main feature of this system is a strong inclination toward teaching as a cultivation of classic professional training with a liberal nature (primarily law and accounting disciplines). Other private universities in the country also emphasize technology, but in the case of ORT this is not a simple reproduction of traditional professional training. Its orientation can be analyzed through an examination of some of its academic programs. In this study, we prioritize biotechnology as a good example of the trends mentioned earlier. In addition, despite the small size of the private university subsector in Uruguay and ORT, it shares some of the features of the previously mentioned entrepreneurial or enterprising universities.

Data for this study came from three kinds of sources: institutional documents or those produced by the institution and its leaders, statistical indicators, and public information about Uruguayan higher education and, especially, ORT. On the other side, the literature review used academic sources and included an annotated bibliography to cover Latin American higher education and private higher education. Furthermore, international support was considered mainly on new ways of providing educational service, in particular the entrepreneurial university described and analyzed by Clark (1998a,b, 2004a) and other authors.

The ORT University

The original ORT Technical High School was founded in 1943 in Montevideo as a civil partnership for technical education in industrial trades (electricity, auto mechanics, blacksmithing, carpentry, and dressmaking). It is an institution of the World ORT Union, which originated in the Society for Agriculture and Handwork, founded in St. Petersburg, Russia, in April 1880. Initially, ORT supported the social integration of Jewish immigrants, but in the 1950s and 1960s, it expanded its educational scope. In Uruguay, over the following two decades, the institution established an international focus and leadership in technology fields, which helped improve and expand its enrolment. In 1985, the ORT presented some of its tertiary programs to the MEC, and in 1988 the Ministry recognized the degree in systems analysis, the first program from a private university of this kind in the country.

In 1989, the ORT Technological Institute, as it was originally named, became the largest nongovernmental technical education institution in Uruguay. Even today ORT offers around 25 short-term degrees (one- to three-year duration). These degrees, implemented across a variety of departments, were consolidated in 1996, leading to the creation of the current "Bernard Wand-Polak" Faculty (School) of Engineering.

In 1995, ORT sought university recognition, which was granted in 1996, becoming the first private college to gain recognition under the procedure established by Decree-Law 15,661 and Decree 308. Subsequently, ORT expanded its leadership in technology and management disciplines and extended its educational offerings to a variety of fields in the social sciences, education, and technology. Consequently, over the past 30 years, ORT has become an institution with a technological mandate and in whose activities the development of entrepreneurialism is an important and frequently emphasized goal in the many avenues of public outreach, such as the institution's website and brochures of the different programs.

Degree Programs

The ORT offerings of nondegree-oriented training are heterogeneous and dynamic. They are adjusted as technology evolves and business demands change. Offerings are increasingly in demand, particularly technical and technological training and skill upgrading required in the workplace.

In 2011, 1,181 students enrolled at ORT, which is 5.15 percent of the total national university enrollment and 32.84 percent of the private sector. The number of graduates (6,991) the same year represents 40.9 percent of the graduates in the Uruguayan private university sector (MEC 2012). The degrees available were concentrated in four faculties: (a) Engineering; (b) Communications and Design; (c) Architecture; and (d) Management and Social Sciences. Traditional liberal degrees are absent (with the exception of architecture), which is an indicator of ORT's orientation toward scientific and technological majors.

Technology as a Core Component

As described earlier, ORT is known for degrees in areas of technology. This includes short-term degree programs (5B training in the International Standard Classification of Education, 1997) in engineering, architecture, and biotechnology. Even though the organizational structure includes the School of Business, the Faculty of Social Sciences and Management, the School of Social Communication, and the Education Institute, course offerings in the social sciences and management are strongly oriented toward the service industry and professional training is linked to creative industries. In this sense, these programs stand out over other public and private university programs whose enrollment leans toward more traditional liberal professions (law, notarial work, public accounting, medicine, and dentistry). Although other private universities created faculties of engineering (the UR has three solid faculties in technology fields: chemistry, engineering, and architecture), ORT, in contrast, developed areas of technology away from the traditional professions.

Guided by this technological vocation, the ongoing development of ORT course offerings since the mid-1990s represents a central characteristic of the institution. In 1996, ORT installed the first classroom network in the country for training via videoconference. The selection of ICTs followed a careful path to avoid large investments in expensive and constantly changing technologies. Basically, the new technologies were employed to support face-to-face education. The next steps were the creation of coordinating units to employ the ICTs and work over the Internet, using materials previously designed at the institution.

ORT has several agreements in place with various organizations, particularly those in the private sector, ranging from large businesses to nonprofit organizations. These agreements, in general, include student internships, training for workers in the private sector, and the implementation of joint projects. Each faculty has specialized areas that are responsible for the relations with businesses and external organizations. This kind of organizational structure is, as we have pointed out, related to the predisposition of the university to focus on technological knowledge. Similarly, the strong orientation of degree programs toward experimental sciences is linked to the institutional origin as a technological institute focused on workplace training. Likewise, this is associated to its directors' training in engineering, which could typify a particular conception of R&D and of its interaction with the demands of the working and social worlds.

Strategies in the Creation of the Program in Biotechnology

The recent creation of a program in biotechnology is an example of a successful experience to create the conditions to train human resources and generate profitable knowledge. Here, the capabilities of ORT to take strategic advantage of the opportunities for institutional development are clear in spite of the context of scarce resources. ORT identified biotechnology as a strategic field and provided funding from diverse strategic sources to create the infrastructure and develop the capabilities for the program.[3] Given the government policies and the potential of biotechnologies, the university decided to fully support this program that did not exist in the country either at the technical or at the bachelor's level. Instead, a master's program in biotechnology was created under the Basic Sciences Development Program (PEDECIBA: *Programa de Desarrollo de las Ciencias Básicas*).[4]

A group of specialists commissioned by the National Research and Innovation Agency (ANII: *Agencia Nacional de Investigación e Innovación*) carried out a study that revealed a lack of development of the field of biotechnology in Uruguay. The report states:

> There are practically no proper biotechnology companies in our country that operate internationally, and few that perform development activities in biotechnology for application to their products or services, and in general those products or services are imported at high cost. Highly-skilled human resources necessary for the development of biotech startups are concentrated

in the academic sector, with little demand from the productive sector and there are no long-term state policies that are oriented toward bringing the two together. (Capdevielle et al. 2008).

In this sense, ORT was able to articulate the outcomes of this analysis and the existing public policies for the development of new academic programs by responding to those emerging trends. In addition, the university brought from abroad a distinguished field researcher with experience in the pharmaceutical industry to oversee the project. The researcher, Carlos Sanguinetti, studied medicine at the UR and completed a master's degree on Chagas disease in Belo Horizonte, Brazil. There, he and a colleague learned, in his own words, "to put a price on science." Upon his return to Uruguay, Sanguinetti took up teaching duties at the UR's Faculty of Science and created a business with a group of his students. Initially, they sold sample analysis services of coagulation factor 5 (associated with spontaneous abortions) to doctors and later reoriented their work to the production of diagnostic kits. As this researcher noted in an interview:

> The laboratory and the doctor do business together, and we were still thinking that it was just our job, and didn't bill them. But once we took a pause to reflect, we saw that we were receiving a large quantity of samples, so the novel idea that arose was to transform services into products, and change the client. Where once we sold to the doctors, we thought it better to sell the technology in a bottle to the clinical analysis labs in the form of *kits*, and let them offer human genetic analysis to the doctors. That's how we began a business producing products. (Madrid 2013, p. 22)

Sanguinetti's business operated for two years within the premises of the UR's Faculty of Science. Later, they moved out of the UR and then a private pharmaceutical laboratory took over the business where Sanguinetti began his career. After an informal meeting with the Academic Coordinator of ORT, Sanguinetti was appointed to develop the project (Madrid 2013). This was a key beginning for the development of graduate studies and research in biotechnology.

With the creation of the Biotechnologist Technician program in 2009, ORT became a recipient of a grant for the "Support for Tertiary Priority Programs of Technical Education" from the ANII.[5] The aim of the program is "training technicians with adequate basic capabilities, laboratory work abilities, and training in business/entrepreneurialism that allows graduates to identify opportunities and create startups with a technological basis in biotechnology" (ANII n.d.). It also intended to prepare technicians with a professional outlook, who would seek to enter the business and industrial sectors.

The funding obtained from the ANII allowed the creation of the Biotechnology Laboratory[6] and later the signing of agreements with institutions like the Technological Laboratory of Uruguay (*Laboratorio Tecnológico del Uruguay*) and the INIA. The former is a parastatal corporation, and the latter is a government agency. This resulted in student access to high-tech scientific equipment to conduct projects and pursue training on the use of technical instruments.

One year later, in November 2010, the Bachelor of Biotechnology program was recognized by official resolution of the MEC. This made possible for graduates to continue studying at the graduate level in the country and abroad. It also meant that graduates could work independently as consultants or as entrepreneurs by developing their own start-ups.[7] The program's teaching staff consists of a group of researchers educated in public universities, some of whom are professors at the UR. Other academics completed graduate studies or worked as researchers in foreign institutions. Career opportunities for the program's graduates are seen primarily in national and international industries that work with living creatures in the production and purification of high value-added bioproducts. Some graduates went into agribusinesses that are the basis of national export industries. The bachelor's program had 49 graduates and 94 students enrolled in 2011. The same year, 6 students graduated from the certificate program, which had 16 enrollments (MEC 2012).

Starting in 2014, the courses of a new program in Biotechnology Engineering will be available at ORT. This program will be presented for approval by the MEC.

Implementation of Policies for Faculty Research Productivity

In an effort to encourage and develop research at the institution, in a national context where the ANII created a new National System of Researchers (SNI-Uru: *Sistema Nacional de Investigadores*),[8] the university undertook a series of initiatives. Through various methods of economic incentive, the ORT is looking for researcher productivity to increase. The amounts of these incentives depend on the results of research and their visibility. These measures include:

1. Research support fund: an annual fund (open window mode) to support scientific research activities of academics and students, which is

run by the dean of each faculty with the support of the university's Academic Development office.
2. Bonuses are awarded for articles published in refereed journals included in the Thomson Reuters' Journal Citation Reports. The amount of the incentive depends on the impact factor of the journal.
3. Incentives for academics' inclusion in the SNI-URU, which are considered a credit toward offsetting the expenses incurred in the course of research through reimbursements (after provision of receipts). To be nominated for these incentives, university researchers or instructors must work a minimum of 12 hours a week and not pursue paid activities or honoraria at another educational institution (some exceptions apply).

As a result of these research promotion policies, as well as other possible factors, intellectual production increased, as shown in table 12.1. It shows the academic production of ORT by research output over selected years. We can see growth in the number of publications.

Research centers and specialized facilities integrating different faculties undertake research at ORT. These centers conduct applied research through projects with high technological content and develop educative material that incorporates the state of the art in curriculum. Some of those centers include the Mathematics Applied to Telecommunications Group, the Theoretical Computation Group, the Centre for Innovation and Research in Software Engineering, the Protein Technology Group, the Centre for Managerial Research, and the Management Accounting Research Group.[9]

Moreover, ORT hosts a center for the promotion and creation of new businesses: the Centre for Innovation and Entrepreneurism (CIE). This center was founded in 2008. Its creation is seen as the continuation of

Table 12.1 Academic production of ORT by category (select years)

Research output	Select Years				
	2003	2006	2010	2011	Total
Peer-reviewed articles	3	11	13	18	45
Conference proceedings	20	33	30	41	124

Source: Author's creation, drawn from the ORT University database.

previous initiatives carried out at the Faculty of Engineering. As its coordinator mentioned:

> Its birth was like the natural evolution of various decisions made by the Faculty of Engineering that were taken more than 20 years ago, when it began to work on the promotion of a proactive attitude among its students that derived from what we know today as an entrepreneurial culture; it was understood that this initiative could be replicated in the other university faculties. (ORT, 2010)

The faculty supports activities of students, professors, entrepreneurs, and organizations by developing opportunities and strengthening university-business ties, in order to produce a positive impact on the society. The CIE specializes in university-business linkages by creating contact networks with the productive sector. It is a place to identify market needs and design innovation projects in order to generate capability-based solutions at the university. Even though most projects involve new technologies, there are no limitations toward other areas, when ideas meet the objectives of the center.

Knowledge Production in Biotechnology

As a result of the policies outlined earlier, in 2010, research in biotechnology began and the Protein Technology Group was created. This group seeks to:

1. Explore recombinant proteins of biotechnological interest
2. Improve enzyme properties in biotechnology applications, for instance, increase their biosensor integration potentials or their use as industrial catalyzers in more sustainable synthesis processes
3. Increase the sensitivity of proteins or other biomolecule detection systems at a nanometric scale
4. Develop new strategies for the purification, immobilization, and stabilization of proteins through the use of custom-made foundations.[10]

Similarly, they have conducted three projects in biotechnology. The ANII provided funding for two of them, through the program "Alliances for Innovation,"[11] an initiative that promotes the implementation of projects that involve linkages between the academia and businesses in order to find solutions to any given problem. The projects are the following:

1. "Development of tailored chromatographic methods to improve bioprocesses: purification of toxoids for the preparation of veterinary

vaccines." 2010–2013. Funding from the ANII (Alliances for Innovation Program in collaboration with Santa Elena Laboratories, S.A.).[12]
2. "Design of lipase preparations for biocatalysis: support for the development of sustainable biotechnologies in Uruguay." 2011–2012. Funding from the Spanish Agency of International Cooperation for Development. Participants: researchers from the University of Barcelona, the High Council of Scientific Research of Madrid and Uruguayan researchers from ORT and the UR.[13]
3. "New approaches for the development of agricultural-use biopesticides." 2012–2014. Funding from the ANII (Alliances for Innovation Program) in collaboration with LAGE Company.[14]

In the biotechnology field, they have published five articles in peer-reviewed journals during 2010–2013.[15] They have also conducted, as a university extension activity, a workshop on biotechnology with high school teachers. During the workshop, the teachers learn to perform experiments and become familiar with the most common techniques in the fields of biotechnology and molecular biology and then reproduce them in the classroom.

Discussion

The twenty-first century is particularly challenging for public and private universities. New public policies and regulations, growing costs, new social demands, and competitive contexts are testing the forces and limits of these institutions. In more developed countries, universities work together with businesses from the productive sector. However, for private universities in less developed countries, with contexts of little investment on R&D, research productivity depends greatly on whether public policies are favorable to the university-enterprise links, or in how much the private sector is able to access public financing.

Latin America has few public universities that appear in the rankings as *research universities* or at the *world-class* level. Only a short list of urban universities of the larger countries in the region enjoy that kind of visibility.

In small countries with poor levels of innovation and few patents, where the university system has a modest reputation, like in Uruguay, innovation has a few characteristic traits: It does not depend much on original and relevant basic research; there is not an established standard for the promotion of basic and applied research; institutions compete for public funding, innovation in teaching programs, and fields of knowledge; and there is a predominant management culture.

Besides the small size of the Uruguayan economy, there are major developments achieved by the country in the fields of biology and biotechnology. The demand for goods from the agricultural sector is another stimulating factor of the progress in research. The explicit and decisive development variables in the production of knowledge rely not only on economic scale or the weight of the university budget, but rather on the specific academic cultures that can be deepened and enriched in the various institutions.

Within a context of growing complexity and flexibility among the various fields of knowledge, science and technology demand and enable the collaboration among diverse actors to attain proposed objectives. As Vessuri et al. (2008, p. 30) noted:

> Currently, science and innovation are, at the same time, at their most competitive and cooperative... Their breadth and scale are achieved less through the size of the investment and more through the sharing of data, knowledge and infrastructure, through associations with their competitors... New science and technologies offer frames of reference that are infinitely adaptable, which stimulates and allows participants with differing abilities, roles and incentives to work together toward common ends.

ORT appears to be a good example of modernization and innovation in the private sector. This university is neither faith-based nor elite; it does not belong to the category of institutions that simply deal with absorption of demand (rather than preparation for employment); and it is strongly oriented toward new technologies, management, and creative industries. This does not mean that ORT is the only private institution that is improving management or implementing new programs. However, the case we present here certainly shows a strong pattern that brings together key diverse policy dimensions for the improvement of research and innovation (Clark 2000).

This pattern results from the particular strategies implemented to develop local capacities in biotechnology and to find resources. This type of innovation seems to have resulted from a number of factors. Four of them are: (a) the selection of professors who studied abroad; (b) the interest in new technologies; (c) the ability to handle global themes via the professionalization of strategic management; and (d) the capability to meet the requirements of public calls for project proposals in science, technology, and innovation.

The reasons for these developments can be attributed to three central variables: (a) the predominant fields of knowledge in the academic program; (b) the vision promoted by the leadership of the university, which depends to a great extent on the field of expertise of the vice chancellor and staff; (c) the capacity of a young private university to design a globally oriented response based on strong relationships with the most dynamic economic and social sectors (e.g., ICTs, biotechnology, nanotechnology, earth sciences, water, telecommunications, strategic management, cultural industries, arts, and social sciences).

An essential feature of the strategies implemented to create the conditions to develop biotechnology at ORT is the collaboration with different private and public organizations. The combination of national policies and institutional strategies has resulted in the generation of new knowledge in the field of biotechnology, even if it is at an incipient stage.

There are, however, some issues that need to be analyzed and developed to meet the institutional goals of the university. The greatest challenges faced by ORT and the graduates of its biotechnology program are the need to increase linkages with the productive sector in Uruguay, both public and private, and to promote the creation of startups in this field that has great potential for innumerable applications. It also requires that the university maximizes the participation of the various local, highly skilled human resources that are currently available within and around of the institution. This could be achieved through the implementation of a synergetic and interdisciplinary working model where technological innovation is considered within a wider social and cultural context. This presupposes internal work toward achieving, as Clark (2004b) notes, a group of professors who are motivated and academically prepared to generate initiatives that respond to the needs of their environment. In doing so, the field of biotechnology can advanced within a project that is sustainable in space and time.

Conclusion

The creation of the biotechnology program has been successfully developed due to a decisive strategic positioning that took advantage of the opportunities found in the ORT University. Biotechnology represents: (a) an area defined as strategic by the government and for which competitive development funding is available; (b) an area in which human resources with advanced training exist across various national and international institutions; (c) the experience of a prestigious researcher who had worked outside public higher education in the private business sector; (d) a field where no undergraduate programs exist, but there are some offerings at the graduate level; and (e) a space where cooperation and alliances among diverse public and private actors are fundamental to participating in the increasingly interconnected and competitive world.

In the case described in this chapter, competitive funding from the ANII was obtained for the creation of the Certificate in Biotechnology and the construction of infrastructure to carry out teaching and research activities. One year after the government provided the funding for the certificate program, the MEC recognized a bachelor's program in the field. An intense coordination among different actors allowed establishing alliances and using resources in a context of cooperation with results that included the creation of a research group, the publication of a number of journal articles, and the development of projects in the 2010–2013 period.

The importance of developing the biotechnology area at ORT cannot be expressed as much in quantitative terms as it is in the consolidation of a research group with sustained outcomes over time. Likewise, the training of human resources with the capability to participate in innovation and development activities in the field of biotechnology is a relevant achievement of this program.

Notes

1. Publications in languages such as Spanish ("La Misión de la Universidad" by José Ortega y Gasset, 1930), French ("Homo Academicus" by Pierre Bourdieu, 2008), English (Robin's Report; Burton Clark 1991; Ben David 1967, 1968, 1971; and Theodore Schultz's works), and German (Karl Jaspers's work).
2. We use the term "inertial" from the perspective of physics as inertia: the property of a mass to resist changes in velocity (speed and direction). It also includes the case of zero speed or no motion.
3. The Uruguayan government, through the ANII, created some mechanisms to foster the links between universities and companies and to attract investment from industry. Competition for these funds is open to all research fields. Some sector funds were created with the participation of public enterprises in different areas: agro-industrial, energy, natural resources, and environment; ICTs; and health. Recently, two projects in biotechnology from the Faculty of Engineering received grants from the ANII Energy Sector Fund.
4. The PEDECIBA was launched in 1986. Its overseeing bodies are the MEC and the UR (Chiancone 1996).
5. In this call for proposals, the creation of nonuniversity, tertiary technical education programs was the desired outcome, in areas defined as priorities by the Ministry of Innovation in 2005. It included the "development of

biotechnological and pharmaceutical potentials, particularly in the field of human health, animal health and matters relating to plants."
6. The laboratory is equipped to work according to the technical principles employed in biotechnology. It is designed to simultaneously provide 20 researchers with personal equipment. It includes additional areas for equipment sharing, such as the bacteria and eukaryotic cell culture rooms for the purposes of DNA and RNA amplification. It also has a room to work with fermenters and large equipment with a space for the operations involving technical assistants and laboratory organization, two air extraction hoods for chemical work, and four laminar flow hoods for microbiology. For more information, see http://www.cuti.org.uy/novedades/910-ort-invita-a-la-inauguracion-de-su-laboratorio-de-biotecnologia.html (retrieved: January 25, 2014).
7. See http://www.ort.edu.uy/index.php?id=AAAHAGAE (retrieved: January 25, 2014).
8. The SNI-Uru was created under the auspices of the ANII in 2007 with the aim of strengthening, expanding, and consolidating the national scientific community dedicated to the task of categorizing and evaluating periodically all researchers, creating a system of economic incentives (see http://www.sni.org.uy). The SNI-Uru is overseen by an honorary commission. The first convocation was held in 2008. The SNI-Uru was preceded by the National Researchers Fund, in the past five years of the twentieth century, and represented an important advance in the policies for research promotion, following the successful national cases of Brazil, Mexico, and Venezuela.
9. For more information, see www.ort.edu.uy/index.php?id=AAAJAF.
10. See http://www.ort.edu.uy/fi/pdf/folletobiotecnologia.pdf.
11. The program "Alliances for Innovation" prioritizes projects created by more than two or more actors in the business sphere, who share risks and benefits. In the proposals, the role of each institution should be clear: applicant or knowledge generator. The alliances finance up to 70 percent of the total cost of the project, to a maximum subsidy of US$200,000. The remaining percentage must be provided by the participating institutions and should be in the form of cash (for more information, see http://www.anii.org.uy/web/node/72).
12. See http://fi.ort.edu.uy/innovaportal/v/2302/5/fi.ort.front/proyectos.html.
13. See http://fi.ort.edu.uy/innovaportal/v/2302/5/fi.ort.front/proyectos.html.
14. See http://fi.ort.edu.uy/innovaportal/v/2302/5/fi.oErt.front/proyectos.html.
15. Betancor, L., G. R. Johnson, and H. R. Luckarift. 2013. "Stabilized Laccases as Heterogeneous Bioelectrocatalysts." *Chem Cat Chem* 5: 46–60; Martínez Luaces, V., and B. Velázquez. 2012. "A Course on Experimental Design for Biotechnology Students." *CULMS Newsletter* 5; Marques, D., B. C. Pessela, L. Betancor, R. Monti, A. V. Carrascosa, J. Rocha-Martin, J. M. Guisán, and G. Fernandez-Lorente. 2011. "Protein Hydrolysis by Immobilized and Stabilized Trypsin." *Biotechnology Progress* 27(3); Fernández-Lorente, G., C. Pizarro, D. López-Vela, L. Betancor, A. V. Carrascosa, B. Pessela, and

J. M. Guisan. 2010. "Hydrolysis of Fish Oil by Lipases Immobilized Inside Porous Supports." *Journal of the American Oil Chemistry Society* 88: 819–826; Sans, Mónica, Gonzalo Figueiro, Carlos Sanguinetti, Lourdes Echarte-Rafaelli, Cecilia Portela, Luis Taranto, Carlos Pizzarossa, Roberto Oliver, Rosana Manikowski, Isabel Barreto, Pedro C. Hidalgo, and Guido Berro. 2010. "The Last Charrua India (Uruguay): Analysis of the Remains of Chief Vaimaca Perú." *Nature Preceedings.* Available online at: http://precedings.nature.com/documents/4415/version/1.

References

Altbach, Philip G. 1999. "Comparative Perspectives on Private Higher Education." In *Private Prometheus: Private Higher Education and Development in the 21st Century*, edited by Philip Altbach. Westport, CO: Greenwod.
———. 2001. *Educación Superior Comparada. El Conocimiento, la Universidad y el Desarrollo* (Comparative Higher Education. Knowledge, University, and Development). Buenos Aires, Argentina: UNESCO Cathedra of History and Future of the University, University of Palermo.
Altbach, Philip G., and Patti McGill Peterson, editors. 2000. *Educación Superior en el Siglo XXI. Desafío Global y Respuesta Nacional* (Higher Education in the XXI Century. Global Challenge and National Response). Buenos Aires, Argentina: Biblos.
Ben-David, Joseph. 1968. *Fundamental Research and University*. Paris, France: Organisation for Economic Co-operation and Development (OECD).
———. 1971. *The Scientist's Role in Society*. New York, NY: Prentice-Hall.
Ben-David, Joseph, and Awraham Zloczower 1962. "Universities and Academic Systems in Modern Societies." *European Journal of Sociology* 3 (01): 45–84.
Bourdieu, Pierre. 2008. *Homo Academicus*. Buenos Aires, Argentina: Siglo XXI.
Brunner, José Joaquín. 2007. *La educación superior en Iberoamérica 2007* (Higher Education in Iberic-America 2007). Santiago, Chile: CINDA-Universia.
Brunner, José Joaquín, and Daniel Uribe. 2007. *Mercados Universitarios: el nuevo Escenario de la Educación Superior* (University Markets: The New Scenario of Higher Education). Santiago, Chile: Diego Portales University Press.
Capdevielle Fabián, Alejandro Chabalgoity, and Rodolfo Silveira. 2008. *Biotecnología: Promoviendo la Innovación en los Sectores Farmacéutico, Agroindustrial y de Salud Humana y Animal* (Biotechnology: Promoting Innovation in the Pharmaceutical, Agroindustrial, and Human and Health Sectors). Montevideo, Uruguay: National Research and Innovation Agency. Available online at: http://www.anii.org.uy/imagenes/biotecnologiainforme.pdf, accessed on November 15, 2013.
Chiancone, Adriana. 1996. *La Definición de Políticas Públicas en un Contexto de Transición Política. El Caso del PEDECIBA de Uruguay* (Definition of Public Policies in a Context of Political Transition. The Case of PEDECIBA from Uruguay). Buenos Aires, Argentina: Latin American School of Social Sciences (FLACSO)-DAAD.

Clark, Burton R. 1991. *El Sistema de Educación Superior. Una Visión Comparativa de la Organización Académica* (Higher Education System. A Comparative View of the Academic Organization). México City, Mexico: Autonomous Metropolitan University-Azcapotzalco, Nueva Imagen, Universidad Futura.

———. 1998a. *Creating Entrepreneurial Universities: Organizational Pathways of Transformation*. Oxford, UK: Elsevier.

———. 1998b. "The Entrepreneurial University: Demand and Response." *Tertiary Education and Management* 4 (1): 5–16.

———. 2000. "Collegial Entrepreneurialism in Proactive Universities." *Change* 32 (1): 10–12.

———. 2004a. *Sustaining Change in Universities. Continuities in Case Studies and Concepts*. London, UK: Open University Press.

———. 2004b. "Delineating the Character of the Entrepreneurial University." *Higher Education Policy* 17 (4): 355–370.

Del Bello, Juan Carlos, and Osvaldo Barsky. 2007. *La Universidad Privada Argentina* (Argentinean Private University). Buenos Aires, Argentina: Libros del Zorzal.

Didou Aupetit, Sylvie. 2004. "Public et Privé dans l'enseignement Supérieur au Mexique" ("Public and Private in Higher Education in Mexico"). *Cahiers de la Recherche sur l'éducation et les Savoirs* (Research Papers on Education and Knowledge) (3): 97–118.

Gabinete Ministerial de la Innovación (Ministerial Office of Innovation). 2010. *Plan Estratégico Nacional de Ciencia y Tecnología* (National Strategic Plan of Science and Technology). Montevideo, Uruguay: Direction of Innovation, Science, and Culture, Ministry of Education and Culture (MEC: Ministerio de Educación y Cultura).

García Guadilla, Carmen. 2002. *Tensiones y Transiciones. Educación Superior Latinoamericana en los Albores del Tercer Milenio*. (Tensions and Transitions. Latin American Higher Education at the beginning of the Third Millennium). Caracas, Venezuela: Development Study Center, Nueva Sociedad.

Gregorutti, Gustavo. 2011. "La Producción de Investigación en las Universidades Privadas: Estudio de un Caso" ("Research Production in Private Universities: A Case Study"). *Enfoques* (Approaches) 23 (2): 5–20.

Knight, Jane. 2002. "The Impact of GATS and Trade Liberalization on Higher Education." In *Globalization and the Market in Higher Education. Quality, Accreditation and Qualifications*, edited by International Association of Universities. Paris, France: UNESCO.

———. 2003. "Comercialización de Servicios de Educación Superior: Implicaciones del AGCS" ("Commercialization of Higher Education Services: Implications for GATS"). In *El Difícil Equilibrio: La Educación Superior como Bien Público y Comercio de Servicio* (Difficult Equilibrium: Higher Education as a Public Good and Service Trade), edited by Carmen García Guadilla. Paris, France: Columbus Program.

Levy, Daniel. 1985. "Latin America's Private Universities: How Successful Are They?" *Comparative Education Review* 29 (4): 440–459.

Levy, Daniel. 1995. *La Educación Superior y el Estado en América Latina: Desafíos Privados Al Predominio Público* (Higher Education and State in Latin America: Private Challenges to the Public Dominance). México City, Mexico: FLACSO México.
Madrid, Patricia. 2013. "Think Different." *Revista Seisgrados*-Diario *El Observador* (*Seisgrados Magazine—The Observer Newspaper*) (March): 21–25.
Martínez Larrechea, Enrique, and Adriana Chiancone. 2011. "La Educación Superior en Uruguay" ("Higher Education in Uruguay"). *Innovación Educativa* (Education Innovation) 11 (57): 123–132.
Ministry of Education and Culture (MEC). 2012. *Anuario Estadístico 2011* (Statistical Yearbook 2011). Montevideo, Uruguay: MEC.
Neave, Guy. 2001. *Educación Superior: Historia y Política. Estudios Comparativos sobre la Universidad Contemporánea* (Higher Education: History and Politics. Comparative Studies on the Contemporary University). Barcelona, Spain: Gedisa.
ORT University. 2010. "Centro de Innovación y Emprendimientos: un Lugar donde las Ideas Valen" ("Center for Innovation and Entrepreneurship: A Place Where Ideas Are Valued"). Montevideo, Uruguay: ORT. Available online at: http://www.ort.edu.uy/index.php?id=AAALBQ, accessed on November 15, 2013.
Programa de Desarrollo Tecnológico (PDT: Program for Technological Development), and MEC. n.d. *¿Qué es el PDT?* Montevideo, Uruguay: MEC. Available online at: http://www.dicyt.gub.uy/pdt/pdt.html, accessed on November 15, 2013.
Rama, Claudio. 2012a. *La Nueva Fase de la Universidad Privada en América Latina* (New Phase of Private University in Latin America). Montevideo, Uruguay: Grupo Magró, University of the Enterprise.
———. 2012b *La Reforma de la Virtualización de la Universidad. El Nacimiento de la Educación Digital* (University Virtualization Reform. Birth of Digital Education) (2nd edition). Santo Domingo, Dominican Republic: University of the Caribbean.
Schultz, Theodore. 1971. *Investment in Human Capital: The Role of Education and of Research*. New York, NY: Free Press.
———. 1972. *Human Resources*. New York, NY: National Bureau of Economic Research.
Shills, Edward. 1997. *The Calling of Education. The Academic Ethic and Other Essays on Higher Education*. Chicago, IL: University of Chicago Press.
Trow, Martin. 1974. "Problems in the Transition from Elite to Mass Higher Education." In *General Report on the Conference on Future Structures of Post-Secondary Education* (pp. 55–101). Paris, France: OECD.
———. 2000. *From Mass Higher Education to Universal Access: The American Advantage*. Research and Occasional Paper Series CSHE.1.00. Berkeley, CA: Center for Studies in Higher Education, University of California Berkeley. Available online at: http://cshe.berkeley.edu/sites/default/files/shared/publications/docs/PP.Trow.MassHE.1.00.pdf, accessed on November 15, 2013.

Vessuri, Hebe, Josè Miguel Cruces, Renato Janine Ribeiro, and José Luis Ramírez. 2008. "El Futuro nos Alcanza: Mutaciones Previsibles de la Ciencia y la Tecnología" ("Future reaches us: Foreseeable Mutations of Science and Technology"). In *Tendencias de la Educación Superior en América Latina y el Caribe* (Higher Education Trends in Latin America and the Caribbean), edited by Ana Lucia Gázzola and Axel Didriksson. Caracas, Venezuela: UNESCO International Institute for Higher Education in Latin America and the Caribbean.

Chapter 13

Conclusion

Gustavo Gregorutti and Jorge Enrique Delgado

Throughout this book, we have argued that the advancement of science, technology, and innovation (STI) has an increasing role in Latin American higher education, particularly for private higher education institutions and universities. This comes as a combination of expected contributions of private institutions to the betterment of the region and a shift from the teaching-oriented university model to a larger focus on research. Thus, research productivity has become more a defining characteristic than an option for universities in the twenty-first century. Worldwide, state and private universities intensively look for ways to generate new knowledge and technologies that can transform economies and the society. In the predominantly Latin American government-funded universities, there is also an increasing interest in engaging private universities in a transformation from a training-focused mindset to an increased emphasis on applied research that can lead to innovation. In several countries, governments are urging private universities to add research to their educational projects. They use different mechanisms such as accreditation that includes research-related measurements. These kinds of requirements constitute a challenge for several private universities that have traditionally emphasized teaching and knowledge transmission over its generation. Macro policies have prompted important changes in some private universities that have somehow split them into a type of segmentation. Those institutions that accumulate accreditations and expand quality assessment with intensive research agendas are standing out as a new kind of elite, redefining their leadership and prestige. One visible sign of this trend is the strategic pursuance of inclusion in main national, regional, and international university rankings. The Monterrey Institute of Technology and Higher Studies in Mexico is a clear example of the competition that is taking place among certain private universities. Some of these institutions fear competition and show a clear interest in research from the time of their foundation. The Brazilian, Chilean, and Peruvian cases confirm that research was at the core of universities' missions and now, with a proresearch policy environment, they are heading even more in that direction. This way, well-positioned universities have rapidly used new government policies and available funding to expand what they believe was a crucial mission of higher education. Newcomers such as the ORT University in Uruguay, Puebla State Popular Autonomous University in Mexico, and Central American institutes are a good example of institutions that can redirect their faculty goals to reinvent themselves under new paradigms. On the other side, less prestigious and demand-absorbing schools seem to struggle to keep pace with all these pressures and stay in business by focusing on training, as one of Marcelo Rabossi's cases exemplifies. This situation may generate a kind of schizophrenia that could actually impede institutional development.

Governments can do several things to help the private sector be more productive. Even though Argentinian quality policies have some limitations, they are another noteworthy example of encouraging research from outside. The comparison between Chile and Colombia government funding systems to promote research across all universities, including private, is instructive. Top Chilean private universities have been receiving abundant grants for long periods of time; these have helped them to establish clear research agendas over the years. It is important to note that public funding for advancing research is vital even in the American and European contexts. Most Latin American governments allow researchers from private institutions to apply for research grants. However, as some authors argue throughout this book, private universities have limited access to public funds. This is a sensitive scenario since available resources are not enough for all projects and competition can be challenging. Nevertheless, if private universities are expected to be more productive, they need to receive more public support as well. Some Latin American countries do not seem to have a plan to make private universities eligible for public research funding. It seems that governments want private universities to find some sort of magic solutions in order to be productive. At the same time, these institutions should become more entrepreneurial by being on the lookout for nongovernmental funding. The two Mexican cases presented in this book are great models of strategic inside-outside funding systems. The dominant model to search for funding and develop innovation involves three actors: universities, government, and the productive sector (triple helix).

Given this rather complex and challenging development of research, we invited authors to find out how some Latin American private universities are able to produce more knowledge than others. In addition, we wanted to know what all these productive universities have in common. According to what authors have showed here, universities with remarkable productivity tend to have at least a combination of the following aspects:

1. *Visionary strategic leadership.* Leaders acting with a clear sense of purpose and strategic thinking were able to unify and redirect all available resources to mission changes. This is not a simple task, but the cases presented here demonstrate that it is doable. Proactive leaders are a key component to engage all involved players to new visions of higher education.
2. *Clear mission purpose.* What does it mean to be a research university? This may be a hard question for some institutions, but those who understand its benefits go for this model even though that implies taking risks.
3. *Funding.* No real transformation or shifting is possible without a solid plan to support the multilevel expenses a research institution will demand. Successful cases had a clear understanding of this and went through different stages to increase revenues and external funding. The search for funding includes not only public grants from local governments but also the private sector and other funders locally and abroad.
4. *Outstanding human resources.* This is also a key aspect to carry out research in the long run. Having the best possible qualified professors is a must. Although some universities may find it difficult to achieve this, frontrunner institutions demonstrate open and highly selective processes to hire new academics.
5. *Balanced teaching loads.* It is almost impossible to produce ideas and transfer them to the society and the private sector if academics have heavy teaching loads. Reversing that is expensive, and tuition-driven institutions would not be able to attain it. The challenges, therefore, are to create the conditions for faculty to engage in research activities and to develop mechanisms to find external funding when there is no public funding available.
6. *Global researcher networks.* Universities cannot do this without highly qualified professors who are globally connected with colleagues with whom they share projects and resources. These scholars think and move in borderless networks that demand time and support from

their departments. Globalization creates competition but also opens the doors to collaboration. Networks can be located at the national, regional, and global levels.
7. *Strong graduate programs.* All of the universities studied here have relied heavily on graduate programs and students to advance knowledge. Like in both Mexican cases, much of their progress can be attributed to graduate degrees and activities.
8. *University-private sector relationships and entrepreneurship.* Beyond finding partners to fund research, the transfer of knowledge and technology also implies developing mechanisms to patent inventions, promoting the creation of spin-offs by the institutions, their faculty members, and graduates, and developing joint revenue creating ventures.

Hence, these basic characteristics seem to be crucial for a university that pursues ways to become successful in producing new knowledge and technology that will impact the knowledge-driven societies. In order to summarize the general findings of this book, figure 13.1 shows that more research-mission-driven institutions with a clear leadership to support research work, solid funding systems, outstanding human resources, lower teaching loads, wide-ranging research networks, graduate programs that involve students in research projects, and university-productive sector partnerships are the ones that are generating more productivity. In addition,

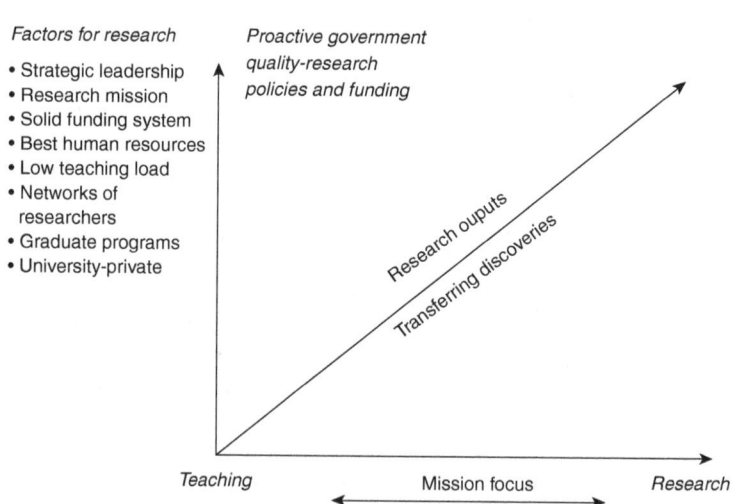

Figure 13.1 Promoting research among private universities in Latin America.

and even though there is limited support in most countries, these universities are flourishing in national policy contexts that help them advance complex and expensive projects.

Universities that are able to create an appropriate research environment, engage their faculty members in STI endeavors, and redirect resources to produce quality research will not only get ahead in this tight competition, but also have a remarkable impact on their local economies by generating jobs and producing better-trained graduates. However, it is important to emphasize that government policies, particularly funding, are central variables that help private universities to advance knowledge creation and innovation in the region. Thus, this is a combination of environmental and internal factors that interact to impact research productivity.

To conclude, we would like to emphasize that not all universities are ready to take these important and, in many cases, far-stretching steps. In a collegial-type discussion, leaders, professors, and constituency must go through an institutional-soul-searching stage. Some private universities serve churches or specific markets and may not want to reconvert all resources after a research university model that can alienate deep and rooted mission purposes. Although learning to carry out research is an important competency and all higher education models should promote it, becoming an institution that produces highly complex STI processes is very expensive and needs serious consideration. Quality training does not always need to be associated with research. If it is done in the proper format and with at least minimum quality assurance, less prestigious and demand-absorbing tertiary educational institutions become crucial for Latin American economy and job markets. Hence, governments need to look at the whole spectrum of higher education and target policies accordingly and not try to impose "one-size fits all" institutions. At the end, as always, this is a matter of collective choices.

Appendix

Satisfaction Scale:

    5. Very satisfied
    4. Somewhat satisfied
    3. Neither satisfied nor dissatisfied
    2. Somewhat dissatisfied
    1. Very dissatisfied
    0. Not applicable

1. Are you satisfied with the kind of research work you conduct at this institution? (kindrese)
2. Are you satisfied with the amount of time you have for doing research at this institution? (timrese)
3. How satisfied are you with the library availability at this institution (journals/books/online resources)? (library)
4. How satisfied are you with your job salary at this institution? (salary)

Recognition Scale:

    5. Strongly agree
    4. Somewhat agree
    3. Neither agree nor disagree
    2. Somewhat disagree
    1. Strongly disagree
    0. Not applicable

5. In my opinion, I believe that the institution offers adequate professional assistance for obtaining internally or externally funded grants. (assifund)
6. In my opinion, the university recognizes and rewards excellent performance in research. (rewresea)

7. In general, the institution provides me with travel funds (totally or partially) to present papers, conduct research, or attend seminars. (travfund)
8. In my opinion, the institution has an adequate policy for providing sabbatical leaves to support training or research activities. (sabbatic)

Contributors

José Anicama is the head of Psychology Training at the School of Medicine and Public Health of the Autonomous University of Peru (*Universidad Autónoma del Perú*) and the Federico Villarreal National University (*Universidad Nacional Federico Villarreal*). He has been an active leader holding positions in different academic levels and Peruvian universities. He holds a PhD in Sciences from the Cayetano Heredia Peruvian University (*Universidad Peruana Cayetano Heredia*), a master's in Public Health from the University of Alabama, and a bachelor's in Psychology from the National University of San Marcos, Peru. His research interests include issues related to psychology and higher education in Peru. janicamag@yahoo.com

Édgar Apanecatl-Ibarra is a PhD candidate in the Higher Education program at Oklahoma State University. His research interests include the internationalization of higher education, best teaching practices, and faculty development. He has worked as a faculty member and administrator at the University of the Americas (*Universidad de las Américas*), in Puebla, Mexico. apaneca@ostatemail.okstate.edu

Elizabeth Balbachevsky is an associate professor at the Department of Political Science at the University of São Paulo, São Paulo, Brazil, and deputy director of the University of São Paulo's Center for Public Policy Research. She collaborates with the University of Campinas' Strategic Thinking Forum, and is an Erasmus Mundus Scholar at the European Master's Program in Research and Innovation in Higher Education, where she teaches the course Systems in Transition. (Danube University Krems—Austria, University of Tampere—Finland, University of Applied Sciences Osnabrück—Germany, and Beijing Normal University—China). She was a Fullbright New Century Scholar in 2005–2006. balbasky@usp.br

Antonio José Botelho is a PhD, full professor, head of the Graduate Program in Political Science and International Relations, and director of Research Units for the Study of Science, Technology, Innovation, and Society and for the Study of Comparative Political Economy at the University Research Institute of Rio de Janeiro, Cândido Mendes University. He is also CEO of Innovastrat Consulting and has been the Brazil correspondent, European Commission Programs' Research Inventory ERAWATCH, Country Report, InnoPolicy Trendchart, and METRIS III. Dr. Botelho has done significant contributions in the area of producing and transferring knowledge through higher education in Brazil. ajjbotelho@gmail.com

Francisco J. Cantú-Ortiz is a professor of Computer Science and Artificial Intelligence at the Monterrey Institute of Technology and Higher Studies (ITESM: *Instituto Tecnológico y de Estudios Superiores de Monterrey*), where he is also the dean for Research, Graduate Studies, and Entrepreneurship. He holds a PhD in Artificial Intelligence from the University of Edinburgh, UK, and a bachelor's in Computer Science from ITESM. Dr. Cantú-Ortiz has published around 50 scientific articles and around 20 edited books. His research interests include knowledge-based systems and inference, machine learning and data mining using Bayesian and statistical techniques for business intelligence, technology management, and entrepreneurial science, as well as philosophy of science, technology, and religion. fcantu@itesm.mx

Adriana Chiancone has a PhD in Social Studies of Science at the Venezuelan Institute for Scientific Research. She is a professor at the University of the Republic of Uruguay and a researcher of the National Research System. She has also worked on nanotechnology in different Uruguayan companies. Her research agenda includes issues of the institutionalization of science, trends and challenges of higher education, and knowledge production and its relationship with social development. achiancouniversidad@gmail.com

Ángela Corengia is an associate professor and researcher at the School of Education of the Austral University in Argentina. From 2005 to June 2013, she was the director of the Office of Institutional Assessment at the Austral University. During the period between 2010 and 2013, she led the Second Institutional Self-Assessment Process of the University. She received a research grant from the National Agency for the Promotion of Science and Technology (2008–2010) and was a postdoctoral fellow of the National Council of Research in Science and Technicology (2010–2012). She holds a PhD and a master's degree in Education and a bachelor's in Business Administration. Her main research focus is on issues regarding quality and funding of higher education. acorengia@austral.edu.ar

Jorge Enrique Delgado holds a PhD in Administrative and Policy Studies in Education (Social and Comparative Analysis in Education) from the

University of Pittsburgh. Dr. Delgado is an instructor of the Department of Administrative and Policy Studies in Education and Affiliated Faculty of the Center for Latin American Studies at the University of Pittsburgh in the United States. He is currently the co-chairperson of the Higher Education SIG of the Comparative and International Education Society and the editor-in-chief of the scientific journal *Universitas Odontologica* of the Pontifical Javeriana University from Bogotá, Colombia. Dr. Delgado's research focuses on the development of research in universities, particularly the communication of research through the publication of scholarly/research journals in Latin American universities. His scholarly work covers topics such as knowledge-based economies and societies; higher education systems; science, technology, and innovation policy; institutional policy; faculty development; and open access and other publication trends. jed41@pitt.edu

Ana García de Fanelli is a senior research scholar of the National Council of Research in Science and Technology at the Center for the Study of State and Society in Buenos Aires, Argentina. She has published widely on comparative policies in higher education in Latin America, the management of public universities, and university financing. She was a senior consultant to the UNESCO International Institute of Educational Planning in Buenos Aires and Paris, the National Commission for University Evaluation and Accreditation, the Inter-University Development Center from Chile, and the Argentine Ministry of Education. Dr. García de Fanelli obtained her master's in Social Sciences from the Latin American School of Social Sciences (FLACSO) and her PhD in Economics from the Universidad de Buenos Aires. anafan@cedes.org

Gustavo Gregorutti worked until recently as an associate professor of the School of Education at the Montemorelos University in Mexico. As part of the Montemorelos graduate program, Dr. Gregorutti has visited several Latin American universities where he has done presentations on higher education leadership and management. He has been conducting postdoctoral research at the Humboldt University Center for Higher Education in Berlin, Germany. Currently, he is an associate professor of the School of Education at Andrews University in Michigan. His research focuses on faculty research productivity, private higher education in Latin America, and quality issues that impact accreditation. Dr. Gregorutti is currently the chair of the Awards Committee of the Higher Education SIG of the Comparative and International Education Society. ggregoru@andrews.edu

José Livia is the head of the Psychology Department at the School of Medicine and Public Health of the Federico Villarreal National University in Peru, where he also chairs the Center for Research on Psychology and Health. Dr. Livia is director and associate editor of several national and international peer-reviewed journals. He is the vice dean of the Psychology Association of Peru. He holds bachelor's, master's, and PhD degrees in Psychology from the Federico Villarreal National University. Dr. Livia has been conducting research in different areas of psychology and teaching in higher education. livsegjo@yahoo.com

Enrique Martínez Larrechea has a PhD in International Relations, a master's in Social Sciences, and a bachelor's in Sociology. Dr. Martínez is the dean of the School of Education at the University of the Enterprise (*Universidad de la Empresa*) in Montevideo, Uruguay. He is the president of the Board of the brand new Uruguayan Society of Comparative and International Education. He is also a visiting professor of many graduate programs in Argentina, Bolivia, and Paraguay and is currently a researcher of the National Research System. Dr. Martínez is the former national director of Education of the Ministry of Education and Culture of Uruguay, where he participated actively in the Mercosur Education Sector. martinez.larrechea@ude.edu.uy

Pedro Pineda is an associate professor at the Externado University of Colombia (*Universidad Externado de Colombia*) in Bogotá, Colombia. Dr. Pineda holds a PhD in Education from the Humboldt University Institute of Education from Berlin. He obtained a master's in Education from the University of Kassel and a bachelor's in Psychology from the National University of Colombia. While in Germany, Dr. Pineda conducted research as a fellow of the German Academic Exchange Service. His academic work has been enriched with ten years of professional experience at schools, private industries, and international organizations. His current research interests in comparative education are related to higher education policy, science and innovation, and human rights education. pc.pineda@uniandes.edu.co

Marcelo Rabossi obtained a PhD in Education from the State University of New York, Albany. At present, Dr. Rabossi is a full-time professor of the School of Government at Torcuato di Tella University (UTDT) in Argentina, where he teaches courses in education finance and economics, and higher education policy. Between 1996 and 2003, he was in charge of the organization and development of Executive Training Courses in Educational Administration for headmasters and developed workshops of research in educational policies and management. From 2000 to 2004, he was director of the Area of Education at UTDT. His research interest include higher education governance and financing, private higher education, and academic labor markets. mrabossi@utdt.edu

Contributors

Claudio Rama is a specialist in higher education and its relationship with economic development. Dr. Rama is the dean of the School of Business at the University of the Enterprise (*Universidad de la Empresa*) in Montevideo, Uruguay. Earlier, he was the director of the Latin American and Caribbean Virtual Education Observatory, which is affiliated to the Organization of American States, and the director of the UNESCO International Institute for Higher Education in Latin America and Caribbean in Caracas, Venezuela. His credentials include two doctoral and three postdoctoral degrees from universities in Uruguay, Argentina, and Brazil. claudiorama@gmail.com

Nanette Svenson is an adjunct professor at Tulane University and independent consultant for the United Nations and other international organizations. Previously, she helped establish the United Nations Development Programme Regional Centre for Latin America and the Caribbean in Panama and headed its research and knowledge management efforts. Her education includes a PhD from Tulane, an MBA from IESE in Barcelona, and a BA from Stanford University. Dr. Svenson is based in Panama, where Tulane recently launched a new master's program in International Development, and her research focuses on capacity development, particularly in relation to higher education programs and international organizations. nsvenson@tulane.edu

Stephen P. Wanger is an associate professor of Higher Education at Oklahoma State University. Dr. Wanger holds a PhD from Purdue University and a master's degree from Duke University. His research focuses on the evolving missions of international and American universities, student success, the leadership of change, and academic program development. He has worked as a faculty member and administrator in both postsecondary and K-12 education. steve.wanger@okstate.edu

Index

2010–2015 Development Plan, 40, 48
2011–2015 Plan for Integral Development, 39, 49
academia, 29, 89, 111, 217, 262
academic achievement, 90, 173
Academic Affairs Director, 65–9, 75
academic community, 31, 99, 178, 194
academic decision-making, 20
academic degrees, 19, 247
academic excellence, 18, 146
academic freedom, 18
academic profession, 18, 20, 96, 188, 200
academic reputation, 40, 174, 175
academic staff, 59, 186, 196, 202
academic units, 33, 43, 72, 95, 201, 234, 235
academicians, 40, 189, 192, 200
  See also academics
academics, 16, 84–6, 90, 92, 125, 163, 186–90, 195–7, 199–200, 202, 207, 209, 211, 213, 215–16, 219, 237, 260–1, 275
  See also academicians
access, 2, 9–11, 27, 52, 70–1, 96, 115, 121, 122, 126, 134, 168, 170, 186, 187, 189, 194–201, 253, 260, 263, 274
accountability, 17, 20, 93, 99, 159
accreditation, 1, 3, 12, 14, 15, 28, 52, 55–9, 63, 65–70, 74, 75, 121, 134, 152, 174, 175, 209, 228, 245, 273
  international, 115

accreditation agencies, 10, 82, 84, 244, 175
accreditation standards, 55, 72
accumulated advantage, 10
adjunct faculty, 119
administrators, 3, 10, 15–20, 35, 68, 71, 79–81, 84, 93, 97, 99, 114–15, 125–6, 131, 135–41, 143–5, 148–51, 245
Africa, 167
Africa Peace and Conflict Journal, 172
agencies, 21, 30, 34, 35, 63, 71, 75, 82–4, 114, 115, 122, 134, 146, 170, 172, 174, 201, 218–20
  government, 114, 122, 146, 172, 174, 218
  international, 82
  international aid, 34
agribusiness, 167–8, 176, 260
agricultural sciences, 165
agricultural sector, 34, 264
agriculture, 17, 33, 87, 162–8, 256
Alberto Fujimori, 208
Alcalá de Henares University, 41
alliances, 29, 112, 146, 165, 173, 262, 266, 267
alumni donations, 117, 121, 126
Álvaro Uribe, 95
Andres Bello University, 89
Andrés Pastrana, 95
anthropology, 162
anticipatory principle, 143
Antonio Nariño University, 86, 89
applied knowledge, 214, 217

applied research, 1, 34, 35, 44, 81,
    84, 91, 93, 96, 97, 100, 124, 157,
    162, 163, 167, 170, 178–80, 195,
    197–8, 208–9, 261, 264, 273
appreciative inquiry, 135, 143, 147
archaeology, 162
architecture, 119, 257
Argentina, 3, 4, 11, 30–3, 35–7,
    39–40, 42–3, 51–76, 168, 169,
    175, 207, 225–47
Argentinean Pontifical Catholic
    University Santa Maria de Los
    Buenos Aires, 40
Argentinian Technological Fund, 60
articles, 28, 30, 33, 39–41, 82, 85,
    115, 117, 122, 124, 170, 194,
    197, 211, 212, 214, 216, 234,
    261, 263, 266
artificial character, 97
assessment, 10, 12, 33, 54, 56–9,
    63–6, 70, 75, 119, 123, 159,
    166, 213, 215, 227, 273
  institutional, 3, 52, 56–8, 63–5,
    72, 76, 200
assistantships, 198
Association of Medical Science
    Schools of Argentina, 72
Austral University (Argentina), 40
Austral University (Chile), 88
Australia, 35
autarchy, 53
autonomy, 17, 20, 96, 173, 208
  academic, 17, 168, 171, 200
  university, 53–4, 80, 202, 207
AVINA Foundation, 170–1

balanced teaching loads, 275
basic sciences, 32, 52, 68, 69, 75
Basic Sciences Development
    Program, 258
Belgian Development Agency, 213
Belize, 158, 160–1, 165
best practices, 79, 80, 97, 101
better-paid jobs, 126

Bicentennial Scholarship, 93
bilingual, 163, 173
Bill Gates Foundation, 213
Biosis, 33
biotechnology, 4, 119–22, 125,
    251–68
Bogotá, 283
Bolivia, 11, 36, 165, 167, 168
Bologna Process, 132, 150
bonus, 194, 243, 261
books, 28, 82, 85, 143, 169, 170,
    228, 279
Brazil, 4, 13, 21, 31–7, 39, 41, 63,
    124, 168, 185–202, 210,
    213, 259, 267, 274
Brazilian Institute of Capital
    Market, 187
Brazilian Petroleum Corporation, 13
budget, 9, 11, 16, 20, 65, 71, 115, 117,
    120, 160, 165, 176, 215 219, 228,
    235, 264
business cluster, 141
business demand, 197, 257

CAB Index, 33
Cambridge University, 90
Canada, 35, 121
capabilities, 1, 5, 112, 144, 149, 192,
    254, 258, 259
capacity development, 27, 179
capitalism, 111
Carlos III University, 41
Carlos Sanguinetti, 259, 268
Carnegie Mellon University, 121
case study, 52, 56, 63, 64, 74,
    112, 118, 124, 133, 136–7,
    151, 206, 233
Catholic Church, 36, 206
Catholic University of Temuco, 88
Catholic University of the Holy
    Conception, 88
Catholic University of the North
    (Chile), 88
Catholic University of Uruguay, 251

Index

Cayetano Heredia Peruvian University, 4, 205–20
Ceiba, 168
Center for Research and Documentation on Contemporary History, 193
Center for the Study of the State and Society, 228
Center for Tropical Agricultural Research and Education, 163
central administration, 35, 67
Central America, 4, 157–81, 274
Central American Academic Link, 169
Central American Bank for Economic Integration, 170, 174
Central American Integration System, 174
Central American Journal of Social Sciences, 169
Central American Tourism Council, 174
Central American Tourism Integration System, 174
certification, 14, 121, 122, 149, 194
Chagas disease, 166, 259
change, 2, 3, 12, 16, 19–20, 29, 34, 35, 52, 54–7, 59, 62–8, 70, 72–5, 79–82, 89–97, 126, 133–7, 140, 143–4, 147–53, 159, 165, 170, 186, 194, 200, 205–8, 210, 214, 219–20, 229, 242, 244, 254, 257, 266, 273, 275
 factual, 56, 57, 65–8, 70, 72–4
 intended, 57, 65, 68, 72, 73
Changing Academic Profession network, 188
Chemical Abstracts, 33
Chile, 3, 13, 15, 31, 33–7, 41, 43, 63, 76, 79–102, 124, 168, 210, 274
Christian institutions, 28
citations, 39, 40, 64, 116, 121, 122
civil engineering, 121, 162
Clark, Burton, 3, 54, 55, 63, 73, 74, 79, 253, 254, 256, 265

Clemente Estable Institute of Biology Research, 252
climate, 165, 170, 219
 organizational, 227, 231–2, 236, 243
clinical sciences, 120
coauthorship, 124
Colciencias, 95, 96
collaboration, 2, 35, 41, 114, 116, 118, 121, 124, 126, 127, 133, 138, 139, 141, 146, 148, 149, 152, 166, 169, 174, 176, 189, 213, 263–5, 276
Colombia, 3, 31, 33, 35–7, 39, 41–3, 76, 79–102, 116, 124, 165, 210, 274
commercial media, 38
commercialism, 17
commercialization, 10, 43, 44, 122, 126, 159, 179
commodity, 29, 35, 148, 158, 186, 199, 200
communication, 147, 148, 173
 scientific, 215, 217, 257
companies, 14, 16, 17, 20, 33, 55, 70, 116, 122, 123, 126, 151, 186, 187, 192, 193, 195–8, 210, 217, 258, 266
Company of Jesus, 28, 36, 45, 51
Compendex, 33
competition, 14, 16, 27–45, 75, 83, 90, 91, 97, 134, 151, 210, 216, 236, 242, 245, 266, 274, 276, 277
 global, 14, 29
competitive grants, 13, 53, 73, 74
competitive market, 12, 14, 90
competitiveness, 3, 14, 28, 29, 35, 38, 43–4, 110, 111, 126, 165, 198, 218, 220, 252, 255
comprehensive university, 118, 185
confessional university, 18, 53, 54
Conicyt Scholarship, 93
constructionist principle, 143

consulting, 44, 93, 121, 123, 163, 169, 170, 173, 175, 187, 192, 194, 195, 201
continuing education, 123, 126, 193
contract, 57, 65–8, 70, 74, 75, 117, 124, 185, 196–8, 228–31, 233–43, 247
convergence, 84, 141
Coordination for Improvement of Higher Education Personnel, 193
copyright, 19, 29, 111, 116, 217
Cordoba reform, 207
Cordoba University (Argentina), 51
Cordoba University movement, 207
Cornell University, 121
corruption, 18
cosmetic changes, 66
Costa Rica, 15, 36, 76, 158, 160, 161, 163–71, 174–8
Council of Chilean University Presidents, 88
countries, 2, 3, 10–13, 15, 17, 31–7, 40, 47, 63, 79–81, 83–5, 88, 89, 97, 99–101, 110, 112, 116, 134, 141, 157–60, 162–70, 176–9, 190, 210, 213, 225, 226, 254, 263, 273, 274, 277
coverage, 13, 28, 159, 160
critical mass, 98, 125, 176, 225, 228
cronyism, 18
Cuba, 36, 43, 168
cultural capital, 30
culture, 2, 13, 16, 20, 97, 100, 113, 117, 122, 125, 135, 136, 146, 147–50, 174, 201, 207, 215, 232, 252, 254–5, 262, 264, 267
research, 16, 20, 100, 117
curriculum, 159, 208, 261
customers, 75

dual degree programs, 134, 151, 152
decentralization, 91, 169
decentralized competitive market, 90
decentralized local adaptation, 135

decision-making, 16, 20, 71
Decree 4 of 1981 (Chile), 91
Decree 308 of 1995 (Uruguay), 252
Decree 1,444 of 1992 (Colombia), 95
Decree 2,912 of 2002 (Colombia), 95
Decree DL 112 of 1981 (Peru), 209
Decree-Law 15,661 of 1995 (Uruguay), 251, 252, 256
Decree-Law 19,326 in 1972 (Peru), 208
demand-absorbing, 11, 54, 63, 88, 89, 91, 100, 201
demand-absorbing institutions, 21, 88, 89, 93, 189, 190, 274, 277
dentistry, 211, 257
Department of Science, Technology, and Innovation (Colombia), 95
developing countries, 157, 158, 168, 179, 190
development, 1, 2, 4, 5, 12, 15–20, 27, 29, 30, 32, 34–7, 39, 43, 44, 52, 55, 57, 59, 63, 64, 73, 74, 79, 81–4, 90, 92–102, 110, 111, 119, 121, 124, 132–3, 137, 141, 143, 145, 146, 150–2, 157–70, 172, 174–81, 187, 193, 205–12, 215, 217–20, 228, 234, 242, 252–66, 274–5
economic, 1, 34, 43, 100, 110, 132, 133, 164, 169, 193, 206
national, 5, 34, 83, 162, 164, 175, 176, 177, 179, 181, 217
social, 30, 111, 169
technological, 84, 93, 94, 97, 177, 205, 218, 252, 253
Diego Portales University, 86, 89
differentiation, 4, 10, 29, 35, 39, 54, 74, 98, 186, 192–9, 200, 201, 229, 239, 254
DiMaggio and Powell, 3, 54, 63, 72, 74, 75
discipline-based departments, 35
disciplines, 9, 15, 42, 75, 89, 109, 125, 126, 139, 140, 196, 207, 208, 229, 230, 253, 255, 256

discourse, 81, 94, 85, 93, 95, 97, 100
discoveries, 10, 17, 110, 116, 122, 205, 225, 226, 245, 276
dissertation committees, 115
diversification, 254
doctoral degrees, 16, 32, 37, 43, 59, 62, 65, 73, 114, 115, 118, 119, 151, 202, 211, 234, 235, 242, 245, 246
doctoral graduates, 117
doctoral programs, 39, 40, 114, 115, 118, 120, 134, 165, 191, 196, 213
doctoral students, 59, 115, 116, 119, 121, 122, 123, 126
doctorates, 30, 42, 43, 94, 197
Dominican Republic, 36, 165, 168
donations, 117, 121, 123, 126, 175

Eafit University, 83, 89
earth sciences, 162, 265
economic activity, 83, 158
Economic Commission for Latin America and the Caribbean, 132
economic growth, 10, 31, 44, 84
economic progress, 2, 210
economics, 83, 188, 192, 193
economy, 2, 13, 15, 29, 75, 91, 96, 132, 141, 186, 194, 195, 208, 225, 254, 264, 277
   national, 5, 218
ecosystem, 3, 109–27
Ecosystems of Innovation, 110
Ecuador, 36, 167, 168, 175, 210
education in the professions, 34
education scholarship, 28
El Mercurio, 83
El Salvador, 36, 37, 43, 61, 158, 160, 161, 164, 165, 169
elite institutions, 186, 188, 191, 201, 226, 234
elite-oriented institutions, 187, 189, 190, 192, 200
elitism, 21
elitist structure, 98–9

Elsevier, 33, 41, 116
employability, 190
employer reputation, 40
endowments, 16, 111, 117, 121
engineering, 32, 33, 55, 56, 68–72, 83, 87, 89, 110, 119–22, 141, 142, 162, 195–7, 257, 258, 260–2, 266
England, 90, 213
English-speaking countries, 34, 35
enrollment, 11–13, 30, 32, 36–7, 42, 52, 56, 62, 63, 92, 119, 120, 161, 185, 211, 227, 228, 233, 234, 257, 260
   tertiary, 12, 159
entrepreneurial, 10, 80, 93, 94, 96, 101, 111, 125, 175, 179, 192, 255, 262, 272
entrepreneurialism, 256, 259
entrepreneurship, 114, 116, 118, 122, 127, 145, 166, 168, 196, 197, 276
environmental studies, 162, 180
epidemiology, 212
equipment, 16, 116, 123, 187, 207, 260, 267
European Union, 213
evaluation, 28, 37, 38, 51, 57, 58, 67, 68, 72, 99, 114, 118, 121, 123, 146, 193, 195, 200, 202, 235, 244, 247
   peer-, 119
   research, 114, 118, 123
evolving curricula, 150
expansion, 1, 9, 10–14, 27, 28, 35, 57, 60, 63, 73, 80, 82–5, 91, 146, 151, 194, 200, 201, 234, 252, 253
extension programs, 117
Externado University, 89, 284
external assessment, 12
external funding, 10, 13, 16, 37, 39, 59, 70, 71, 117, 123, 124, 219, 226, 275
external networks, 17

face-to-face education, 257
facilities, 12, 14, 16, 53, 113, 116–18, 123, 126, 176, 197, 226, 261

faculty (school), 53, 211, 216, 256–66
faculty members, 12, 16, 18, 37, 42, 57, 64, 65, 67, 68, 70, 72–5, 117, 119–20, 127, 134, 138, 142, 145, 190, 194, 200, 211, 228–9, 233–47, 276, 277
faculty mobility, 114, 150, 151
faculty promotion, 29
faculty qualifications, 42
faculty research, 4, 16, 18, 20, 113, 231, 242, 243, 245, 260–3
faculty salaries, 30, 37
faculty/student ratio, 40
 See also faculty/student relation; student/faculty productivity ration
faculty/student relation, 30
Federal Council of Engineering Deans (Argentina), 72
federal government, 53, 185, 196, 199, 200
Federal University of Minas Gerais, 39
Federal University of Rio de Janeiro, 39
Federal University of Rio Grande do Sul, 39
fellowships, 210, 216
Fields Medals, 39
financial aid, 54, 115
financial sustainability, 79, 201
flexibility, 27, 44, 140, 254, 264
food science, 119, 162, 167
Ford Foundation, 83, 169, 188
foreign companies, 33, 151
foreign-trained graduates, 83
forestry, 162, 165
for-profit sector, 13
Foundation for Latin American Economic Research, 228
foundations, 70, 110, 115, 117, 172, 173, 174, 246
France, 59, 85, 90
full-fledged researcher, 189, 190
full-time faculty, 14, 32, 57, 68, 114, 118, 119, 138, 139, 229
 See also full-time professors

full-time professors, 16, 18, 66, 68, 114, 235, 237, 239, 242, 243, 246
full-time researchers, 246
Fund for Construction and University Research (Chile), 91
Fund for Innovation and Development Projects (Colombia), 95
Fund for Innovation for Competitiveness (Chile), 93
Fund for Scientific and Technological Research (Argentina), 37, 60
funding, 1–3, 10, 13, 16, 17, 19, 20, 29, 31, 32, 35, 37–40, 43, 51–76, 83, 85, 90–9, 111, 113, 114, 117, 118, 121–6, 132, 134, 159, 168, 170, 171–3, 175, 177, 181, 187, 194, 195, 198, 210, 212–19, 225, 226, 229, 230, 239, 241, 244–6, 252, 254, 258, 260, 262–6, 274–7
government, 29, 55, 57, 64, 70, 71, 91, 92, 117, 177, 226, 274

Galileo University, 162
Genesis Technology Incubator, 196
genetic epidemiology, 212
German Organization for Technical Cooperation, 171
Germany, 85, 90, 174
Gerontology Institute, 213
Getulio Vargas Foundation, 187, 193
global markets, 14, 153
global researcher networks, 275
globalization, 28, 29, 132, 141, 151, 169, 276
globalized scholarship, 17
governance, 4, 36, 53, 80, 95, 96, 101, 158, 164, 165, 169, 172, 200, 201, 230, 241
government, 1, 2, 5, 9, 11–13, 16, 21, 27–9, 31, 32, 34, 35, 38, 40, 43, 51–5, 57, 59, 60, 62–5, 69–71, 73–5, 80–101, 110–15, 117, 122, 124–6, 136, 137, 141,

INDEX

146, 159–61, 164, 165, 168–70, 172–4, 176, 178, 181, 185, 190, 192, 194, 196, 197, 199, 200, 207, 209–11, 217, 218, 225–8, 246, 251, 252, 256, 258, 260, 265–6, 273–7
graduate education, 4, 20, 31, 35, 92, 119, 164, 167, 186, 189, 190, 192, 195, 198, 199, 207, 236, 243
graduate programs, 3, 14, 18, 19, 32, 55, 58, 72, 115, 119, 134, 137, 139, 141, 142, 186, 190, 191, 193, 196, 198, 199, 202, 233, 266, 276
grant, 13, 16, 32, 53, 59, 62, 66, 69, 71–6, 81, 84, 90, 115–17, 124, 138, 139, 187, 202, 208, 216, 218, 219, 237, 241, 246, 252, 256, 259, 266, 274, 275, 279
Great Britain, 226
Guadalajara, 119
Guatemala, 11, 37, 158, 160–2, 164, 165, 167–9, 180

half-time professors, 42
Harvard Business School, 170
health care administration, 211
High Council of Scientific Research of Madrid, 263
higher education, 1–5, 9–15, 21, 27–36, 38, 39, 41, 44, 51–4, 57, 58, 63, 64, 72, 73, 75, 76, 79–82, 84, 85, 88, 90–5, 97–102, 111, 112, 117, 126–7, 131, 132, 134, 136, 141, 149–51, 153, 157, 159, 162–4, 171, 173, 175, 177, 185, 187–90, 193–5, 198, 202, 206–10, 225–8, 245–7, 251–6, 266, 268, 273–5, 277
Higher Education Act of 1995 (Argentina), 51, 53, 58, 72
higher education coordination, 253
higher education expansion, 27

higher education institutions, 14, 27, 63, 151, 153, 159, 162, 189, 198, 209, 227, 254, 273
Higher Education Law 24,521 of 1995 (Argentina), 72
higher education reform, 94
higher education system, 4, 11, 33–8, 52, 53, 64, 111, 117, 185, 228, 246, 253–5
higher education vice-ministries, 82
high-income families, 186
high-level administrators, 114
h-Index, 81
Hipólito Unanue Foundation, 216
hiring practices, 55, 57, 67, 68, 76
Honduras, 11, 31, 37, 158, 160, 161, 164–5, 167, 168
human capital, 29, 37, 177, 218
human resources, 4, 5, 12, 17, 18, 30, 32, 61–3, 73, 113, 115, 127, 173, 175, 176, 211, 213, 218, 220, 226, 229, 232, 246, 252, 258, 265, 266, 275, 276
humanistic values, 148–50
humanities, 32, 75, 87, 119, 120, 245
Humboldtian principle, 89

Iberic-American Network of Accreditation Agencies, 175
Iberic-American University, 37, 41
immunology, 212
impact factor, 123, 261
Imperial University, 90
import substitution, 34, 43
INCAE Business School, 164, 170
incentive, 2, 4, 13, 16, 29, 51, 52, 59, 73, 149, 159, 180, 199–201, 216, 219, 225–47, 260, 261, 264, 267
inclusion, 134, 137, 144, 147, 152, 169, 261, 274
Incubation Cell Program, 122
incubators, 14, 44

indicators, 28, 30, 32, 36, 38–41, 56, 65, 73, 74, 76, 81, 82, 88, 92, 102, 119, 120, 123, 127, 138, 139, 187, 210, 256
industrial partner funding, 126
industrial property, 30, 122
industrial revolution, 110
industrial sector, 93, 259
industrialization, 34
industry, 39, 43, 44, 91, 93, 110, 111, 118, 138, 139, 141, 148, 149, 151, 152, 257, 259, 266
information and communication technologies, 120, 147, 252
information asymmetries, 231
information society, 206
information technology, 119–21, 125, 162
infrastructure, 2, 16, 27, 40, 54, 80, 84, 89, 91, 92, 94, 96–8, 100–2, 114, 116, 117, 121, 126, 160, 196, 197, 207, 218, 258, 264, 266
innovation, 1–5, 10, 15, 16, 18, 20, 28–30, 34, 35, 39, 42, 43–4, 54, 55, 60, 83, 84, 93, 95, 96, 110, 114, 118, 121, 124, 126, 127, 145, 177, 188, 206, 209, 217, 218, 252–5, 262–6, 273, 275, 277
innovation ecosystem. *See under* research and innovation ecosystem model
innovative leadership, 119
innovative programs, 11, 113
Inspec, 33
Insper Institute for Teaching and Research (Brazil), 187
Institute for Educational Credit and Technical Studies Abroad (Colombia), 94
Institute for Educational Development (Brazil), 193
Institute of Higher Studies (Uruguay), 251
Institute of Philosophy, Science, Literature, and Linguistics (Uruguay), 251

Institute of Tropical Medicine in Antwerp (Belgium), 213
institutional arrangements, 42, 188
institutional development, 258, 274
Institutional Development Fund (Chile), 92
institutional differentiation, 29, 54, 254
institutional frameworks, 3, 51, 79–102, 192
institutional legitimacy, 54
institutional performance, 27
institutional research, 27
institutional rules and norms, 232
institutionalization, 80–5, 89–97, 99, 101, 102
intellectual production, 33, 210, 219, 261
intellectual property, 44, 81, 111, 116, 117, 122, 124, 217, 218
Inter-American Institute of Cooperation on Agriculture (Costa Rica), 164
interdisciplinarity, 139, 140, 150
interdisciplinary, 96, 99, 111, 139, 140–2, 145, 146, 152, 165, 168, 171, 173, 214, 253, 265
Interdisciplinary Center of Graduate Programs (Mexico), 137, 139–42
interinstitutional, 142, 149
internal approach (Burton Clark's), 3, 54, 74
internal evaluation, 146
international collaboration, 41, 114, 118, 121, 124, 127
international conferences, 116
international consortiums, 14
international cooperation, 4, 157–81
international faculty, 40, 163, 173
international foundations, 117
international networks, 4
international outlook, 39
International Scientific Index, 212
See also Science Citation Index

International Standard Classification of Education, 257
international students, 35, 40, 134, 151
international university, 165, 167, 178, 179
internationalization, 29, 113, 132, 141, 146, 152, 254
inventions, 17, 276
investment, 1, 9, 12, 16, 30–2, 44, 98, 114, 116, 157, 160, 162, 163, 175, 210, 227, 257, 263, 264, 266
isomorphic pressures, 55, 84
isomorphism, 3, 21, 63, 72
  coercive, 54, 72
  competitive, 75
  institutional, 54, 55, 75
  mimetic, 55
  normative, 55, 72
Ivy League, 63

Jesuits. *See under* Company of Jesus
John F. Kennedy, 61, 170
Johns Hopkins University, 121
journal article *or* publication, 28, 33, 115, 124, 175, 213, 214, 234, 266
Journal Citation Reports, 261
journals, 14, 28, 33, 39, 40, 41, 114, 116, 124, 169, 194, 197, 210, 211, 279
  academic and professional, 165
  high-impact, 116, 194, 201
  indexed, 30, 116
  peer-reviewed *or* refereed, 172, 228, 234, 236, 261, 263
  scholarly, 30, 33
  technical, 168
Julio Sanguinetti, 252

knowledge creation. *See under* knowledge generation
knowledge dissemination, 15, 29, 45, 132, 172, 174, 225, 273

knowledge generation, 1, 4, 5, 9, 10, 12, 15, 29, 86, 114, 116, 121, 126, 127, 132, 140, 146, 151, 175, 185–93, 195, 198–201, 212, 219, 220, 234, 251, 262, 277
knowledge production. *See under* knowledge generation
knowledge property. *See under* copyright
knowledge transfer, 35, 43, 152, 167
knowledge transmission. *See under* knowledge dissemination
knowledge-based economies, 27, 132, 205, 283
knowledge-based societies, 10, 17, 28, 29, 206, 276
knowledge-driven societies. *See under* knowledge-based societies

La Paz, 36
labor contract, 57, 65–8, 70, 75, 231
labor market, 11, 159, 199, 226, 230, 242, 244, 246
laboratory, 15, 19, 34, 67, 71, 110, 116, 121, 162, 166, 196–8, 211–14, 219, 259, 260, 263, 267
Latin American Center for Competitiveness and Sustainable Development (Costa Rica), 170, 180
Latin American School of Social Sciences—FLACSO, 163–4, 168–70, 175, 176, 178, 181
Law 29 of 1990 (Colombia), 94, 96
Law 1,286 of 2009 (Colombia), 96
Law 1,530 of 2012 (Colombia), 96
Law 4,004 of 1920 (Peru), 207
Law 11,575 of 1954 (Chile), 91
Law 15,738 of 1985 (Uruguay), 252
Law 19,021 of 1991 (Chile), 92
Law 28,740 of 2006 (Peru), 209
Law for Investment Promotion in Education (Peru), 208

leadership, 4, 20, 72, 119, 122, 124, 125, 127, 133, 135, 145, 147, 148, 150, 206, 207, 209, 214, 256, 265, 273, 275, 276
league tables. *See under* rankings
learning environment, 38
Leloir Institute Foundation, 228
liberalization, 34, 43
library, 30, 67, 71, 219, 237–9, 279
licensing, 44, 117
life-long learning, 201
Lima, 36, 211
local community, 133, 151, 166, 185
local government, 126, 275
lottery, 117

mainstream, 14, 35, 72, 79, 101, 219
management, 19, 20, 53, 61, 76, 110, 112, 114, 117, 119, 120, 123–4, 126, 127, 143, 147, 149, 152, 164–8, 171, 174, 176, 193, 200, 206, 208, 211, 213, 215, 217–19, 231, 256, 257, 261, 264, 265
Mariano Gálvez University (Guatemala), 180
market, 11–15, 17, 20, 28
marketing, 10, 11, 15, 152, 190
massification, 91, 132, 210, 254
master's programs, 32, 165, 191
Matthew effect, 10
medical sciences, 32, 75, 98
medicine, 56, 65, 67, 72, 83, 87, 89, 109, 119, 120, 122, 206, 211, 212, 214, 257, 259
Medline, 33
meritocracy, 17, 18, 20
Mexican Federation of Private Higher Education Institutions, 134
Mexican Institute for Industrial Property, 122
Mexico, 3, 14, 19, 31–3, 35–7, 39–43, 76, 109–27, 131–54, 165, 168, 181, 213, 267, 274
Mexico City, 119, 133
microbiology, 212, 267

Microsoft, 197
middle-income countries, 158
Ministry of Education (Argentina), 53, 57, 65, 69, 72
Ministry of Science, Technology and Innovation (Argentina), 59
mission
  institutional, 16, 62, 64, 70, 125, 131, 132, 137, 144
  research, 82, 101, 253, 276
  teaching, 79, 131, 133, 276
model, 3, 5, 10, 12, 14, 15, 18–21, 29, 37, 55, 59, 72, 89, 109–27, 132, 144, 146, 153, 162, 163, 169, 178, 179, 197, 201, 202, 206, 207, 219, 226, 230, 234, 244, 246, 253–5, 265, 273–5, 277
  cultural change, 135, 147
  economic, 28, 34–5, 43, 84
  German university, 253
  mainstream university, 72
  market-oriented, 29, 38, 53, 54, 74, 75, 84, 89–92, 94, 97, 100, 102, 111, 153, 159, 166, 168, 169, 179, 186, 187, 189, 190, 192, 194, 195, 198–201, 226–31, 234, 242, 244–6, 254, 262, 277
  Napoleonic, 34
  professor-researcher, 37
  research, 20
  research and innovation ecosystem, 3, 109–27
  triple helix, 29, 35, 43, 110–12, 114, 125, 275
  "want-to-be," 21
Monterrey Institute of Technology, 3, 14, 37, 109–27, 274
Morrill Land-Grant Act, 90
Motorola, 197

National Accord on Development Priority Policies (Peru), 218
National Accreditation Commission (Chile), 84

Index

National Accreditation Council (Colombia), 84
National Aeronautics and Space Administration—NASA, 166
National Agency for the Promotion of Science and Technology (Argentina), 52
National Assembly of Rectors (Peru), 209
National Autonomous University of Mexico, 39, 132
National Biodiversity Institute of Costa Rica, 166
National Center for Scientific Research (France), 59
National Commission for Atomic Energy (Argentina), 228
National Commission for University Evaluation and Accreditation (Argentina), 51, 241
National Council for Operation Authorization of Universities (Peru), 208
National Council for Science and Technology (Mexico), 120, 134
National Council for Science and Technology (Peru), 209
National Council of Innovation for Competitiveness (Chile), 93
National Council of Scientific and Technological Research (Argentina), 37
National Evaluation, Accreditation, and Quality Assurance in Education System (Peru), 209
National Fund for Scientific and Technological Development (Chile), 92
national identity, 29
national (bibliographic) indexes, 33
National Institute for Agricultural Technology (Argentina), 228
National Institute for Industrial Technology (Argentina), 228
National Peruvian University Council, 208
National Program of Quality Programs (Mexico), 120–1
national repositories, 33
National Research and Innovation Agency (Uruguay), 258
National Research Institute of Farming (Uruguay), 252
National Researcher System (Mexico), 37, 120, 132
National Science, Technology, and Innovation Strategic Plan (Uruguay), 253
National System of Researchers (Uruguay), 260
National System of Science, Technology, and Technological Innovation (Peru), 209
National University of Costa Rica, 169
National University of San Marcos, 206, 212
natural sciences, 89, 110, 229
Nature, 39, 268
neoinstitutional theory. See under new institutionalism
neoinstitutionalist approach. See under new institutionalism
neoliberal reform, 91
nepotism, 18
networks, 4, 17, 41, 115, 122, 173, 175, 178, 215, 216, 252, 254, 262, 275–6
new institutional economic theory, 226
new institutionalism, 3, 54, 55, 74, 101
New Zealand, 35
Nicaragua, 36, 158, 160, 161, 165, 168, 170
Nobel Prize, 39
North America, 124, 151, 158
notarial work, 257
nursing, 211

open access, 283
Open Knowledge Network, 172
open system, 54
operational costs, 16
Organic Law of Peruvian Universities-Decree 17,437 of 1969, 207
Organic Law of Science and Technology (Venezuela), 37
Organization of American States, 82, 168, 176
organizational challenges, 20
organizational culture, 150
organizational effectiveness, 38
organizational theory, 226
organizations, 1, 2, 4, 9, 10, 21, 53–5, 59, 63, 64, 70–2, 74, 75, 80–4, 109, 132, 146, 162, 163, 170–4, 177–9, 185, 213, 226, 230–2, 253, 258, 262, 265
  international, 4, 9, 10, 70, 82, 84, 132, 171, 173, 179
ORT University, 4, 255–68, 274
outcomes, 1, 4, 5, 28, 30, 33, 35, 81, 116, 117, 120, 124–6, 134, 149, 188, 194, 210, 259, 266
Outliers, 4, 157, 159, 162, 174
Oxford University, 90

Panama, 31, 158, 160, 161, 165, 167, 168, 177
Pan-American University, 38
paradigm, 1, 10, 15, 17, 37, 110, 150, 228, 236, 274
Paraguay, 36, 165, 168, 210
partnerships, 39, 42, 43, 116, 165, 167, 168, 174, 180, 196–9, 210, 256, 276
part-time instructors, 32, 42
Pascal, 30, 33
patents, 15, 17, 19, 30–3, 44, 81, 82, 84, 86, 87, 111, 116, 117, 121, 122, 139, 201, 263, 276
Paul Standley Herbarium, 167
Peace and Conflict Monitor, 172
peer-reviewed presentations, 116
peer-reviewing publication, 17
performance assessment, 227
performance-based Fund, 94, 97, 98, 101
per-hour professors, 186
personnel, 19, 20, 30, 150, 189, 192, 193, 195, 200
Peru, 4, 36, 37, 41, 167, 205–20, 274
Peruvian Network of Universities, 217
Petrobras, 13, 197
pharmaceuticals, 252
planning, 39, 40, 59, 70, 96, 102, 115, 135, 137, 138, 143–9, 152, 177, 196
poetic principle, 143
policy
  academic, 219
  accreditation, 57, 65–8
  economic, 193
  governmental, 97
  higher education, 91, 93, 100, 101
  international, 158
  national, 15, 59, 158, 163, 265, 277
  neoliberal, 9
  public, 3, 28, 29, 51, 56, 63, 73, 120, 169, 217, 218, 245, 252, 253, 255, 259, 263
  repatriation, 210
  research funding, 3, 51, 52, 59–62, 70–1, 73–4
  science, 80, 97, 100
policy decision-making, 71
policy framework, 194, 199
political power, 54
politicization, 132
polytechnic and technical institutes, 159
Pontifical Catholic University of Chile, 83
Pontifical Catholic University of Parana (Brazil), 41
Pontifical Catholic University of Peru, 41, 212

Index

Pontifical Catholic University of Rio de Janeiro (Brazil), 40, 188
Pontifical Catholic University of Rio Grande do Sul (Brazil), 41
Pontifical Catholic University of Sao Paulo (Brazil), 40–1
Pontifical Catholic University of Valparaiso (Chile), 41
Pontifical Javeriana University (Colombia), 41, 88
Portuguese, 33
Portuguese-speaking Latin America, 36
positive principle, 144
postdoctoral positions, 114, 117, 119, 123
postdoctoral programs, 115
postdoctoral researchers, 115, 118, 119, 120, 121, 125, 127
postdoctoral scholars. *See under* postdoctoral researchers
postsecondary education. *See under* higher education
president, 53, 56, 65, 66, 70, 71, 75, 76, 81, 88, 93, 95, 143, 144, 152, 167, 171, 235
prestige, 4, 14, 16, 18, 33, 37, 39, 40, 43, 53, 58, 63, 64, 83, 88, 89, 99, 113, 115, 174, 175, 177, 186, 192, 194, 195, 201, 225, 263, 273
private higher education, 2, 4, 9, 10–15, 21, 27, 28, 41, 52, 53, 80, 85, 91, 99, 102, 111, 134, 162, 187, 194, 209, 226, 246, 251, 254, 256, 273
private investment, 31, 227
private sector, 1, 2, 4, 11–13, 21, 29, 31, 35, 39, 42–4, 52, 53, 56, 58, 59, 62, 63, 73, 85, 88, 94–7, 100–2, 114–16, 124, 151, 159, 160, 162, 163, 165, 169, 172, 174, 179, 185–202, 229, 230, 234, 245, 246, 254, 257, 258, 263, 264, 274–6
privatization, 34, 43, 151, 253, 254

productive institutions, 10, 114
productive sector. *See under* private sector
productivity, 1–4, 12–14, 67, 71, 79–102, 117, 170, 225, 232
 mainstream scientific, 31
 research, 2–4, 9, 12, 13, 16, 18, 20, 21, 27–44, 79–82, 85, 95, 113, 115, 125, 127, 136, 138, 149, 151, 152, 163, 178, 201, 231, 234–6, 242–6, 260, 263, 273, 277
 scientific, 3, 31, 79–102
professional development, 18
professional graduate programs, 186
professionalization, 35, 55, 72, 264
professions, 32, 34, 207, 257
program accreditation, 52, 56, 67, 72
program isomorphism, 3
project co-funding, 95
psychology, 211
public accounting, 257
public funding, 2, 3, 29, 31, 32, 69, 90, 117, 125, 132, 181, 187, 194, 198, 230, 245, 264, 274, 275
public good, 41, 98, 192, 195
public health, 211, 214
publications, 15, 28, 30–3, 35, 44, 45, 71, 85, 88, 89, 92, 94, 95, 97, 99, 114, 116–18, 121–5, 138, 139, 157, 164, 168, 169, 175, 178, 194, 212–14, 216, 242, 243, 247, 253, 261, 266
 scholarly, 44, 124
 scientific, 114, 118, 124
Puebla State Popular Autonomous University (Mexico), 3, 4, 131–54, 274

Quacquarelli Symonds, 40
qualitative assessment, 123
quality, 2, 3, 9–12, 14, 15, 21, 28, 30, 38–40, 43, 44, 51–67, 71–6, 84, 88, 89, 91–3, 100, 112, 113, 117, 132, 144, 159, 166, 169, 175, 178,

181, 186, 187, 192–5, 198, 199, 208–10, 212–13, 229, 234, 237, 241, 273, 274, 276, 277
quality assurance, 2, 3, 51–76, 92, 113, 277
quantitative assessment, 123
Quito, 36

Rafael Landívar University, 162
rankings, 35, 38, 41
  Academic Ranking of World Universities, 38, 48, 112
  international rankings, 14–16, 27, 35, 157, 274
  Latin American University Ranking, 40, 83
  Leiden University Ranking, 38
  national, 83
  QS Latin American University Rankings, 83
  QS University Rankings, 38, 40
  SCImago Institutions Rankings, 38, 83
  Shanghai Jiao Tong University Academic Ranking of World Universities, 38–40
  Taiwan Higher Education and the Accreditation Council Ranking, 38
  Times Higher Education World University Ranking, 38–9
  US News & World Report, 112, 124
recognition, 10, 18, 38, 44, 52, 53, 89, 99, 101, 119, 123, 146, 174, 175, 227, 232, 233, 236, 237, 239–41, 243, 252, 256, 279
regional clusters, 150–2
regional (bibliographic) indexes, 33
regional networks, 173
regional repositories, 33
Registry of *Quality* Graduate Programs, 134
reputation. *See under* prestige

research activities, 3, 35, 43, 52, 56, 57, 59–60, 62–75, 79, 81, 82, 85, 90, 93, 95, 97, 98, 101, 114, 160, 169, 172, 174, 187, 188, 190, 195, 196, 201, 229, 233, 234, 236–8, 240, 241, 243, 244, 247, 260, 266, 275, 280
research administration, 114, 118, 123
research and development, 1, 30, 55, 98, 119, 157, 166, 180, 187, 210, 229, 252
research capacity, 30, 73, 113, 126, 131, 133, 157, 162, 163, 170, 179
research centers, 28, 33, 44, 85, 99, 101, 112, 116, 141, 149, 165, 175, 181, 229, 245, 246, 261
Research Chairs, 119–27
research committee, 67
Research Excellence Centers (Colombia), 95
research function, 52, 56, 57, 65, 70, 84
research groups, 29, 53, 75, 95, 99, 114, 115, 119–21, 126
research infrastructure, 89, 91, 92, 96–8, 101, 114, 116, 121, 196, 218
Research Institute on Altitude (Peru), 214
research institutions, 38, 67, 169, 177, 226, 264
research laboratory, 67
research outcomes, 4, 116, 117, 120, 124, 210
research performance, 3, 71, 73, 125, 192, 244
research production, 79, 97, 134, 139, 192
research projects, 13, 16, 19, 21, 37, 67–9, 71, 75, 76, 92, 96, 97, 116, 117, 146, 151, 168, 173, 176, 196, 216, 218, 219, 228, 235, 246, 276
research support fund, 260

Index

research university, 2, 3, 10, 14–21, 32, 54, 59, 89, 96, 124, 132, 139, 151, 153, 195, 225, 263, 275, 277
researcher, 14, 16, 17, 30–3, 37, 39, 52, 53, 56, 57, 59–63, 67–76, 99, 111, 115–27, 132, 134, 137, 142, 149, 152, 162, 171, 189–91, 205, 206, 209, 210, 212, 215–19, 225, 227, 229, 231–3, 245–6, 253, 259–61, 263, 265, 267, 274–6
researcher promotion and evaluation systems, 37
research-intensive institutions, 4, 228, 234
revenue, 13, 37, 43, 44, 115–18, 165, 175, 193–5, 275, 276
Revista Médica Herediana, 216
Rockefeller Foundation, 83
Rosary University (Colombia), 41, 88
royalties, 44, 96, 116, 117, 122, 139

Sabana University (Colombia), 89
salaries, 12, 18, 30, 37, 114, 115, 232, 235–7, 242, 246, 247
Samuel Zemurray, 167
San Andrés University (Argentina), 62
Santo Domingo, 36
scholarships, 14, 16, 52, 53, 60, 74, 92, 93, 97, 115, 196
School of Tropical Agriculture (Costa Rica), 163
Science, 39
science, technology, and innovation, 1, 28–38, 95, 252, 264, 273
science, technology, and innovation systems, 27, 28, 34, 254
Science and Technology Mission (Colombia), 94
science and technology systems. *See under* science, technology, and innovation systems
Science Citation Index, 30, 39, 81, 157, 212
See also SCI-Expanded

science systems. *See under* science, technology, and innovation systems
scientific databases, 85, 93, 95
scientific impact, 41, 117
scientific knowledge, 111, 135, 174, 206, 207, 217, 218, 220
scientific networking, 99
Scientific Researcher Career Program (Argentina), 37
scientific-technical knowledge, 252
scientometrics, 80
SCI-Expanded, 39
See also Science Citation Index
SCImago Research Group, 41
Scopus, 33, 40, 41, 116, 121, 122, 210, 212
Secretariat of Science and Technology (Argentina), 59
secular university, 54, 88, 162, 163, 234
seed money, 70, 119, 123
segmentation, 2, 13, 14, 21, 273
self-assessment, 52, 57, 58, 59, 63–5, 70, 72
simultaneity principle, 143
social inequality, 100
social recognition, 38, 89
social science databases, 85
social sciences, 32, 75, 119, 120, 164, 168, 169, 229, 245, 256, 257, 265
Social Sciences Citation Index, 39
Solectron, 197
Southern Association of Colleges and Schools, 174
Spain, 41, 76, 207, 213
Spanish Agency of International Cooperation for Development, 263
Spanish Institute for Policy and Public Goods, 41
Spanish-speaking Latin America, 94
specialization, 41, 140, 186, 229
specialization programs, 186

specialized researcher, 37
spin-off companies, 3, 116, 122, 197, 276
standards, 15, 21, 55, 58, 63, 64, 66, 67, 72, 73, 96, 100, 118, 121, 159, 163, 173, 235–6
start-ups, 198
State University of Campinas (Brazil), 39
strategic decision-making, 16
strategic planning, 39, 70, 115, 135, 137, 138, 143–9
strategies, 1, 2, 4, 14, 19–21, 52, 57, 73, 74, 91, 112–14, 117, 126, 127, 131, 133, 135–8, 145–7, 151–3, 177, 190, 206, 215, 217, 219, 242, 251–68
student enrollment, 30, 36, 228
student mobility, 134, 146
student/faculty productivity ratio, 245
supply-and-demand relationship, 252
Suriname, 168
sustainability, 79, 126, 138, 171, 201
sustainable development, 121, 164–6, 170, 172, 177, 178, 180
sustainable economic development. *See under* sustainable development
sustainable funding, 123
Swedish International Development Agency, 169
systemic discrimination, 239

teaching, 1, 13, 16, 30, 38, 42, 43, 56, 63, 64, 69, 74, 80, 94, 113–15, 120, 123, 125, 131, 132, 144, 146, 153, 159, 166, 168, 172, 177–80, 187–91, 193–7, 206, 212, 213, 215, 216, 218, 225, 228, 234–6, 241–7, 253, 255, 259, 260, 264, 266, 273, 275–6
teaching-intensive institutions, 188
teaching-oriented institution, 3, 4, 14, 228, 234
TEC Millennium, 119

TEC Research Group, 119
technical schools, 159
Technical University Federico Santa Maria (Chile), 41, 88
Technical University of the State (Chile), 91
Technological Autonomous Institute of Mexico, 37
technological innovation, 34, 60, 209, 217, 218, 265
technological knowledge, 112, 208, 217, 218, 255, 258
Technological Laboratory of Uruguay, 260
technological research, 93, 100, 217
technology
    foreign-generated, 31
    locally generated, 31, 252
technology transfer, 30, 44, 82, 121, 206
    vertical, 44
technology transfer offices, 44, 82, 121
technology-based companies, 126
technoscience, 111
tenure, 18, 194, 242
tertiary education. *See under* higher education
The Peace and Conflict Review, 172
think tank, 28, 193
Thomson Reuters, 33, 39, 116, 261
Thomson Scientific. *See under* Thomson Reuters
top-down strategies, 20
Torcuato Di Tella University (Argentina), 61, 62
traditional institutions, 13
training
    doctoral, 198, 243
    graduate, 74, 172
    professional, 132, 255, 257
transferable knowledge, 5
transference, 110
transformation, 3, 11, 19, 34, 55, 118, 136, 153, 201, 253, 254, 273, 275

Index

transnational institutions, 14
transparency, 18, 76
traveling expenses, 121
tuition, 11, 37, 43, 53, 63, 69, 70, 74, 83, 96, 115, 117, 123, 132, 187, 234, 247
tuition-driven institutions, 13, 16, 275
tuning project, 150
twenty-first century socialism, 34

uncertainty, 55
undergraduate programs, 3, 32, 52, 58, 65–70, 72, 134, 165, 191, 196, 199, 266
United Fruit Company, 167
United Kingdom, 35
United Nations Human Rights Centre, 172
United States, 35, 59, 83, 85, 111, 121, 134, 164, 166, 167, 174, 213, 214, 225
universities
  Catholic, 41, 88, 89, 187
  decentralized, 90
  elite private, 12, 63
  elite-type, 72, 73
  emerging research, 16
  enterprising, 254–5
  entrepreneurial, 79, 254–6
  foreign, 115, 146
  government-funded, 273
  megauniversities, 27, 33, 39
  multi-branched, 159, 169
  national, 34, 116, 169, 208
  public, 1, 2, 11, 12, 13, 15, 27, 32, 34, 37, 39, 42, 53, 58, 60, 62–4, 70, 75, 84, 91, 94, 95, 98, 117, 118, 125, 132, 159, 160, 186, 200, 218, 226, 228–30, 245, 260, 263
  religion-affiliated, 28
  religious, 4, 36
  research-driven, 225
  research-intensive, 21, 42

research-oriented, 21, 116
state-funded, 11
successful private, 3, 27, 29, 38, 42, 43
teaching-oriented, 119, 126, 244, 273
teaching-oriented french, 81
traditional, 11
traditional Catholic, 88
tuition-free public, 186, 200
world-class, 29, 35, 111, 112, 118, 119, 124, 127, 226
University for Peace (Costa Rica), 164
University Law 23,733 of 1983 (Peru), 208
University Law of 1960 (Peru), 207
University of Barcelona (Spain), 263
University of British Columbia (Canada), 121
University of Buenos Aires (Argentina), 39, 63
University of Chile, 39, 91
University of Conception (Chile), 88
University of El Salvador, 169
University of Extremadura (Spain), 41
University of Florida, 166
University of Granada (Spain), 41
University of Houston, 121
University of Porto (Portugal), 41
University of San Carlos (Guatemala), 162
University of Sao Paulo (Brazil), 39, 41
University of Texas Austin, 121
University of the Americas (Mexico), 38, 41
University of the Andes (Chile), 89
University of the Andes (Colombia), 39, 83, 116
University of the North (Colombia), 83, 88
University of the Republic (Uruguay), 251
University of the Valley of Guatemala, 162

University of Toronto (Canada), 121
university reform, 12, 207
university systems, 34, 179
university-industry cooperation. *See under* university-private sector partnerships
university-private sector partnerships, 42, 44, 276
university-private sector relationships. *See under* university-private sector partnerships
upper-middle class, 199
Uruguay, 4, 11, 31, 34, 36, 168, 251–68, 274
US Agency for International Development, 83, 165
US Department of Agriculture, 167
utilitarianism, 111

value-added products, 126
Venezuela, 31, 36, 37, 165, 267
Venezuelan Institute for Scientific Research, 37
veterinary medicine, 211, 262

vice-presidents, 81, 82
virtualization, 254
visibility, 4, 10, 35, 93, 134, 260, 263
visionary strategic leadership, 275
vocational schools, 159

W. K. Kellogg Foundation, 165
Western Europe, 35
Whirlpool Foundation, 83
Whole Foods Market, 166
Wilson Popenoe, 167, 168
workforce, 115, 120, 126, 127
World Bank, 82, 92, 132, 158, 174, 205
World Declaration on Higher Education, 206
World Economic Forum, 171
world economy, 29
World Health Organization, 213
World ORT Union, 256
world-class scientific research, 43

Zamorano Pan-American Agricultural School (Honduras), 163, 167

GPSR Compliance

The European Union's (EU) General Product Safety Regulation (GPSR) is a set of rules that requires consumer products to be safe and our obligations to ensure this.

If you have any concerns about our products, you can contact us on

ProductSafety@springernature.com

In case Publisher is established outside the EU, the EU authorized representative is:

Springer Nature Customer Service Center GmbH
Europaplatz 3
69115 Heidelberg, Germany

www.ingramcontent.com/pod-product-compliance
Lightning Source LLC
LaVergne TN
LVHW051915060526
838200LV00004B/153